GROWTH AND STRUCTURAL CHANGE
IN THE EGYPTIAN ECONOMY

Publications of
The Economic Growth Center

LLOYD G. REYNOLDS, *Director*

Growth and Structural Change in the Egyptian Economy

by **DONALD C. MEAD**
Makerere University College
Kampala, Uganda

A Publication of
The Economic Growth Center
Yale University

1967
RICHARD D. IRWIN, INC.
Homewood, Illinois

© RICHARD D. IRWIN, INC., 1967

First Printing, January, 1967

Library of Congress Catalog Card No. 66–27466

Printed in the United States of America

Introduction

In some ways it is presumptuous to write a book attempting to analyze a whole economy. In discussing the present study with numerous individuals in Egypt and the United States, the first question asked was always the same: "But with what aspect of the Egyptian economy do you plan to deal?" The answer, "The whole economy," is somewhat shocking to both interrogator and respondent. Yet the attempt to encompass the whole economy rather than concentrating too quickly on individual sectors or problem areas makes sense, we believe, for a number of reasons. For one thing, it is often quite difficult to keep a sense of proportion as to the relative importance of a question with which one is dealing, unless one has an adequate national framework in which to place the analysis. More detailed studies of specific sectors often try to handle this with a few introductory paragraphs or pages, but it is tempting for reader and researcher alike to forget this overall framework thereafter. In fact, until one has some overall view of how the economy operates, it may be difficult to know which specific problems are worthy of more detailed attention, which are of serious importance, and which are irrelevant. Furthermore, an economy is interrelated in such a way that it is often impossible to understand developments in one sector without knowing a good deal about what is going on in the rest of the economy. Finally, and by far most important, there is a goal which one can set oneself which concerns an understanding not of how the industrial sector has changed or whether there is underemployment in agriculture, but how the economy as a whole operates, what the dynamic forces for development are and how they spread through every corner of the economy. This is an ambitious target; returning to our opening words, perhaps it is presumptuous even to try to reach it. We make no claims at having succeeded, and in fact we are well aware of a thousand problems of both a micro-economic and an aggregative nature which remain unanswered; yet it has been the aim of this study to see how far we can move in this direction.

Our main concentration has been on the period from 1945 to

1960. Historical antecedents are important, and we have referred to them at numerous points in the study; but we have neither the time nor the competence to write a thorough history of the Egyptian economy since 1800, or even during the whole 20th century. With regard to the post-1960 period, the closer we come to the present, the more difficult it is to evaluate the ever-increasing flow of information which is pouring from almost countless government departments; officials are much more ready to talk about the level and estimation of national income for 1954 than for 1964. Once again Egypt under the Plan has intruded into nearly every chapter of the book; but our main attention has been devoted to the preceding period.

Since we have started this study, two books have been published on the economy of the U.A.R.: One by Charles Issawi of Columbia University,[1] and one by Bent Hansen and Girgis Marzouk, of the Institute of National Planning and the Central Bank, respectively, in Cairo.[2] Had we known at the outset that these two studies were under preparation, we might have been tempted to concentrate our energies elsewhere, but such is the insularity of economics that we knew nothing of the first until it had gone to the publishers, in the fall of 1963, nor of the second until we had already invested well over a year of work on the study. From our point of view the timing of these other books has been quite unfortunate; if they had been started somewhat later, some form of coordination or collaboration might have been possible; had they been finished earlier, we could have taken their work as given and gone on from there, without being lead into needless duplication of effort and unexplained statistical inconsistencies, sometimes for trivial reasons. Wherever possible we have attempted to eliminate or at least explain any remaining discrepancies.

One of the most difficult problems facing an analyst working on the Egyptian economy is to provide an adequate understanding of the changing role of the government. Final statements of actual receipts and expenditures have not been published since 1956/57, which means that any fiscal analysis of developments since then must rely on the budget estimates.[3] To make matters worse, the

---

[1] C. Issawi, *Egypt in Revolution: An Economic Analysis* (New York: Oxford University Press, 1963).

[2] B. Hansen and G. A. Marzouk, *Development and Economic Policy in the U.A.R. (Egypt)* (Amsterdam: North-Holland Publishing Company, 1965).

[3] It seems that closed accounts for more recent years are available for internal governmental use; in Chapter IX we have made some use of the limited and highly aggregated figures which have been released.

growth of the government sector has been accompanied by a proliferation of annexed and independent budgets, with a complex
web of transfers and subsidies among these various entities and
little consistency through time as to how a given function was
treated. It would be a Herculean task to attempt to disentangle
this web, and since budgeted figures have not in the past been very
closely reflected in actual expenditures—and we suspect this gap
may be widening—the task seems not to be worth the toil. Of course
this is disappointing, since it means that we have only limited and
indirect measures of the precise role of the government in the
economy since 1957; unfortunately at the moment this seems to be
an unavoidable situation.

Somewhat similar considerations apply to our discussion of planning. A great deal of work has been done in Egypt on planning
techniques, setting forth and attempting to estimate a large number
of different planning models of quite a high level of sophistication.
While this work is of considerable interest to students of the theory
and methodology of planning, we shall see in Chapter X that it has
generally been quite irrelevant to the economic development of the
country, and even to the plan itself. For this reason, our discussion
of these planning models is rather cursory.

It goes without saying that a study such as this could never be
undertaken without substantial help from others. The author is glad
to acknowledge with thanks the help and encouragement he has received from the directors and staff of three different institutions:
The Economic Growth Center at Yale University, the Institute of
National Planning in Cairo, and the Department of Statistics and
Census of the Egyptian Government. In Cairo, Dr. Ibrahim Hilmy
Abdel Rahman and Dr. Hassan Hussein have opened innumerable
doors in facilitating our research work. Special thanks go to the
following individuals, who have given detailed and helpful comments on all or portions of an earlier draft of this study: Professors
Lloyd Reynolds, Gustav Ranis, Gerald Helleiner, Shane Hunt; Professor Bent Hansen, Mr. Patrick O'Brien, Professor Simon Kuznets,
Mr. John Gunter, and Professor Richard Porter. Where we have
failed to listen to their good advice, the responsibility is entirely
our own.

Kampala, Uganda   DONALD C. MEAD
April, 1966

TABLE OF CONTENTS

ix

STATISTICAL APPENDIX

BIBLIOGRAPHY

INDEX

LIST OF TABLES

UNITS OF MEASUREMENTS

£E refers to the Egyptian pound. This was officially virtually at par with the Sterling pound through the whole period of this study until May 1962, when the official selling rate was changed from £E1 = $2.838 to £E1 = $2.30. As we indicate in Chapter VII, in effect this devaluation took place gradually during the 1950's, relying on a changing combination of taxes, subsidies, and multiple effective exchange rates. The Egyptian pound is made up of 100 piasters (pt.) or 1,000 millièmes (mms.).

1 feddan = 1.038 acres = 4,300.833 square meters

1 cantar = 44.928 kg = 99.05 lbs

1 ardeb = 198 litres; the approximate weights of 1 ardeb of different crops are as follows:

wheat:	1 ardeb	=	150 kg
maize:	1 ardeb	=	140 kg
beans:	1 ardeb	=	155 kg
millet:	1 ardeb	=	140 kg
barley:	1 ardeb	=	120 kg

1 dariba of rice = approximately 935 kg.

Ħistorical Background

For a country with as long and rich a history as Egypt's, to refer to a brief look at the past sixty years as providing historical perspective may seem like a misnomer; not only Egyptologists, but also students of the interaction between the Arab world and medieval Europe, as well as historians of the Ottoman Empire, will take offense at this restricted vision. The purpose of this chapter is the limited one of showing the nature of the Egyptian economy in the first decade of the twentieth century, with some brief remarks on how this situation arose out of the late nineteenth century, and how it developed during the following thirty years.

In discussing the Egyptian economy in the year 1913, one commentator said that "nearly everything which Egypt consumes, with the exception of a good part of her food, comes to her from abroad."[1] This is an exaggeration which is characteristic of statistical department officials, who tend to regard anything which is difficult to measure as being unimportant; at that time, there were significant rural industries and handicrafts, not to mention the service sector. Yet the observation has a measure of truth to it and serves to emphasize one of the most important characteristics of the Egyptian economy of the time: its heavy dependence on the agricultural sector as a source of both domestic food supply and export earnings.

---

[1] M. I. G. Lévi, "Le Commerce Extérieur de l'Egypte: Mouvement de l'Année 1913," *L'Egypte Contemporaine*, No. 19 (May, 1914), p. 413.

During the last twenty years of the nineteenth century, Egyptian pletion of the Delta Barrage, a dam across the Nile at the mouth of the fertile Delta area, it was possible to introduce double and agriculture underwent a remarkable transformation. With the comtriple cropping into areas where formerly the water was only high enough to be brought to the fields during one season of the year. The results were dramatic, as Table 1–1 shows. These figures make clear the striking increase in cropped area which took place during this period, primarily as a result of the extension of the area growing several crops a year.

TABLE 1–1

Area under Crops

(Feddan)

	1879	1899
Winter crop	3,139,228	3,906,299
Summer crop	813,012	1,712,276
Flood (autumn) crop	809,938	1,414,136
Total cropped area	4,762,178	7,032,711
Total cultivated area	4,742,610	5,087,887

Source: A. E. Crouchley, *The Economic Development of Modern Egypt* (New York: Longmans, Green & Co., Inc., 1938), p. 153; United Arab Republic, Central Statistical Committee, *Basic Statistics*, June, 1962, p. 62. Cropped area counts any feddan where two crops are grown during the year as two feddan; cultivated area shows the total area where crops are grown at least once during the year. Figures for total cultivated area (from *Basic Statistics*) refer to 1877 and 1897; this source also gives the 1879 total cropped area figure shown above referring to 1877. (One feddan equals 1.038 acres.)

Data on yields are available only for cotton during this period. These estimates are rough, but they show a marked rise in output per acre—perhaps 70 to 100 percent—from the 1870's to the peak period, 1895–99. In the following decade, yields declined by some 20 percent, due in large part to the inadequate drainage which accompanied the new irrigation system.[2] These changes in yields sharply reinforced the increase in cotton supply due to the expanding acreage through the 1890's, while partially offsetting the continuing increase in acreage in the following decade. The net results of these two factors was that cotton production and exports developed as shown in Table 1–2. The marked rise in the quantity of cotton exports during the 1890's was offset by a sharp fall in

---

[2]Crouchley, *op. cit.*, pp. 154–61 and 263–64; also J. I. Craig, "Statistics of the Yield of Cotton," *L'Egypte Contemporaine*, No. 8 (November, 1911), pp. 587–90. See also C. H. Brown, *Egyptian Cotton* (London: Leonard Hill, Ltd., 1953), pp. 14–19.

prices, with the result that during the 1890's export receipts rose very little; during the following decade, on the other hand, cotton prices recovered from their depressed levels, while the quantity of cotton shipped abroad continued to rise, with the result that the average receipts from merchandise exports in the period 1900–1909 were 60 percent higher than in the preceding decade. Cotton's share in total export receipts rose from below 75 percent in the early 1880's to over 90 percent in the first decade of this century.

TABLE 1–2

COTTON PRODUCTION AND EXPORTS

	Production (000 Cantar)	Exports (000 Cantar)	Export Prices (£E/ Cantar)	Export Value (£E Million)	
				Cotton	Total Merchandise
1880–89.........	2,890	2,915	2.648	7.7	11.8
1890–99.........	5,321	5,139	1.775	9.1	13.1
1900–1909......	6,236	6,210	3.214	19.9	21.2

SOURCE: *Annuaire Statistique*, various issues, except total exports, 1880–84, from Crouchley, *The Economic Development of Modern Egypt* (New York: Longmans, Green & Co., Inc., 1938), p. 263. Total exports exclude specie and reexports. Prices have been computed by the author.

With exports rising sharply, imports increased apace; Egypt maintained the small if fluctuating balance-of-trade surplus which had characterized the economy since the American Civil War. Although full balance-of-payments estimates are not available, it seems reasonable to assume that this trade surplus, supplemented by some long-term capital inflow (primarily into agriculture, trade, and finance), was needed to cover the continuing payments of interest on Egypt's extensive foreign private and public debt. No doubt, it was this substantial rise in imports, made possible by the plentiful foreign exchange earnings from expanding cotton exports, which explains the view that all Egypt's needs except her food supply were secured from overseas. As Appendix Table V–A–1 (page 342) shows, there were substantial increases in all major categories of imports, although the import of producer goods rose more rapidly than the total. It seems fair to say that virtually all the capital inputs to the small industrial sector, a major part of the physical needs for the expanding construction activity, and a large part of the increase in nonfood consumption, as well as some food items (e.g., sugar, flour, tea), were supplied from outside the country. In view of the crucial place of cotton in the country's exports, it is easy to see why this commodity was thought of as the pivotal point around which the whole economy turned.

In some ways, this seems like a classic case of a one-crop, export-oriented economy; yet we should remind ourselves that at the turn of the century, only 16 percent of the cropped land was used to produce the export crop, cotton. In spite of a population increase which during this period was probably between 1 and 1.5 percent per annum, Egypt continued to be able to feed herself, with relatively small exceptions. In large part, the explanation for this lay in the rapid increase in the production of maize, which in turn can be associated with the extension of multiple cropping into the autumn season, when maize is virtually the only crop grown (see Tables 1-1 and 1-3). The main thing which permitted Egypt to

TABLE 1-3

CULTIVATED AND CROPPED AREAS

(000 Feddan)

	1906-7	1916-17	1926-27	1936-37
Summer:				
Cotton	1,603	1,677	1,516	1,978
Rice	156	232	358	243
Sorghum	n.a.	180	180	223
Others	301	163	158	146
Total	2,060	2,252	2,212	2,590
Winter:				
Wheat	1,218	1,076	1,594	1,369
Clover	n.a.	1,372	1,490	1,742
Beans	596	472	447	386
Barley	458	429	362	261
Others	1,591	268	256	262
Total	3,863	3,617	4,149	4,020
Autumn:				
Maize	1,624	1,656	2,115	1,554
Others	89	125	151	128
Total	1,713	1,781	2,266	1,682
Orchards	27	28	34	66
Total cropped area	7,662	7,677	8,661	8,358
Cultivated area	5,403	5,269	5,544	5,281

SOURCE: *Annuaire Statistique*, various issues. Totals may not add due to rounding.

raise enough food domestically for her growing population during this period was the extension of the practice of multiple cropping.

Accustomed as we are to thinking of Egypt as an overpopulated

country, it is worth recalling that this was not always so. Mohammed Ali was constantly struggling with a shortage of men to work
his fields, maintain the irrigation works and industrial establishments, and fight in his army. Issawi reports that "as late as the
1860's plans for large-scale immigration of Italians, Chinese, and
other laborers were seriously considered."[3] By the turn of the century a number of important changes had taken place in this sphere.
The first was the growth of the population itself. Estimates of the
rate of population increase are quite rough, since the first reliable
census was taken only in 1897; over the course of the whole nineteenth century the average population growth rate may have been
of the order of 1.3–1.4 percent per annum,[4] implying that the total
population may have expanded by some 50 percent from 1870 to
1900. With nearly 70 percent of total employment in the economy
concentrated in the agricultural sector in 1907,[5] we may surmise
that the agricultural labor force grew at approximately the same
rate as total population. An additional factor working in the same
direction was the completion (in 1890) of the Delta Barrage. By
making it possible to raise the water level in the canals at flood time,
this system of dams sharply decreased the labor requirements for
maintaining and cleaning the irrigation system; the corvée was
abolished in 1892 and replaced by hired labor, but the total labor
requirement was far smaller.[6] On the other hand, we have seen that
this change in the irrigation system was accompanied by an expansion of both cropped and cultivated areas. Perhaps it is a fair if
rough generalization to say that an increase in the cultivated area
creates a need for more agricultural workers, while increasing the
cropped area means that existing laborers work harder, i.e., they
are busy a larger part of the year. It is clear that the total population—and in all probability the agricultural labor force as well—
was growing substantially more rapidly than cultivated area during
the last three decades of the nineteenth century. On the other hand,
with total cropped area growing faster than the labor force, there
may have been a tendency developing already during this period to
share the work as well as the increased total income. In short, it
may be that while the growing practice of multiple cropping sus-

---

[3]C. Issawi, *Egypt in Revolution: An Economic Analysis* (New York:
Oxford University Press, 1963), p. 33.
   [4]Using a population estimate for 1798 of 2.5 million; see *ibid.*, p. 20.
   [5]See Appendix Table II–B–1 (p. 304).
   [6]See B. Hansen, *Marginal Productivity Wage Theory and Subsistence Wage
Theory in Egyptian Agriculture,* Memo No. 547 (Cairo: Institute of National
Planning, March, 1965), pp. 31–32.

tained the per capita consumption levels in agriculture and permitted the country to feed its expanding population, it did this only by converting seasonal unemployment of the agricultural labor force (which was in large measure unavoidable) into year-round underemployment. This hypothesis is based largely on conjecture; further research in this area should be both fruitful and fascinating.

A further characteristic of the country during this period which bears special comment is the nature of the government. In 1876 the country was no longer able to meet the payments on its massive external public debt; "an international Caisse de la Dette Publique was set up, with British and French commissioners to receive the Egyptian revenues, supervise the railways and the port of Alexandria, and maintain the payments due to the creditors."[7] The underlying aim here was to provide the necessary financial organization and control to make sure that foreign debts were paid, starting from the idea that "no sacrifice should be demanded from the creditors until every reasonable sacrifice had been made by the debtors."[8] It soon became clear that the only way to carry out this task was to restrict other expenditures and increase the stringency of tax collection, tasks which required far more authority than could be exercised within a restricted financial sphere. It should not surprise us that in 1882 the British stepped in to take virtual control of the country, in political as well as financial matters. First as proconsul and later as high commissioner, the chief British representative was the de facto ruler of Egypt for the following forty years.

For its revenue the government depended heavily on receipts from the land tax; during the 1880's and 1890's, this tax alone provided some 60 percent of total tax revenues. Since the tax rates were fixed by international agreement and the expansion of land area was limited, total government receipts rose only slowly until after the turn of the century, when other taxes began to assume more prominence. The authorities seem to have paid more attention to a "wiser" allocation of their revenue than to attempts to increase the level of government receipts, although considerable effort was devoted to making the tax structure more equitable.[9]

On the expenditure side, the regular payment of interest on the

---

[7]G. E. Kirk, *A Short History of the Middle East* (London: Methuen & Co., 1955), p. 110.

[8]*Ibid.*, p. 112.

[9]See the Earl of Cromer, *Modern Egypt* (London: MacMillan & Co., Ltd., 1908), Vol. II, chap. liii.

public debt was a major preoccupation of the fiscal regime. In 1881, over 45 percent of the government's ordinary expenditure was devoted to this one item; by 1897, this share had fallen somewhat, but was still over 37 percent. Cromer indicates that up to 1888, all energies of the government were concentrated on the avoidance of bankruptcy; any question of reform or improvement of the administrative system had to be postponed until a later date. It is noteworthy, however, that one of the first acts of the British authorities during this period was to *increase* public debt outstanding by £E1 million, in order to finance improvements in the irrigation system. This policy was justified in terms of its direct impact on government revenues, although it clearly had a major effect on the income of the population of the country; as we have seen, the results achieved were impressive. For the rest, government expenditures might best be considered as a holding operation: maintaining public buildings and streets in good repair, keeping the administration and the courts going, with some relatively minor attention to health and education. This pattern was a clear reflection of the conception of "good colonial government" in fashion at the time.[10]

With this brief background, let us trace the main developments in the economy into the 1930's. Starting once again with the agricultural sector, it is clear from the figures in Table 1–3 that the expansion of agricultural land area was relatively insignificant; from 1907 to 1937, cultivated land area actually fell slightly, largely as a result of the depressed market for agricultural products during the 1930's. Cropped area rose by less than 10 percent from 1907 to 1937, in sharp contrast to the 60 percent rise during the preceding thirty years.

With the extensive margin expanding only slowly, there was pressure to use the existing land more intensively. This was reflected in a number of ways, as other inputs to the agricultural

---

[10]See *ibid.*, especially chaps. liii and liv. For a rather critical appraisal of British policy during this period, see S. Young, *Egypt* (London: Ernest Benn, Ltd., 1927). El Gritly has said that during this period "the sole aim of the British Administration was the extension of perennial irrigation and the area under cotton with a view to providing sufficient foreign exchange to meet the service of the large external debt" (A. A. I. el Gritly, "The Structure of Modern Industry in Egypt," *L'Egypte Contemporaine*, Nos. 241–42 [November-December, 1947], p. 367). Whether or not this was the sole aim of British policy, it surely was a dominant one; see United Kingdom, Foreign Office, *Reports on the Finances, Administration and Condition of Egypt, and the Progress of Reforms* (London: H.M.S.O., May, 1898), pp. 20–21, where the Earl of Cromer justifies government expenditure on the construction of a dam at Aswan in these terms.

sector rose substantially. The use of chemical fertilizer, for example, increased from negligible amounts at the turn of the century to a level in the late 1930's among the highest in the world.[11] A second important input is labor; although, as we shall see, this is a variable which is difficult to measure precisely, still it is clear that there was a very substantial increase in the man-land ratio in Egyptian agriculture from the turn of the century to the late 1930's. One measure of this comes from the employment data in the population censuses, as indicated in Table 1–4. Combined with the data in Table 1–3, these figures imply a rise of 45 percent in the agricultural labor force per cropped acre, or an increase of over 60 percent in the more relevant measure, workers per unit of cultivated land, from 1907 to 1937.[12]

TABLE 1–4

EMPLOYMENT IN AGRICULTURE

| | Total Population | Males Engaged in Agriculture and Livestock | | Ratio |
| | A | B | C | B/A |
	(Thousands)	(Thousands)	(Index)	
1907................	11,287	2,258	100	0.20
1917................	12,751	2,387	106	0.19
1927................	14,218	2,916	129	0.20
1937................	15,933	3,560	158	0.22

SOURCE: Population Censuses.

A third area where inputs to agriculture rose substantially during this period was in the system of irrigation and drainage. As Table 1–5 shows, irrigation canals were extended approximately in proportion to the increase in cropped area; in the case of drains, however, the increase was much more substantial, amounting to over 40 percent from 1917 to 1937, over a period when the cropped area rose by less than 10 percent. This extension of the drainage system should probably be thought of as a necessary measure to

---

[11]See U.S. Department of Agriculture, *Pre-War World Production and Consumption of Plant Foods in Fertilizers,* Miscellaneous Publication No. 593 (Washington, D.C.: U.S. Government Printing Office, April, 1946), p. 56. This study gives figures for total plant food used per acre of arable land, over the period 1936–39; of fifty-one countries examined, Egypt ranked tenth, following only countries of western Europe, New Zealand, and Japan.

[12]These estimates agree reasonably closely with those given in M. M. el Imam, *A Production Function for Egyptian Agriculture, 1913–1955,* Memo No. 259 (Cairo: Institute of National Planning, December, 1962), p. 43. These employment data are discussed in more detail in Chapters 2 and 4 below.

offset the decline in yields which took place in the early years of the century, when there was a major extension of the irrigation system, but without adequate attention to the problem of drainage.

TABLE 1–5

LENGTH OF IRRIGATION CANALS
AND DRAINS

(000 Kilometers)

	Canals	Drains
1917	18,634	6,290
1927	18,711	7,088
1937	20,170	9,168

SOURCE: *Annuaire Statistique*, various issues. This series is not available before 1913.

The result of all these factors, along with the use of improved varieties of seeds, was to bring about an increase in yields per cropped acre of approximately 20 percent from 1913–19 to the late 1930's.[13] When combined with the relatively small increase in cropped area during this period, we find an overall increase in agricultural output of some 30 percent from the pre-World War I years to the peak year of the thirties, 1937. Let us see how this increase is distributed among the major crops.

Table 1–3 shows that if we compare 1936–37 with 1906–7, more than half of the increase in cropped area was devoted to the cultivation of cotton. The level of production of this crop showed substantial annual fluctuations during this period, due to variations in both acreage and yields; one would be hard pressed to show that there was any significant upward trend in the level of production, although high yields resulted in large crops for a few years in the late 1930's (See Table 1–6). As we shall see, the sluggish increase in the production of this important crop has caused problems in recent years as well; during the 1950's, average annual production of raw cotton came to only 8.5 million cantars, well below the levels attained in the late 1930's.[14]

When we move on from the volume of cotton exports to their value, the figures in Table 1–6 show that price fluctuations were generally so large as to dominate the production variations.[15] By

---

[13] *Ibid.*, p. 42. See also Brown, *op. cit.*, p. 18.

[14] See Appendix Table V–A–6 (pp. 359–62).

[15] The fact that the fluctuations were frequently offsetting suggests that the Egyptian supply may have been a major factor in the determination of world price; however, Egypt supplied less than 10 percent of total world production during this period, while the major price changes shown in Table 1–6 were shared by all staple lengths.

far the highest total earnings from cotton exports came during the period when export quantities were lowest, during the First World War; conversely, depressed prices during the late 1930's resulted in a low level of export earnings, in spite of very high volumes. Egypt's other exports—primarily rice, vegetables, and other raw materials—did not suffer such a large price decline during the depression as did cotton, attaining the same value in the late 1930's as in the late 1920's; the result was that by the late 1930's, cotton's share in the country's exports had dropped from its pre-World War One peak of 92 percent to about 75 percent. As we shall see, this downward trend has continued in the post-World War II period.

TABLE 1–6

COTTON PRODUCTION AND EXPORTS

	Area (000 Feddan)	Yield (Cantar/ Feddan)	Production (000 Cantar)	Exports (000 Cantar)	Average Price (£E/ Cantar)	Value of Cotton Exports (£E000)
1900–1904	1,305	4.67	6,093	6,062	2.738	16,683
1905–9	1,583	4.03	6,379	6,359	3.642	23,233
1910–14	1,711	4.27	7,301	7,182	3.521	25,707
1915–19	1,482	3.58	5,304	5,328	9.007	47,775
1920–24	1,684	3.67	6,181	6,097	7.188	44,432
1925–29	1,761	4.34	7,661	7,144	5.117	38,822
1930–34	1,679	4.28	7,144	7,545	2.635	18,851
1935–39	1,754	5.20	9,137	8,361	2.792	25,367

SOURCE: *Annuaire Statistique*, various issues. See also Appendix Table V–A–6 (pp. 359–62). Export figures here differ somewhat from those in the Appendix, since the latter refer to calendar years, while these refer to cotton crop years (September 1–August 31).

Appendix Tables V–A–1 to V–A–4 (pages 342–57) indicate how these developments were reflected in Egypt's trade balance over this period. During the period of rising export receipts, the level of imports also rose sharply, but with a lag, so that there was a continuing export surplus; this surplus was particularly large during the First World War, when a scarcity of shipping limited the supply of imported goods. Furthermore, during the war years the British made substantial payments (estimated at £80 million)[16] to Egypt to cover expenses of British troops stationed there. These payments, combined with the large trade surpluses of this period, put the

---

[16]A. E. Crouchley, "The Visible Balance of Trade since 1884," *L'Egypte Contemporaine*, Nos. 155–56 (March-April, 1935), p. 495. The sterling pound and the Egyptian pound were at par throughout this period.

current account of the balance of payments heavily in surplus. Egypt's net indebtedness to the rest of the world was substantially reduced, partly through purchases by Egyptians of the country's own national debt, partly through the accumulation of substantial foreign assets. Complete balance-of-payments estimates are not available, so we cannot determine the extent of change in her net payments of interest and profits to the rest of the world, but the fall in this item must have been substantial.[17] This, in turn, would imply a significant change in Egypt's overall balance-of-payments situation. An unofficial estimate of the balance on invisible current account, made by a French economist for 1935, is as shown in Table 1–7. This seems like too optimistic a picture; it leaves out of ac-

/. 2 5

TABLE 1–7

Invisible Current Account Items in Egypt's Balance of Payments, 1935

(£E millions) *Ɫ ℒ*

Receipts:	
Return from capital invested abroad...................	1.0
Tourist expenditures in Egypt........................	1.0
British army expenditures............................	3.0
Local expenditures of Suez Canal Company..............	1.7
Port charges of foreign ships, profit from transit trade and reexports......................	1.0
Payments:	
Interest and profits of foreign capital invested in Egypt...............................	−5.0
Overall surplus on invisible current account..............	2.7

SOURCE: G. Blanchard, "Du Redressement de la Balance Commerciale de l'Egypte en Temps de Crise," *L'Egypte Contemporaine*, No. 157 (May, 1935), pp. 622–24.

count, for example, expenditures abroad by Egyptians for tourism, pilgrimage, business, and government, the sum of which Issawi puts at about £1 million.[18] On the whole, it seems probable that,

---

[17]"It is a matter of considerable labour and difficulty to ascertain the proportion of the Debt respectively held in Egypt and elsewhere, owing to the fact that the quantity of coupons presented for payment in London, Paris, Cairo and Alexandria forms no guide to the whereabouts of the holders, but, according to an authoritative statement, it was estimated that quite a substantial proportion of the public debt of Egypt was held in Egypt towards the end of 1923, and that the public fortune of the country stood at about £E95 millions." This presumably refers to holdings within Egypt of Egyptian public debt as well as foreign securities; it might be compared to the country's total public debt outstanding at the time, £E84 million. United Kingdom, Department of Overseas Trade, *Report on the Economic and Financial Situation of Egypt* (London: H.M.S.O., April, 1924), p. 8.

[18]Issawi, *op. cit.*, p. 39.

taking one year with another, Egypt's current invisibles normally ran a small surplus during the interwar period.

We have traced the impact of the changing pattern of one particular crop, cotton, on the Egyptian economy, and particularly on its exports, moving on from there to the full international trade situation; let us now return to look briefly at the pattern of development of the other major crops. These are virtually all food crops, providing the main source of nourishment to the Egyptian population. Of these, three stand out as of particular importance: wheat, maize, and rice. These three have consistently accounted for over two thirds of the gross value of all agricultural output other than cotton.[19] The supply of rice is highly variable, depending heavily on year-to-year fluctuations in the height of the Nile flood. Output of the other two crops was more stable, although for these as well there were substantial variations in output, due both to fluctuations in yield and to changes in the area planted. The trends in the annual production volume for these three crops developed as shown in Table 1-8. To interpret these data, we need to compare them

TABLE 1-8

INDICES OF OUTPUT OF MAJOR FOOD CROPS

(1913–19 = 100)

Annual Averages	Rice	Wheat	Maize
1913–19.	100	100	100
1920–29.	99	112	112
1930–39.	189	131	100
Value of gross output, annual average, 1913–19 (£E million). . .	4.3	13.6	20.0

SOURCE: M. M. el Imam, *A Production Function for Egyptian Agriculture, 1913–1955*, Memo No. 259 (Cairo: Institute of National Planning, December, 1962), pp. 39 and 41.

with two other pieces of information. The first concerns food imports. Looking at the main categories of food imports, including all food except animal products and "colonial products" (sugar, spices, coffee and tea, etc.), the value of food imports rose markedly up to 1913, but showed no continuing upward trend since then (see Appendix Tables V–A–1 [page 342] and V–A–3 [pages 344–

---

[19]Of the ten most important crops other than cotton (and clover, which is used for fodder and for which statistics are very shaky), these three accounted for 72 percent of gross value of product in each of the years 1913, 1937, and 1955. See el Imam, *op. cit.*, p. 41.

53]).[20] One partial explanation for this result is that from the early 1930's Egypt introduced a prohibitive tariff on the import of wheat and flour, causing imports of this category to drop from over £E2 million in the late 1920's to negligible quantities in the 1930's. Issawi explains this policy as a move on the part of landlords to try to recoup their losses from falling cotton prices by raising the price of cereals; the repeal of this legislation in 1950 had "the same symbolic importance as did the repeal of the Corn Laws in Britain."[21]

The second bit of information to be brought in here concerns the size of the population. As Table 2–1 (page 21) shows, this total rose by some 25 percent from 1917 to 1937. It is difficult to judge what happened to the distribution of income during this period; Issawi indicates that there are reasons to believe it may have become more unequal.[22] Our figures give some support to the conclusion that there was a fall in average food consumption per capita from 1913 to the late 1930's. This fall seems to have been of the order of magnitude of 10 to 15 percent,[23] although it seems likely that shifts in income distribution may have caused a substantially greater drop in food consumption for a large part of the population.

Hansen has recently pointed out that one of the determinants of income distribution within Egypt is the relative price of cotton and foodstuffs.[24] To the extent that the money wage rate is influenced by the total value of output, a rise in the relative price of cotton will cause an increase in real wages (in terms of food), and vice versa.[25] The broad outlines of the Egyptian developments in relative prices are shown in Table 1–9. We have seen that Egypt was nearly self-sufficient in grains during this period; as a result,

---

[20]Before 1930, this was listed as cereals, flour, and agricultural products (category 4); the classification used in Appendix Table V–A–3 does not show total food imports explicitly.

[21]Issawi, *op. cit.*, p. 36.

[22]*Ibid.*, p. 34.

[23]See J. I. Craig and M. Abdel Karim, *Cereals Consumption in Egypt* (Cairo, 1947), cited in Issawi, *op. cit.*, p. 121 n.; also A. F. Sherif, *General Tendencies in the Development of the National Economy in the Last Quarter Century*, Memo No. 121 (Cairo: National Planning Committee, January, 1959).

[24]Hansen, *op. cit.*, pp. 14–19.

[25]Conversely, if the real wage is stabilized in terms of food prices, a rise in the relative price of cotton will shift the distribution of agricultural income away from wage earners and toward landlords. Hansen compares these two approaches in an attempt to determine which theory is better able to explain actual developments in agricultural wage rates. This study is discussed in the Appendix to Chapter 4; see pp. 91–94 below.

the sharp rise in world price of wheat and maize in the 1920's was not strongly felt within the country. Conversely, grain prices in Egypt fell less than the world price during the 1930's. In the case of cotton, at least during this period, the Egyptian price is in fact the world price; the divergencies indicated reflect only the difference between medium and long-staple fibers. In this situation the Egyptian laborer benefits from world boom conditions, while during the 1930's the shift in relative prices added to his misery; there is no doubt that during this period, his lot was miserable indeed.

TABLE 1–9

RATIO OF COTTON PRICES TO GRAIN PRICES: EGYPTIAN AND WORLD PRICES
(1913 = 100)

	Egypt			World		
	Cotton	Grain	Ratio	Cotton	Grain	Ratio
1913...................	100	100	100	100	100	100
1920–29...............	161	119	135	174	152	114
1930–39...............	57	78	73	80	82	98

NOTES AND SOURCES: Egyptian price data are from M. M. el Imam, *A Production Function for Egyptian Agriculture, 1913–1955*, Memo No. 259 (Cairo: Institute of National Planning, December, 1962), p. 40. The grain price is a simple average of the price index for wheat and maize, with 1939 = 100. World price ratios are computed in the same way, using for maize Yellow Platte, London, and Liverpool; for wheat, Winnipeg Manitoba No. 1; for cotton, New Orleans Middling. The ratios show cotton/grain × 100.

In the field of public finance, important changes took place during this period, from the point of view of both expenditures and receipts (see Appendix Tables VI–E–1 [page 380] and VI–E–2 [page 381]). On the expenditure side, education and public health rose from less than 3 percent of the total government budget in 1900 to over 20 percent in 1938–39.[26] The share of irrigation and agriculture rose as well, although not to the same extent. Interest payments on the public debt, on the other hand, stayed nearly constant in absolute terms, with the result that the relative share of this item fell quite sharply. Clearly, the government was devoting more of its energies to what might be called "developmental" expenditures. These were still restricted primarily to agriculture, health, and education; but by the late 1930's, this broad category accounted for over 35 percent of the government's current expenditures, surely an impressively high figure.[27]

With regard to receipts, the most important change which took

---

[26]Excluding the railroads, telephone, and telegraph.
[27]See Appendix Table VI–E–2 (p. 381).

place was the growing importance of customs duties. Rising from 28 percent of tax revenues in 1900 to nearly 60 percent by 1938–39, this item provided the backbone of the tripling of tax revenue over this period. Up to 1930, this increase was a result of sharply rising import values with ad valorem tariffs which were generally constant for all commodities except tobacco. Until that time, Egypt was bound by international agreements to hold customs duties on most imported articles at 8 percent ad valorem or less. When these conventions expired early in 1930, Egypt rushed to take advantage of her new freedom to set her own tariffs. By 1938–39, the ratio of customs receipts to import values for all goods except tobacco products had more than doubled compared to a decade earlier, rising to 25 percent. In broad outlines, the marked rise in government tax revenues up to 1930 was a result of rising import values, with tariff rates nearly constant (with the major exception of tobacco products). After 1930, the increase in tariff rates was large enough so that tax receipts (as distinct from other government revenues) were higher in 1933–34 than in 1928–29, although imports had fallen by 50 percent. Total government revenues from all sources declined slightly (allowing for removal from the budget of the railroads, telephone, and telegraph). Expenditures were held down as well, so that in only two years of the depression did the government budget show a deficit.[28]

It is clear that the rising tariff rates were quite significant in sustaining the revenue of the government; their protective impact is more difficult to judge. In the case of food grains, import tariffs kept prices high during the 1930's relative to other crops, but it is difficult to find any reflection of this in the allocation of land; Table 1–3 suggests that the movement may have been in the opposite direction. With regard to industrial products, the tariffs brought about the first steps toward import substitution in a few specific lines (e.g., textiles, fertilizers, cement, sugar refining); in most of these cases, however, Egyptian producers supplied only a very small portion of the domestic market during this period. In general, it seems fair to say that while much was made during the 1930's of the government's new right to protect domestic industry, and while this development was quite important from the point of view of its effects on the government budget, the protective impact of the change was not particularly significant. It was not until the following period, during World War II, when imported supplies were

---

[28] In 1930–31 and 1938–39.

drastically curtailed and domestic demand was greatly increased, that Egyptian industry made any real headway.

We have seen that during the final decades of the nineteenth century the increase in agricultural output kept pace with population growth primarily as a result of the rapid extension of multiple cropping. During the first third of the twentieth century, this clearly was not the case; total output grew by roughly 30 percent, largely through increasing yields per acre, while the growth of the population was close to 50 percent. In spite of this, the dependence of the country on agriculture showed no signs of abating; the share of agriculture in total employment remained virtually constant at 70 percent, while its share in total income in the late 1930's was nearly 50 percent.[29] Changes in internal relative prices meant that the resulting decline in real income per capita was shifted onto the shoulders of the lower classes: agricultural workers and urban laborers, for whom the relatively expensive basic foods formed a higher portion of total outlays. By the late 1930's, Egypt had only taken the first steps to break out of this box. The government aimed at a strictly orthodox, balanced-budget policy; until the mid-1930's, international conventions sharply restricted the country's taxing abilities, while these same agreements effectively ruled out any protection of domestic industry. It is easy to exaggerate the importance of these legal restrictions; even if they had not existed, it seems doubtful that the picture would have been very different. Neither the British nor the Egyptian ruling elite showed much concern for the longer run economic problems of the country. It is true that the government made some use of its increased freedom to finance new projects, even to make loans to an industrial bank, as well as to protect domestic producers from the cold realities of international competition; still, the use of these new tools in the prewar period was generally limited and ineffectual.

The growth in the Egyptian economy during the first three decades of the twentieth century might be characterized by proportional expansion, with agriculture playing a consistent and predominant role from both income and employment points of view. Since the 1930's, by contrast, the basic characteristic of the growth of the economy has been one of structural transformation. In absolute terms, agriculture has retained a primary role in the economy,

---

[29]See Appendix Tables I–A–1 (pp. 270–71) and II–B–1 (p. 304). There is no way of knowing agriculture's share in national income at the turn of the century, although it can hardly have been much over 50 percent.

but the major impetus for growth has come from other sectors of the economy. Manufacturing industry has grown rapidly, although from a small base, to the point where today it accounts for some 20 percent of national income. Perhaps more significant, however, has been the explosive growth of the services, accounting for over 60 percent of all new jobs in the economy from 1937 to 1960. Our concern in the remainder of this study is to explore the nature of this transformation, to see how it has taken place, what problems it has created, and how viable a base it has provided for the future growth of the economy.

Population and Employment

In the great debate over the nature of economic development in countries with unlimited supplies of labor, Egypt is invariably cited as one country which is, in some sense, heavily overpopulated. As early as 1936, a careful student of the demographic situation in Egypt estimated that "one might envisage with fair assurance the reduction of the agricultural population by at least 50 percent without reducing the total products from the land and without much more mechanization than at present."[1] Since that time, the population has continued to grow substantially more rapidly than cultivable area; and although alternative employment opportunities outside of agriculture have expanded considerably, still within the agricultural sector the man-land ratio has continued to rise. Clearly, the country provides an interesting case study for those wishing to test theories about the interrelationship between population and economic growth, whether these be of the older Malthusian variety or of the newer Arthur Lewis line. Furthermore, as we shall see, Egypt has extensive demographic data of all kinds. For both these reasons, population analysis in Egypt constitutes a relatively heavily worked field. In spite of this fact, it still has many puzzles and questions outstanding. There is still substantial disagreement, to take one obvious example, as to the extent —or even the existence—of agricultural unemployment. We shall

---

[1] W. Cleland, *The Population Problem in Egypt* (Lancaster, Pa.: Science Press Printing Co., 1936), p. 106.

postpone consideration of this particular question until Chapter 4, concerning the agricultural sector. In this chapter, we set forth a general picture of the Egyptian demographic situation, first in terms of the overall level and rate of growth of the population, birth and death rates, and the age and sex structure of the population; then, in terms of health and education; and finally, from the point of view of employment and its geographical distribution.

A. THE DEMOGRAPHIC BACKGROUND

Egypt is unusual among developing countries in that it has a long history of censuses; referring to a long string of population counts starting more than five thousand years ago and continuing through the "modern" censuses of recent years, Cleland says that "Egyptians have been counted perhaps more times than any other people."[2] Estimates of the population of Egypt in Pharaonic and Roman times range from three million to twenty-seven million;[3] perhaps the most reasonable guess would be in the range of six to eight million, although this is subject to substantial error.[4] By the beginning of the nineteenth century, the population had fallen to two or three million, probably due primarily to the centuries of misrule and oppression under the Mameluke rulers. During the nineteenth century the population more than tripled, so that by the time of the first "modern" census in 1897 the country found itself with 9.7 million people.[5] Since that year, censuses have been held regularly every ten years, except that the Suez crisis forced the postponement of the 1957 census until 1960.

There were substantial improvements in techniques, in detail, and in organization of the censuses in the early twentieth century; by 1927, the coverage was officially stated to have been "well over 99 per cent."[6] The published figures, as given in the last seven

---

[2]*Ibid.*, p. 3.

[3]For a listing and evaluation of a number of these estimates, see Abdelmegid Moustafa Farrag, *Demographic Developments in Egypt during the Present Century* (Ph.D. dissertation, London School of Economics and Political Science, 1957), p. 6.

[4]See *ibid.*, p. 6; Cleland, *op. cit.*, pp. 3–6; C. Issawi, *Egypt in Revolution: An Economic Analysis* (New York: Oxford University Press, 1963), p. 20; and references cited in each of these sources.

[5]There was a census of the population taken in 1882, but the country was in such a turmoil at the time, with a new nationalistic government in power and a British invasion impending, that the results are considered to be virtually worthless.

[6]Farrag, *op. cit.*, p. 23; this study contains an excellent survey of the development of census techniques during the twentieth century.

censuses, are shown in Table 2–1. There has been considerable discussion as to the accuracy of the 1947 census. Two reasons have been advanced for believing that it was an overcount. In the first place, as we shall see below, the statistics showed no increase in fertility and mortality rates in the country, a fact which makes the rise in the population growth rate in the decade 1937–47 look rather suspicious. Furthermore, in 1945 a population count was made and used as the basis for distributing rationed commodities;[7] in 1947, people may have exaggerated the numbers in their household, either in the expectation that the census would be used for the same purpose or for fear that the two counts would be cross-checked. On the basis of an assumption of growth rates over the decade 1937–47 equal to those in the period 1907–37, el Badry has concluded that the official figures for 1947 are 5.6 percent too high.[8] The validity of this adjustment depends in part on one's judgement of the relative accuracy of annual vital statistics and decennial censuses. Let us look at the nature and sources of these vital statistics.

TABLE 2–1

POPULATION

	(Thousands)	Annual Compound Growth Rate from Previous Census (Percent)
1897	9,715	
1907	11,287	1.5
1917	12,751	1.2
1927	14,218	1.1
1937	15,933	1.1
1947	19,022	1.8
1960	26,089	2.5

Registration of all births and deaths has been compulsory in Egypt, in rural as well as urban areas, since 1912.[9] In areas where there exists a health bureau, the registration is done with the local medical officer, and this is one of his primary responsibilities. In

---

[7] This rationing count yielded a total of 24 million people, 35 percent too high a figure compared to later estimates of the population in that year. See M. A. el Badry, "Some Demographic Measurements for Egypt Based on the Stability of Census Age Distributions," *Milbank Memorial Fund Quarterly,* Vol. XXXIII, No. 3 (July, 1955), p. 275.

[8] *Ibid.*

[9] For a discussion of the reporting of births and deaths, see Introduction in United Arab Republic, Department of Statistics and Census, *Vital Statistics,* Vol. I (Cairo annual).

areas not blessed with a health officer—where over half of the population lives—this registration is done with the local tax official, a man whose primary interests and responsibilities lie in quite different lines. Probably this is the main explanation for the fact that both birth and death rates in rural areas with health bureaus have been consistently and substantially higher than in areas without health offices, a divergence which must be attributed to difference in degree of coverage of the statistics, rather than to basic health or fertility conditions. Furthermore, detailed studies indicate that the statistics of births and deaths may be rather inaccurate even in the villages where a health center is located.[10] Both of these limitations restrict the usefulness of the figures as they stand.

TABLE 2–2

ANNUAL AVERAGES OF CRUDE BIRTH AND DEATH RATES

(Numbers per Thousand of Population)

	Reported Figures			Adjusted Figures		
	Birth Rates	Death Rates	Natural Increase	Birth Rates	Death Rates	Natural Increase
1927–36	43.6	27.0	16.6	n.a.	n.a.	n.a.
1934–36	42.6	27.7	14.9	47.7	34.2	13.6
1937–46	41.0	26.6	14.4	45.2	32.5	13.7
1947–51	43.5	20.2	23.5	47.2	24.6	22.5
1951–60	41.7	17.7	24.3	44.4*	20.8*	23.6*
1947–60	42.3	18.4	23.9	45.5*	22.3*	23.2*

*Terminal year is 1959.
SOURCES: Reported figures: United Arab Republic, Department of Statistics and Census, *Vital Statistics*, various issues. Adjusted figures: M. A. el Badry, "Trends in the Components of Population Growth in the Arab Countries of the Middle East: A Survey of Present Information," *Demography*, Vol. II (1965).

Recently, an attempt has been made to improve the accuracy of these vital statistics by adjusting them on the assumption that true birth and death rates in rural areas without health bureaus are equal to those in rural health bureau areas, rather than distinctly lower (as the original figures imply).[11] These adjusted estimates

---

[10]J. M. Weir and Associates, "An Evaluation of Health and Sanitation in Egyptian Villages," *Journal of the Egyptian Public Health Association*, Vol. XXVII, No. 3 (1952), pp. 55–122. For the village adjacent to the health center, Sindbis, Weir's characterization of the vital statistics as "grossly inaccurate" seems too harsh, on the basis of the figures given on pages 104–6 of the article.

[11]M. A. el Badry, "Trends in the Components of Population Growth in the Arab Countries of the Middle East: A Survey of Present Information," *Demography*, Vol. II (1965).

still understate the true figures to the extent that reporting in urban and rural health bureau areas is incomplete, and to the extent that these diverge from the situation in areas without health bureaus; but they constitute a distinct improvement over the original reported figures. A further problem arises with regard to the infant mortality rate; in 1958, this was reported at 151 per thousand in Cairo, compared to 147 for all urban areas, 136 for rural areas with health bureaus, and only 81 for rural areas with no health offices. El Badry has argued that health conditions in Cairo are the best in the country, and that the lower rates in other areas are due simply to underreporting of deaths of infants. If this is so, we might make the further adjustment of imputing the Cairo rates of infant mortality to the rest of the country as well. These two adjustments give us revised estimates of birth and death rates for the whole country, as shown in Table 2-2.[12] Neither the original figures nor the adjusted ones give any reason to believe that there was any rise in the natural rate of increase from the 1927–36 period to 1937–46;

TABLE 2–3

POPULATION GROWTH RATES

(Average Annual Increase)

	Computed Directly from Population Censuses	Registration Statistics	
		Original Figures	Adjusted Figures
1927–37...........	1.1	1.7	n.a.
1937–47...........	1.8	1.4	1.4
1947–60...........	2.5	2.4	2.3

if anything, the figures might suggest the reverse. This could be taken as a substantiation of the need for a downward adjustment of the figures in the 1947 population census, with a resulting fall in the indicated growth rate in the decade preceding that census and a sharp rise in the following period. When we go on to look at the implied growth rates over a longer period, however, the question becomes more complicated. The various estimates are as shown in Table 2–3. The problem with accepting the downward

---

[12]Commenting on these adjustments, el Badry makes the following interesting comparison: "It is found that in rural areas without health bureaus, adoption of the infant mortality rate of Cairo gives a total of 95,000 underreported infant deaths, and the adoption of the crude birth rate of rural health bureau areas gives a total of 98,000 underreported births. The closeness of the two figures is indicative of the possibility that missing infant deaths had not been reported at either birth or death" (*ibid.*, p. 6).

revision of the 1947 census is that it would imply a growth rate in the following period of over 2.9 percent per annum,[13] which seems far out of line with the vital statistics of the period. In what follows, we shall work with the 1947 figures as published in the census.

The breakdown of the total population by sex shows that the ratio of males to females has never diverged markedly from 1.0. With regard to age, the distribution of the population for recent census years has been as indicated in Table 2-4. Detailed studies of el Badry[14] and Farrag[15] have indicated that there is a consistent

TABLE 2-4

AGE DISTRIBUTION OF THE POPULATION

	1917	1927	1937	1947	1960
0-9	28.0	27.4	27.1	26.3	30.6
10-19	20.3	20.3	20.4	21.7	20.5
20-29	15.6	16.4	15.2	15.1	14.3
30-39	13.5	14.1	14.7	13.8	13.1
40-49	9.0	9.3	10.1	10.4	9.3
50 and over	13.7	12.5	12.5	12.7	12.2
Total	100.0	100.0	100.0	100.0	100.0

NOTE: Totals may not add due to rounding.

tendency to report ages wrongly in the replies to the census questioners. From our point of view, the most serious inaccuracy concerns males aged 20-29; both studies found this cohort to be consistently too small, perhaps as young men sought to avoid the draft (which runs from ages 19 to 27) by reporting their actual ages as below 19 and (according to Farrag) above 30. In 1937, these studies estimate the degree of underreporting of males aged 20-29 to be 9 percent (el Badry) or 13 percent (Farrag). We shall have to bear this in mind in our discussion of employment statistics. It should be made clear, though, that neither study suggests that these men were missed by the census, but rather that they are wrongly reported as being in a younger or older age group. Since most of our employment analysis is concerned with adult males taken as a whole, this shifting should not be a major problem for us.[16] In 1960 the relatively stable age structure of the population over the preceding four censuses was broken, as a fall in death

---

[13]Unless the 1960 census is also an overcount, which seems highly unlikely.

[14]El Badry, "Some Demographic Measurements . . .," pp. 278-86.

[15]Farrag, *op. cit.*

[16]Except to the extent that they are wrongly reported to be under 15, which is probably not a serious exception.

rates and a consequent rise in the rate of natural increase brought about a marked change in the share of young people in the total population. We shall have more to say about this in the discussion of employment below.

Perhaps we should say a word about the importance of birth control in Egypt. There is some evidence to indicate that in spite of government equivocation and indecision, the use of birth control techniques has found fairly ready acceptance, at least among certain groups. In a sample survey taken in the period 1956–58, and reaching 6,067 women, the results shown in Table 2–5 were found. The question asked in the survey was whether the wives had "made some effort to prevent pregnancies," surely as sweeping a definition of birth control as one could imagine. As the table indicates, the incidence of controlling is heavily concentrated in urban families with well-educated husbands. It is also significant to note that the share of controllers in the total is substantially higher for incomplete than for completed urban families, an indication that the practice of birth control is more widespread among younger wives.

The practice of birth control must have spread somewhat since the time of the survey; in 1962 the government began a serious campaign to convince the public of its importance and to educate them on various possible methods. In recent years, since the government has taken over the importing of pharmaceuticals, the domestic price of contraceptive pills has been cut to equal the import cost (i.e., they are subsidized to cover domestic distribution costs), so that the domestic price for a month's supply is now 20 piasters (46 cents, at the official exchange rate), compared to over three times that amount a year earlier.[17] During the first quarter of 1963, some 150,000–200,000 women were receiving these pills regularly, of whom about one third received them free of charge through rural health centers. From the point of view of the birth rate of the country, this is a small but not negligible amount;[18]

---

[17]This might be compared with an average *weekly* wage rate of industrial laborers of 221 piasters (in July, 1961), or an average *daily* wage of paid agricultural laborers of 11–14 piasters (1959). In 1966 the price was further reduced to 10 piasters for a month's supply.

[18]Assuming 25 percent of these users would have had children in the absence of pills, the birth rate in 1963 would have risen from 4.4 percent to 4.58 percent. Some of these women may have switched from other techniques of birth control to using pills, so these figures exaggerate the net increase in the number of controllers. It seems likely, though, that switching to the use of the pills increases the effectiveness of controlling, a factor which Rizk found to be of considerable importance as a determinant of fertility (Rizk, *op. cit.*, pp. 38–45).

TABLE 2-5

PERCENTAGE OF WIVES WHO EVER PRACTICED FAMILY LIMITATION, BY EDUCATION OF HUSBAND

Level of Education	Urban		Semiurban		Rural	
	Number of Wives Interviewed	Percent Controllers	Number of Wives Interviewed	Percent Controllers	Number of Wives Interviewed	Percent Controllers
Completed families:						
University and secondary..............	71	33.8	0	...	0	...
Primary and elementary...............	150	18.7	17	17.0	123	3.0
Illiterate...........................	158	8.9	8	0.0	527	1.0
Total..........................	379	17.4	25	12.0	650	1.5
Incomplete families:						
University and secondary..............	310	51.0	0	...	0	...
Primary and elementary...............	755	23.0	502	17.5	470	3.0
Illiterate...........................	440	10.7	87	10.3	1,291	0.8
Total..........................	1,505	25.2	589	16.4	1,761	1.0

NOTES: Education level refers to highest level started but not necessarily completed by husband. A completed family is one where the wife has passed 45. For incomplete families, another variable, duration of marriage, is important; duration of marriage. Data in source provide breakdown according to this variable, but these details do not basically alter the pattern shown above. Total figures for incomplete families were computed by the author.

SOURCE: H. Rizk, *Fertility Patterns in Selected Areas in Egypt* (Ph.D. dissertation, Princeton University, 1959), pp. 120–21.

looking to the future, the groundwork is being laid for an expansion which might reach significant proportions five to ten years hence.

With regard to the expected future growth rate, the government of the United Arab Republic has made official population projections, but these seem rather implausible from a number of points of view.[19] In outline, their basic premise seems reasonable; in the coming twenty-five years, the Egyptian demographic picture will be dominated by some decline in mortality, with fertility rates constant or falling very little. This would imply a steady rise in the rate of growth of population. If the current rate of increase is in the range of 2.5 to 3 percent per annum, perhaps a reasonable guess would be that by 1985 the growth rate would be in the range of 3 to 3.5 percent per annum. Clearly, the Egyptians cannot look for solace from the demographers in their own particular version of the race between mouths to feed and hands with work to keep them busy.

B. HEALTH AND EDUCATION

Perhaps the most important characteristic of Egypt's health situation is the prevalence of poverty and of debilitating diseases. The statistics and studies available make it clear that the major epidemic diseases—malaria, typhoid, and the like—are not so much of a threat to the country's health as are the enervating parasites which infect the vast majority of the populace. The most widespread of these infections is bilharzia, a parasitic disease which is said to reduce the productivity of the patient by 25 to 50 percent.[20] There is no general agreement as to what proportion of the population suffers from this disease; perhaps a fair estimate would be

---

[19]See United Arab Republic, Presidency of the Republic, Central Statistical Committee, *Population Trends in the U.A.R.* (Cairo, 1962). For the maximum and expected estimate (No. I), which is based on the assumption of constant fertility and declining mortality, the expected quinquennial average per annum compound growth rates are as follows:

$$1960–65 = 2.78$$
$$1965–70 = 2.89$$
$$1970–75 = 2.89$$
$$1975–80 = 2.83$$
$$1980–85 = 2.84$$

The pattern of change in the growth rate looks implausible, and the implied increase in the growth rate over the period is negligible. Furthermore, the age and sex breakdowns in these estimates are quite unreasonable. I am indebted to Etienne van de Walle for a careful and helpful appraisal of this study.

[20]Issawi, *op. cit.*, p. 92. For a description of the nature of this disease, how it is spread, and its effects, see Cleland, *op. cit.*, pp. 82–87.

close to 60 percent. In a detailed study of one village in Lower Egypt, Weir found that rather sophisticated techniques were needed to discover the full extent of this malady; when he applied these techniques to 215 randomly chosen males from this village, the infection rate was found to be 95 percent.[21] This ratio cannot be generalized to the whole country, since the disease is known to be more prevalent in Lower than in Upper Egypt, and more prevalent among men than women; still, it is clear that the disease is quite widespread. Bilharzia can be cured, but this involves a series of painful injections coupled with a period of complete inactivity, neither of which seems within reach for most rural Egyptians; furthermore, the reinfection rate is quite high.[22] Weir's study also indicated a heavy incidence of other intestinal parasites and amoebic infections, not to mention eye infections such as trachoma, which affected nearly 90 percent of the villagers examined in this same study.[23]

Information on causes of death (Appendix Table II–A–9) bears out the idea that Egypt's main health problem is not one of major killer diseases, but rather of general poverty and weakness of the population, making them susceptible to bronchitis, gastroenteritis, and colitis, for example, three sicknesses which are relatively minor in developed countries, but which have accounted for 50 percent of all deaths in Egypt in recent years. The discouraging thing about this situation is the great difficulty of bringing about any major improvement. Where the primary health problem of a country is malaria, for example, it is possible to introduce DDT and virtually solve that problem (as in the case of Ceylon); but where the population has a low level of health generally, due both to widespread poverty and to ubiquitous parasitical diseases, progress is sure to be much more slow, dependent on advance on a number of fronts together. This was clearly brought out in Weir's study, from which the following quotation is taken:[24]

> The burden of disease carried by the population is heavy. Nutritional deficiencies, epidemic and chronic eye diseases, enteric fevers and dysenteries, tuberculosis, syphilis, and bilharzia are all found at extremely high levels in the village population.
>
> The possibility of any effective control is dependent upon a number of factors. The bulk of the conditions are the result of poor sanitation in

---

[21]Weir, *op. cit.*, pp. 90–91.
[22]*Ibid.*, p. 93.
[23]*Ibid.*, p. 77.
[24]*Ibid.*, pp. 109–11.

all its aspects. Under the present situation in the villages it was possible to improve sanitation only through installation of water supplies and latrines. Such installations in a village, without parallel improvement in housing, social and economic status do not appear to have a marked effect upon the death rate in infants and therefore presumably little or no effect on the rate of dysenteries in infants.

Fly control will prevent the spread of acute eye diseases and will lower the dysentery and the infant mortality rates. However it has been shown that fly control by insecticides cannot be maintained for a period of over two years. Basic fly control through improvement in handling manure and control of other breeding areas cannot be achieved under the present conditions of housing and of handling animals and manure for the fields.

Overcrowding and poor ventilation and lighting are probably major factors in the spread of tuberculosis and no real improvement can be made in the present villages.

In general it would appear that any improvement in the nutritional status will require a long term program in home economics and an agricultural extension program to reorganize the planting and dietary habits of the villagers.

Clearly, Weir is correct in concluding that any basic improvement in the health of the Egyptian population "must necessarily be a long term program extending over many decades and coordinated with educational, economic, and social improvements."[25]

TABLE 2-6

ILLITERACY

	Total Persons Aged 10 and Over	Persons Not Able to Read and Write Aged 10 and Over	Illiteracy Rate		
			Total	Male	Female
1907	7,848,024	7,277,303	92.7	87.0	98.6
1917	9,161,944	8,357,461	91.2	84.8	97.7
1927	10,268,404	8,816,601	85.9	76.1	95.6
1937	11,603,488	9,885,300	85.2	76.6	93.9
1947	13,489,946	10,407,972	77.2	66.1	88.2
1960	17,914,323	12,587,686	70.3	56.6	83.8

NOTE: Total excludes nomads and those for whom literacy is not stated.
SOURCE: UNESCO, *Progress of Literacy in Various Countries*, Monographs on Fundamental Education, No. VI (Paris, 1935), pp. 83-84; and population censuses.

With regard to education, Egypt has made substantial progress in reducing its illiteracy rate, although in absolute terms the number of people who cannot read and write has continued to increase (see Table 2-6). As the table shows, far greater progress has been

[25]*Ibid.*, p. 110.

made for males than for females. Another aspect of this picture can be seen in Table 2–7, which shows the number of students as a proportion of children of school age. This table shows a particularly remarkable and important expansion of schooling in the provinces, for boys as well as girls; in the governorates, on the other hand, even with an expansion of 80 percent in the number of students, the ratio fell somewhat.[26] A partial explanation for this

TABLE 2–7

STUDENTS AND POPULATION OF STUDENT AGE

(Thousands)

	1947			1960		
	Boys	*Girls*	*Total*	*Boys*	*Girls*	*Total*
Governorates:						
Population aged 5–14	377	391	768	780	765	1,545
Students	286	165	451	468	345	813
Ratio	0.76	0.42	0.59	0.60	0.45	0.53
Provinces:						
Population aged 5–14	1,975	1,871	3,846	2,843	2,589	5,432
Students	773	372	1,145	1,698	881	2,579
Ratio	0.39	0.20	0.30	0.60	0.34	0.47
Total:						
Population aged 5–14	2,352	2,262	4,614	3,623	3,354	6,977
Students	1,059	537	1,596	2,166	1,226	3,392
Ratio	0.45	0.24	0.35	0.60	0.37	0.49

NOTES: Students include total enrollment in primary, preparatory, secondary, and technical training schools, private and public, but exclude all higher education. The fact that 14 is too low a cutoff point makes all the ratios somewhat too high. Furthermore, the numbers of students refer to the school year 1948–49 for the earlier period, and as of November 15, 1961, for the later one, once again giving an upward bias to all ratios.

SOURCE: Population figures from the population censuses. Students: 1947: United Arab Republic, Department of Statistics and Census, *Statistique Scolaire: Année Scolaire 1948–49* (Cairo, 1950). 1960: United Arab Republic, Ministry of Education, Statistical Section, *Agenda Statistique, 1961–62* (Cairo, 1963).

pattern lies with the high rate of increase in population in the governorates, due primarily to internal migration; it is also true, however, that the number of students in the provinces rose at a faster rate than in the governorates. The marked expansion of education outside the major cities is surely a remarkable achievement; one hopes that the nature of the educational program will be such as to have some impact on the pattern and level of living of the rural population.

With the substantial expansion of universities in recent years,

---

[26]The governorates are the five major urban areas, while the rest of the country is divided into provinces. This breakdown is discussed in more detail on pages 34–35 below.

the Egyptian education system might be characterized as a "steep pyramid." One out of every 250 people in the Egyptian population is a student in higher education, a figure equal to that in West Germany, Sweden, and the United Kingdom. There have been complaints that with this rapid expansion—the number of university students has doubled in the last ten years—the quality of the education has deteriorated; with admissions requirements falling off while teaching loads are increasing to levels which no American or British teacher would attempt, it is inevitable that the quality of education should fall. The decision to follow this path of rapid expansion was not without vocal dissent from the academic community, but the decision to expand—to permit all secondary school graduates with a C average or better to enter a university if they chose, without cost—was a political one, overruling all objections of the educators. From the point of view of the quality of education, the decision has clearly been an unfortunate one. Egypt has no shortage of people who have sat through four years of university lectures, although, as in all countries of the world, there is a real need for imaginative and well-trained college graduates. If this "open-door" policy is thought of as a means of helping to solve the overpopulation problem by keeping the young people out of the labor market for four additional years, surely the policy is shortsighted in the extreme. The help obtained in this way is very temporary, while the cost, in terms of decreased quality, is permanent and serious.[27]

C. EMPLOYMENT

Before beginning a detailed examination of the pattern of employment in recent years, perhaps we should say a word about the various sources of data available for this examination. The analyst working on this question is blessed—or cursed—with a large diversity of sources, varying widely in coverage, in classifications, and in concepts of employment used. A discussion and brief appraisal of a number of these sources is given in Appendix II-B. For most purposes, we prefer to rely primarily on the population

---

[27] It is an interesting exercise to look at the impact of this supply-demand situation on rates of remuneration. One approach to this, suggested by Richard Jolly, is to compare the starting annual wage of a college graduate with average income per capita of the whole population (gross national product divided by total population). In Egypt the ratio is approximately 4:1, compared to, perhaps, 3:1 in the United States and 25:1 in Uganda.

censuses, the source providing the most comprehensive and consistent set of figures. The main weakness of these census figures, we believe, concerns the treatment of female workers. Although the dividing line between employed, unemployed, and those outside the labor force has ostensibly remained the same over the last three censuses, a brief look at the figures is enough to convince one that this line has in fact varied from year to year. This is particularly clear in the case of farm wives, a group which it is virtually impossible to treat with precision and consistency. Once we have eliminated such obvious slips as the inclusion of 3.3 million women listed in the agricultural sector in 1947 as engaged in "home duties," the employment picture for females is as shown in Table 2–8. It seems clear that the drop in farm employment of

TABLE 2–8

EMPLOYMENT OF FEMALES

	Agriculture and Livestock	All Others	Total Employment
1937	673,385	163,413	836,798
1947	587,236	212,002	799,238
1960	270,064	315,158	585,221

NOTES: Figures exclude unemployed, ill-defined, unproductive, and those engaged in house owning, as well as women doing family household work both on and off the farms.
SOURCE: Population censuses.

females is a statistical phenomenon to which no analytical significance should be attached. With regard to the steady increase in other employment of women, in 1960 78 percent of these workers were in the service sector, primarily as domestic servants; one quarter of the total were young girls under 15 years of age. When we come to consider employment and output in the service sector in Chapter 6 below, we shall have to take account of this expansion in the employment of women. With regard to young people, we have already seen that the proportion of this group in schools has risen markedly in recent years, although it still is only about 50 percent. In absolute terms, the number of young people (below 15 years of age) who are listed as employed has continued to rise slowly, in spite of laws forbidding the employment of children under age 12. In 1960, only 14 percent of the population aged 6–14 were listed as employed. Of this group of employed young people, 80 percent were in the agricultural sector, while most of the others were in the services. The demand for young people to

TABLE 2–9

POPULATION AND EMPLOYMENT

(In Thousands)

	1937	1947	1960
A. Total population...................	15,933	19,022	26,085
B. Total employment.................	5,783	6,590	7,833
1. Agriculture*....................	4,020	4,075	4,406
2. Industry†.....................	377	589	771
3. Services‡.....................	1,386	1,927	2,656
C. Total adult§ males................	4,806	5,761	7,333
D. Employment, adult§ males...........	4,457	5,246	6,594
1. Agriculture*....................	2,976	3,139	3,560
2. Industry†.....................	330	514	715
3. Services‡.....................	1,151	1,593	2,318
E. Participation ratio:			
1. Total population................	0.36	0.35	0.30
2. Adult§ males, total..............	0.93	0.91	0.90
a) 15–19......................	0.82	0.79	0.65 ‖
b) 20–29......................	0.93	0.91	0.88 ‖
c) 30–39......................	0.97	0.96	0.97 ‖
d) 40–49......................	0.97	0.97	0.97 ‖
e) 50 and over.................	0.92	0.90	0.84 ‖

*Agriculture, forestry, hunting, and fishing.
†Mining, manufacturing, electricity, gas, and water.
‡Construction, commerce, transportation, communications, and other services.
§Aged 15 and above.
‖Age-specific participation rates for 1960 exclude military employment, although this is included in the ratio for total adult males.
SOURCES: Population censuses. Figures in Section B are revised figures from United Arab Republic, Department of Statistics and Census, *Population Census, 1960* (Cairo, 1963), Vol. II, p. xiv, adjusted to exclude unemployed workers and to include an estimate of 1960 military employment (see Table 6–2 [page 134]). For Sections D and E, see Tables 2–10 and 2–11 for notes and sources. Totals may not add due to rounding.

work in agriculture is highly seasonal, reaching one peak in June (for planting rice and combating cotton worms), a second in September (when cotton is picked). The significance of this seasonal pattern is that the population censuses of 1947 and before were taken in March, a period of low demand for young people, while the 1960 census was taken during a month of peak demand, September.[28] This makes us hesitant to attach much significance to the reported employment figures for young people. In the remainder of this chapter, we shall concentrate our attention primarily on the employment pattern for adult males, leaving aside further considerations of both young people and women until the detailed discussion of specific sectors in later chapters.

[28]See M. el Tomy and B. Hansen, *The Seasonal Employment Profile in Egyptian Agriculture*, Memo No. 501 (Cairo: Institute of National Planning, October, 1964), pp. 7–12. This study suggests that the labor requirements for women and children in agriculture in September are roughly five times the level for March.

During the decade 1937–47, Egypt's population rose by nearly 20 percent, while the number of people employed increased at approximately the same rate (Table 2-9, p. 33); the participation rate for the whole economy remained virtually unchanged.[29] With the stable age structure to which we have referred, the number of adult males grew at approximately the same rate as did total population, while jobs for this group increased only fractionally less than proportionally, so that the participation rate for men fell slightly, in the aggregate as well as through all specific age groups. This aggregated picture of proportional growth, however, conceals considerable structural change which was taking place in the economy during this period. Employment in agriculture increased very little, while the service sector expanded rapidly; it was primarily the services, along with a more moderate expansion of employment in the industrial sector, which absorbed the great majority of the natural increase in the labor force in the economy.

The details of the population census permit us to be somewhat more precise about the nature of these developments. As the census figures show, the territory of Egypt falls into two fairly clear and distinct groups. The first of these consists of the five urban governorates of Cairo, Alexandria, the Canal Zone, Suez, and Damietta.[30] The urban nature of these agglomerations is made clear by the fact that within the five of them as a whole, the agricultural sector has accounted for 3 to 5.2 percent of total employment over the past three censuses. The rest of the country is divided into provinces, where the agricultural sector has provided between 70

---

[29]There was a negligible fall, from 0.363 to 0.346. Strictly speaking, the participation rate refers to the ratio of labor force to population; with unemployment figures either unavailable or unreliable, we use this term to refer to the ratio of employment to population.

[30]The demarcation lines of the governorates have been changed often over the course of past censuses, primarily to take account of the growth of urban areas. In the 1960 census, several changes were introduced, two of which are particularly significant here. The Canal Zone was broken into two parts, Ismailia and Port Said; the area of Ismailia was expanded substantially so that the estimate for the population in that city in 1947 as stated in the 1960 census is over 100,000 higher than the estimate for the same year in the 1947 census. This expansion took in a substantial rural—or at least agricultural—population, although the 1960 census lists them all as urban.

The second change was in Damietta, which was broadened to include the surrounding agricultural area, and hence was included as of 1960 in the provinces. In what follows, we have used the urban-rural division of the census for that province for 1960, including urban Damietta with the governorates (as in earlier years) and the rural population with the provinces.

Finally, in the 1960 census the terminology "governorates" and "provinces" has been dropped, but we prefer to follow the older usage.

and 80 percent of total employment.[31] In these circumstances, it does make sense to speak of the division between governorates and provinces as if it were an urban-rural division, and to examine the nature of the population transfer in terms of these figures.[32]

From the point of view of the whole population, we can surmise that there has been a substantial internal migration from the fact that between 1937 and 1947 the population in the governorates rose by some 52 percent, while rural population grew only by 14 percent over the same period. If the rate of natural increase was the same in the two areas, these figures would imply that some 760,000 people migrated from the provinces to the governorates during that decade.[33]

It is possible to check this estimate against another set of data, that on internal migration, as shown by the population censuses. This source tells, for each census year, the number of people who were enumerated in a given district but born elsewhere. For example, in 1937 there were 588,000 people enumerated in the governates who were born in the provinces; by 1947, this figure had risen to 1,053,000. In order to be able to estimate from these two figures the number of immigrants to the governates, one would have to know the number of people from the original group —and from those who migrated during the interim period—who died before 1947. As an approximation, we might assume that the death rate of the original migrants was the same as that of the rest of the urban population, and ignore those who migrated and died during the period;[34] on this basis, we can state that at least 615,000 migrated from the provinces to the governorates during the decade. The discrepancy between this figure and the estimate in Table 2–10 is primarily a result of our assumption that the rate of natural

---

[31]At a detailed level (taking each province and governorate separately), there was more variation, but the general characterization shown by the aggregates is still valid. The only significant exceptions came in 1960, when agricultural employment in Ismailia (a governorate) reached 46 percent of the total (see n. 30 above), and agriculture's share in the two provinces adjacent to Cairo—Kalyubia and Giza—fell to 59 percent and 48 percent, respectively.

[32]The official urban-rural breakdown in the 1960 census has not been used, since it is not available for earlier years, with the necessary cross-classifications. That breakdown is on administrative lines: Capitals of provinces and districts were considered urban and all other areas rural. It passes the "economic test" we have applied fairly well: in urban areas outside the five governorates, agriculture's share of employment was 23 percent, compared to 81 percent in rural areas.

[33]See Table 2–10.

[34]These people are not counted in the estimates of migration in the preceding paragraph either.

increase was equal in the two areas; in actual fact, this increase was probably somewhat higher in the governorates and lower in the provinces, implying a somewhat smaller internal migration than that indicated.[35]

The figures in the table permit us to say something about the relationship between this geographical movement and the economic transfer between sectors of the economy. In general, the overall picture is clear; out of an increase of some 810,000 in the number of adult males in the provinces, barely 20 percent went to work in agriculture, although in 1937 nearly 80 percent of all working men in the provinces were employed in this sector. Of the remainder, a substantial number found work in the growing service sector in the provinces, while more than 25 percent moved to the governorates, finding employment primarily in the rapidly expanding service sector there. In both rural and urban areas the growth of industrial employment was relatively small.

In percentage terms,[36] the expansion of employment in the governorates was far greater than in the provinces. This expansion in the urban areas was substantially in excess of the natural increase in adult males in those districts and was made possible only by the influx of men from the countryside. It is not obvious whether it was the large number of men looking for work (including those who had migrated) which caused employment to expand—a not implausible chain of events, particularly in the services—or whether it was the rising demand for workers which pulled people in from the countryside. We shall return to this question in Chapter 6, where we take a more detailed look at employment in specific areas within the service sector. In either case, it is clear that during this decade, as in the following period, it was the rapid expansion of employment in the services which kept the country from facing more serious pressure from growing underemployment in agriculture, as well as more overt unemployment both in the cities and in

---

[35]Statistics of births and deaths in all urban areas and rural areas with health bureaus (where the reporting is presumably more accurate), averaged over the period, imply that the rate of natural increase in urban areas was some 20 percent above that in rural areas, due primarily to the higher death rate in rural areas. This would imply average per annum growth rates of 2.08 percent in governorates and 1.74 percent in the provinces, instead of the 1.79 percent average figure of Table 2–10; this, in turn, would imply an internal migration of only 650,000 (the natural increase is higher in urban areas and lower in rural ones). This approach is not followed in the table in the interest of consistency, since it does not seem feasible to estimate the relative rates of natural increase of adult males in the two areas in a comparable way.

[36]Although not in terms of absolute numbers.

rural areas. Whether or not this created an equally serious problem of underemployment in the services is a matter which we shall consider at some length in Chapter 6.

TABLE 2–10

POPULATION SHIFTS, 1937–47

(In Thousands)

	1937	Natural Increase	Actual Increase	Surplus or Deficit	1947
Governorates:					
Population	2,332	452	1,212	760	3,544
Adult males:					
A. Total number	735	146	378	232	1,113
B. Employment, total	617		325		943
1. Agriculture	26		1		27
2. Industry	130		91		221
3. Services	461		233		694
C. Not employed	118		53		171
Provinces:					
Population	13,601	2,636	1,877	−759	15,478
Adult males:					
A. Total number	4,071	809	577	−232	4,648
B. Employment, total	3,840		463		4,303
1. Agriculture	2,950		162		3,112
2. Industry	200		93		293
3. Services	690		209		899
C. Not employed	231		114		345

NOTES AND SOURCES: Governorates refer to Cairo, Alexandria, Canal Zone, Suez, and Damietta. All others are included in provinces.
Total population breakdown is from 1960 census (United Arab Republic, Department of Statistics and Census, *Population Census, 1960* [Cairo, 1963], Vol. II, Table 1). All other figures are based on the original data in the 1937 and 1947 population censuses.
The following adjustments have been made: Those listed as unemployed have been excluded from the employment figures, as have all domestic workers engaged in "home duties." Land owning (in agriculture) and house owning (in commerce) have been excluded. Irrigation has been shifted from manufacturing to agriculture; men's tailoring, shirtmaking, women's dressmaking, and uphostering have been shifted from manufacturing to services; domestic service in farmers' houses (as domestic servants, not "home duties") has been shifted from agriculture to services.
In some cases the published figures did not give sufficient detail for subtracting out boys and unemployed men according to the breakdown used here; in these cases, where the numbers involved were always relatively small, we have freely used an assumption of proportionality, using as close a sectoral breakdown as was available. For example, in 1937 there were 8,874 unemployed males in "transformation industries," but no breakdown of this group to governorates or provinces; we have allocated them between these two in the same ratio as total "occupied" males (employed plus unemployed) in transformation industries in that year. The same approach was used to derive the 1937 participation rates, by age groups, in Table 2–9 above.
Natural rates of increase are assumed to be the same for governorates and provinces, but are calculated separately for total population and adult males. Sectoral groupings are as in Table 2–9.
Totals may not add due to rounding.

Perhaps we should say a word about the group which we have entitled "not employed." This includes all those who are truly unemployed, in the sense that they are looking for work and unable to find it, as well as those who are not in the labor force; it is equal to the difference between total employment of adult males and the total number of men in this group. The rise in this category in 1947 is matched by sudden expansion—from a negligible figure to about 340,000—in those listed as being employed in "ill-defined industries." This category poses a serious problem for any analyst working with Egyptian data. We have found it best to exclude these people from our employment statistics, for a number of reasons. Seventy-five percent of this group in "ill-defined industries" were in the provinces, and the largest number were in the age group 10-29. If this group is included as employed, the age-specific participation rates look unreasonably high, compared to earlier and later years. It seems plausible to assume that this group is made up primarily of men who have no regular employment, but who are happy to take any temporary job they can find. Of the whole category "not employed," the majority are young men, with perhaps 60 to 70 percent between 15 and 30 years of age; as the table indicates, they stay predominately in the rural areas, where there are good prospects of finding some work, at least at certain peak seasons of the year, and where in the meantime they can share in the produce of their family. In some ways the continuing expansion of this group is a measure of the frustration which Egypt faces in attempting to increase the number of jobs fast enough to keep pace with the number of people wishing to work.[37]

When we move on to the following intercensal period (1947-60), a new variable assumes some importance: the share of adult males in the total population (see Table 2-11). The rise in the growth rate of population during this period brought about a marked increase in the proportion of the population who are below 15 (see Table 2-4). The result is that while the participation rate for adult males stayed nearly unchanged, that for the whole economy fell quite sharply. One result of this is that the average employed worker had nearly 25 percent more dependents in 1960 than in 1947.[38] This is a measure of one of the strains which an increasing population growth rate and the concomitant shift in age structure put on the economy.

---

[37] In the governorates a substantial number of those listed as not employed —perhaps as many as 60 percent of the total, in 1960—were students; in the provinces, by contrast, where the number of people in this category was much larger and the number of students aged 15 and above smaller, this factor is of minor importance.

[38] The ratio of not employed to employed in the whole population rose from 1.88 to 2.33. In terms of dependents of adult male workers only, the rise was only about 13 percent.

In terms of economic and geographical shifts taking place during this period, the picture is similar to that of the preceding decade. In the provinces, less than one third of the increase in the adult male population was absorbed into agriculture; nearly two thirds of the rest found employment in the services, either in the provinces or by migration to the major urban areas. Within the governorates the expansion of industry began to grow in significance, although it was still very much overshadowed—at least from an employment point of view—by the service sector. The group which we have entitled "not employed" continued to expand. Particularly in rural areas, where the demand for temporary agricultural laborers was falling off as a result of the land reform, the plight of this group must have been serious indeed.

TABLE 2–11

POPULATION SHIFTS, 1947–60

(In Thousands)

	1947	Natural Increase	Actual Increase	Migration	1960
Governorates:					
Population	3,544	1,316	2,151	835	5,695
Adult males:					
A. Total number	1,113	304	540	236	1,653
B. Employment, total	943		469		1,412
1. Agriculture	27		38		65
2. Industry	221		125		346
3. Services	694		307		1,001
C. Not employed	171		71		242
Provinces:					
Population	15,478	5,747	4,912	−835	20,391
Adult males:					
A. Total number	4,648	1,268	1,032	−236	5,680
B. Employment, total	4,303		879		5,182
1. Agriculture	3,112		383		3,495
2. Industry	293		77		370
3. Services	899		418		1,317
C. Not employed	345		153		498

NOTES: See notes to Table 2–10.

Looking back at the two intercensal periods we have discussed, it is surprising to note that internal migration in the second was only slightly larger than the first; in fact, on a per annum basis, the absolute size of the internal transfer—and hence, a fortiori, the proportion of the total rural population moving into the cities— was larger in the earlier period.[39] This would seem to imply that

[39]The first period covers 10 years, while the second covers 13.

the rate of urbanization has been slowing down. There are a number of explanations for this. It is worth recalling that the first period includes the war years, which provided a large if temporary demand for workers in the governorates;[40] thereafter, the movement to the cities may well have fallen off, only to increase again in recent years as the industrialization program has picked up speed. Besides this, we shall see in Chapter 5 that a substantial amount of industrial employment has been located outside the governorates. The Delta textile towns and the growing industrial complexes of Aswan and Helwan are examples which come to mind here, while the processing of foods—a not inconsiderable component of the industrial sector—has always been widely dispersed throughout the countryside. Finally, the growth of suburban and semiurban centers such as Giza and Kalyubia, which are counted here with the provinces, means that the distinctions we have used cannot be pushed too far. On the whole, there is every reason to believe that the rate of urbanization has been increasing during the postwar period; the figures in the tables serve to remind us that there was very heavy migration into the governorates during the war years as well.

The employment figures in Tables 2–9 to 2–11 give us some indication of the way in which the economy responded to the predicament of the 1930's, one major characteristic of which was a heavy concentration of economic activity in the agricultural sector, where there was little prospect of being able to supply either employment opportunities or increased output to keep pace with the growth of the population. During the period from 1937 to 1960, agricultural employment was nearly stagnant, increasing by less than 20 percent over the twenty-three-year period; the small industrial sector expanded at a very rapid rate, but far more important than this was the creation of over 1.1 million new jobs for men in the services. It was primarily the rapid expansion of employment in this area which made it possible to halt the earlier trend whereby the largest part of the population increase had been absorbed almost automatically into the agricultural sector, in spite of the fact that these additional workers were hardly needed there and contributed very little in the way of additional output, with

---

[40]Anis estimates that civilian employment by British and American military forces in Egypt amounted to over 200,000 workers in 1944; presumably, virtually all of these were in the governorates. M. A. Anis, "A Study of the National Income of Egypt," *L'Egypte Contemporaine*, Nos. 261–62 (November-December, 1950), p. 775.

a resulting decline in per capita income. In following chapters, we should like to see if the newly evolving structure of the economy was any better than the old in providing improvements in the economic well-being of the population.

Aggregate Output: A Summary View

In this chapter, we should like to present an overall picture of the changing structure of income and production in Egypt during the period since the late 1930's. In addition, we shall be concerned with the changing role of the government in the economy over this period. This provides us with a background for the more detailed discussion of the major sectors of the economy in following chapters.

Perhaps the best place to start such an examination is with the national accounts of the country. In the field of national income data, as in a number of statistical areas, Egypt is provided with an impressive abundance, or even superabundance, of estimates. In the Statistical Appendix to this study (pages 263–69), we have commented at some length on what we feel are the most important of these figures, showing gross national product at current prices for the years from 1937 to the present, and from 1945 to the present at constant prices. For present purposes the most important of these figures are the constant price estimates, reproduced in Tables 3–1 and 3–2 of this chapter. These two tables, along with the average growth rates in different sectors shown in Table 3–3, provide us with a good starting place for examining the growth of aggregate real income in the economy, along with some indication of which sectors were primarily responsible for increases in output, and which were lagging behind.

With regard to the levels of real income during World War II,

TABLE 3-1

GROSS NATIONAL INCOME AND PRODUCT AT MARKET PRICE, 1945–54

(£E Million, at Constant 1954 Prices)

	Agriculture	Industry and Electricity	Construction	Transport and Communications	Housing	Commerce and Finance	Other Services	Gross Domestic Product	+ Net Factor Income from Abroad	Gross National Product	Net Gains or Losses (−) from Terms-of-Trade Changes	Gross National Income
1945	303	91	19	38	50	122	117	740	− 8	732	− 38	694
1946	302	92	22	43	51	142	121	773	− 9	764	− 40	724
1947	299	101	25	46	53	147	126	797	− 5	792	− 45	747
1948	328	113	31	61	56	169	133	891	− 3	888	31	919
1949	325	126	25	72	59	190	145	942	− 9	933	10	943
1950	303	133	22	78	62	210	157	965	−11	954	68	1,022
1951	304	132	36	81	65	209	167	994	−13	981	113	1,094
1952	334	132	30	81	68	193	181	1,019	−12	1,007	9	1,016
1953	315	134	37	86	73	181	178	1,004	−11	993	− 25	968
1954	312	146	33	88	77	188	192	1,036	−13	1,023	0	1,023

NOTES AND SOURCES: See Appendix Table I–A–6 (p. 286).

TABLE 3-2

Gross National Income and Product at Market Price, 1952–53 to 1962–63
(£E Million, at Constant 1954 Prices)

	Agriculture	Industry and Electricity	Construction	Transport and Communications	Housing	Commerce and Finance		Other Services	Gross National Product		Net Gains from Terms-of-Trade Changes	Gross National Income	
						I	II		I	II		I	II
1952–53	325	140	25	54	59	170	142	217	990	962	+ 8	998	970
1953–54	315	143	27	55	56	161	158	232	989	986	0	989	986
1954–55	318	152	26	58	62	164	163	235	1,015	1,014	+ 8	1,023	1,022
1955–56	329	163	25	62	65	174	165	237	1,055	1,046	+10	1,065	1,056
1956–57	339	174	28	58	67	175	151	236	1,077	1,053	+17	1,094	1,070
1957–58	355	190	33	62	68	193	167	240	1,141	1,115	+14	1,155	1,129
1958–59	376	202	38	69	70	209	172	245	1,209	1,172	+17	1,226	1,189
1959–60	392	213	42	88	73	217	184	259	1,284	1,251	+26	1,310	1,277
1960–61	390	239	39	97	74	227	197	289	1,355	1,325	+30	1,385	1,355
1961–62	361	262	55	111	76	233	198	289	1,387	1,352	+30	1,417	1,382
1962–63	412	279	63	121	78	280	211	302	1,535	1,466	+20	1,555	1,486

Notes and Sources: See Appendix Table I–A–8 (pp. 288–89).

TABLE 3–3

AVERAGE ANNUAL COMPOUND GROWTH RATES OF AGGREGATE OUTPUT AND ITS COMPONENTS

	Agriculture	Industry and Electricity	Construction	Transport	Housing	Commerce and Finance	Other Services	Gross National Product	Gross National Income
1945–51............	0.0	6.4	11.3	13.5	4.5	9.4	6.1	5.0	7.9
1951–54 *reconstruction*	0.9	3.4	– 2.9	2.8	5.8	–3.5	4.8	1.4	–2.2
1953–54 to 1959–60...	3.7	6.9	7.6	8.1	4.5	5.1	1.9	4.5	4.8
1959–60 to 1962–63...	1.7	9.4	14.5	11.2	2.2	8.9	5.3	6.2	5.9
1945–62............	1.4	6.6	8.3	9.6	4.2	5.4	4.4	4.3	4.7

SOURCES: See Tables 3–1 and 3–2. Sectoral figures refer to real domestic product to 1954, real national product thereafter. As explained in Appendix I (p. 268), the divergence between gross national product and gross national income is due to changes in the terms of trade. For this table, we have used measurement I of commerce and finance, and the corresponding GNP and GNI totals (see Appendix Table I–A–8, pp. 288–89).

information is scant indeed. There is a current price estimate of national income, which can be deflated by any of several rather inadequate price indices; in the case of agriculture and manufacturing, the resulting series can be compared with independent output indices. The implication of this exercise in statistical guesswork is that national income at constant prices was virtually the same in 1945 as in 1939; this implies a fall in real income per capita of close to 10 percent over this period. These figures are extremely rough, but we feel that the order of magnitude is correct.[1]

During the immediate postwar years the structural shift into the services which we found in the employment data is clearly reflected in the income estimates; it was the marked expansion of the services which produced the major share of growth in real output. The industrial sector also grew fairly rapidly, but the increase in production here accounted for barely 10 percent of the total expansion in real income. Agricultural output fluctuated fairly widely from year to year, but showed no upward trend. We shall have a great deal to say in Chapter 6 about the various components of the services; perhaps we should point out here that the rapid growth of the transport sector was primarily due to the reopening of the Suez Canal, while the expansion of commerce and finance reflects the rebuilding of the export and import trade. The rapid growth of construction reflects a rush to make up for the wartime neglect of repairs and new construction of dwellings as well as factories and office buildings. In other services the largest part of the expansion came from the growth of the government sector; real income from household services was assumed to be constant throughout this period.

One of the most striking changes which took place in the economy from the war's end up to 1951 was the great improvement in the terms of trade of the country. This was primarily the result of a rise in the price of cotton substantially in excess of the increase in the world price of the goods Egypt imported. There are various ways of estimating the extent of the resulting gain to the country, although the results are not markedly different in magnitude. The method followed here (which is explained in Appendix I [page 268]) suggests that this improvement in the terms of trade boosted real national income by an additional 2.9 per cent

---

[1]See B. Hansen and D. Mead, *The National Income of the U.A.R. (Egypt), 1939–1962*, Memo No. 355 (Cairo: Institute of National Planning, July, 1963), pp. 2–3; also Appendix Tables III–A–1 (p. 318) and III–A–3 (p. 320), and Appendix IV–A–2 (p. 337).

per annum during this period, an improvement equal to more than 50 percent of the concurrent growth in real product. The annual figures in Table 3–1 indicate that a large part of this improvement was associated with the heavy demand for cotton during the Korean War, although there was a substantial improvement in Egypt's terms of trade even before 1948.

During this period between the end of the war and the revolution in 1952, the Egyptian government took a number of steps to promote the economic development of the country.[2] A five-year plan was drawn up in 1945, with projects estimated to cost £E96 million; these were generally typical public works projects: roads and bridges, irrigation and drainage, water and sewerage; there were also expenditures on low-cost public housing, and an electricity-generating station.[3] These expenditures were to be financed half from current revenues, half by drawing on reserves. In actual fact, there seems to have been a serious problem in keeping expenditures up with appropriations; over the first three years, little more than half the amounts allocated to those years had been spent. The underspending was attributed to "difficulties encountered in importing the requisite materials and the inability of certain government departments to cope with the additional tasks involved by the new projects."[4] Whether within the framework of this plan or outside it, public capital formation accounted for approximately 25 percent of total gross investment in the country during this period.[5]

Aside from these investments in public works, the government's intervention in the economy took a number of forms. In agriculture, there were acreage controls, attempting to make sure that enough food was produced for the growing population, as well as to prevent the overcropping of the soil; there were price controls aimed at holding down the price of basic foods and holding up the price of raw cotton. In industry, there was a whole complex of legislation involving such things as railroad rebates and tax benefits, as

---

[2]For a more detailed discussion of the role of the government in the economy during this period, see P. K. O'Brien, *The Revolution in Egypt's Economic System, 1952–1965* (London: Oxford University Press, 1966), chap. ii.

[3]United Kingdom, Overseas Economic Survey, *Egypt*, November, 1947, pp. 3–4; and October, 1951, pp. 23–24.

[4]*Ibid.*

[5]S. H. Abdel Rahman, *A Survey of the Foreign Trade of Egypt in the Post-War Period, with Special Reference to Its Impact on the National Economy* (Ph.D. dissertation, Faculty of Commerce, Cairo University, 1959), Appendix C: "Estimates of Gross Domestic Fixed Capital Formation, 1945–1953."

well as generous tariff protection.[6] These policies were designed in such a way that they often led to the creation and encouragement of private monopolies; in fact, the government's economic policies during this period can largely be interpreted as a response to the demands of the wealthy elite: the big land owners, industrialists, and traders. Of course, the interests of these various groups did not always agree. The prohibition on imports of raw cotton benefited the landlords at the expense of the manufacturers, since textile mills were forced to use high-quality Egyptian cotton even to produce the simplest cloth. In general, the government gave generous encouragement to private enterprise, although this was often very different from encouraging private competition.

During the years 1952–54 the economy experienced a sharp reversal. Real product grew hardly at all, while the deteriorating terms of trade caused a significant drop in real national income; on a per capita basis the drop amounted to 4–5 percent a year. This downturn was partly a result of the internal uncertainties following the revolution, along with the temporary reduction of current expenditures by the new regime. Far more important, however, was the halving of cotton prices between 1950 and 1953. The resulting decrease in purchasing power touched virtually every sector of the economy, although it shows most clearly in commerce and finance, where the reduction in income reflects the smaller quantity of goods exported and imported. The decline in the construction sector is primarily the result of the institution of government controls over the erection of luxury homes and apartment houses. The turning point in this cycle came in 1954; thereafter, supported by solid increases in output in the commodity-producing sectors, the economy moved steadily forward, with real product rising by 30 percent from 1954 to 1960. Terms-of-trade shifts were relatively minor during this period, improving somewhat up to 1960, with a small deterioration since then.

The members of the Revolutionary Council which overthrew the government of King Farouk had no sharply defined economic ideology when they came to power in 1952.[7] It is clear that the new leaders were unhappy about the privileged position of the wealthy elite, and the power of this group to manipulate the government for its own ends; the land reform may best be seen as an attempt

---

[6]See A. A. I. el Gritly, "The Structure of Modern Industry in Egypt," *L'Egypte Contemporaine*, Nos. 241–42 (November-December, 1947).

[7]For a documentation and discussion of the ideas of this paragraph, see O'Brien, *op. cit.*, chap. iii.

to break the power of this group. It is also clear, though, that in the early years the new regime was only too happy to leave the largest part of the economy in private hands, not just temporarily and for lack of qualified managers, but for lack of a strong feeling that any alternative way of organizing the economy was preferable. There is no reason to doubt the statements of President Nasser and others that the policy of the government was to eliminate the special privileges of the wealthy, but beyond this to encourage the private sector in every way possible. O'Brien has aptly referred to the period 1952–56 as the "free enterprise phase" of the revolution.[8]

The years 1956–60 saw a gradual encroachment of the government on the private sector of the economy. This took two forms: increasing controls over private production and expansion of the scope of activity of public enterprises. In the agricultural sector, traditional government controls over cropping patterns and water usage were extended and strengthened in areas affected by the land reform by the appointment of government officials with strong supervisory powers. A number of the leading financial institutions were placed under sequestration in the wake of the Suez crisis of 1956; these have remained in government hands since that time. For all other financial institutions a law was passed in 1957 requiring that they be "Egyptianized" within five years. This meant that all shares were to be owned by Egyptians, while all members of the boards of directors as well as those responsible for the banks' management were to be Egyptians.[9] The newly formed Ministry of Industry was given extensive authority over pricing and output decisions of private manufacturing firms. Besides this, the government's responsibilities in the industrial sector were given a substantial boost with the adoption in 1957 of a five-year plan for industrial development. This preceded the overall five-year plan for the whole economy, which only came into effect from July 1, 1960; the industrial plan was based on the assumption that the rest of the economy would grow steadily at 2 percent a year. Like Egypt's earlier five-year plans, it was basically a list of projects to be undertaken;[10] yet it differed from the earlier plans in a number

---

[8]*Ibid.*

[9]National Bank of Egypt, *Economic Bulletin,* Vol. X, No. 3 (1957), p. 251.

[10]Besides the plan for 1946–47 to 1950–51, which we have discussed above, there was also a plan covering the years 1935–39, to be financed from current revenues and reserves; 60 percent of the expenditures in this earlier plan were designated for irrigation alone. See United Kingdom, Department of Overseas Trade, *Economic Conditions in Egypt,* (London: H.M.S.O., July, 1935), pp. 8–9.

of important respects. Concentrated solely in the industrial sector, the size of the undertaking was very much larger than its predecessors. While the cost of the plan for 1946–47 to 1950–51 was originally envisaged to be £E96 million and was substantially underspent, net investments in the five-year industrialization plan were set at £E221 million. Furthermore, the financing of this expenditure was left entirely up in the air. The *Economic Bulletin* of the National Bank of Egypt suggested that projects included in the plan implied domestic investment in industry alone roughly equal to total domestic savings—i.e., ignoring all needs for capital formation in other sectors.[11] When the Minister of Industry was asked about problems of financing his numerous projects, he is reported to have answered: "Finance is not my field; I don't understand it. Go see Dr. Kaissuny."[12] While the government was expected to provide some 60 percent of the financing for this investment, both private savings and private entrepreneurs were assigned an important role as well.[13] When the private sector did not live up to the ambitious targets set for it by the minister, there was a proliferation of controls and an extension of the role of public enterprises, culminating in the nationalizations of 1960 and 1961, which brought all major industrial establishments under government ownership.

The figures in the later comprehensive national plan indicate that in the base year of the plan (1959–60), aside from public administration proper, some 8 percent of value added in the country originated in enterprises either fully under state ownership or partially publicly owned but "effectively controlled" by the state.[14] For the most part, these public enterprises were under the supervision of two large authorities: the Economic Development Organization, which had been set up primarily to manage the British and French firms nationalized in the wake of Suez; and the Nasr Organization, which was primarily responsible for the firms set up under the five-year industrial plan. The other major holding company, Bank Misr, was still considered as a private institution until

---

[11]National Bank of Egypt, *op. cit.*, pp. 229–31. Our estimates would indicate total domestic gross savings of well over twice that amount.

[12]K. Wheelock, *Nasser's New Egypt* (New York: Frederick A. Praeger, Inc., 1960), p. 153. Kaissuny was then Minister of Economy and Commerce.

[13]O'Brien, *op. cit.*, chap. iv.

[14]United Arab Republic, Presidency of the Republic, National Planning Committee, *General Frame of the Five-Year Plan for Economic and Social Development, July 1960–June 1965* (Cairo, 1960; hereafter referred to as *General Frame*), pp 43 and 162. See also O'Brien, *op. cit.*, Table 1.

its nationalization in 1960, although the government already exercised substantial control over its operations.

The largest single enterprise under government ownership at that time was the Suez Canal, accounting for 40 percent of value added in all public enterprises. In the industrial sector, government-owned or -controlled enterprises accounted for less than 7 percent of total value added. If we add to this the income earned in public administration, we find that the government sector in this broad sense accounted for less than 20 percent of income earned in the country in 1959–60. Capital formation in the government sector—defined in the same inclusive way—was expected to account for approximately 60 percent of total investment during the planning period, but only about a fourth of this total was slated for industry and electricity, with the largest part going for land reclamation and irrigation, as well as education and other social services. There is no indication in the plant itself that there were projects afoot to expand the government sector in more than a rather marginal way.[15]

In 1960 and 1961, this picture was changed in a fundamental way. Starting with the nationalization of Bank Misr in early 1960, and culminating in a series of laws promulgated in July, 1961, the government expanded its purview until, by late 1961, the government had controlling ownership—and in most cases complete ownership—in the following areas: the whole financial sector, including insurance companies as well as all specialized banking institutions; all foreign trade of the country, as well as the major commercial houses engaged in internal trade; an overwhelming share of the industrial sector, leaving in private hands only the smaller manufacturing establishments (many of which have also since been nationalized); buses and the country's one shipping company; all newspapers; and the major construction companies.[16] What remain—and remains—in private hands is the whole of the agricultural sector, house ownership, many of the services, and innumerable small establishments in trade and manufacturing.[17] The result of this

---

[15] All of these estimates are based on figures in the plan, using data only for the first and last year; by 1964–65 the government business sector was slated to grow from 8 to 10 percent of national income, and from 7 to 13 percent of total income in the industrial sector. See General Frame, pp. 23, 43, 139–42, 158–62.

[16] For details, see National Bank of Egypt, Economic Bulletin, Vol. XIV, No. 3 (1961) pp. 322–35.

[17] Of course, there are widespread government controls in these sectors as well, ranging from price and rent controls to the extensive and close government supervision of agricultural production.

change is that the share of the government sector—enterprises plus administration—in national income may have risen from less than 20 percent in the base year of the plan to 40 percent in 1962–63.

Aside from this expansion in the activities of public enterprises, the role of the government in the economy was further extended by the institution of comprehensive economic planning. The base year of this first economy-wide five-year plan was 1959–60; the next-to-last line of Table 3–3 therefore gives us some indication of the increase in real output achieved during the first three years of the planning period.[18] These estimates were made by the National Planning Committee, using methods which have only partly been made public; as a result, it is rather difficult to appraise the accuracy of the figures. It seems likely that growth rates in industry and construction are somewhat exaggerated; except for this, we believe the data to be reasonably accurate.

Turning to the figures themselves, the picture is clearly one of remarkable growth. It is a mark of the transformation which the economy has undergone that in spite of an agricultural sector which was virtually stagnant, the aggregate real income of the country grew at close to 6 percent per annum. By 1962–63, the latest year for which such data are available, agriculture's share in total output had fallen to below 27 percent, while the industrial sector had risen to over 18 percent. The service sectors, broadly defined to include

---

[18]The following further estimates have recently been released of Egypt's national income:

	1959–60	1964–65
	(£E million)	
Agriculture	405.0	477.0
Industry	256.3	385.0
Electricity	9.8	22.4
Transport and communications	92.9	157.6
Housing construction	73.0	80.1
Services	265.5	387.9
Others, not specified	182.5	252.2
Total	1,285.0	1,762.2

These figures would imply an annual average compound growth rate over the planning period of 6.5 percent. We have not used these in our analysis, since we have not been able to check on sources or accuracy of the figures. If they are correct, they would not alter the analysis of the text, either here or in Chapter 10, in any fundamental way. The figures are taken from Ali Sabri, *The Years of Socialist Transformation: an Evaluation of the First Five-Year Plan* (Cairo: Dar el Maaref, 1966, in Arabic), p. 50 and pictorial insert. For an alternative estimate showing constant price GNP growing at 6.4 percent during the five years of the plan, see B. Hansen, *Planning and Economic Growth in the U.A.R. (Egypt)* (mimeograph), p. 4. On the whole, it seems likely that real income grew at an average rate of between 6 and 6.5 percent per annum over the full plan period, although this is nothing more than an educated guess.

construction, transportation, and housing, as well as commerce, finance, and other services, expanded from 42 percent of national income in the late 1930's to 55 percent in 1962–63. These figures point once again to the major structural change which has taken place in the Egyptian economy during the past twenty-five years. In the following chapters, we shall look in greater detail at each of the major sectors of the economy, examining such questions as why the agricultural sector has failed to grow more rapidly; what special problems have resulted from the rapid expansion of industry, especially in view of the relative stagnation in agriculture; and whether the indicated expansion of real income in the services will stand up to closer scrutiny. If this transformation in the structure of income and employment is real rather than just a statistical phenomenon, and if it is sustainable in the future, surely it is a remarkable achievement.

Agriculture

In the late 1930's the agricultural sector of the Egyptian economy provided directly some 70 percent of total employment and close to 50 percent of the income of the country. Since that time, both output and employment in agriculture have continued to expand, but at a rather slow rate, so that the center of gravity of the economy has shifted slowly but decisively away from agriculture toward manufacturing and the services. In spite of this fact, Egypt is in many ways still very much dependent on agriculture. Not only is over 25 percent of the country's income and 50 percent of her employment currently derived directly from this sector; aside from this, a large part of her growing industrial base as well as a substantial portion of the activities in the fields of commerce, finance, and transport are centered around the processing and handling of agricultural produce.[1] This dependence on agriculture is most clear in the area of foreign trade; the overwhelming majority of the country's exports are agricultural, at least in origin, although some have gone through substantial processing before export. In this chapter, we should like to examine the changing level and commodity breakdown of agricultural output, as well as the production conditions and resource usage in this important sector.

---

[1] The 7 × 7 input-output table in Appendix Table I–A–3 (pp. 274–75) indicates that in 1954, 42 percent of all domestic current intermediate purchases of the industrial sector were from agriculture.

A. OUTPUT

There are a number of different indices of agricultural output available, but the divergencies are not serious, and the general picture is reasonably clear (see Table 4–1). Starting from a fairly high level in the late 1930's—perhaps 30 percent above the pre-

TABLE 4–1

INDEX OF AGRICULTURAL OUTPUT

(1953 = 100)

1935–39 = 102.0	1951 = 98.9	1958 = 125.5
1945 = 87.0	1952 = 108.1	1959 = 130.6
1946 = 90.8	1953 = 100.0	1960 = 134.4
1947 = 94.9	1954 = 112.2	1961 = 118.0
1948 = 110.2	1955 = 111.2	1962 = 145.9
1949 = 108.1	1956 = 110.2	1963 = 161.3
1950 = 104.0	1957 = 123.4	

SOURCE: Appendix Table III–A–1 (p. 318), using National Bank of Egypt and (since 1960) Department of Statistics and Census indices (chained to the earlier series). See also Appendix Table III–A–3 (p. 320) for an alternative, longer period index. The 1963 figure is preliminary.

World War I levels—agricultural output fell sharply during the Second World War, dropping by approximately 25 percent. In large part, this fall was a direct result of the shortage of fertilizers during the war. El Imam has shown, however, that another factor was important as well; this was the reallocation of land from one crop to another, as a result of direct government controls as well as changing price relationships. If the quantum index uses as weights the value of the crop in some base period, switching land from a more valuable to a less valuable crop would cause the index to fall, even if yields per acre of each crop remain constant.[2] During World War II, it was difficult to export cotton because of the disruption of shipping routes, while the large number of British troops stationed in the country led to a great increase in the demand for foods, which it was difficult to import. The result was a marked reallocation of land away from cotton to the production of grain foods, with the former falling form 23 percent of crop area in 1937 to only 9 percent in 1944, while the area devoted to wheat, maize, and rice rose from 38 percent to 45 percent over the same period.

---

[2]For a careful discussion of this problem in the construction of index numbers, see M. M. el Imam, *A Production Function for Egyptian Agriculture, 1913–1955*, Memo No. 259 (Cairo: Institute of National Planning, December, 1962), pp. 12–16.

In large part, this reallocation was brought about by direct production controls, while price controls prevented relative scarcities from being fully reflected in the prices of different commodities. El Imam has indicated that up to 60 percent of the fall in output which the quantum index shows can be attributed to this reallocation factor, leaving a much smaller margin—a 10 percent fall in total output—due directly to falling productivity per feddan, mostly as a result of the shortage of fertilizers.[3]

Output rose rapidly in the immediate postwar years; and by 1948, aggregate output was a bit above the prewar average.[4] From then until 1953, the picture was one of near stagnation of output; since that year, the increase has been rather remarkable, with aggregate output rising some 30 percent between 1953 and 1960.

To interpret this information, the first thing we need to do is to separate agricultural production into food and nonfood components. Nonfood agricultural production in Egypt means virtually one thing: cotton. In the late 1950's, some 17 percent of the total cropped area was devoted to the cultivation of this crop. Gross and net returns per feddan of cotton are high; its share in the gross value of agricultural output was 27 percent. Excluding animal products, cotton's share in the value of output of field crops was 34 percent, just double its share in cropped area.[5] The share of cotton in Egypt's exports has declined throughout the twentieth century, although it still accounted for 65 percent of total merchandise exports in 1963.[6] Turning to changes through time in the production of this crop, the wartime drop in cotton output was larger than for the rest of agriculture (some 35 percent), and the postwar recovery was slower; it was not until 1958 that the prewar peak output was reached, while output in 1962—the year after the crop which was badly hit by insects—was barely 10 percent above the 1935–39 average.[7]

---

[3]*Ibid.*, pp. 22–24.

[4]Part of this increase can be attributed to the elimination of the distortions in land allocation just discussed, as wartime conditions of both supply and demand were eased.

[5]These figures are averages for the 1955–59, based on the value of the cotton crop shown in the *Annuaire Statistique* and the value of total output shown in United Arab Republic, Department of Statistics and Census, *National Income from the Agricultural Sector for the Years 1958–1960* (Cairo, n.d.), p. 21. The share of cotton in total value of agricultural output has fluctuated widely, primarily as a result of variations in the price of cotton; it reached 45 percent in 1950 and fell to 22 percent in 1953.

[6]Raw cotton as well as cotton textiles. See p. 159 and Table 7–2 (p. 163).

[7]See Appendix Table III–A–4 (pp. 321–22).

The reason for the relatively slow increase in cotton production is clear. A major part of the overall growth in agricultural output in Egypt can be attributed to increases in the cropped area (i.e., multiple cropping); for most crops, average yields per feddan per crop have increased very little. While there have been substantial annual variations in the cotton acreage, the maximum area which can be planted with this crop in any one year without seriously overworking the soil seems to have remained fairly stable at close to two million feddan. This total has only been surpassed once (in 1930), although it was closely approached in two other interwar years (1925 and 1937); but in the years 1950 and 1951, when there were no acreage controls and cotton prices were quite high relative to those of alternative crops, the area planted with cotton was only 1.98 million feddan. These figures suggest that while the increasing cropped area has been primarily a result of changes in the rotation pattern whereby farmers have been able to grow two or more crops a year on a unit of land, it has not been possible to increase the frequency with which cotton can be planted in a given area without seriously reducing the productivity of the soil.

With regard to the production of food crops, the general picture is similar to that described above for total agriculture. By 1948, output was about 15 percent above the prewar level; thereafter, there was a slow decline to 1952, when the output index turned sharply upward, rising some 35 percent from that year to 1960. During the following three years the index shows a further rise of 28 percent. Appendix Table III–A–2 (page 319) gives an indication of the commodity composition of this increase.

It is revealing to compare these figures with those on population growth, trade, and food consumption. From 1937 to 1947 the population grew by about 20 percent; food production seems to have risen by slightly less than this.[8] The result was that food consumption per capita in 1948 was somewhat below the prewar level (in calories per day).[9] During this period, there was also a slight increase in Egypt's small net exports of food products. Thereafter, with the continuing and rather marked retrenchment in the area planted with food crops from their artificially high wartime levels, food production declined, while the rate of increase of population moved up markedly. Two results followed. The first was that from being a net food exporter of some £E3 million in 1947 (excluding

---

[8] See Appendix Table III–A–2 (p. 319). Food production in 1947 was approximately the same as in 1948; see el Imam, *op. cit.*, p. 39.

[9] See Appendix Table II–A–10 (p. 303).

beverages and tobacco), Egypt shifted to become a net food importer to the extent of about £E27 million in 1950 and nearly £E35 million in 1951. Even these large-scale food imports were only just adequate to maintain the level of food consumption of the population; per capita caloric intake remained virtually constant.[10]

From 1952 to 1960 the situation was sharply different. As we indicated, food production rose by some 35 percent over this period, while the population increase was only 22 percent. Daily caloric intake rose, while net food imports fell to £E12 million. Since 1960, the discussion becomes more conjectural. The output index shows a sharp rise in food production; we suspect, however, that the actual increase may be somewhat less than that shown in the index.[11] Estimates of caloric intake have not been made. What we do know is that there has been a massive increase in net food imports, reaching £E62 million in 1963. The share of net imports in the total domestic food supply may have risen from 2–3 percent in 1960 to 10–12 percent in 1963.[12]

In broad outlines, then, the changing pattern of agricultural output is clear. Production for export has grown slowly; the average size of the cotton crop in the years 1955–59 was below the average for 1935–39, and although there have been some increases since then, these do not change the basic picture of limited expansion. With regard to food production, there were periods when the growth of output kept ahead of the population; but in general, the race has been the other way. Over the whole period from 1937 to 1960, food production rose by 46 percent, while the population increase was 64 percent, resulting in a 10 percent fall in per capita food supply from domestic production.

Taken by themselves, these facts can tell us nothing about whether the development effort has been successful, whether the average standard of living of the population or the capital stock of the country increased during this period. It is theoretically possible that the slow expansion in agricultural output was accompanied by a transfer of resources to other sectors, making it possible

[10]The statistics indicate a fall of 0.5 percent from 1948–49—1950–51 to 1951–52—1953–54; see Appendix Table II–A–10 (p. 303).

[11]Figures in Appendix Table III–A–4 (pp. 321–22) show a rise in output of several important grains; on the other hand, the indicated growth in output of vegetables, fruits, and particularly animal products (see Appendix Table III–A–2 [p. 319]) seems suspiciously high.

[12]For 1960, see Table 8–6 (p. 212). In 1963, total food consumption may have been in the range of £E550–600 million; as we have indicated above, net food imports came to £E62 million.

for the economy to grow through the increase in output in these other sectors. The main problem with this growth path—which in large measure describes the path Egypt has followed—is that the structure of demand generally does not correspond to the structure of production, while price rigidities, including the price of foreign exchange, prevent the market from moving toward equilibrium. To take a specific example, given the production trends in the agricultural sector, the maintenance or improvement of average real consumption per capita necessarily involves increasing food imports. This is nothing to worry about, and may indeed be desirable, as long as a portion of the increase in nonagricultural output made possible by a transfer of resources out of agriculture can be exported, or can replace goods formerly imported. But when this increase in production is concentrated in services, which cannot be exported,[13] and in manufacturing industries, which are often quite inefficient, balance of payments problems are bound to arise. These external difficulties are generally blamed on the failure of agricultural output to rise fast enough; logically, they could equally well be blamed on overexpansion of the services and international noncompetitiveness of the new manufacturing output. This change of emphasis becomes all the more plausible if we can show that agricultural techniques are relatively advanced, while productivity in agriculture—output per unit of factor inputs—has continued to improve over this period. To this discussion we now turn.

B. INPUTS TO AGRICULTURE

We have seen in Chapter 2 that the number of adult males actively engaged in agriculture rose from 2,976,000 in 1937 to 3,560,000 in 1960, growing at the slow average rate of 0.8 percent per annum (compounded). The result of this relatively slow growth was that agriculture's share in total employment of men fell from 67 percent in 1937 to 54 percent in 1960. While this is probably the best single measure of labor inputs into Egyptian agriculture, it is subject to several important qualifications. There is a considerable degree of flexibility in Egypt as to whether a given agricultural task is performed by men, women, or children. Young people are especially adept at performing certain types of work where manual dexterity is important, such as caring for the young cotton plants,

---

[13]Although foreigners can be encouraged to come and consume them within Egypt (tourism), which amounts to the same thing.

while the heavy work (e.g., hoeing) is generally done exclusively by the men; yet there is also a large intermediate zone of work which can equally well be done by men, women, or children. In this situation, what we really need as a measure of labor inputs to the agricultural sector is either three separate series on employment of men, women, and children, or a total figure, perhaps weighting women and children according to their adult male equivalents. Unfortunately, as we have seen in Chapter 2, information on agricultural employment of women is completely inadequate, while in the case of young people, for whom agricultural work is particularly seasonal in character, the change in the period of the year when the census was performed casts serious doubt on the accuracy of the employment figures. This leaves us no practical alternative but to concentrate our attention primarily on employment of men, where we believe the statistics are considerably more reliable. As a measure of the significance of this omission, the 1960 population census gives the following breakdown of total employment in agriculture, forestry, hunting and fishing:

	(Thousands)
Men, aged 15 and above	3,560
Women, aged 15 and above	131
Boys and girls, aged 6–14	715
Total	4,406

This means that when we concentrate our attention on employment of adult males, we are leaving aside nearly 20 percent of the reported agricultural labor force in 1960; the figure would be higher for earlier years. This is unfortunate, but the data leave us no real alternative.[14]

A further difficulty in this area of employment statistics concerns the rising number of men in the provinces who are listed in the population censuses as not employed. It seems probable that most of these were at least marginally in the agricultural sector, doing temporary jobs whenever they were available, either on a daily

---

[14]Surely, this approach makes more sense than the alternative of working with total agricultural employment, including the nonsensical drop in employment of females. For example, Hansen and Marzouk emphasize the stagnation of employment in agriculture since 1937; see their *Development and Economic Policy in the U.A.R. (Egypt)* (Amsterdam: North-Holland Publishing Co., 1965), particularly secs. 3.1 and 3.2.5. Yet we are confident that the 20 percent increase which employment figures of adult males suggest is closer to the truth than their figure of 3 percent, which in fact they feel may be an overestimation (see p. 61).

wage basis or on family farms. The numbers involved are considerable, reaching nearly 15 percent of reported employment in agriculture in 1960.[15] On the whole, the preceding discussion should serve to remind us that we have only a rough and imprecise measure of the pattern of labor inputs into the agricultural sector in Egypt.

One characteristic of the recorded agricultural labor force which bears special comment is the employment status of the workers. The categories used in the different censuses have changed, so no comparable series through time is available; the figures for 1960 are revealing (see Table 4-2).

TABLE 4-2

EMPLOYMENT STATUS, ADULT MALE
AGRICULTURAL WORKERS, 1960

	Number of Workers
Employers	423,343
Self-employed	1,096,101
Paid employees	1,301,505
Unpaid family workers	707,781
Other unpaid workers	7,186
Total	3,535,916

NOTES AND SOURCES: United Arab Republic, Department of Statistics and Census, *Population Census, 1960* (Cairo, 1963), Vol. II, p. 271. Figures refer to Egyptian Arabs aged 15 and over in *occupation* group 4: farmers, fishermen, hunters, loggers, and related workers. A similar breakdown by economic activity (ISIC) is not separately available for those aged 15 and above. Divergence between the two totals is slight.

The precise breakdown between employers and self-employed is not clear. In principle, self-employed are said to be in charge of farms where no additional laborers are employed, whether paid or unpaid; employers, then, are heads of farms assisted either by unpaid family members or by paid laborers. In fact, it seems probable that this distinction has not been strictly adhered to; one million farms with only one worker each is unlikely.[16] Perhaps the most interesting thing about this table, though, is that in 1960 over 35 percent of the men in the agricultural labor force were paid

[15]See Table 2-11 (p. 39).
[16]With regard to the total number of holdings, data for 1956 put this figure at 1.25 million (see Appendix Table III-C-3 [p. 326]; preliminary figures from the 1960 agricultural census show 1.8 million holdings. See United Arab Republic, Department of Public Mobilization and Statistics, *Handbook of Basic Statistics* (Cairo: S.O.P. Press, October, 1963), p. 75.

employees. The picture of the typical farm laborer as being engaged in peasant agriculture on family farms using exclusively family labor is only partially correct.

There has been a considerable divergence of opinion, both in the theoretical literature on economic development and in the discussion of the Egyptian economy in particular, as to the existence and extent of underemployment of labor in the agricultural sector. We have discussed this question at some length in the Appendix to this chapter (pages 80-98). As we argue there, our interpretation of the available evidence suggests that there is a substantial amount of disguised unemployment in the agricultural sector. The rapid expansion of employment opportunities outside of agriculture may have drained away considerable numbers of people who had previously worked as paid agricultural workers, with the result that there were sharp increases in the wage rates for this group during seasons of peak demand in the mid-1960's; on the whole, though, we think it fair to say that the agricultural sector has more workers than it can use, that there are considerable numbers in the sector whose marginal physical product is virtually zero, who could be permanently withdrawn from the sector with no loss of output and only minor organizational changes in the production process. This is a debatable conclusion based on conflicting evidence; for our evaluation of this evidence, the reader is referred to the Appendix to this chapter. If it is correct, it means that while additional people might be absorbed in agriculture—although with decreasing standards of living, unless this is offset by technological change—no more workers are needed; and if, in fact, more people are absorbed in the sector, their net contribution to output will be zero.

The second major factor input to the agricultural sector is land. As we saw in Chapter 1, there was a substantial expansion of multiple cropping from the 1870's to the pre-World War I period, leading to a 60 percent increase in cropped area, although the cultivated area rose very little; in the following period, up to 1937, the expansion in both series was much more modest, with cropped area rising by less than 10 percent, while the cultivated area actually fell somewhat. The period since 1937 has seen a slow increase in both these variables, as Table 4-3 shows. This means that from 1947 to 1960, while the cultivated land area rose by only 150,000 feddan, the area was used more intensively, so that the cropped area rose by over 1.2 million feddan.

In the careful study of the agricultural sector to which we have referred, M. M. el Imam has suggested a further measure of land as an input to agriculture.[17] He argues that the crop-times-feddan measure (cropped area) is inadequate, since it takes no account of the length of time the crop uses the field. For example, if sugar cane occupies the land for twelve months while lentils need only six months, we might substitute two lentil crops for one crop of sugar cane (rotation questions aside) and thereby double the cropped area, even though the "feddan-year" of land use has remained unchanged. To meet this problem, el Imam suggests the use of a new variable, the exploitation area, which he defines as follows: In a given year the area planted with each product is multiplied by the proportion of the year during which that product utilizes the field; added together for all crops, this gives us a measure of the number of feddan-years employed in agriculture that year. The measure is fully comparable to the more familiar variable, man-hours of work.

TABLE 4–3

CULTIVATED AND CROPPED AREAS

	Cultivated Area		Cropped Area	
	000 Feddan	Index	000 Feddan	Index
1937	5,281	100	8,358	100
1947	5,761	109	9,167	110
1960	5,918	112	10,397	124

SOURCE: United Arab Republic, Central Statistical Committee, *Basic Statistics*, June, 1962, p. 62.

Unfortunately, a number of problems arise in the computation of this exploitation area, particularly with regard to the large number of relatively minor crops. No one of these is of major importance; but along with Egyptian clover, they made up over 30 percent of the total crop area in 1960. It is hard to devise a suitable "average length of growing time" for this mixed bag, particularly since the composition of the total has been changing over the years. In addition, clover—called berseem in its local variant—presents a special problem. Besides enriching the soil, it is the major source of fodder for the livestock of the country, accounting in recent years for over 20 percent of the total crop area. The special problem with this crop from our present point of view is that there is substantial flexibility in the length of time it is left on the

---

[17]El Imam, *op. cit.*, pp. 4–8.

fields.[18] For both these reasons, we have found it necessary to restrict our computation of the exploitation area to the major crops, as el Imam has done. For the 11 most important crops[19] (other than clover), the figures are as shown in Table 4–4. As the table indicates, the 11 percent rise in the crop area of these 11 products was accompanied by an approximately equal increase in the exploitation area of the same crops; there is no evidence that the rise in cropped area for these particular products was achieved by substituting shorter for longer crops, or that the figures on the cropped area are a misleading measure of the input of land to agriculture.

TABLE 4–4

CROPPED AND EXPLOITATION AREA, SELECTED CROPS

	Cropped Area		Exploitation Area*	
	000 Feddan	Index	000 Feddan-Years	Index
1937	6,414	100	3,843	100
1947	6,691	104	3,852	100
1960	7,131	111	4,202	110

*For each of the eleven crops included, the crop area is multiplied by the number of months that crop uses the field, divided by twelve. These "utilization periods" are as follows:

Sugar cane	12 months	Rice, barley	6.5 months
Cotton	9 months	Lentils	6 months
Wheat, helbeh	7.5 months	All others	5.5 months

SOURCE: See M. M. el Imam, *A Production Function for Egyptian Agriculture, 1913–1955*, Memo No. 259 (Cairo: Institute of National Planning, December, 1962), p. 6. El Imam goes on to take the ratio of the exploitation area for these eleven crops to total cultivated area, a ratio which loses much of its meaning due to the exclusion of 30 percent of the crop area; his statement that the land is "left idle for the rest of the year" (p. 7) is clearly wrong.

Although closely related to the question of income distribution, perhaps this is the best place to examine the system of land ownership and land holding in Egypt. Throughout the following discussion, we shall use the term "holding" to refer to farms, to working units, as distinct from ownership of the land; many confusing and misleading statements in the discussions of land tenure in Egypt are due to a failure to keep these two concepts separate.

Looking first at land ownership, there has been continuing fragmentation of the land into smaller and smaller units, primarily as a result of the inheritance laws, which require that at least two thirds of the land be divided equally among all male heirs (un-

---

[18]See Central Bank of Egypt, *Economic Review*, Vol. I, No. 2 (1961), p. 211.
[19]Barley, beans, cotton, helbeh, lentils, maize, millet, onions, rice, sugar cane, and wheat.

married females receiving half a man's share). Baer[20] has shown that there are some offsetting tendencies to this fragmentation process: wakf land (religious endowments) and land owned by foreigners have not followed this inheritance law; newly reclaimed land and government holdings transferred to the private sector were usually sold to large owners; and there has been some taking-over of small owners by their creditors in default of payments on loans, although there is a law protecting the peasant from loss of his last five feddan in this way. In spite of these offsetting tendencies, the continuing fragmentation of ownership can be seen from Table 4–5. Shifting from the percentage of area to the number of owners, the outcome of this process was that by 1962 there were 3.1 million landowners in Egypt, of whom 2.2 million owned less than one feddan each.

TABLE 4–5

PERCENTAGE OF PRIVATELY OWNED AND WAKF AREA OWNED BY
SMALL, MEDIUM, AND LARGE LAND OWNERS

	1896	1916	1936	1962
Up to 5 feddan	19.9	26.6	31.5	44.3
5–50 feddan	36.3	30.3	29.9	32.6
Over 50 feddan	43.8	43.1	38.6	23.1
Total	100.0	100.0	100.0	100.0

SOURCE: G. Baer, *A History of Landownership in Modern Egypt, 1800–1950* (New York: Oxford University Press, 1962), p. 77; and United Arab Republic, Department of Public Mobilization and Statistics, *Statistical Yearbook*, (Cairo, 1964), pp. 58–61. The statistics exaggerate the degree of fragmentation of ownership, since a man owing land in two villages is usually counted twice; see Baer, *op. cit.*, pp. 70–73.

The pattern of land holdings—of working units—is quite different. Table 4–6 gives the overall picture as of 1950, shortly before the land reform. A number of things stand out in this table. First, looking at the breakdown of all farms by size, the share in the total area of farms with less than two feddan—a completely uneconomic farming unit—is quite small, amounting to only 7 percent of the total area.[21] Nearly 30 percent of the total was worked in units of two to ten feddan, yielding somewhat more than bare subsistence income.[22] An additional 25 percent of the area was in farms of

---

[20]G. Baer, *A History of Landownership in Modern Egypt, 1800–1950* (New York: Oxford University Press, 1962), pp. 71–120.

[21]It is true that they constituted 46 percent of the total number of farms; this is more important from the point of view of income distribution than from the standpoint of our present concern of land usage.

[22]The average size of the farms distributed as a result of the land reform of 1952 was approximately 2.5 feddan; see D. Warriner, *Land Reform and Development in the Middle East* (New York: Oxford University Press, 1962), p. 193.

10–50 feddan, enough to make well-to-do men of the villagers. The remaining 40 percent was in large and very large farms, in many cases providing their owners with a place in city society and national politics.

TABLE 4–6

LAND HOLDING, 1950

Area per Holding, in Feddan	Total Area, in 000 Feddan				Number of Farms (000)
	Owned	Leased	Mixed	Total	
Less than 2.........	322	88	38	447	463
2–10...............	1,020	403	371	1,794	446
10–50..............	802	303	392	1,497	79
50–200.............	626	263	252	1,142	12
Over 200...........	949	166	148	1,263	2
Total...........	3,720	1,223	1,201*	6,144	1,003

*Of which 494 were owned and 707 leased.
SOURCE: Republic of Egypt, Ministry of Agriculture, *Agricultural Census of Egypt, 1950* (Cairo, 1958), pp. 14–15. Totals may not add due to rounding.

In terms of productivity, there seems to be remarkably little difference among farms of different sizes in Egypt; the gross value of output per feddan per year has been estimated for 1947 as follows:[23]

Farm Size	Gross Value of Output/Feddan
Less than 5 feddan................	£E35.4
5–50 feddan......................	£E39.9
Over 50 feddan...................	£E36.9

These figures are not particularly helpful in evaluating the impact of the land reform on aggregate agricultural output and income. For one thing, the figures show gross output; yet we know very little about the relationship between farm size and other inputs per feddan. Beyond this, many of the large owners had rented their land in smaller working units before the reform, while on land which has been redistributed, the farmers are very much guided by the agricultural cooperatives. In many ways the decision-making farming unit was made larger rather than smaller because of the land reform. As a result, the familiar argument that land reform means land fragmentation, which in turn means lower output per feddan, loses much of its force in the Egyptian context.[24]

[23]M. A. W. Ezzat, "The Land Tenure System in Egypt," in K. H. Parsons *et al.* (eds.), *Land Tenure* (Madison: University of Wisconsin Press, 1956), pp 101–2. We have not been able to locate the original source or methods of estimation of these data.
[24]See Warriner, *op. cit.*, p. 44.

Turning again to Table 4–6, it is rather striking what a high proportion of the land was worked by its owners; including the owned portion of mixed holdings, over two thirds of all Egyptian farmland was owned by the farmers working it. Furthermore, of the 1,930,000 feddan leased in 1950 (either entirely or as part of mixed holdings), about half were leased from proprietors whose total ownership was less than five feddan. The picture of the typical Egyptian farmer renting his few feddan from the large-scale absentee landlord is clearly incorrect. The majority of the land is worked by its owners; for the portion which is rented, a substantial part is held in such a way as to offset the extreme fragmentation of ownership to which we have referred above.[25]

We have been talking of fragmentation of holdings as if it were primarily a problem of too many, too small farms. From this point of view, at least with regard to land usage, there does not seem to be a serious problem of overfragmentation in Egyptian agriculture. There is another aspect of fragmentation which is more serious; this concerns the division of individual farm holdings into noncontiguous plots of land. The magnitude of this problem can be seen from Table 4–7. The total figures are most impressive; 45 percent

TABLE 4–7

FRAGMENTATION OF LAND HOLDINGS, 1950, BY AREA

(000 Feddan)

Area of Total Holding, in Feddan	In One Piece	In Two Pieces	In Three Pieces	In Four or More Pieces	Not Stated	Total
Less than 2	217	153	55	21	1	447
2–10	330	510	467	480	6	1,794
10–50	186	202	275	827	7	1,497
50–200	185	130	136	679	11	1,142
Over 200	244	123	103	767	26	1,263
Total	1,163	1,118	1,037	2,775	51	6,144

SOURCE: Republic of Egypt, Ministry of Agriculture, *Agricultural Census of Egypt, 1950* (Cairo, 1958), p. 25. Totals may not add due to rounding.

(by area) of the farms were divided into four or more separate plots. This exaggerates the extent of the problem, however. The degree of fragmentation rises sharply with farm size; for very small farms, over 80 percent of the area was in farms of one or two plots; for very large farms, on the other hand, 60 percent of the land was

[25]For figures on types of leases on rented land, see Appendix Table III–C–5 (p. 329).

in farms of four or more plots. If a holding of 500 feddan is divided into five equal plots, this is no particular cause for concern; each one may well be large enough to be worked efficiently as a separate unit, allowing for effective use of fertilizers and insecticides. Since each plot may be worked by different people, the usual argument that time is lost going from one plot to another is not convincing, even if it were relevant in a labor-surplus country. The substantial fragmentation in the middle-sized farms is more serious. With 53 percent of the land in farms of two to ten feddan and 74 percent of the total in the 10–50 feddan group broken into three or more plots, we might clearly expect this fragmentation to have a significant impact on agricultural productivity.

The government is attempting to meet this problem in two ways. In the land reform area, each district is divided into three blocks, each of which is at a different phase in the triennial crop rotation which is used in those areas; the farmer gets a piece in each block, so that perhaps at a moment of time, one third of his land would be under cotton, one third under wheat, and one third under clover. Thus the farm fragmentation continues, but it is rationalized and controlled. Outside of land reform areas, attempts have been made to achieve the same results by arranging for the swapping of land or its produce so that the same three-way split is achieved, and the land can be cultivated in large blocks. This was tried in the village of Nawag in 1955 and proved so successful that attempts are being made to extend the project to the whole country within the first five-year plan. Since the implementation of the project relies heavily on the agricultural cooperatives and (being entirely voluntary) is contingent on winning the confidence of the farmers, it seems unrealistic to hope to be able to move so fast; if it is true that by 1961–62 the project had been extended to one third of the total cultivated area, as had been claimed, this is most impressive.[26]

With this brief review of the land-owning and land-holding patterns in 1950, perhaps it should not surprise us that the land reform instituted by the new government did not represent as revolutionary a change, at least from the point of view of land ownership, as is sometimes claimed. In Warriner's words: "The area officially redistributed amounts to only about 7 percent of the total cultivated land area. About 150,000 families . . . have received land in conditional ownership and have gained considerably in income, security and social responsibility, but they represent only a small

[26]National Bank of Egypt, *Economic Bulletin*, Vol. XV, No. 4 (1962), pp. 216–18. See also Warriner, *op cit.*, pp. 204–7.

fraction of the farm population."[27] This should not be taken as an attempt to belittle the importance of the land reforms. Besides this transfer of property ownership, which was relatively minor, they have increased the security of other tenant farmers, by requiring three-year written leases; as we shall see, they effected some re-distribution of income via rent controls; they eliminated the eco-nomic base from which a small number of wealthy families had attained political power; perhaps most important, they are both the expression and the source of a new spirit in Egyptian agricul-ture, which hopefully will have deep and lasting economic reper-cussions. Economists often speak of the agricultural sector in de-veloping countries as the traditional sector; if the land reforms succeed in shaking Egyptian farmers out of their tradition-bound patterns, the contribution will be great.

In large part, this means that the economic impact of the land reform is very much dependent on the work of the agencies that follow, the agricultural cooperatives. Membership in a cooperative is required for a farmer who receives land through the land reform; yet membership in the cooperatives is by no means restricted to these people. The government is using every means to induce others to join them. By providing cheaper credits,[28] lower cost inputs such as seeds and fertilizers, marketing facilities which give higher prices to the farmers by eliminating a number of intermediaries, farmers have every incentive to join; this, in turn, gives the gov-ernment an important foothold for improving seed, fertilizer, and water usage, controlling crop rotation, and introducing more ad-vanced agricultural techniques. There seems to be every reason to believe that the agrarian reform, in the broadest sense of the word, will have a major impact on the Egyptian agricultural sector, even though the land reform itself has only touched a small minority of the total.[29]

---

[27]Warriner, *op. cit.*, p. 193. As of December 31, 1961, total land redis-tributed was 479,239 feddan, about 8 percent of the cultivated area; see United Arab Republic, Department of Statistics and Census, *Ten Years of Revolu-tion: Statistical Atlas* (Cairo, July, 1962), Table 22. The extension of the land reform in 1961, when completed, will probably affect an additional 250,000 feddan, thereby bringing the total to about 12 percent of the cultivated area.

[28]For an interesting and rather critical appraisal of these credit arrange-ments, see A. M. el Tanamli, "Agricultural Credit and Cooperative Organiza-tion," *L'Egypte Contemporaine*, No. 310 (October, 1962), pp. 5–39.

[29]See also J. S. Oweis, *Agricultural Development in the United Arab Re-public (Egypt)*, working paper prepared for U. S. Department of Agriculture, Economic Research Service, Development and Trade Analysis Division (Wash-ington, D. C.: U. S. Government Printing Office, n.d.) (mimeographed), pp. 52–61; also K. H. Parsons, "Land Reform in the United Arab Republic," *Land Economics*, Vol. XXV, No. 4 (November, 1959), pp. 319–26.

The other inputs to the agricultural sector can be treated more briefly. With regard to fertilizers, the statistics tell the story fairly clearly; the annual average supply of chemical fertilizers, from domestic production as well as imports, was as shown in Table 4–8. As we saw in Chapter 1, in the late 1930's Egypt was among the heaviest users of fertilizers in the world. Since most of her fertilizers were imported, the blocking of trade during the war cut the supply drastically, with major repercussions on the level of output. Thereafter, fertilizer usage climbed rapidly to return Egypt to its position as a heavy user of fertilizer. By 1960, consumption figures per acre of arable land in Egypt were considerably above those for most developing countries, although still far below the levels of a number of more advanced countries, such as Belgium and the Netherlands.[30]

TABLE 4–8

FERTILIZER SUPPLIES

(Annual Averages)

	Total Supply (000 Tons)	Kilograms per Cropped Feddan
1935–39	567.4	68
1940–44	202.5	22
1945–49	431.5	47
1950–54	779.5	79*
1955–59	875.7	85*

*Consumption per cropped feddan (in kilograms). These are rough figures based on unsystematic surveys of fertilizer usage undertaken by the Ministry of Agriculture.

SOURCE: B. Hansen and G. Marzouk, *Development and Economic Policy in the U.A.R. (Egypt)* (Amsterdam: North-Holland Publishing Co., 1965), Table 3.10.

It may seem strange to consider water separately as an input to agriculture; yet in the Egyptian circumstances, water must be considered as one of the most crucial of the scarce resources. Our discussion can be separated into two parts: the supply of water available in the Nile, and the efficiency with which the water is brought to the fields. On the first point, the main determinants are the supply of rainfall in the northeastern part of Africa and the

---

[30]See United Nations Food and Agriculture Organization, *Fertilizers: An Annual Review of World Production, Consumption and Trade, 1960,* Table 15. Intercountry comparisons are made difficult by the use of different types of fertilizers in different countries; in 1960, Egypt used five times as much nitrogenous fertilizer per acre of arable land as the United States, approximately the same amount of phosphates, but only one twelfth as much potassium-base fertilizer *(ibid.).*

storage capacity available for evening out untimely flows both between years and within any given year. It is in this respect that the High Dam is expected to make one of its major contributions. With the completion of the coffer dams as part of the first stage of construction, the height of the Nile flood, which has blessed the farmers for untold centuries, has already been reduced. The stated goal of bringing a million (or even more) new feddan under cultivation seems too high because of both the likely increase in the amount of "timely" water which will be available and the supply of land which could economically be brought under cultivation; but even if the expansion is only half that amount (which seems like a fair target), it would represent a 10 percent increase in the cultivated area.[31] This will make a marked change, even if not a revolutionary one, in the output of Egyptian agriculture, when the water can be fully used in this way, some five to ten years hence.

Besides allowing for an extension of cultivated area, the completion of the High Dam will make it possible to regulate the flow of water over the course of the year in virtually any way which the authorities choose. In the past the cropping pattern in the agricultural sector has been closely determined by water availability; now that this natural flow pattern need no longer dominate, the country faces the possibility of reorganizing its crop rotation without being constrained by the seasonal pattern of water availability. In a highly stimulating and informed discussion of the problems and possibilities of this restructuring, Owen has argued that Egypt should stop producing wheat, concentrating her land and water in areas where she has greater comparative advantage, such as rice, maize, and oil crops, as well as sugar and vegetables.[32] This would imply a growing dependence on imported wheat; but if this is matched by exports of alternative crops, with higher value, it is no cause for concern, but rather for satisfaction. In this situation, care must be taken that the American aid program, with its requirement that PL 480 wheat imports not be matched by increasing

---

[31]Preliminary results of studies undertaken under United Nations auspices indicate that there are not much more than 500,000 additional feddan of land economically suitable for cultivation; the factors which they considered were the quality of the surface (i.e., ruling out rock or extremely porous sand), distance from the Nile, and height above the Nile. Final results of these studies have not yet been published. In June, 1964, an agreement was negotiated with a group of foreign firms for the reclamation of 312,000 feddan, to be irrigated from the High Dam; see *International Financial News Survey*, Vol. XVI, No. 25 (June 26, 1964), p. 209.

[32]W. F. Owen, "Land and Water Use in the Egyptian High Dam Era," *Land Economics*, Vol. XL, No. 3 (August, 1964), pp. 277–93.

exports from land previously devoted to wheat production, not become a force holding back a desirable structural change. This complex of problems is currently being investigated by an advisory group to the governor of Aswan, using techniques of linear programming; the results of that study should be particularly interesting.[33]

The other aspect of the water supply concerns the irrigation system. The relevant figures are indicated in Table 4–9. The length of the canals and drains in the country has risen since the 1930's at a faster rate than that of cultivated area, even slightly faster than the increase in the cropped area. With regard to irrigation machinery, this has risen at a substantially higher rate, with a marked substitution of motor-driven equipment for the older machines using animal- or manpower. It seems clear that from an irrigation point of view, Egyptian agriculture is better supplied today than it was 10 or 25 years ago.

TABLE 4–9

IRRIGATION FACILITIES

	Length of Irrigation Canals (Kilometers)	Length of Drains (Kilometers)	Licensed Irrigation Machinery* (Installed Horsepower, 000)
1937............	20,170	9,169	304
1947............	22,073	12,064	339
1960............	24,804	13,330	460

*Irrigation and drainage.
SOURCE: *Annuaire Statistique*, various issues.

There are two other components of the agricultural capital stock to be mentioned. The first is the number of farm animals. Appendix Table III–D–1 (page 332) shows that there has been a steady increase in the number of buffaloes and cows ("other bovines"); these are are the major working animals, used for preparing the fields and turning the waterwheels, among other things. For the rest, the number of animals may have been declining over the past 25 years. The decline is clearest in the basic meat animals, sheep and goats, but probably includes donkeys and camels as

---

[33]An additional consideration which is relevant here concerns the demands of water for electricity generation; electricity cannot be stored, and the seasonal pattern of demand for electricity (higher in winter than in summer) does not correspond to the seasonal needs of water for irrigation. Once again, this is a question which can best be solved by the use of linear programming.

well, at least since 1947. Finally, Appendix Table III–D–4 (page 334) gives the scanty figures available on the supply of agricultural machinery. As the notes to that table indicate, these figures can do little more than give a rough idea of orders of magnitude. Still, we might point out that 10,000 tractors is a surprisingly large number, averaging one for every 600 feddan in 1950.[34]

C. AGRICULTURAL PRODUCTIVITY

We now have before us the major elements of the agricultural sector. In summary index form, the basic components are as shown in Table 4–10. The broad outlines of this picture are clear. During

TABLE 4–10

SUMMARY TABLE OF AGRICULTURAL PRODUCTION

	1937	1947	1960
Agricultural output................	100*	94	139
Inputs:			
Land:			
Cultivated area...............	100	109	112
Cropped area................	100	110	124
Labor, adult males......../........	100	105	120
Capital:			
Canals and drains.............	100	116	130
Irrigation machinery...........	100	112	151
Fertilizers†....................	100	72	167

*In 1935–39.
†Fertilizer *supply* in the year shown, a rough proxy for fertilizer *consumption* in that year and immediately preceding years.

the first decade the shortage of fertilizer was so significant that it more than offset increases in all other inputs. Some of the indicated fall in output may have been statistical, resulting from the remaining reallocation of land; yet, even making allowance for this, there was clearly a significant drop in output, which must be attributed primarily to the reduced supply of fertilizers. During the following period, there was a rapid expansion in the domestic production of chemical fertilizers; the total fertilizer supply per cultivated feddan, from imports as well as from domestic production, more than doubled between 1947 and 1960. The resulting increase in output exceeded the expansion of either land or labor inputs, so that the output productivity of each of these factors increased.

Not only were yields per acre of land rising during this period;

---

[34]Alternatively, and more precisely, in 1950 there were, on the average, 0.937 tractors for each square mile of cultivated area.

they were also quite impressively high in absolute terms. Of all the countries for which yield figures are available from the Food and Agriculture Organization, output per acre in Egypt in 1962–63 ranked fourteenth for wheat, twelfth for maize, third for rice (8 percent above Japan), first for chick-peas, lentils, and millet, and fifth for cotton (nearly 30 percent above the United States.)[35] It is easy to underestimate the importance of these high yields. Economists might be tempted to say that this is a natural result of the law of diminishing returns; with heavy application of fertilizers and labor-intensive methods of production, yields per acre should be high. Yet we should remember that there are a number of countries with a high man-land ratio, but which still have very low yields per acre.[36] Egyptian agriculture is not primitive and backward, awaiting simply the application of more advanced technology to yield massive increases in output; on the contrary, given the factor supplies available, production techniques are advanced and efficient. This means that rural poverty is primarily a result of unfortunate factor proportions, and hence is perhaps correspondingly more difficult to eliminate than in countries where there is more scope for improvement through the introduction of better production techniques.

This is not to deny that increases in agricultural output could be achieved through such means as more widespread use of higher yielding seeds.[37] We suspect, however, that the scope for such relatively simple and cheap improvements is limited. Beyond this, perhaps with the application of substantial additional capital in the form of better irrigation control and better implements, and (perhaps most important) with better educated farmers, more ready to adopt new production techniques of all kinds, Egypt might attain the 30 percent higher yields reached in the advanced and intensive farming of southern California. Yet, in large measure, this amounts to a statement that if Egypt weret not an underdeveloped country, she would have a more advanced agricultural sector, with higher yields per acre. It is questionable whether such advances represent an achievable

---

[35]See United Nations Food and Agriculture Organization, *Production Yearbook, 1963*, Vol. XVII (Rome, 1964).

[36]The Republic of Korea, Indonesia, India, and Pakistan may be cited as examples. It is true that except for Korea, these countries have a lower man-land ratio than Egypt; see Table 4–15 (p. 83). Japanese yields per acre are at roughly the same level as in Egypt for all major crops grown in both countries.

[37]There is a project under way for the introduction of hybrid corn which may well result in a striking increase in yields of this crop; at present, only 12 percent of the maize area is planted with hybrid seed.

target for the second five-year plan, and even if attainable, whether this would be a wise use of the scarce resources of the country. This is a matter on which a great deal more evidence is needed, particularly from the agricultural economists; the author is skeptical that such a large-scale increase in agricultural output represents an attainable and wise short-run target. Once again, this is not to say that efforts should not be made to raise agricultural output; quite the contrary. The point is rather that to try to turn Egypt into a giant, highly capitalized truck farm, as some have suggested, does not make sense at her present stage of development.

D. AGRICULTURAL INCOME

Let us turn to an examination of the level and distribution of income earned in agriculture. First looking at the trend in the development of real income, it is clear that this is closely associated with the quantum index of output. These two series can diverge for either or both of two reasons. If the "terms of trade" between agriculture and the rest of the economy change, workers in the agricultural sector might find that they have a higher or lower real income, even if the real product remained unchanged. As we shall see in Chapter 8, there does not seem to have been any significant shift in this measure of internal terms of trade in the postwar period. A divergence between real income and output would also result if there were a nonproportional change in the inputs of intermediate products delivered to the sector from outside of agriculture; for example, in the late 1940's, there was a substantial increase in fertilizer usage, with the result that real income in agriculture rose less rapidly than did agricultural output.[38] In general, though, in the postwar period in Egypt the two series moved in parallel; after a modest rise in the immediate postwar years, income showed no sustained increase until 1953–54; from then until 1960, real income rose by some 30 percent. As we saw in Chapter 3, agriculture's share in the total income of the country fell from 40 percent in 1945–47 to 30 percent in 1954, a share which it maintained until 1960. Since then, there has been a further decline, with agriculture's share currently close to 25 percent.[39]

---

[38]See B. Hansen and D. Mead, *The National Income of the U.A.R. (Egypt), 1939–1962*, Memo No. 355 (Cairo: Institute of National Planning, July, 1963), p. 6.

[39]According to M. A. Anis' estimate, agriculture's share in national income was 48 percent in 1939. This seems plausible, in view of agriculture's output decline during the war and the relative share of agriculture (42 percent) in 1945. See Chapter 3 and Appendix I Table I–A–1 (pp. 270–71).

With regard to the allocation of this income, the usual division among various types of factor income is not helpful; for the small farmer owning his own land, all factor incomes are merged. The most that we can hope to do is to break agricultural income into that which is paid to wage laborers, that which is paid as rent to landlords, and the remainder, which is primarily the income of the farmer himself. With regard to the wages shares, the wage rate data in Appendix Table II–B–9 (page 313) can be combined with figures on the number of paid laborers and a rough estimate of the average number of days worked per year, to give us an estimate of the share of agricultural income going to wage earners. In recent years, this share has remained close to 5 percent of total agricultural income. An estimation of the share of agricultural income going for rental payments presents other problems. Until the land reform, land was often rented for one crop at a time; the rental payment depended on the quality of the land, the crop to be grown on it, and the current price of the crop. Of the 1.9 million feddan of land leased in 1950, about 85 percent were rented on a cash basis.[40] Using the figures in the 1950 agricultural census and a rough estimate of the average rent of land in that year, we can obtain the breakdown of value added in agriculture shown in Table 4–11.

How has this picture changed since 1950? It is unfortunate that the 1960 agricultural census has not been released, so that comparable figures must be rough; all we can do is make some guesses as to what developments have taken place since then. With regard to labor income, perhaps a slight rise in wage rates offset a fall in the demand for laborers, leaving unchanged the total amount paid to wage workers. Average rents per feddan declined by some 25 percent, partly as a result of the agrarian reform law, partly because of the decline in agricultural prices, particularly cotton.[41] Finally, there has been a transfer of ownership of nearly 500,000 feddan to small owner-operators. If we assume that half of this land was formerly rented to "medium farmers" (two- to fifty-feddan farm size) and the rest worked by the owners as large holdings, and if we ignore all other changes in land ownership which may have taken place during the decade, the picture would be changed by 1960 to look as in Table 4–12. This implies a sharp fall in the income of absentee landlords, due primarily to the fall in rental values, but also as a result of the transfer of formerly

---

[40]See Appendix Table III–C–5 (p. 329).

[41]Weighted average of rents for ten crops given for 1951 and 1961 in National Bank of Egypt, *Economic Bulletin*, Vol. XVI, Nos. 1–2 (1963), p. 23.

rented land to new owners through the land reform. Total income of large farmers rose fractionally, as rising value added per feddan and falling rents more than offset the transfer of some land formerly worked as large holdings to smaller owner-operators. The income

TABLE 4-11

DISTRIBUTION OF AGRICULTURAL INCOME, 1950

	£E Million	Share in Total (Percent)
Wages	20.0	5.4
Rental payments	48.3	13.1
Other income, by size of holdings:		
Below 2 feddan	24.1	6.5
2-50 feddan	160.7	43.7
Over 50 feddan	114.9	31.2
Total, other income	299.7	
Gross value added	368.0	100.0

NOTES AND SOURCES: All laborers are assumed to work 150 days per year (see C. Issawi, *Egypt in Revolution: An Economic Analysis* [New York: Oxford University Press, 1963], p. 155). Wage rates are from Appendix Table II–B–9 (p. 313). Laborers are assumed to be hired in proportion to area on all farms of ten or more feddan.

Average rental is estimated at £E25/feddan. Figures refer to rent actually paid (in cash or kind), excluding imputed rent of owner-occupied land, which is therefore included with "other income."

Value added per feddan is assumed to be equal for all farm sizes; this gives some downward bias to income figures for most productive farms (probably two to ten feddan) and upward bias to all others (see p. 67). The figures are gross in the sense that they make no allowance for capital consumption. For roughly comparable figures, see *ibid.*, p. 120.

Totals may not add due to rounding.

TABLE 4-12

PROVISIONAL ESTIMATE, DISTRIBUTION OF
AGRICULTURAL INCOME, 1960

	£E Million	Share in Total (Percent)
Wages	20.0	5
Rental payments	31.7	7
Other income, by size of holdings:		
Below 2 feddan	28.7	7
2-50 feddan	218.1	52
Over 50 feddan	123.5	29
Total, other income	370.3	
Gross value added	422.0	100

received by the poorest group—wage earners and those working tiny farms—remained virtually unchanged (partly by assumption). The biggest change came in the situation of the "middle-range" farmers; as a group, their income increased by some 35 percent, with their share of total agricultural income rising to over 50 percent.[42]

In order to be able to interpret these figures from a welfare point of view, we should need to know something about the numbers of people with claims on the income in each of these categories. Inevitably, the figures here are extremely rough. It is clear that income per capita of both the very poor and the very rich in agriculture has dropped markedly during the 1950's. The 35 percent increase in money income of "middle-class" farmers was accompanied by both an increase in the number of these farmers and a rise in the income of each one, although in what proportion is difficult to determine; judging from the transfer of land into this category and the changing man-land ratio in the whole agricultural sector, rising income per capita may have accounted for 15 to 20 percent of this extra income. With a price rise of between 5 and 10 percent, the average real income per capita of these "middle-class" farmers may have risen by some 10 percent over the course of the decade.

As we made clear in Chapter 3, relative to the rest of the economy agriculture has been a slow-growing sector. The result is that in spite of a substantial increase in nonagricultural employment in the provinces as well as heavy migration to the cities (the joint result of which was a quite slow rate of increase in agricultural employment), and in spite of a significant redistribution of income within the agricultural sector, the per capita real income of those who benefited most from this redistribution—those whom we have called "middle-class farmers"—rose by only about 10 percent over the decade of the 1950's. For the remainder—the very rich, the very poor, and the landlords—real incomes declined, hitting a few of the first and third quite hard (averages have little meaning here), hitting all of the second very hard (even small decreases constitute a real threat). Perhaps our conclusion should be that while structural change and income redistribution have helped to allevi-

---

[42]These figures exaggerate their improvement to some extent, since beneficiaries of the land reform had to pay annual installments of interest and principal on the land they received. The average value of the land distributed by 1961 was £E193/feddan, or a total of nearly £E100 million; with interest at 1½ percent and amortization over forty years, this would put the beneficiaries' annual debt to the government at about £E4 million. All of these would fall in the two- to fifty-feddan range. See C. Issawi, *Egypt in Revolution: An Economic Analysis* (New York: Oxford University Press, 1963), p. 161. In 1964, however, interest payments were eliminated, and the amortization value of the land was reduced to one quarter of the original level; see Central Bank of Egypt, *Economic Review*, Vol. IV, No. 1 (1964), p. 73.

ate the pressure of population growth on rural incomes, they have not solved the problem of rural poverty, and probably cannot solve it as long as the factor proportions within the agricultural sector remain so heavily weighted against labor.

APPENDIX

Underemployment in Agriculture

Egypt is generally cited as a classic case of a country with substantial underemployment in agriculture. Past estimates, official and unofficial, have ranged from near 20 percent to over 50 percent, although in general the definitions and specifications underlying these estimates were either inadequate or lacking completely. On one point only has there been wide agreement: that underemployment is quite substantial, and is growing.[43] In recent years, on the other hand, a few significant dissenters have advanced evidence which they feel points in the opposite direction.[44] We have no new definitions or original measurement techniques to add to the immense theoretical literature on this subject; rather, we should like to bring together and evaluate a number of independent pieces of empirical evidence which bear on this question. No one of these alone will prove that x percent of the agricultural labor force was redundant, but perhaps taken together they will permit us to form a judgment as to the existence or extent of disguised unemployment in Egyptian agriculture.

1. *Man-Land Ratio.* In a country with limited cultivable land and a predominantly agricultural population, even a moderate rate of growth

[43]See, among others, W. Cleland, *The Population Problem in Egypt* (Lancaster, Pa.: Science Press Printing Co., 1936), pp. 104–6; M. R. el Ghonemy, "The Investment Effects of the Land Reform in Egypt," *L'Egypte Contemporaine,* No. 278 (October, 1954), p. 14; C. Issawi, *Egypt in Revolution: An Economic Analysis* (New York: Oxford University Press, 1963), pp. 298–99; United Arab Republic, Presidency of the Republic, National Planning Committee, *General Frame of the Five-Year Plan for Economic and Social Development, July 1960–June 1965* (Cairo, 1960), p. 118.

[44]The major proponent here is Bent Hansen; see his *Marginal Productivity Wage Theory and Subsistence Wage Theory in Egyptian Agriculture,* Memo No. 547 (Cairo: Institute of National Planning, March, 1965); B. Hansen and G. Marzouk, *Development and Economic Policy in the U.A.R. (Egypt)* (Amsterdam: North-Holland Publishing Co., 1965), chap. iii, sec. 3.2.5; M. el Tomy and B. Hansen, *The Seasonal Employment Profile in Egyptian Agriculture,* Memo No. 501 (Cairo: Institute of National Planning, October, 1964); H. Kheir el Dine, *The Cotton Production Function in the U.A.R. and Its Relation to Technical Progress and to Disguised Unemployment,* Memo No. 370 (Cairo: Institute of National Planning, September, 1963); A. J. Meyer, *Middle Eastern Capitalism* (Cambridge: Harvard University Press, 1959), p. 116.

in the total population, maintained over fifty years or more, will result
in a substantial increase in the number of workers on each acre of land.
Let us see to what extent this was the case in Egypt. The figures are as
follows:

	"Man" (000)	Land (000 Feddan)	Ratio
1917.............	2,898	5,269	0.55
1960.............	4,343	5,918	0.73

In this tabulation, the figures for "man" refer to the total number of
people whose economic activity was classified in the population census
as being in agriculture;[45] it is basically a labor force concept. As for the
denominator, the most meaningful series for this purpose refers to cultivated area. Those who would rest their case on figures such as these, as
some have, would argue that the 33 percent increase in the number of
workers on each cultivated acre was "clearly" more than could be productively absorbed; by the end of the period the presumption is that
the marginal worker would add little or nothing to total output.[46]

This line of reasoning might lead one to believe that the man-land
ratio has been rising steadily and consistently over the past forty years
or more. If we include an observation in the 1930's, this picture changes
substantially:

	"Man" (000)	Land (000 Feddan)	Ratio
1917.............	2,898	5,269	0.55
1937.............	4,232	5,281	0.80
1960.............	4,343	5,918	0.73

These figures show a large increase in the man-land ratio in the first
twenty years of the period; since the late 1930's, by contrast, the agricultural labor force has stagnated, while the cultivated area was extended
somewhat, implying that the pressure of population on the land may
have been decreasing.

Our discussion thus far has treated the agricultural labor force as if
it were homogeneous; in Chapter 2, we pointed out the weakness of this
approach, which is illustrated in the breakdown of the total shown in
Table 4–13. The author's discussions with informed people in Egypt
leave him convinced that the indicated drop in the number of females
in the agricultural labor force—and probably the declining number of

---

[45]Agriculture and livestock (i.e., excluding forestry, hunting, and fishing),
adjusted as explained in notes to Table 2–10 (p. 37). Beyond this, female
"agricultural laborers inferred from schedules" (in 1917) are excluded.

[46]This statement might be strengthened by pointing out that in 1917, output
per acre in Egypt was quite high by world standards, while output per worker
was very low; this implies that even at that time the land was being worked
intensively. See Issawi, *op. cit.*, p. 299.

boys as well—is purely a statistical phenomenon, resulting from changing interpretation on the part of the census takers as to when a farm wife should be included in the agricultural labor force. This dividing line cannot be defined in any unique, theoretically correct way; one must rely on rules of thumb, and it seems most probable that these rules have been changing in recent years.[47]

TABLE 4-13

	Total Agricultural Labor Force	Males		Females, Total
		Aged 5-14	Aged 15 and Above	
1917	2,898	465	1,921	513
1937	4,232	621	2,938	673
1960	4,343	571*	3,502	270

*Aged 6-14.
NOTE: In thousands.

The discussion of underemployment in agriculture is normally concerned with the stimulus to the economy which would result if these people were withdrawn from the agricultural sector and given productive employment elsewhere. For women and children in Egypt, this is not an important consideration; the 1960 population census showed less than 5 percent of all women aged 15 and above as being "economically active," while all the pressures in the society are aimed toward reducing the employment of young people. It seems plausible to argue, then, that the concept of agricultural unemployment in which we are interested—and, to the extent that it bears on this question, the "man" part of the man-land ratio—refers to adult males only, not to the total agricultural labor force.

This approach to the question would clearly be misleading if we believed that a rising number of men were finding productive work on each acre of land by replacing women and children formerly working there. The data are not accurate enough for us to know if this was the case; it may well have been so, to a limited extent. Still, it seems preferable to use this concept, being aware of the possible bias which it introduces, rather than the meaningless aggregate of the total agricultural labor force. On this basis, the figures are as shown in Table 4-14.

---

[47]This problem arises for men as well, but is probably not so serious for them. Men "on the margin" of the agricultural sector (i.e., with no other jobs, but working only irregularly in agriculture) might be counted by the census either as part of the agricultural labor force or as employed in "ill-defined industries" (which was relatively small in all the years shown in Table 4-13), or else in the category "not specified"; this latter was abnormally large in 1937, implying some understatement of the men in the agricultural labor force in that year.

TABLE 4–14

	Adult Male Agricultural Labor Force (000)	Land (000 Feddan)	Ratio
1917	1,921	5,269	0.36
1937	2,938	5,281	0.56
1960	3,502	5,918	0.59

These figures imply that the rise in the man-land ratio is very much greater, amounting to over 60 percent, while the break in the 1930's becomes a reduction in the rate of increase, rather than a change in the direction of movement.

It may be of some interest to present comparative figures on the man-land ratio for other countries. This is a hazardous exercise, since definitions of both numerator and denominator differ widely from country to country. The figures in Table 4–15, however, may give some idea of orders of magnitude. These figures make it clear that the concentration of labor in Egypt is substantially higher than in a number of Asian countries which are generally considered to be heavily populated, such as India or Pakistan, not to mention western Europe. Of the countries shown, only Japan and Korea had comparable or higher ratios.

TABLE 4–15

Man-Land Ratio in Selected Countries

(Workers per Hectare)

	A	B
Belgium	0.46	0.40
Denmark	0.18	0.13
India	0.81	0.52
Indonesia	1.33	0.98
Japan	3.00	1.43
Korea (Republic)	3.12	1.70
Netherlands	0.45	0.40
Pakistan	0.66	0.63
Philippines	0.51	0.37
United Arab Republic	1.71	1.61

SOURCE: United Nations Food and Agriculture Organization, *Production Yearbook*, 1963, Vol. XVII (Rome, 1964), Tables 1 and 5. For series A, the numerator is the total population engaged in agricultural occupations, while series B refers only to males so engaged. The denominator for both is "arable land and land under permanent crops." All are for the most recent data available.

There seems to be a general presumption, which is part of our standard toolbox of economic theory but which agrees with our intuition as well, that if the number of workers on a unit of land rises continuously, the marginal productivity of additional workers will decline, eventually, to zero. A priori, there is no way of knowing whether that word "eventually" means a 60 or a 600 percent increase in the man-land ratio; surely, the factor proportions at the start of the exercise, and the levels and types of technology actually adopted, are important considerations here. The discussion above clearly does not constitute proof, perhaps does not even create a presumption, that the marginal productivity of labor had declined to zero in Egypt by 1960. For the moment, let us treat the data presented simply as facts, and go on to other information which may bear on this question.

2. *Agricultural Production Function.* In Section 1 of this Appendix, we have considered only the relative abundance of two factors of production, land and labor. We should like to broaden this discussion to consider other inputs as well, and to examine in a systematic way the relationship between these inputs and the real product of the agricultural sector. The basic work here has been done in the careful study referred to earlier, by M. M. el Imam at the Institute of National Planning in Cairo;[48] el Imam has used multiple regression analysis to fit a Cobb-Douglas type of production function to the Egyptian agricultural sector, covering the period 1913–55. One weakness of this study, we believe, lies in el Imam's use of the same total labor force series which we have objected to above, lumping together men, women, and children. We have recomputed these estimates, using only adult males in the agricul-

TABLE 4–16

ESTIMATED PRODUCTION FUNCTION FOR EGYPTIAN AGRICULTURE, 1917–55

$\text{Log } Y = -2.4115 + 0.3523 \log A + 0.0876 \log W + 0.0150 \log F$
$\qquad\qquad\quad (0.3172) \qquad\quad (0.0709) \qquad\quad (0.0151)$
$\qquad -0.0074\, t + 0.9323 \log L \qquad\qquad\qquad\qquad R = 0.8594$
$\qquad (0.0034) \quad (0.2799)$

$\text{Log } Y = -0.8188 + 0.2967 \log A + 0.0211 \log F - 0.0065\, t + 0.8354 \log L$
$\qquad\qquad\quad (0.3165) \qquad\quad (0.0144) \qquad\quad (0.0034) \quad (0.2708)$
$\qquad\qquad\qquad\qquad\qquad\qquad\qquad\qquad\qquad\qquad\qquad R = 0.8523$

$\text{Log } Y = \quad 1.8718 + 0.3596 \log A + 0.0269 \log F + 0.3482 \log L$
$\qquad\qquad\quad (0.3266) \qquad\quad (0.0146) \qquad\quad (0.0981)$
$\qquad\qquad\qquad\qquad\qquad\qquad\qquad\qquad\qquad R = 0.8347$

$\text{Log } Y = -0.5584 + 0.6209 \log A + 0.4650 \log L$
$\qquad\qquad\quad (0.3039) \qquad\quad (0.0774)$
$\qquad\qquad\qquad\qquad\qquad\qquad\qquad\qquad\qquad R = 0.8169$

Y = Agricultural output
A = Area: feddan-years
W = Water: Discharge from Aswan
F = Chemical fertilizer in previous year
t = Time
L = Labor

[48]M. M. el Imam, *A Production Function for Egyptian Agriculture, 1913–1955*, Memo No. 259 (Cairo: Institute of National Planning, December, 1962).

tural labor force,[49] covering the period 1917–55, with the results shown in Table 4–16.

One might object to these calculations from a number of points of view. With regard to the data used, one might say that there are other important inputs which should have been considered, such as capital or entrepreneurship; one might argue that women and children do have an important role to play in agriculture and should at least be considered as a separate input. These criticisms make sense, although one is at a loss to find data to take account of them in practice; surely, in view of the bad statistics, leaving out the women and children is more reasonable than adding them to the number of adult males in the labor force. A further objection might be made to the functional form specified; in particular, in a Cobb-Douglas type of production function the marginal product of a factor can never reach zero. On the other hand, this formulation does permit us to say that, given the average labor productivity at some point in time, the marginal productivity is or is not significantly positive.[50] An additional difficulty concerns the estimation of such a function for the agricultural sector as a whole; the dependent variable is an index comprising a number of different crops, each one of which may in fact respond quite differently to an increase in a given factor of production.[51] Perhaps the most important challenge, at least for our purposes, concerns the use of a labor input series which is basically a capacity concept: labor *available* for use, rather than labor actually employed. If these two concepts diverge widely, it would be difficult to justify using this measure of labor inputs. If the divergence was large and we persisted in computing the production function using these labor force figures, we should expect this to show in the regression results by yielding a labor coefficient which was statistically insignificant.

Turning to the results of the estimation, there are a number of aspects which are questionable. Three of the four cases specified imply increasing returns to scale, which surely is not plausible; the insignificant

---

[49]Interpolating between census years by assuming exponential growth rates.

[50]In the Cobb-Douglas production function the coefficient for any factor of production tells the ratio of its marginal to average product. Since the average product of labor is consistently positive (although declining), the question whether the marginal product is also positive comes down to a question of whether the labor coefficient is significantly different from zero. We have also estimated the production relationships using two other functional forms, quadratic and square root production functions, both of which do allow for the possibility that the marginal products may go to zero (and even become negative). Unfortunately, although the multiple correlation coefficient was high—virtually the same as for the Cobb-Douglas form—the coefficients of the variabes were economically meaningless and statistically not significant.

[51]See M. Bronfenbrenner, "Production Functions: Cobb-Douglas, Interfirm, Intrafirm," *Econometrica*, Vol. XII (1944), pp. 35–44.

coefficients for fertilizers and the negative ones for the time need further explanation.[52] Yet perhaps the most striking result, which shows in all formulations, is the highly significant coefficient for labor. Expressed in simple terms, this means that when we consider labor as one of several inputs to the agricultural sector, there is a highly significant relationship between changes in labor inputs—as measured by the number of adult males in the agricultural labor force—and total output. This seems like a basic challenge to the idea that there were substantial numbers of redundant workers in Egyptian agriculture.

One of the problems with the Cobb-Douglas production function is that it implies a constant elasticity of output with respect to each input over the whole period of estimation. There is no way of finding from these figures whether the relationship between labor and output was becoming more or less significant through time, or whether a very close relationship in the early part of the period was strong enough to yield significant coefficients for the period as a whole, even though by the end of the period this relationship had weakened, or even disappeared. One way of testing this is by recomputing the function over various subperiods. If we break the data into two periods of 20 years each, for example, we get the results shown in Table 4-17. During the first

TABLE 4–17

1917–36

$$\text{Log } Y = -0.3296 + 0.5151 \log A + 0.0108 \log F + 0.5325 \log L$$
$$(0.3379) \qquad (0.0206) \qquad (0.1873)$$

$$R = 0.8892$$

1936–55

$$\text{Log } Y = 5.9664 + 0.5809 \log A + 0.0332 \log F - 0.4763 \log L$$
$$(1.0307) \qquad (0.0214) \qquad (0.6030)$$

$$R = 0.4554$$

period the correlation coefficient is higher than for the full 39 years, while the labor coefficient is quite significant. The Cobb-Douglas type of production function is not a very satisfactory way of explaining changes in agricultural output in the second 20-year period. The case would have been clearer if the multiple correlation coefficient had remained high, while variables included in the function other than labor had come to "explain" the major part of the variation in output. These data are consistent with the proposition that the marginal product of labor was significantly positive early in this period, but has fallen to zero in recent years. We must admit, though, that the weakness of the

---

[52]Part of the explanation might lie in the fact that only chemical fertilizers are included, thereby exaggerating the increase in total fertilizer usage; furthermore, while the man-land ratio rose substantially over this period, as we have seen, yields per acre rose by less than 20 percent, making the implied "negative technological progress" not implausible.

output index during the war years, along with the low correlation coefficient during this period, makes us suspicious of this interpretation. When we break the data into four periods of 10 years each, the labor coefficient becomes insignificant in all four periods.[53] On the whole, we feel that the figures in Table 4-16 do present a challenge to those who believe there is a significant amount of disguised unemployment in Egyptian agriculture; breaking the data into subperiods does not fully answer this challenge, although it does make us somewhat suspicious of the stability and significance of the underlying relationship between labor inputs and output.

3. *Seasonal Agricultural Employment Data.* A further set of information which bears on this question concerns the average number of days worked per month by the agricultural labor force. The Ministry of Agriculture has made a special study of this question.[54] First, the district officers were requested to estimate the average number of man-days and of boy-days normally employed per acre in that district, for each stage in the production of each crop.[55] For example, they estimated how many man-days and how many boy-days were normally used in their province in preparing an acre of land for seeding with cotton, how many of each were used per acre for planting, for weeding, and for harvesting cotton. This information was combined with data on land usage in each province—how many acres were used for each crop and at what stage each was in the production process each month—yielding monthly figures

---

[53]More precisely, it is completely insignificant in all periods but one, when it has the wrong sign. The estimated equations are as follows:

1917–26

Log $Y = -1.9640 + 1.3088$ log $A + 0.0114$ log $F - 0.0525$ log L
$\qquad\qquad\quad (1.1535) \qquad (0.0229) \qquad (0.6667)$
$\qquad\qquad\qquad\qquad\qquad\qquad\qquad\qquad\qquad\qquad R = 0.8141$

1927–36

Log $Y = -5.0009 + 0.9573$ log $A + 0.0621$ log $F + 0.7291$ log L
$\qquad\qquad\quad (1.0477) \qquad (0.1121) \qquad (1.1251)$
$\qquad\qquad\qquad\qquad\qquad\qquad\qquad\qquad\qquad\qquad R = 0.5364$

1937–46

Log $Y = 32.6329 - 0.9639$ log $A + 0.0180$ log $F - 2.8163$ log L
$\qquad\qquad\quad (1.5478) \qquad (0.0215) \qquad (1.1116)$
$\qquad\qquad\qquad\qquad\qquad\qquad\qquad\qquad\qquad\qquad R = 0.7992$

1947–55

Log $Y = -3.0242 - 0.3886$ log $A - 0.0616$ log $F + 1.8898$ log L
$\qquad\qquad\quad (1.8375) \qquad (0.1221) \qquad (2.7672)$
$\qquad\qquad\qquad\qquad\qquad\qquad\qquad\qquad\qquad\qquad R = 0.3414$

[54]United Arab Republic, Ministry of Agriculture, *Monthly Bulletin of Agricultural Economics and Statistics*, June, 1960, pp. 10–17 (in Arabic).

[55]"Boys" here actually refers to the total of boys, girls, and women. In fact, there is some flexibility here, as a number of tasks can be performed either by men or by "boys"; this is not of major importance to the analysis that follows, since the periods of peak demand for men and "boys" do not coincide, although it does introduce a degree of ambiguity into the figures.

on the total number of man-days and boy-days of actual agricultural work performed, province by province. This figure was then divided by the reported agricultural labor force in that province, to measure the average number of days actually worked by the agricultural labor force in that province during that month.[56]

Before looking at the resulting statistics, perhaps we might comment on the nature of this measure of agricultural underemployment. Labor redundancy in agriculture could be defined as the total number of workers who can be permanently removed from the agricultural labor force with no change in productive techniques and no fall in agricultural output. The catch phrase here concerns the lack of change in techniques; surely, there must be some change, at least in the organization of production, if workers are to be removed. The approach outlined above permits us to specify more clearly which changes are and which are not permitted. Specifically, we might say that the number of man-days actually employed per acre for a given crop is assumed to remain unchanged; altering that would mean getting people to work more efficiently and hence would involve technological change, which is ruled out of the analysis. On the other hand, we do permit a reorganization which concentrates the given number of man-days in as few hands as possible, implying that each man who remains in the sector can be induced to work every day (or 26 days, or whatever standard of "full employment" we choose to adopt) for at least one month in the year.

Unfortunately, this distinction, which is clear in theory, is blurred in practice; if ten man-days of work to be done today are shared among 30 men not by letting one third work and the rest stay in the coffee-house, but by having all 30 work for three hours, then the measure becomes less clear-cut. Is the reorganization which induces fewer men to work longer hours a "minor" one, similar to getting those remaining to work every day, or is it a "major" one, an example of technological change which we have ruled out by assumption? There is no clear-cut answer. Perhaps this problem is somewhat less serious in Egypt than in countries whose agricultural sector is organized on a purely peasant, family farm basis; as we have seen, more than one third of the agricultural labor force in Egypt is made up of daily paid wage workers. All of these, as well as the small numbers of family workers on farms where additional wage labor is hired, can be assumed to work a full day. The problem still remains, though, and should remind us that the statistics are not unambiguous.

Turning to the data themselves, Table 4–18 indicates that in six of

---

[56]This study has been examined critically, and some further similar estimates have been made, in el Tomy and Hansen, *op. cit.* However, the basic criticism of the study which we make below applies to their analysis as well. As they point out, in the estimates of the agricultural labor force, "seasonal and occasional workers are not included" (p. 4); but this robs the exercise, as it stands, of all significance.

TABLE 4-18

Average Number of Days Worked per Month by Adult Males, 1955

	Jan.	Feb.	Mar.	Apr.	May	June	July	Aug.	Sept.	Oct.	Nov.	Dec.	Labor Force Adjustment*
Bahera.	9	12	13	15	27	30	13	15	18	19	15	12	0.70
Gharbia.	5	9	9	10	13	9	6	6	13	13	9	9	0.84
Kafr-el-Sheikh. . . .	5	8	11	13	26	30	11	7	16	20	12	10	0.75
Dakahlia.	6	16	11	24	30	30	31	20	30	28	14	9	0.51
Sharkia.	8	17	10	20	25	30	29	19	30	22	13	12	0.55
Munufia.	4	6	5	6	13	7	8	7	6	10	5	6	0.89
Kalyubia.	8	14	8	12	14	15	15	16	13	13	7	10	0.65
Giza.	10	13	8	14	17	14	11	14	13	15	9	9	0.61
Beni-Suef.	11	18	14	29	29	19	22	21	30	16	14	15	0.46
Fayum.	9	13	11	18	26	19	23	18	29	16	17	17	0.69
Menia.	7	18	16	30	31	15	17	20	30	14	14	12	0.41
Asyut.	4	10	11	17	18	8	5	6	26	9	9	5	0.63
Suhag.	3	6	10	24	16	8	6	8	22	8	4	4	0.62
Qena.	8	10	19	23	16	7	4	11	8	6	10	7	0.53
Aswan.	11	11	14	17	17	8	3	7	11	10	8	8	0.72

*Ratio of "permanent agricultural labor force," as used in deriving these figures, to total labor force derived by interpolation from population censuses (all for adult males only).

Source: United Arab Republic, Ministry of Agriculture, *Monthly Bulletin of Agricultural Economics and Statistics*, June, 1960, pp. 10–17 (in Arabic).

the fifteen provinces, the full labor force worked in the fields every day during at least one of the twelve months of the year. In the remaining provinces, we can estimate the number who could be removed from the agricultural labor force, with no change in the total number of man-days worked, assuming we could induce those remaining to work every day during at least one month in the year. This gives us an estimate of redundancy in the total agricultural labor force of slightly less than 20 percent. Surely, this is an impressively low figure, when we remember the assumptions underlying it: Those remaining will work every day (i.e., have no free days) for at least one consecutive month, while all work other than field work (e.g., care of cattle, work on the irrigation systems, transporting of crops to the market for sale, etc.) is ignored. This study clearly lends support to those who would argue that there is little or no redundant labor force in Egyptian agriculture.

Unfortunately, this conclusion is unwarranted. In dividing the number of man-days of work by the agricultural labor force, the figures for the denominator were taken from a table in the 1950 agricultural census entitle "Permanent Agricultural Laborers";[57] this table indicates that the number of adult males in agriculture was some 30 percent below the level shown in the 1947 population census. Presumably, the Ministry of Agriculture concluded that some of the people whom the census takers counted in the agricultural labor force were not *permanent* agricultural laborers, but rather were seasonal or occasional workers; yet it is precisely these marginal workers with whom we are concerned.

By interpolating between the 1947 and 1960 population censuses, we can estimate the total number of adult males in the agricultural labor force (including seasonal workers) in 1955, the year in which this study of employment was made. These figures, in turn, can be used to recompute the extent of labor redunancy in agriculture, on the same assumptions as we specified above, i.e., ignoring all work other than field work and assuming that those remaining can be induced to work every day for at least one month of the year. On these assumptions, the statistics imply that between 30 percent and 50 percent of the total agricultural labor force was redundant in 1955.[58] Alternatively, if we adopt as our standard of full employment twenty-six days a month—in effect, saying that farmers take one day off a week, even during the busiest month—the range drops to 25–45 percent.[59]

---

[57]Republic of Egypt, Ministry of Agriculture, *Agricultural Census of Egypt, 1950* (Cairo, 1958), pp. 254–55.

[58]The wide range comes from the six provinces with "full employment" during some months in the original statistics; presumably, "30" in these cases should read "30 or more," but published data do not tell us what the actual computed figure was.

[59]El Tomy and Hansen, op. cit., argue that the 1955 figures are not representative, since in that year the area sown with cotton and rice—the two labor-intensive crops—was unusually small; as Appendix Table III–A–4 (pp. 321–22) shows, however, the 1955 area figures for these two crops were larger than the average for the 1950's, although there have been some increases since then.

As we have indicated, one problem with these figures concerns their exclusion of all work other than on field crops. Four other types of work done by agricultural laborers which might be mentioned concern care of cattle, maintenance of the irrigation system, construction of farm buildings, and transport of crops to the market. While precise data are lacking, we feel that including these tasks would not change the picture presented above in any fundamental way. Most farmers do not own more than a few animals, and these are generally entrusted to the care of wives and young people.[60] In the case of irrigation and construction work, surely by far the largest part of this can be concentrated in periods of slack demand for labor, while market transactions (purchasing inputs and selling produce) would normally take place primarily before and after the busy season. In short, including these additional tasks clearly would add to labor requirements in agriculture; we see no reason to believe they would add significantly to these needs during the peak season of the year.

We feel that it is quite important to distinguish clearly between seasonal unemployment in agriculture and year-round unemployment, whether open or disguised. Surely, the economic implications of these two are fundamentally different, and they must be analyzed separately.[61] Our concern in this Appendix is solely with nonseasonal, year-round unemployment in Egyptian agriculture. We might point out in passing, however, that the extent of purely seasonal unemployment is probably small in Egypt relative to many other countries. Multiple cropping means that there is no equivalent of winter, when no field work whatsoever is done. Even during the slack period, November-March, the full Egyptian agricultural labor force (not just "permanent workers") was occupied approximately six days per month, on the average, in the fields.[62] If similar figures for the full year were available for other countries, we suspect that Egypt could be shown to have less seasonal unemployment than, say, the United States or Great Britain.

4. *Agricultural Wage Rates.* There are two aspects of the pattern of wages which are of relevance to us: the long-term trend in real wages, and short-term variations from month to month as well as between provinces. On the first of these questions, Tables 4–19 and 4–20

---

[60]United Arab Republic, Department of Statistics and Census, *Population Census, 1947* (Cairo, 1954), which lists these separately, shows 33,375 males caring for animals in various ways, less than 1 percent of the male agricultural labor force that year (p. 110). Admittedly, this is not a full answer to the question, though, since we are concerned with men who are engaged primarily in field work but who spend part of their time caring for animals.

[61]For a contrary view which we find thoroughly unconvincing, see J. Fei and G. Ranis, *Development of the Labor Surplus Economy: Theory and Practice* (Homewood, Ill.: Richard D. Irwin, Inc., 1964), p. 13, n. 3. If we consider the meeting of peak seasonal needs as "a lesser, 'technical' problem," as they do, we introduce technological change into our definition of labor redundancy in a way which robs it of all precision.

[62]Weighted average, based on Table 4–18, adjusted.

are revealing. The near stability of real wages is remarkable, in view of the quadrupling of retail prices during these years; once again, it is what we should expect in a country with a substantial surplus agricultural labor force.

TABLE 4–19

AVERAGE DAILY MONEY WAGE OF PAID
AGRICULTURAL LABORERS

(In Millièmes)

	Men	Women	Boys
1937–40...........	30	20	15
1945..............	93	57	46
1950..............	116	n.a.	n.a.
1959..............	110–140	n.a.	60–70

SOURCE: See Appendix Table II–B–9 (p. 313).

TABLE 4–20

AVERAGE DAILY REAL WAGE OF PAID
AGRICULTURAL LABORERS*

	Men	Women	Boys
1939.............	30	20	15
1945.............	29	17.5	14
1950.............	35	n.a.	n.a.
1959.............	30.5–38.9	n.a.	16.7–19.4

*In this table, money wages in Table 4–19 have been deflated by the retail price index (1939 = 100). This is extremely rough, since the index is based on city prices and a city dweller's consumption basket of food, fuel, and soap.

In a stimulating study of this question, Hansen has emphasized that relative stability of real wages in agriculture in itself proves nothing about the existence of disguised unemployment and subsistence wages.[63] An alternative theory of wage determination says that workers are paid the value of their marginal product, equal to their marginal physical product times the price of agricultural output. If agricultural output prices generally move in parallel with the cost-of-living index, and to the extent that the marginal physical product per worker is constant,[64] wage determination according to marginal productivity would also result in stable real wages. The question Hansen poses, then, is the following: Which is more closely correlated with the agricultural money wage rate: the cost of living of an agricultural worker or the value of his marginal product? The results of his regression analysis, using seventeen

---

[63]B. Hansen, op. cit.
[64]Or to the extent that movements in these two series offset each other.

observations scattered irregularly through the period 1914–61 (using all years when wage rate estimates are available), are as shown in Table

TABLE 4–21

$W_t = \quad 31.31 + 0.88\,(O/L)_t$ $\quad\quad (15.21)\ (0.05)$	$R = 0.973$	$\delta = 32.00$
$W_t = \quad -5.09 + 1.33\,(Pm)_t$ $\quad\quad (32.74)\ (0.16)$	$R = 0.907$	$\delta = 57.63$
$W_t = -21.5 \ + 1.41\,(Pc)_t$ $\quad\quad (26.88)\ (0.13)$	$R = 0.941$	$\delta = 46.25$

4–21. Using first differences, the results are as indicated in Table 4–22.

TABLE 4–22

$\Delta W_t = \quad 1.30 + 0.91\,\Delta(O/L)_t$ $\quad\quad (14.50)\ (0.24)$	$R = 0.712$	$\delta = 55.18$
$\Delta W_t = \quad 9.98 + 0.68\,\Delta(Pm)_t$ $\quad\quad (16.24)\ (0.25)$	$R = 0.584$	$\delta = 63.80$
$\Delta W_t = \quad 7.11 + 0.86\,\Delta(Pc)_t$ $\quad\quad (15.43)\ (0.27)$	$R = 0.645$	$\delta = 60.08$

In both tables:

W = Money wage rate.
O/L = Value of the average product; in a Cobb-Douglas production function, this is equal to a constant times the value of the marginal product
Pm = Price of maize.
Pc = Cost-of-living index.
t = Subscript, for time.
R = Correlation coefficient.
δ = Standard error of estimate.

As Hansen points out, the marginal productivity wage theory comes out here consistently on top, with the highest correlation coefficient, the lowest standard error of estimate, and coefficient of the independent variable closest to its theoretical value (one in all cases).

Our reaction to this study is that the underlying statistical data are so weak that the difference between the size of the various coefficients cannot be considered as significant. As an example of the statistical problems involved, we present the wage rate index used in the estimation and the underlying statistical data, for the first seven years of the series (see Table 4–23). The two series A and B were originally estimated independently by different authors;[65] the 1914 figure in series A actually refers to the average of 1912 data for the Delta and the 1913–14 data for Upper Egypt. By assuming that the differential between the two series is constant through time, we get some paradoxical results;

---

[65]For full sources and detailed discussion of the figures, see Hansen, *op. cit.*, pp. 37–40 and Table III.

for example, although reported wage rates rose by 23 percent from 1933 to 1934, the index fell by 32 percent.[66] Surely, with underlying data as weak as these, we can attach very little significance to the difference between correlation coefficients of 0.97 and 0.94. Hansen's basic point is a valid and important one, that stability of real wages is by itself no proof that marginal productivity considerations are irrelevant. We feel, though, that the data are not precise enough and the results not clear-cut enough for us to use this approach in order to say which theory most accurately describes the process of wage determination in Egypt.

TABLE 4–23

AVERAGE DAILY MONEY WAGE RATES IN AGRICULTURE:
EARLY ESTIMATES

| | Series A | Series B | Index |
	(In Millièmes)		(1914 = 100)
1914...............	42	26	100
1920...............		67	258
1928...............		42	161
1929...............	50		117
1933...............		22	85
1934...............	27		58
1939...............		25	96

SOURCE: B. Hansen, *Marginal Productivity Wage Theory and Subsistence Wage Theory in Egyptian Agriculture*, Memo No. 547 (Cairo: Institute of National Planning, March, 1965), Table III. We present only average figures for Upper and Lower Egypt, available separately in original sources, but not used separately by Hansen.

A further set of information in Hansen's Memo concerns seasonal and regional variations in wage rates. Table I in that Memo records the daily wage of agricultural laborers once a week during the last six months of 1964, for each of three widely scattered Egyptian villages. The range of daily wage rates for men over this period was as follows (in piasters per day):

Kilishan (Behera).....................12–22
Abu el Gour (Gharbia)................. 8–24
Bakour Abu Tig (Asyut)...............15–30

Surely, these are impressively large fluctuations, far too large to be explainable in terms of changing prices of consumption goods in the villages. In fact, it is difficult to find any explanation for these variations other than one of market response to changing supply and demand conditions.

---

[66]This procedure of chaining together information from various sources is not confined to the earlier years. The figures for 1955 and 1956 are introduced in the same way; and as Hansen suggests, "this chaining is a bit doubtful" (*ibid.*, p. 37); if the chaining had been based on 1959 (when comparable published figures are also available) rather than 1950–51, the wage index would be quite different for those two years.

We find it more than surprising that earlier investigators did not discover or comment on these wide fluctuations in wage rates. A number of economists and statisticians have explored and discussed the question of agricultural wage rates in the past. The most recent and thorough study before the project on which Hansen's data are based was undertaken by the Ministry of Agriculture, yielding the results shown in Table 4-24. One might try to explain the relatively small variations in this table by overaggregation, both geographically and temporally, in the Ministry of Agriculture study; yet the breakdown in Table 4-24 was specifically chosen in such a way as to group together areas and periods similar in character, from a wage point of view. This makes us rather suspicious of the idea that actual wage fluctuations in 1959 were more than twice as large as those shown in Table 4-24, but Ministry of Agriculture economists either failed to notice them or thought them so unimportant that they were not worth mentioning. Hansen's data were based on preliminary results of a study undertaken jointly by the Institute of National Planning in Cairo and the International Labor Organization. Discussion by the writer in September, 1965, with those responsible for this survey indicates that these large wage fluctuations are by no means confined to a few select villages, but are a general characteristic of the whole country.[67] Surely, these fluctuations do suggest a widespread if temporary tightening in the market for paid laborers during periods of peak demand.

TABLE 4-24

WAGE RATES PER DAY OF ADULT MALE AGRICULTURAL LABORERS, 1959

(In Millièmes)

	Dec.-Mar.	Apr.-May	June-Aug.	Sept.-Nov.
North Delta...............	120	135	140	130
South Delta...............	120	125	125	120
North Upper Egypt.........	110	110	115	110
South Upper Egypt..........	115	125	120	120

SOURCE: United Arab Republic, Ministry of Agriculture, *Monthly Bulletin of Agricultural Economics and Statistics*, March, 1962, pp. 39-42 (in Arabic). Of the villages mentioned on pp. 4-65, Kilishan is in North Delta, Abu el Gour in South Delta, and Bakour Abu Tig in South Upper Egypt.

5. *Conclusions.* We have presented and explored a number of different sources of information which bear on this question of labor redundancy in Egyptian agriculture. For better or worse, they do not

---

[67]We might point out that if such large variations in wage rates over the course of the year are not a new development but have in fact been taking place for some time, they would cast doubt on the meaning and validity of the preceding correlation analysis, which relates either prices or productivity to some one wage rate, presumably an average for certain districts or even the whole country over the whole year.

point clearly to one conclusion. How are we to put together the various pieces of this puzzle? We find the most challenging and important data to be those in Section 3, on seasonal employment patterns, and in Section 4, on seasonal wage variations. These two studies clearly appear to conflict. The first says that during periods of peak demands, not more than 85 percent of the agricultural labor force was actually used in 1955; this is the maximum estimate, and most probably the true figure was somewhat below that.[68] The other study, on the other hand, indicates that in 1964, during periods of peak seasonal demand, there was some shortage in the supply of paid agricultural laborers, reflected in substantial seasonal increases in agricultural daily wage rates. Our interpretation of these facts, expressed briefly, is as follows. First, there has been a marked tightening in the market for paid agricultural workers in recent years; but secondly, this tightening was confined to the market for paid workers, leaving considerable disguised unemployment on family farms. On the first point, aside from the data on wage variations themselves (for 1959 as well as 1964), we base our conclusion on discussions with a number of informed people in Egypt, including several farm operators, during the late summer of 1965. Virtually all commented on the marked change which had taken place, perhaps since 1962 or 1963, in the rural employment situation. Laborers are more difficult to find, they reported, working shorter hours and demanding higher pay. On one farm some fifty miles north of Cairo, the owner indicated that in 1960 he could find more workers than he needed, at the peak season of the year, for 12 piasters a day; in 1965, he had difficulty in obtaining enough laborers at periods of peak demand, although the wage rate during this period rose to 30 piasters a day. Our discussions were decidedly unsystematic and in no sense give a representative sample of the whole country; yet, among those with whom we did speak, there was universal agreement that there had been a sharp tightening in the rural labor market during the early 1960's.

It is clear that the process of urbanization and the expansion of non-agricultural employment in general have continued at a high rate during this period; just how rapid this growth has been is a matter of conjecture. Let us give some actual and illustrative figures, and their implications. Over the period 1947–60, nonagricultural employment rose at an average annual rate of 2.8 percent;[69] if, during the 1960's, this rate

---

[68]This maximum figure is derived by taking the highest point in the range, assuming farmers are free one day a week (25 percent redundancy, the remaining 75 percent needed for field work), plus what we feel is a generous allowance of 10 percent of the labor force at periods of peak demand for other agricultural work. The opposite end of the range, allowing 5 percent of the labor force for nonfield work and no days off in the busiest month, would indicate employment of 55 percent of the agricultural labor force at the seasonal peak.

[69]All figures in this paragraph refer to adult males only.

jumped to 4.5 percent per annum, this would be enough to absorb all new net entrants to the labor force, leaving agricultural employment constant. If employment outside of agriculture grew by as much as 5.6 percent per annum, just double the rate of growth in the 1960's, the result would be a 5 percent *fall* in the agricultural labor force over the period 1960–65. In view of these figures, we can hardly believe that the exodus from the agricultural sector could have been of the magnitude necessary to eliminate the labor surplus which we found above, for 1955. But in fact, there is no evidence to suggest that there was an overall shortage, but only a shortage in the specific category of paid laborers. If a 5 percent fall in the total agricultural labor force had been concentrated in this category, the number of paid laborers would have decreased by 15–20 percent, perhaps resulting in seasonal and regional shortages of this particular category of workers. If there were a flexible and responsible national market for agricultural workers, we might find some adjustments taking place, as workers from labor surplus areas moved to districts where demand was high, and, more significantly, as underemployed workers on family farms turned to paid employment in response to high wages. In general, though, one might expect this market to be somewhat compartmentalized as a result of lack of knowledge as well as tradition-bound preferences for working one's own land. Besides this, taking paid employment means working harder and longer hours, for the person who takes the new job as well as for those remaining on the family farm. We should not like to push this argument too far; surely, we should expect a considerable spill-over from one category to another, particularly if the high seasonal wage rates are repeated for several years. We do think it reasonable to believe, however, that the market is sufficiently imperfect for shortages of hired workers to occur at the same time that there is a considerable amount of underemployment of unpaid workers on family farms.

Turning to the future, it does not seem realistic to expect secondary and tertiary employment to continue to expand at 4.5 percent per annum, much less the 5.5 percent growth rate which would keep agricultural employment constant once the increased rate of aggregate population growth spreads to the higher age brackets. The expansion of cultivated area following the construction of the High Dam at Aswan will increase the absorptive capacity of the agricultural sector somewhat, although, as we have indicated, the area expansion might amount to only 10 percent, hopefully with a smaller proportionate increase in labor inputs. On the whole, our expectation is that when further data become available, they will show a sharp expansion during the early 1960's in nonagricultural employment as well as in the number of people whom we referred to in Chapter 2 as "not employed," probably with a small absolute decrease in the level of employment in agriculture, but with a larger absolute decrease in the number of paid laborers in agriculture. On the other hand, we suspect that this high rate of growth of nonagricultural employment (and perhaps unemployment outside of agriculture as well) is temporary, and that the main characteristic of the next ten years will be not a shortage but a continuing surplus of agricultural workers, both paid laborers and unpaid workers on family farms.

In concluding, we should like to emphasize once again that this discussion has been heavily based on preliminary data and on conjecture. The different sets of data do contradict each other, and we must either choose the set which seems most reliable or attempt to find some way of reconciling the different approaches. Surely, the most interesting episode in this narrative is the most recent one, concerning events during the mid-1960's; the facts on which to hang the analysis here are all particularly uncertain. We shall be watching with great interest for further data on wage rates and employment patterns both inside and outside the agricultural sector, which should permit us to judge further if our tentative hypotheses are in fact correct.

Industry

To most observers in the underdeveloped world, economic development is nearly synonymous with industrialization. Egypt is no exception; she was already well into her five-year industrial plan when the first comprehensive development plan was launched. Most general comments as to the nature of the Egyptian economy, whether they relate to the degree of public control, the pattern of wage developments, or future growth rates, refer primarily— and sometimes exclusively—to the industrial sector. Rightly or wrongly, and like so many other countries at a similar stage of development, Egypt is a country with "industry on the brain."

In some ways, this is entirely natural. Industrialization looks like the way of the future; this sector has had one of the highest growth rates of any portion of the Egyptian economy in recent years; value added per capita here is among the highest in the country.[1] Yet, if industrialization is proposed as a quick way of avoiding balance-of-payments problems, we must sound a note of warning and scepticism; and any suggestion that industrialization in itself will solve the problem of overpopulation and underemployment must receive an even clearer negative response. Throughout this chapter, we shall be concerned with the question of the help which Egypt can hope to get from the industrial sector in achieving its multiple goals of raising the levels of national income, employ-

---

[1]See Appendix Table I–A–10 (p. 291).

ment, and savings, as well as freeing the country from its omnipresent balance-of-payments problems.

A. OUTPUT

As in the case of agriculture, there are several different indices of industrial production available, which are discussed in some detail in Appendix Tables IV-A-1 and IV-A-2 (pages 336 and 337). Perhaps the best series would be as shown in Table 5-1.

TABLE 5-1

INDEX OF MANUFACTURING PRODUCTION

(1953 = 100)

Prewar = 36	1950 = 100	1956 = 125
1945 = 70	1951 = 99	1957 = 132
1946 = 71	1952 = 99	1958 = 143
1947 = 78	1953 = 100	1959 = 147
1948 = 86	1954 = 107	1960 = 162
1949 = 96	1955 = 117	1961 = 188

SOURCE: See Appendices IV-A-1 and IV-A-2 (pp. 336 and 337).

As the discussion of these figures in the Appendix indicates, the wartime increase may be somewhat exaggerated, but the restrictions of imports and the additional demand of the British troops in the country during this period clearly provided a great stimulus to the small domestic manufacturing sector. Output of textiles more than doubled; and while production in the other major industry—food processing—rose more slowly, there were a number of small industries—beer, matches, and petroleum refining might be cited as examples—which were negligible before the war, but which in the aggregate made a significant addition to value added in manufacturing by 1945.

If the artificial wartime conditions provided a major stimulus to the growth of industry in Egypt, it is remarkable that the industrial sector was quite successful in maintaining itself and even increasing its output after the war's end. Admittedly, import duties, already fairly high on domestically produced manufactures in the later 1930's, were raised further during the immediate postwar period;[2] yet, at these tariff rates, imports were freely available (at

---

[2] See United Nations, Department of Economic and Social Affairs, *The Development of Manufacturing Industry in Egypt, Israel, and Turkey* (New York, 1958), p. 129.

least from the sterling area). The reduction in demand from the troops led to excess capacity in some specific lines—brewing and sugar refining are clear examples;[3] yet the expansion in domestic demand, and the growth in domestic productive capacity to meet this demand, resulted in an increase of over 40 percent in manufactured output between 1945 and 1950.

TABLE 5–2

INDUSTRIAL PRODUCTION: VALUE ADDED, BY SECTORS
(Constant Prices of 1954, £E000)

	1945	1947	1950	1954
A. Consumer goods:				
Food, drink, and tobacco	38,188	42,509	54,915	58,990
Ready-made clothing	3,963	3,807	3,690	3,885
Furniture	1,154	1,239	2,778	4,274
Spinning and weaving	7,898	8,962	12,000	15,189
Others	541	580	710	1,490
Total	51,744	57,097	74,093	83,828
B. Producer goods:				
Basic chemicals	10,448	10,345	7,823	5,147
Cement	966	1,434	2,290	2,758
Basic metals	0	0	2,106	4,270
Metal products	2,517	3,997	6,168	4,934
Machinery repair	4,428	5,141	5,734	8,122
Building materials	939	1,007	2,036	1,868
Others	2,223	2,676	3,406	4,205
Total	21,521	24,600	29,563	31,304
C. Others (mixed and export):				
Petroleum products	5,098	5,000	8,825	9,805
Ginning and pressing	1,484	1,816	2,437	2,215
Paper and printing	1,709	2,661	3,085	3,668
Other industry	2,523	2,451	2,905	3,034
Total	10,814	11,928	17,252	18,722
Grand total	84,079	93,625	120,908	133,854

SOURCE: United Arab Republic, National Planning Committee, Memos No. 1 and No. 22 specially prepared for the plan (Cairo, November, 1959). For a description and appraisal of sources used, see Appendix I–A–5.

Table 5–2 gives an indication of the composition of this increase in output. As the table shows, nearly 60 percent of the increase was concentrated in two lines: food, drink, and tobacco; and spinning and weaving. This degree of concentration is not surprising, since it is only slightly more than the proportional share of these industries in total output in 1945. Virtually all of the remainder of

---

[3]*Ibid.*, p. 81.

the increase was concentrated in the production of construction materials of one kind or another, petroleum refining, and metal products.[4] Food, textiles, and building materials—these three form the backbone of the industrialization base in most underdeveloped countries.

One might ask whether there is any evidence that this increase in output resulted in import substitution. Trade statistics during this period indicate that with few exceptions, for each of the categories where production was rising, imports were rising as well. This was true of processed foods, in the aggregate as well as in the more detailed breakdown; it was also true of textiles. Exceptions include some items for which demand had been strongly influenced by the large numbers of British troops, such as cigarettes and beer, so that imports fell partly as a result of increased domestic production, but even more because of a fall in demand. For some other items, such as cement, domestic production was adequate to meet virtually all of the demand (except for some specialty products) throughout the period. There were some examples of true import substitution (matches, for example), where domestic production rose faster than the increase in domestic demand, so that imports fell; but these seem like the exception rather than the rule. In general, we might say that the increase in domestic production was import-replacing only in the sense that, given the level or rate of growth of demand, if domestic production had not risen as much as it did, imports would have had to increase even more than they did. This is a rather uninteresting concept of "import substitution," since it implies that any increase in domestic production, unless it is for export, is import-replacing.

In large part, the particular circumstances of this period can be explained by the sharp restrictions of imports during the war years; this fact, combined with the substantial expenditures in the country by the British both during and after the war, meant that the war's end found the country with a large pent-up demand for many types of goods, including manufactured consumer goods. This is reflected in the very low savings rates for 1946 and 1947 shown in Table 9–1 (page 216), as well as the high marginal import propensities of Table 7–1 (page 159); while the average propensity to import consumer goods was only 0.06 in 1945, the marginal figure over the period of 1945–48 was 0.43. Clearly, there was a sub-

---

[4]Primarily iron and lead pipes and fittings, and other small household articles. The fall in basic chemicals was primarily a result of a decline in the output of caustic soda.

stantial backlog of demand for manufactured consumer goods which was met partly by a sharp rise in the imports, but also by a marked increase in domestic production.

The question might be asked why local production had not expanded further during the war to meet this domestic demand. The answer seems to be that the growth in local production required an expansion of productive capacity via capital goods imports which were not available during the war. As we shall see, there were substantial imports of machinery and equipment in the late 1940's, as the manufacturing sector was expanded and modernized. The blocking of trade routes was a major component of the inflationary wartime situation, partly because consumer goods imports were limited, but also because these trade restraints made it difficult to expand capacity to meet the extra demand from domestic production.

From 1950 to 1953, industrial production rose very little. The growing stringency of exchange control, which made it increasingly difficult to obtain imported intermediate inputs, machinery, and spare parts, may have been a partial explanation for this slowdown. In some other cases (e.g., matches), import substitution may have been virtually completed by 1950, so that further growth was limited to the rate of expansion of the domestic market. A third group of industries—ginning and pressing, and cottonseed oil pressing—are directly tied to the local cotton crop, which rose sharply to 1950, then leveled off and declined somewhat thereafter. The most important cause, though, was simply the fall in demand, as the Korean boom reached and passed its peak. The figures in Table 5–2 indicate that the increases which did occur were mainly in the consumer goods industries, particularly those relying on domestic raw materials such as spinning and weaving and sugar refining.

After 1954, manufacturing output again turned sharply upward, rising by 50 percent between that year and 1960. Data are not available to permit the same detailed sector-by-sector analysis of the components of this increase. Table 5–3 gives an indication of the structure of the sector in 1959–60. These figures are somewhat more complete, and hence are only roughly comparable with those in Table 5–2; calculated growth rates of individual industries from 1954 to 1959–60 are generally not reliable,[5] but the figures do per-

---

[5]For example, the official index of textile production rose less than 40 percent from 1954 to 1959. Industrial prices rose by about 12 percent over this period, according to our calculations, and those of textiles only about 6 percent; see Appendix Table VI–F–1 (pp. 400–401).

mit us to get some idea of the changes which were taking place in the sector. Food and textiles were still predominant, accounting for nearly 60 percent of total value added; in the rest of the industrial sector, on the other hand, a noticeable diversification was taking place. The production of fertilizers and other chemicals was growing rapidly; output of the petroleum industry nearly doubled between 1954 and 1960; the contribution of the iron and steel mill

TABLE 5–3

INDUSTRIAL PRODUCTION: VALUE ADDED, BY SECTORS

(Approximately Constant Prices of 1959–60, £E Million)

	1959–60	1960–61	1961–62
A. Consumer goods:			
Food, drink, and tobacco............	74.3	75.9	78.6
Clothing..........................	10.1	10.6	13.8
Textiles..........................	56.9	60.6	64.1
Total........................	141.3	147.1	156.5
B. Producer goods:			
Chemicals.......................	13.5	16.9	20.3
Basic metals......................	7.3	8.5	10.0
Metal products....................	6.6	6.6	8.6
Machinery and its repair............	3.9	8.8	8.1
Rubber..........................	2.3	2.5	3.2
Nonmetallic products..............	9.5	10.0	11.5
Means of transport................	6.5	10.0	12.2
Total........................	49.6	63.3	73.9
C. Others (mixed and export):			
Petroleum.......................	23.4	24.5	26.5
Ginning and pressing..............	3.9	4.1	3.0
Paper and printing................	11.0	11.0	13.6
Leather and products..............	2.7	0.8	2.2
Wood and wood products...........	7.6	9.3	9.6
Others..........................	2.8	7.2	7.3
Total........................	51.4	56.9	62.2
Grand total...........................	242.3	267.3	292.6

SOURCE: United Arab Republic, Ministry of Planning (unpublished estimates). These figures represent a revision and extension of those found in United Arab Republic, Presidency of the Republic, National Planning Committee, *General Frame of the Five-Year Plan for Economic and Social Development, July 1960–June 1965* (Cairo, 1960), p. 107. They purport to be at constant price, although there are probably some price increases remaining.

to domestic income reached £E7 million in 1960, while production of automobile tires added another £E2 million of income. In short, Egypt was developing a remarkable diversified industrial sector, with a significant amount of output in a wide range of products, both producer and consumer goods.

The question might be raised as to the costs and efficiency of this sector. It is not possible to answer this question at present with any degree of accuracy. In 1955 a study by the United Nations concluded that a number of important industries, including fertilizers, cement, and several food-processing industries, could probably dispense with tariff protection without danger;[6] since that time, output per man has continued to increase in many of these industries, while wage rates have risen only slowly. Output was similarly rising somewhat more rapidly than the capital stock, as measured in Table 5-6 (page 113). On the whole, there is every reason to believe that these expanding industries maintained or even improved their international competitiveness during this period.[7]

The situation is different for a number of the newer products, such as automobile tires, kitchen equipment, and small consumer goods, the costs of which are generally above and quality often below that of the world market. In these cases the government is quick in providing whatever protection is necessary to the domestic industry. In basic outline the policy seems to be to determine the country's productive capacity of a given commodity, and then to set the prices of domestic production on a cost-plus basis, assuming full-capacity operation; customs duties are then adjusted so that the prices of the imported commodity are somewhat above those of the local product. According to officials in the Ministry of Industry, this differential is normally around 20 percent, but casual observation indicates that there are substantial variations in the differential, perhaps reflecting in part the Ministry's evaluation of the difference in quality between imported and locally made products. This tariff policy is reinforced by import quotas on all industrial products, although, since the government is now the sole importer, the concept of quotas changes in character somewhat; the decision to permit the import of a certain quantity of a certain good is merged with the decision to do the actual importing, and the distinction between the two becomes primarily a matter of timing. The objective of all these policies is to make sure that within the limits of the domestic market, production of each good is raised to capacity and all of the output is sold; in effect, the domestic industry gets complete protection from the world market.

---

[6]United Nations, *Economic Developments in the Middle East, 1945–54* (New York, 1955), pp. 40–41.

[7]Productivity in industry is discussed in B. Hansen and G. Marzouk, *Development and Economic Policy in the U.A.R. (Egypt)* (Amsterdam: North-Holland Publishing Co., 1965), chap. v, sec. 5.

It is extremely difficult to evaluate this policy of "industrialization at all costs." To do so in any comprehensive way would involve an appraisal of alternative uses of factors of production, as well as an estimate of the quantity and quality of resources which would be available if other approaches were followed. A forced march toward industrialization surely brings improvements in the technical skills of the labor force; perhaps it puts the country in a better bargaining position in asking for foreign grants, as well as providing an almost limitless absorptive capacity for foreign loans of a more or less commercial nature. The infant-industry argument for tariff protection can provide only ex post justification for those who either attack or support the establishment of a given industry. To make matters worse, there is no specification of "how far" ex post we should go; proponents of protectionism are always ready to say that "we haven't waited long enough," although this argument begins to lose its force after ten years or more.

One might approach this problem with three different questions in mind. The first is a question of overall development strategy: Is it wise for Egypt to concentrate so much attention on industry, or would the country be better off to let this sector more or less alone and concentrate its efforts on some other aspect of the economy, such as agriculture, or tourism, or extraction of natural resources? We shall return to this question in the concluding chapter; but perhaps we can anticipate that discussion by saying that while one might want to argue about details, in broad outline Egypt had no real alternative to giving industrialization a major role in the country's development plan.

Secondly, given the fact that she has chosen a path of rapid industrialization, one might ask further whether the specific industries chosen were the best ones for raising income and employment. This familiar question of investment criteria might be approached by reference to factor endowments or to natural resources. One is tempted to propose some simple rule of thumb for Egypt, that investment should be allocated to industries where the capital-output ratio, or the capital-labor ratio, is as low as possible. As anyone who has struggled with the literature on this subject will agree, however, this is far too complex a subject to be settled by recourse to simple rules of thumb. Neither capital nor labor is homogeneous; both come equipped with specific skills and skill requirements, so that at the very least we need to take account of these differences, which may be quite substantial. Capital-output ratios in different industries can only be compared in value terms, which means that we must make some assumptions about prices, present and future, and hence about the demand for the product. Furthermore, there may well be a range of possible production techniques using different factor combinations in a given industry, which might make it impossible to say that Egypt "ought to" go into cotton weaving but not into spinning simply because the capital-labor ratio is high in the latter. In short, any search for an optimal investment pattern based on some simple rule of thumb is not likely to be very satisfactory.

In examining the way this problem has been approached in Egypt, one soon becomes aware of the marked divergence between the analytical framework set up for this purpose and the actual investment decisions. In this area, as in the whole field of planning methodology, it seems clear that the models and variants of models which foreign observers take such pleasure in analyzing and dissecting bear only a faint relationship to the decisions which were actually made. As we shall see in Chapter 10, the approach to this question of investment criteria which received most attention among the planning theorists in Egypt was one which concentrated on the impact of a given investment program on the balance of payments; the goal was to maximize income, given the constraint on foreign indebtedness. In practice, it seems that the investment projects were chosen by a process of bargaining and struggling among ministries as well as within them, with politics playing a role equal to that of economics. The results are extremely difficult to evaluate, partly because data are almost unobtainable, partly because of the argument that in due course, domestic costs per unit will fall, so that an evaluation based on present cost comparisons is inconclusive. There are some examples where it seems quite improbable that the investment will make economic sense, even in the long run. In the case of automobiles, the cost of assembling the cars—that part of the production process actually brought into the country—may be as much as four times the cost of having the assembling done in Italy, where the parts are made. The size of the market seems unlikely to grow enough in the forseeable future to bring these costs down close to equality with those in Italy, and it seems improbable that Egypt will become so efficient in the production of parts as to offer an offsetting justification. In the case of the iron and steel works, Egypt must import all her coal, while her ore is of the lowest iron content of the ten African countries discussed by the United Nations Economic Commission for Africa.[8]

---

[8]United Nations Economic Commission for Africa, *Industrial Growth in Africa: A Survey and Outlook* U.N. Document E/CN.14/INR/1/Rev. 1 (1963), p. 31.

This same study states that "an iron and steel industry is the foundation of a modern integrated industrial complex."[9] If this is so, does it mean that every country seeking to industrialize should have one? If we justify the creation of a steel industry by pointing to external benefits such as improving the technical skills of the labor force, we should be aware that other industries might provide these external benefits as well, and at lower costs. All this points to a rather pessimistic conclusion with regard to the possibility of applying any "scientific" rules to the question of investment criteria, either in the sense of determining an optimal investment pattern or by indicating how much the deviation of actual from optimal investment is "costing" in terms of income, employment, or foreign exchange forgone. The author can find very few cases where he feels there has been a clear misallocation in the decision to produce a specific item; the assembly of cars and the production of rubber tires are perhaps the clearest examples. Beyond this, he feels that the misallocation of investment among various types of capital and consumer goods has been relatively minor compared to the overriding political decision to allocate scarce resources for the production of military goods. Very little is known about this in terms of specific costs, but it is clear that no country at Egypt's stage of development (or at any other stage, for that matter) can devote the resources necessary to develop rockets and jet planes without this having a major impact on the development processes and prospects.

The third question one might ask about the industrialization program concerns the speed with which it has been pushed. The main restraining factor here is the balance of payments, although there are other aspects as well. Setting up a new industry puts strains of three types on the balance of payments. First of all, the capital equipment for the industry is generally not available domestically; secondly, the current inputs—raw materials or intermediate products—may have to be imported; thirdly, the income received from the production of the plant may be spent on the consumption of imported goods. These foreign exchange costs may be partially or fully offset by exchange benefits derived from the project: If the production of the plant is exported, or substitutes for imports, this helps to meet the foreign exchange shortage. If a plant is set up to process imported materials or to assemble imported parts, the foreign exchange cost per unit is likely to be

[9] *Ibid.*, p. 30.

below the import price of the finished article; yet the establishment of a domestic assembly plant is often associated with an increase in the number of units sold, so that the total amount of foreign exchange spent on that particular commodity may rise substantially. This is a familiar phenomenon in Egypt; examples of cars, radios, and kitchen equipment come readily to mind. This form of import substitution, if one wants to call it that, would result in higher total foreign exchange expenditures, although foreign exchange costs per unit would fall.

With regard to the need for capital imports, a number of the industries which Egypt has been pushing are normally quite capital-intensive. Recent unpublished estimates by the National Planning Committee imply that for 1963–64, needed imports of capital goods would come to over 30 percent of domestic capital formation of all types, including construction; for manufacturing industry alone, the share of imports may have been closer to 50 percent. The attainment of the recent rapid rates of industrial growth has necessitated a large increase in manufacturing investment, currently running at well over £E100 million a year (see Appendix I–A–9 [page 290]); clearly, this is an important source of strain on the balance of payments.

With regard to current inputs, the 1954 studies brought together in the input-output table for that year indicated that for manufacturing industry as a whole, the ratio of imported intermediate products to total value of output was about 6.5 percent.[10] For some specific industries which have been growing rapidly, such as basic metals and metal products, the ratio was over 20 percent. As the industrial complex grows, we should expect that more of the needed inputs could be obtained locally, so that this ratio would fall for any given industry; recent studies by the National Planning Committee imply that this may in fact have occurred, to a limited extent.[11] If there was a decline in this ratio for specific industries, however, it was more than offset by the shifts in the composition of the industrial sector toward the more heavily import-using lines,

---

[10]This figure, as well as the following ones in this paragraph, include only current imports going directly to the sector specified; excluded, for example, are imports of fertilizers, which cause an increase in agricultural output, making possible in turn an expansion of the food-processing industry.

[11]In basic metals industries, for example, the ratio of current imports to output fell from 23 percent in 1954 to 21 percent in 1963–64, according to input-output studies for those years. In view of the roughness of these figures, particularly for the later years—see comments in the text above—this might best be interpreted as virtual constancy of the ratio.

with the result that for the industrial sector as a whole the ratio of current imports to output rose to a level of about 13 percent. This is heavily influenced by the large imports of wheat, used in the grain-milling industry; if we exclude food, drink, and tobacco, the ratio falls to close to 10 percent, compared to about 8 percent a decade ago. In interpreting these figures, we should be well aware of their high margins of error; the estimates for 1963–64 were made before that year had started and should be considered as planning targets rather than reports of actual developments. However, since these targets were formulated by capable economists and estimated on the basis of an examination of developments in the preceding period, they probably provide a rough approximation to the actual structural relationships. It seems probable that as a result of the change in the structure of Egyptian industry, imports of raw materials and intermediate products currently form a somewhat higher proportion of total manufacturing output than they did ten years ago, even if we exclude the substantial imports of foods for processing. With manufacturing output rising at over 9 percent per annum during the planning period, this clearly puts substantial further strains on the balance of payments.

The third aspect of industry's negative effect on the balance of payments concerns the resulting increase in purchases of imported consumer goods. This is something which can generally be kept under control, via tariffs and quotas. As we shall see in Chapter 7, the government has made some efforts to restrict imports of consumer goods, thereby cutting down somewhat on the importance of this aspect of the problem.[12]

In general, it seems clear that, to date, the negative impact on the balance of payments of the industrialization program—the increased needs for imports of capital goods, intermediate products, and raw materials—has far outweighed the positive aspect—import substitution and export of manufactures. In a sense, there is a race going on in Egypt. On the one hand are the mounting balance-of-payments deficits, which, with foreign exchange reserves exhausted, must be met by ever-growing indebtedness, with the further problem of impending interest and amortization payments superimposed; on the other hand is the growing industrial output, which one hopes will begin to be less and less dependent on im-

---

[12]See Tables 7–1 and 7–8 (pp. 159 and 172). We might point out that this aspect of the problem is not confined to industrial expansion, but would result from any increases in income, no matter in which sector they occur.

ported capital goods and intermediate products, and which may in time even be able to reach out into the export market. So far, there is little evidence that the country is nearing the payoff period.

B. INPUTS

As we indicated in Chapter 2, there is a very great multiplicity of employment statistics in Egypt, particularly those referring to the industrial sector. Since these differ so widely in coverage, approach, and definitions, we prefer to rely primarily on the population censuses, which we feel are most likely to provide comparable statistics. Unfortunately, the periods between censuses are quite long; for this reason, we have felt it worthwhile to attempt to make one interim estimate, for 1954.[13] The figures on employment in manufacturing (ISIC 2 and 3) are as shown in Table 5–4. As the table indicates, total employment and employment of adult males developed about in the same way; in what follows, we shall concentrate on the total figures, since in this case these seem to be more reliable.

TABLE 5–4

MANUFACTURING EMPLOYMENT

(In Thousands)

	Employment, Total	Employment, Adult Males
1937	353	320
1947	561	502
1954	569	n.a.
1960	713	658

SOURCE: United Arab Republic, Department of Statistics and Census, *Population Census, 1960* (Cairo, 1963), Vol. II, p. xiv; Appendix II–B–3 (p. 305); and figures in Table 2–9 (p. 33), adjusted to exclude mining, electricity, gas, and water.

With regard to the capital stock, two different approaches are possible. One is to work with figures of installed horsepower. Any firm operating any nonelectric motor must obtain a permit from the government; figures on permits issued are published annually, with details on installed horsepower, sector by sector. In the case

---

[13]The approach used in making this estimate is explained in Appendix II–B–3 (p. 305).

of electric power, we have converted industrial usage into installed horsepower equivalent,[14] yielding the results shown in Table 5-5. These figures indicate that there was a substantial increase in industrial motive power during the war; thereafter, the increase continued, but at a surprisingly moderate rate, in view of the substantial reequipping of industry and expansion of output which took place during this period. This should serve to remind us that these figures can give us a useful indication of motive power per worker, or motive power per unit of output, but not of total capital or investment per worker, which may develop quite differently. For this, we must turn to a second way of measuring the capital stock.

If we have an investment series covering a number of years, it is possible to combine this with an assumption as to the rate at which the capital stock is being used up—the depreciation rate—to generate figures on real capital stock. For the earlier years in the series, it is necessary to make some further assumption as to the capital stock at the start of the series (unless we are only in-

TABLE 5–5

INSTALLED HORSEPOWER IN MANUFACTURING

(Thousands)

	Electrical	Nonelectrical	Total
1937	50	329	379
1947	148	395	543
1950	228	408	636
1954	321	454	775
1960	822	513	1,335

SOURCE: Estimates by the author (see n. 14); and *Annuaire Statistique*, various issues.

[14]Industry's share in total generated electricity is estimated on the basis of a detailed examination of sales by major companies. The conversion to installed capacity is on the basis of average load factors, estimated for earlier years. The detailed figures are as follows:

	Generated Electricity Total (GWH)	Industrial Usage (GWH)	Load Conversion Factor	Installed Horsepower
1937	226	90	0.240	50
1947	560	280	0.255	148
1950	881	440	0.260	228
1954	1,247	625	0.263	321
1960	2,638	1,670	0.2725	822

The 1937 figure is considerably less reliable than those for the later years, which are probably quite accurate.

The author is indebted to Kamal Nabih of the Electric Power Commission for assistance in preparing these figures.

terested in a stock figure starting D years after the investment series, where D is the depreciation period). Working with figures on the book value of capital assets as shown in corporate balance sheets, Hansen and Marzouk have estimated that the value of capital stock in manufacturing industry may have been in the range

TABLE 5–6

ESTIMATED CAPITAL STOCK IN MANUFACTURING
INDUSTRY, ASSUMING 1939 STOCK = £E40 MILLION

(Index, 1939 = 100)

	$D = 15$	$D = 20$	$D = 25$
1939	100.0	100.0	100.0
1945	82.1	94.9	102.6
1950	159.0	187.2	202.6
1954	205.1	251.3	282.1
1960	282.1	341.0	394.9

(Index, 1945 = 100)

1945	100.0	100.0	100.0
1950	193.8	197.3	197.5

(Index, 1950 = 100)

1950	100.0	100.0	100.0
1960	177.4	182.2	194.9

NOTE: Besides the indicated assumptions as to original capital stock and depreciation rates, the inputs to this table are annual figures on real investment. For this, we have taken the current price series of the National Planning Committee, discussed in Appendix Table I–A–9 (p. 290), and deflated them by the price of capital goods exports from the United Kingdom ("metal goods," later changed to "engineering products"), as computed by the Board of Trade. This seems like the best approach, since most capital goods are imported; and indeed, the investment series is constructed by applying a constant markup to the current value of capital goods imports.

For a critical appraisal of this deflator, see E. Devons, *An Introduction to British Economic Statistics* (Cambridge: Cambridge University Press, 1961), pp. 150–154. This approach assumes that the share of machinery and equipment in total capital formation in industry is constant.

Hansen and Marzouk have made an estimate of this same type, but using as price deflator the domestic wholesale price subindex for industrial products and materials. Our approach seems more reasonable, in spite of its own limitations: Not all capital imports come from the United Kingdom, and United Kingdom export prices may not be a good measure of changing world prices of capital goods. Finally, the United Kingdom index covers only a portion of British capital goods exports. Hansen and Marzouk's figures generally show a smaller increase in the capital stock (B. Hansen and G. Marzouk, *Development and Economic Policy in the U.A.R. [Egypt]* [Amsterdam: North-Holland Publishing Co., 1965], Table 5.10).

of £E30–40 million in 1939.[15] Using the higher of these figures, and assuming straight-line depreciation over various numbers of years (D), we can estimate the changes in capital stock in manufacturing industry, as shown in Table 5-6.

---

[15]Hansen and Marzouk, *op. cit.*, p. 129.

It is hard to say which of these depreciation rates is the most accurate. Rough estimates for Argentina put the average useful life for industrial and agricultural machinery at 20 years, while for public and private construction the figure was 50 years.[16] In principle, the investment estimates for Egypt include both plant and equipment; while wear and tear may be substantially higher in Egypt than in countries at intermediate stages of development, such as Argentina, it seems unlikely that the average length of life for the total capital stock, including industrial construction, would be as low as 15 years, except perhaps during the war years. It may be that the heavy use of the capital stock during these years resulted in unusually rapid depreciation rates, in which case the capital stock may have fallen by 10 percent or more. Thereafter, the capital stock began to grow rapidly, approximately doubling in size between 1945 and 1950, and nearly doubling again from 1950 to 1960.

A number of commentators have pointed to the rapid rate of investment in the early postwar years, citing this as evidence that there was a large-scale shift either to more capital-intensive production techniques or to industries which were heavily capital-using. Yet these figures, combined with those in Table 5–4, imply that the heavy wartime usage and shortage of imports may have resulted in a fall of nearly 40 percent in the capital-labor ratio during the war; it was not until 1950 that the prewar ratio was reattained. Thereafter, the capital stock continued to grow rapidly, while employment was virtually constant until 1954, so that by that year the capital-labor ratio may have been some 50 percent above the prewar level.

The figures in Table 5–2 indicate no major change in the structure of production over this period, although some capital-intensive industries, such as petroleum, metals, and metal products, did grow substantially faster than the average for all industry. For the rest, there seems to have been a significant reequipping and modernization of the industrial sector, so that by 1954 a substantial part of the sector seems to have been on sound footing, with modern equipment and efficient production techniques.[17] From 1954 to

---

[16]R. Goldsmith and C. Saunders (eds.), *The Measurement of National Wealth*, International Association for Research in Income and Wealth, Series VIII (London: Bowes and Bowes, 1959), p. 282. The same volume gives figures which are virtually the same for Australia (p. 329).

[17]See United Nations, *Economic Developments in the Middle East, 1945–54* (New York, 1955), pp. 40–41; also Hansen and Marzouk, *op. cit.*, chap. vi, sec. 6.5.

1960, the capital-labor ratio rose by an additional 10 percent, probably largely a reflection of the continuing growth of more capital-intensive heavy industry.

It is possible to use the same general estimation techniques, inflating earlier investments rather than deflating them, to get the current value, or replacement cost, of the capital stock. This, in turn, can be compared with the data on value added in the industrial sector, to yield an estimation of the average capital-output ratio for this sector. Concentrating on the series based on a twenty-year average useful life, the figures are as shown in Table 5-7.

TABLE 5–7

CAPITAL STOCK AND VALUE ADDED IN MANUFACTURING AND ELECTRICITY

(£E Million, All in Current Prices)

	Capital Stock*	Gross Value Added†	Computed Depreciation*	Net Value Added	Ratio, Capital Stock to Net Value Added	Book Value of Depreciation‡
1953	273	133	20	113	2.41	n.a.
1954	295	147	22	125	2.36	n.a.
1955	331	162	25	137	2.42	n.a.
1956	366	179	29	150	2.44	n.a.
1957	388	205	32	173	2.24	13
1958	410	229	36	193	2.12	13
1959	439	234	35	199	2.21	16

*Assuming twenty-year useful life. The capital stock figures show the constant price series underlying the figures in Table 5-6, multiplied by the price index for capital goods.

†United Arab Republic, Department of Statistics and Census, *Ten Years of Revolution: Statistical Atlas* (Cairo, July, 1962), Table 9; calendar years derived by averaging fiscal years.

‡United Arab Republic, Department of Statistics and Census, *Census of Industrial Production* (Cairo, years specified).

This inflation of the value of the capital stock by an import price index is a tenuous exercise at best; yet the figures are not implausible, and they do give us some indication of the amount of capital which would be needed to produce a certain amount of income in the industrial sector, if the capital had to be purchased at current prices. The figures indicate some fall in the capital-output ratio in the late 1950's, probably reflecting a fuller utilization of capacity during these years.

C. INCOME

Let us turn to the question of the distribution of income earned in the industrial sector. The main point of interest here concerns the level of wage rates and the share of total value added going to profits. There are a number of sources of information on the pattern of industrial wage rates; Table 5-8 presents the picture in outline. This table shows a drop of more than 20 percent in the industrial real wage during the early war years, as the rise in money wage rates failed to keep up with the increase in prices; thereafter, there was a steady and significant rise in the real wage rate, reaching a point in 1954 just twice the wartime low point.

TABLE 5–8

WEEKLY WAGE RATES IN INDUSTRY AND AGRICULTURE

(In Millièmes)

| | Manufacturing Industry | | Agriculture, | |
	Money Wage*	Real Wage†	Money Wage‡	Ratio 1:3
	(1)	*(2)*	*(3)*	*(4)*
1938........	440	440	170	2.6
1943........	830	340	350	2.4
1945........	1,110	380	520	2.1
1947........	1,275	455	n.a.	n.a.
1950........	1,500	510	650	2.3
1954........	1,940	680	670	2.9
1959........	2,185	720	700	3.1

*See Appendix Tables II–B–5 to II–B–8 (pp. 207–13). For 1943 and later years, the figure shown is the average of the wage rate at the beginning of the year shown and the following year; i.e., 1943 refers to average of January, 1943, and January, 1944. As the notes to the Appendix tables indicate, these figures are not fully comparable; before 1950, they include clerical and administrative workers, while in 1950 and thereafter the figures refer only to operatives. Between 1950 and 1957, there is a shift from a 25 percent sample of firms of all sizes to full coverage of firms with 10 or more employees; the significance of this change is discussed in Appendix II–B–8 (pp. 312–13).

†Money wage deflated by cost-of-living index; 1939 = 100.

‡Appendix Table II–B–9 (p. 313) shows agricultural wage rates per day; we have converted these to a weekly rate by multiplying by 5.6, the average number of days worked per week by industrial workers in 1938. These figures refer to rates for men only, while those in column 1 refer to all workers.

Since 1954, industrial wages have risen more slowly, both in money and in real terms. It is interesting to compare this with the pattern of wages in agriculture. During the war period, money wages in agriculture increased more rapidly than money wages in industry (although not as rapidly as prices); the differetial between the two sectors fell by nearly 20 percent. Thereafter, industrial wages continued to rise rapidly, while wages in agriculture remained roughly constant, so that by 1954 the differential had increased by 25 percent, with a further small increase since then; by 1959, it was some 20 percent above the prewar level.[18] In actual fact, the ratio of industrial to agricultural wages in 1959 was substantially higher

[18]In fact, the increase was probably somewhat larger than this. The manufacturing wage figures for 1947 and earlier years have a relative upward bias, since they include clerical and administrative workers as well, while the later figures refer only to operatives.

than the 3:1 level shown in Table 5–8, for two reasons. The agricultural figures refer only to men, while the industrial data include all laborers; furthermore, the agricultural workers' weekly wage is computed on the assumption that they work the same number of days per week as in industry. In view of the substantial underemployment in agriculture which we found in Chapter 4, it seems surprising that this differential is so high; given the fact that it *is* so high, it is surprising that more people in the agricultural labor force do not rush to the cities, in the hope that they will be lucky enough to find jobs in manufacturing industry. Perhaps the most surprising thing, though, is the increase in this differential, particularly between 1950 and 1954. Why was it that industrial wages rose during these years, relative to both price increases and agricultural wages?

TABLE 5–9

SHARE OF WAGES IN VALUE ADDED

	Wages (£E Million)	Gross Value Added (£E Million)	Ratio 1:2
	(1)	(2)	(3)
1947............	21.0	54.2	0.39
1950............	22.7	57.7	0.39
1954............	29.5	74.9	0.39
1958............	33.7	108.4	0.31
1960............	42.2	136.1	0.31

NOTES AND SOURCE: All figures are taken from United Arab Republic, Department of Statistics and Census, *Census of Industrial Production* (Cairo, for years specified). Inclusions are ISIC 2 and 3, except that we have subtracted 207 (sugar refining) and 321 (petroleum refining); annual figures in these two lines are wildly erratic, due to inconsistent methods of valuing intermediate inputs, probably due in turn to differing ways of treating customs duties, as well as changing internal pricing policies for integrated industries.

We have used gross value added, since depreciation is not included in the censuses of 1952–56.

One possible explanation is that productivity per worker was rising very rapidly, and the laborers were given a share in the rising profits. In fact, this was true; real product per worker rose by 40 percent from 1947 to 1954, probably due in large part to the heavy capital investment which took place during this period. When combined with a rise of 30 percent in the prices of industrial products, it is clear that the 50 percent rise in money wage rates of industrial workers was one which the employers could well afford to pay. One way of putting this is that in spite of the marked increase in wage rates, the share of wages and salaries in industrial value added stayed roughly constant during this period (see Table 5–9).

This explanation for the increase in wage rates is not very satisfying, however. If there was an unlimited supply of unskilled workers, all of whom would presumably be willing to work at the given real wage rate, it is hard to see why employers increased real wages by 40 percent or more, as they did during this period; the argument that they did so because they could afford to is hardly convincing. In the following period, from 1954 to 1960, real output per worker rose by nearly 20 percent. Taking account of the slow price rise, the value of output per worker rose by 33 percent. Yet, wage rates during this period rose only slightly, moving virtually in step with the consumer price index; labor's share in total value added in the industrial sector fell quite sharply (see Table 5–9). Why is it that the real wage rate rose by nearly 35 percent between 1950 and 1954, while staying virtually unchanged in the following six years?

An alternative explanation of this rise in real wages might run in terms of the power of unions to restrict the supply of labor which can be employed by a firm, even though there are large numbers of workers who would gladly take jobs if they were available, with no increase in wages. Once again, though, this argument is far from convincing. In the early 1950's, somewhat less than a third of the industrial labor force was nominally unionized; it seems clear, however, that the great majority were in company unions. Where the workers did attempt to assert their independence, there was a web of legal control which sharply restricted their ability to demand and obtain additional benefits. The government scrutinized the finances of the unions and required that one third of all funds collected be used for social welfare; union officials had to have full-time employment in the plant; most serious of all was the law which, in effect, made all strikes illegal.[19] In these circumstances, it hardly seems plausible to attribute the rising real wages to effective collective bargaining by the unions.

We are brought one step closer to an understanding of this puzzle if we look at the detailed industrial breakdown, to see which specific sectors accounted for the jump in wage rates. Such an examination shows that there were two industries with wage increases substantially above those in the rest of the sector, namely, textiles and clothing. For these two sectors, average weekly money

---

[19]See F. Harbison and I. A. Ibrahim, *Human Resources for Egyptian Enterprises* (New York: McGraw-Hill Book Co., Inc., 1958), pp. 181–83; also A. A. I. el Gritly, "The Structure of Modern Industry in Egypt," *L'Egypte Contemporaine*, Nos. 241–42 (November-December, 1947), pp. 546–54.

wages rose between 1950 and 1954 by 60 percent and 89 percent, while the nearest competitors were six sectors with increases between 30 and 40 percent.[20]

In the case of clothing and footwear, the explanation for this sharp increase is almost entirely statistical. As we have indicated, between January and June, 1953, there was a change in the coverage of the wage statistics from 25 percent of all establishments to complete coverage of all firms with ten or more employees; in the case of clothing and footwear, 80 percent of the increase from 1950 to 1954 came at the time of this change in coverage and was due primarily to the exclusion of many small establishments with very low wages. This sector was so small, however, that the influence of this statistical aberration on average wage rates in the industrial sector was insignificant.[21]

This means that our problem comes down to an explanation of the sharp rate of increase in wage rates in the production of textiles. The central importance of this industry from this point of view might be expressed by saying that if wage rates in textiles had been constant from 1950 to 1954, the average money wage rate for all industry would have risen by only 12 percent, rather than the actual increase of 30 percent.

Once again, the indicated wage increase is partly simply a statistical phenomenon; yet this statistical aspect is not of primary importance here. Approximately a third of the indicated wage increase between 1950 and 1954 took place at the time of the change in coverage of the survey; this exaggerates the significance of the change in coverage, however, since wages rose steadily throughout this period, and presumably a portion of the reported increase from 1952–53 to 1953–54 was a real one, and not simply a result of changing survey techniques. We must look for more fundamental explanations.

---

[20]Basic metals (39 percent), beverages (38 percent), paper and paper products (38 percent), nonelectrical machinery (34 percent), wood products (32 percent), and electrical machinery (31 percent). These are two-digit ISIC categories. (See Appendix Table II–B–7) [pp. 310–11]). Prices in 1954 were virtually the same as they were in 1950, although there was a cyclical upswing and decline in the meantime.

[21]As we have shown in Appendix II–B–8 (pp. 312–13), this is one of four industries where this change in coverage was accompanied by a substantial increase in reported wage rates; since three of these four are quite insignificant in the industrial sector as a whole, particularly as weighted by 1954 employment in firms employing ten or more persons, the resulting upward bias in the wage series shown in Table 5–8 is insignificant. The remaining industry is textiles, and here the upward bias in the statistics is more serious (see discussion in the text).

The textile industry in Egypt is dominated by a relatively small number of very large establishments, most of which are run by companies affiliated with the Bank Misr. This group of companies is known for its forward-looking management, as well as for its desire to use the most advanced machinery and equipment; Harbison and Ibrahim cite several examples where the introduction of more capital equipment in Misr companies resulted in marked increases in textile production while employment stayed constant or even fell.[22] In this situation, it seems reasonable to attribute a large part of the increase in wage rates in this industry to a shift to the use of more highly skilled workers.[23] Aside from this, a number of people have commented on the high costs resulting from excessive labor turnover, particularly in the textile industry;[24] this might well have led the more forward-looking managers to raise their wage rates in an attempt to stabilize the work force and bring forth a greater industrial commitment of their employees. It seems that these two forces accounted for a large part of the rise in industrial wages in the early 1950's, as well as the rising differential between agricultural and industrial wage rates during this period.

With the share of wages in industrial value added falling sharply in recent years, one might ask what has happended to the resulting profits. Have they been reinvested by the firms to finance their own capital expansion, or have they been paid out as dividends? The data to answer this question are far from ideal, but the picture that they show is quite striking (see Table 5-10). These figures are based on a detailed analysis of the income and expenditure statements of a sampling of industrial limited-liability companies. As the first column shows, the size of the sample has increased through time; there is no indication as to how the inclusions were chosen. Yet, even in 1954, "as many of the large firms are included, substantially more than 50% of aggregate assets and profits of limited companies are covered."[25] In this situation the

---

[22]"Since the end of World War II, for example, the Mehalla company has doubled its production and decreased its total labor force by 40 percent. Within eight years the Kafreldawar company tripled its output with no net additions to its labor force, and Misr Rayon is constantly adding new facilities for greater production without contemplating any new labor." See Harbison and Ibrahim, *op. cit.*, p. 53.

[23]The wage statistics refer to all production workers, whether skilled or unskilled.

[24]Harbison and Ibrahim, *op. cit.*, chap. iv; Gamal el Din Said, "Productivity of Labor in Egyptian Industry," *L'Egypte Contemporaine*, Nos. 259-60 (May-June, 1950), pp. 501-3.

[25]National Bank of Egypt, *Economic Bulletin*, Vol. X, No. 2 (1957), p. 88.

variations in the number of companies included in the sample may not be too serious. What the figures indicate is that the share of net profits which were paid out as dividends rose from around 60 percent in 1954 to about 80 percent in 1959. These are extremely high figures; the rise in the late 1950's implies that a substantial part of the increasing industrial profits resulting from falling labor costs and rising prices was paid to the stockholders as dividends.

TABLE 5–10

SHARE OF DIVIDENDS IN NET PROFITS IN
INDUSTRIAL COMPANIES

	Number of Companies	Dividends/Net Profits
1954	61	0.59
1955	61	0.60
1957	88	0.75
1958	88	0.78
1958'	89	0.80
1959	89	0.79

SOURCE: National Bank of Egypt, *Economic Bulletin*, Vol. X, No. 2 (1957), p. 100; Vol. XII, No. 2 (1959), p. 104; Vol. XIII, Nos. 3–4 (1960), p. 286. Net profits are equal to gross profits, plus investment revenues, plus other revenues, minus total expenditures, excluding losses brought forward. Only industrial companies are included here. O'Brien points out that studies by the National Planning Committee also indicate a fall in the share of gross profits which were retained in the organized business sector, over the period 1955–59; see P. K. O'Brien, *The Revolution in Egypt's Economic System* (London: Oxford University Press, 1966), chap. vii; and United Arab Republic, National Planning Committee, Memos No. 4, No. 32, and No. 134 (Cairo, 1959).

This rise was probably the result of growing fear of nationalization and increasing government control, making the owners anxious to take their profits out of the business while they could still get them. On the other hand, they provide one of a number of motives for the nationalizations themselves, to enable the government to tap this rich source of potential savings.

D. GEOGRAPHICAL AND SIZE DISTRIBUTION

The 1960 population census indicates that in that year, over 50 percent of all industrial employment was concentrated outside the five major governorates. This figure is biased upward by the fact that the urban areas have sometimes expanded over the borders of the neighboring administrative units; a large portion of the manufacturing employment in Giza should be considered as being part of the Cairo urban area, for example. Comparison of the employment figures in Tables 2–10 (page 37) and 2–11 (page 39) show that the degree of industrial concentration in the five governorates has been rising steadily, from 39 percent in 1937 to 48 percent in 1960. Still, it seems clear that there is a substantial decentralization of industrial production. This is quite plausible, once we remember that over 60 percent of industrial value added was in food and textiles, two sectors which are widely scattered through the countryside.[26] Further growth of such industrial centers as Aswan and Helwan will continue the pattern of decentralization set in the past, when the major spinning and weaving establishments were located in the heart of the cotton-growing areas of the Delta.

With regard to the size distribution of the establishments in the industrial sector, virtually all data available refer to establishments with 10 or more employees. Information on establishments with less than 10 employees or on production outside of establishments can only be derived residually. For example, we might estimate employment by starting from manufacturing employment in the population census, subtracting employment in firms with 10 or more workers, as shown in the census of industrial production. Alternatively, we can start from figures on total value added in industry, subtracting that portion derived from the larger firms, as shown in the census of industrial production. This residual approach is extremely hazardous, since small differences in definitions or inclusions might affect the size of the residual quite substantially; yet it seems worth doing, at least to give us an idea of the degree of inclusiveness of the various sources of data. The figures appear in Table 5–11. From a size point of view, most of the government establishments probably fall in the category with 500 or more workers. If we include them with that group, it is clear that Egyptian industry is dominated, both from the employment and from the value-added point of view, by very small and very large establishments. The prevalence of the small-scale firms is a result of many forces; perhaps the most important are the difficulty of obtaining loans to finance an expansion and the prevalence of handicrafts industries, where economies of scale are of little importance. The importance of the very large firms, on the other hand, is primarily a reflection of two factors: the modern, highly capitalized textile industry, where nearly 70 percent of em-

---

[26]In each of these two industries, 55 percent of employment in firms with ten or more workers was outside the five governorates, according to the 1960 census of industrial production.

ployment in very large firms is located;[27] and the willingness of the
government to tolerate, and even strengthen, the monopoly position
of the firms that succeed in rising above the mass of small firms in
the industry.[28] As the table shows, there is a sharp rise in value
added per worker as the firm size increases, although this is not
an entirely smooth progression.

TABLE 5–11

EMPLOYMENT AND VALUE ADDED IN MANUFACTURING,
BY SIZE OF ESTABLISHMENT, 1960

Establishments Employing:	Persons Employed (000)	Gross Value Added (£E Million)	Gross Value Added per Person (£E)
Under 10, and outside establishments	366	100	274
10–49	55	12	224
50–499	97	53	545
500 and over	173	82	472
Government establishments	21	8	380
Total	713	255	358

NOTES AND SOURCES: This table is modeled on Table V–9 in B. Hansen and G. Marzouk,
Development and Economic Policy in the U.A.R. (Egypt) (Amsterdam: North-Holland Publishing
Co., 1965); these figures differ from those given there in several respects. We refer only to manufacturing (ISIC 2 and 3). All figures for firms of size 10–500 and over are from United Arab Republic, Department of Statistics and Census, *Census of Industrial Production 1960* (Cairo, 1962); for the
government sector, we have included value added in industry by the government business sector,
exclusive of municipal lighting and water, with employment derived by assuming that wage rates
there are as in large private firms, as suggested by Hansen and Marzouk; see United Arab Republic,
Presidency of the Republic, National Planning Committee, *General Frame of the Five-Year Plan
for Economic and Social Development, July 1960–June 1965* (Cairo, 1960), p. 167. Total employment
is from United Arab Republic, Department of Statistics and Census, *Population Census, 1960*
(Cairo, 1963), Vol. II, p. xiv; total value added from Table 5–3. The first line is derived residually,
in all cases. Totals may not add due to rounding.

With regard to rates of change in employment of small versus
large enterprises, there seems to us to be no adequate way of
measuring the relative rates of growth of these two components.
Hansen and Marzouk have concluded that small-scale industry is
continuing to expand, with employment rising perhaps by as much
as 35 percent from 1947 to 1960, compared to an employment increase of less than 30 percent for all industry over the same period;[29] however, the data underlying this estimate are so weak,
having been officially disavowed by the sources that originally

---

[27]Although, surprisingly, less than 50 percent of value added in very large
firms was in textiles; value added per worker was far higher in large-scale
establishments producing fertilizers and tobacco products, to pick two important examples.

[28]See Section E below.

[29]Hansen and Marzouk, *op. cit.*, p. 125.

produced them, that they can only be taken as an unverified guess, which we feel may err on the side of exaggeration of the growth of small industry.[30]

E. GOVERNMENT POLICIES

There is a long tradition in Egypt of government encouragement of monopolies. Already in the early nineteenth century the country made a valiant attempt at industrialization via state-owned monopolies;[31] Mohammed Ali's successors followed the policy of selling these companies—and the rights to form new ones—to private monopoly firms. During the late nineteenth and early twentieth centuries, when freedom to vary tariff rates was sharply restricted by international agreements, these monopolies were generally in service lines (e.g., railroads, utilities); the government used various means to allocate to itself a share of the net revenues, in spite of the fact that direct taxation had been virtually ruled out by the capitulations.[32] Since the 1930's, when Egypt regained her fiscal autonomy, tariff protection has been the major instrument for government aid to industry. There are other types of government assistance, such as railroad rebates and tax benefits, but these have been relatively minor by comparison.

As we have seen, until quite recently the industrial base in Egypt was heavily concentrated in a few lines: food, textiles, and building materials. For virtually all of these, tariff protection was a major factor in permitting the industry to get established, although as they expanded, several were able to dispense with this protection. In recent years, when the growth surge has resulted in the creation of large numbers of new "infants" pleading for governmental assistance, the level of tariffs has continued to rise; Hansen and Marzouk have estimated that from 1952 to 1961 the ratio of import duties paid to dutiable imports[33] rose by 60 percent, to reach an average tariff rate of over 100 percent. As they point out, the degree of protection has been further reinforced by licensing procedures, which means that only limited quantities of these goods can be purchased, even at the high after-tariff prices.[34]

---

[30]See Introduction to 1947 *Industrial and Commercial Census.*

[31]For an interesting appraisal of these efforts, see C. Issawi, "Egypt since 1800: A Study in Lopsided Development," *Journal of Economic History,* Vol. XXI, No. 1 (March, 1961).

[32]See el Gritly, *op. cit.,* pp. 522–25.

[33]Excluding imports of capital goods, raw materials, and essential foodstuffs, all of which enter at very low rates, or even duty-free.

[34]Hansen and Marzouk, *op. cit.,* chap. vi, sec. 6.2.

As we have seen, in July, 1961, there was a major change in the structure of ownership of industry. Our rough estimate is that since that time, some 60 percent of industrial output (including all large-scale establishments) is either fully under state ownership or else partially publicly owned, but controlled by the state. It is difficult at this stage to say much about the impact of this change on production and productivity. In the short run, we should expect it to make very little difference; in general, the same people are now making operating decisions, on largely the same bases as in the past. With regard to pricing, as we have seen, this was under virtually complete government control even before 1961. Production decisions as well were already subject to extensive centralized decision making; in principle, approval of the Ministry of Industry had even previously been required for any firm either to expand or to restrict production.[35] In the labor market the nationalizations were accompanied by a shortening of the work week in large establishments to a maximum of 42 hours; the average in all manufacturing establishments (ISIC 2 and 3) was 44 hours per week in January, 1963, compared to 45 hours in July, 1961.[36] Employers were required to take on additional workers so as to keep the total number of man-hours of work per week unchanged. Since the new workers were probably less skilled than those previously employed, there may have been a decline in labor productivity per man-hour, although this is impossible to document. With regard to wages, an effort was made to standardize wage rates for each skill level in all nationalized firms. Since no one had his pay cut in this process, while a number of workers were given raises, the average wage rate per week must have gone up. According to the *Survey of Wages and Working Hours*, cash wages (excluding profit shares) of laborers rose from 214 piasters per week in January, 1962, to 236 piasters per week in January, 1963.[37] Beyond this, in cases where the work week was shortened, the weekly pay check was not decreased, with the result that the hourly pay rate was raised. Finally, there was instituted a system of profit sharing whereby workers were entitled to receive 25 percent of the profits of the company, either as cash benefits or as funds set aside for the provision of social services. With output per man-hour subject to downward pressures while

---

[35]See Law 21 of 1958 for organizing and encouraging industry.

[36]See *Survey of Wages and Working Hours*, July, 1961; and United Arab Republic, Department of Public Mobilization and Statistics, *Statistical Yearbook, 1964* (Cairo, 1965). Hansen and Marzouk estimate a fall in the average work week for all industry of 4 percent from 1960–61 to 1962–63 (*op. cit.*, chap. v, secs. 5.5.3 and 5.6.3).

[37]See Appendix Table II–B–7 (pp. 310–11).

the hourly pay rate was rising, we should expect labor's share in value added to rise.[38] Until more recent industrial production censuses are available, this must remain only a surmise.

With regard to savings and investment, two questions arise. One concerns the share of value added which is saved, the other the allocation of new investments among different industries. On the latter point, in principle this was under government control before the nationalizations, although the effectiveness of the control was strengthened by government ownership. It is too early to tell the extent to which the structure of investment, and hence of industrial production, will be changed in the postnationalization period. To the extent that there is such a change, however, it cannot be directly tied to the nationalizations themselves; the structure of the industrial sector would undoubtedly have altered with time in any case. Perhaps the most important result of the nationalizations has been to give manufacturing establishments more possibilities of borrowing from commercial and Central banks, thereby raising the rate of investment in industry.

It is difficult to say whether the rate of savings in the sector has risen or fallen. We have already indicated that the share of wages in value added has probably increased; yet, if the government is a better saver than private capitalists, aggregate savings of the sector may well have risen. This seems quite possible if we look at the situation just prior to the nationalizations, when the private sector may have been more intent on withdrawing profits in anticipation of greater government control than in continuing expansion. The figures in Table 5-10 seem to point in this direction, although unfortunately they are not available for more recent years; as a result, these remarks must remain conjectural.[39]

F. INDUSTRY AS PANACEA?

Before concluding this chapter, perhaps we might return to the question of the extent to which the authorities can look to the industrial sector for help in solving the country's most pressing problems. The first of these has to do with the balance of payments. As

---

[38]According to estimates by Hansen and Marzouk, there was no absolute fall in output per man-hour, but only a reduction in the rate of increase (*op. cit.*, Table 5.15).

[39]For a further discussion of the interaction between private and public sectors during this period, see P. K. O'Brien, *The Revolution in Egypt's Economic System, 1952–1965* (London: Oxford University Press, 1966), chaps. iv–vii.

we have seen, there is little indication to date that the rapid rate of industrial growth has helped the country's payments position, or will be able to do so in the near future; on the contrary, all indications are that the rapid increase in output in this sector has put heavy strains on the payments situation of the country, to supply the capital goods and intermediate products to fuel this engine of expansion. Secondly, we might ask what hope there is that rapid expansion here will solve the problem of overpopulation in the country. Perhaps the figures speak for themselves in this regard; in spite of an extremely high increase in industrial output, additional employment in this sector absorbed less than 15 percent of the increase in the number of adult males in Egypt from 1947 to 1960[40] There is virtually no prospect that in the forseeable future the sector will be in a position to employ enough workers to reduce the degree of overpopulation in the rest of the economy. A third question relates to the impact of industrial growth on the level of income in the country. As Appendix Table I-A-10 (page 391) shows, value added per worker in industry is substantially above that in virtually any other sector of the economy. Yet, from 1947 to 1960 the share of industrial workers in total employment of adult males rose only from 9.8 percent to 10.8 percent. If that rate of structural change is greatly accelerated so that by 1970 an additional 2 percent of total employment is shifted from agriculture into industry, while real product per capita in each sector remains unchanged, the result would be a rise in average real income per capita in the economy of some 2.6 percent over the ten-year period. Clearly, there is not much mileage to be gained in trying to raise the income of the country simply through this type of structural transformation. Finally, we might ask about the role of the industrial sector as a source of savings in the economy. As we have seen, the high rate of distribution of corporate profits provided one of the justifications for the nationalization of industry, thereby putting this potential source of savings under direct governmental control; recently, gross profits of nationalized companies may have been as high as 40 percent of domestic gross savings. This function of making funds available and accessible to finance further capital formation has been one of the most important aspects of the rapid growth of the industrial sector in the United Arab Republic in recent years.

General discussions of economic development often state that

---

[40]See Table 2-9 (p. 33).

a marked increase in agricultural output is a necessary precondi-
tion—or at least a necessary simultaneous development—for a major
expansion in industry and the services. In Egypt, we found that
even in the 1930's, agricultural techniques were relatively advanced,
while income per capita in the sector was low primarily as a
result of unfortunate factor proportions. In this context, perhaps
the concept of balanced growth between agriculture and industry
will need to be reinterpreted. Rostow, for example, lists three reasons why agricultural growth is a necessary concomitant to industrial expansion: to supply food for the growing urban population, to provide a market for the output of manufactured consumer
goods, and to provide a surplus to be invested in the rest of the
economy.[41] If our analysis is correct, there is little prospect that
the agricultural sector will be very successful in filling any of these
roles in Egypt. Looking at developments to date, we saw in Chapter 4 that imports currently account for some 10–12 percent of the
total food supply of the country; with the exception of textiles and
fertilizers, the agricultural sector has provided only a negligible
market for industrial products. In the case of savings, the question
is more debatable. In the past the large-scale landlords provided
one of the main sources of funds to finance an expansion in the industrial sector; with the substantial income redistribution which
has taken place as a result of the land reforms, it seems likely—
although far from certain—that the supply of savings from agriculture made available to the rest of the economy has fallen.[42]

It is clear that the failure of agricultural output to expand rapidly has made it more difficult for the rest of the economy to maintain a high growth rate; to say, though, that it is *impossible* for a
country to undergo a successful industrialization program without
a concomitant agricultural revolution seems to us prematurely to
prejudge the outcome of the present development effort in Egypt.
This does not mean that we regard current efforts to raise agricultural output as inevitably doomed to failure; the £E300 million
to be invested in agriculture during the second five-year plan at-
tests to the earnest desire of the government to bring about just
such an expansion. We do feel, however, that there is a good

---

[41] W. W. Rostow, *The Stages of Economic Growth: A Non-Communist Mani-
festo* (Cambridge: Cambridge University Press, 1960), pp. 22–24.

[42] This does not necessarily imply that total savings in the agricultural sector
have fallen; it may be that small farmers have the same marginal propensity
to save as rich landlords but devote more of their savings to the improvement
of their own farms.

chance that the actual increase in agricultural output will be relatively modest, perhaps just keeping pace with population growth. If this is the case, food imports will necessarily remain large and will grow with any rise in the standard of living; but foreign aid, along with a decreasing dependency of industry on imports and some increase in manufactured exports, could well mitigate the seriousness of this problem. The manufacturing and service sectors of the economy seem wholly capable of providing the necessary market for industrial output; finally, the supply of savings from the industrial sector—once again, along with foreign aid—may well be adequate to finance a continuing high level of industrial investment. Clearly, a low rate of growth of agricultural output would make the attainment of all these tasks substantially more difficult; we do not believe that it would make a continuing industrial expansion impossible.

Services

In 1960 the population of Egypt numbered about 10 million more than it had in 1937; of this increase, some 2.5 million were adult males. In 1937, over 65 percent of all working men were employed in agriculture, where for perhaps a century the man-land ratio had been steadily increasing to a point where it seemed clear that additional workers would add very little to the output of the sector. The industrial sectors was so small that even a very substantial expansion could hardly have been expected to provide jobs for more than a small minority of the men seeking them. The result was that an ever-growing number of people were pushed to seek employment in the services. From 1937 to 1960 the number of men working in this sector approximately doubled, rising by more than a million and accounting for well over half of all the new jobs in the economy during the period. This pattern of events has led some to conclude that the problem of underemployment was transferred—or at least spread—from the agricultural sector into the services, with the substantial increase in employment being matched by a very much smaller—or even negligible—increase in real output. In this chapter, we shall look in some detail at the major components of the service sector, in an attempt to evaluate the accuracy of this appraisal. Beyond this, we shall be concerned with the changing role and structure of the government sector, particularly with regard to its functions in the provision of current services, as well as the financing of these expenditures. Summary figures on employment in the various branches of the services are given in Table 6–1.

TABLE 6–1

Employment in Services

	1937	1947	1960
A. General government............	222,417	376,848	896,396
B. Commerce.....................	436,074	587,542	641,408
C. Transport and communications...	137,148	201,582	260,210
D. Construction..................	116,525	111,693	158,885
E. Personal services..............	326,699	473,808	567,027
(Paid domestics)............	(130,073)	(234,645)	(191,627)
F. Other services.................	147,187	175,787	131,865
Total..................	1,386,050	1,927,260	2,655,791

Sources: *Line A.* See Table 6–2.

Lines B, C, and D. Revised figures from United Arab Republic, Department of Statistics and Census, *Population Census, 1960* (Cairo, 1963), Vol. II, p. xiv, after deducting unemployed from earlier censuses.

Line E. 1937 from *Population Census, 1947* (Cairo, 1954), pp. 138–42, 202, 206; includes men's tailoring and shirtmaking, women's dressmaking, and upholstering. 1947: *ibid.*, pp. 138–42, 276–77; excludes home duties. 1960: *Population Census, 1960*, Vol. II, p. 84; "domestics" is total on p. 146, plus all young girls and all Sudanese (pp. 84–85). Referring to a somewhat more comprehensive total (including besides domestics "photographers, shoeshiners, domestic servants, exchange bureaus, etc."), the five-year plan gives a total of 324,000 (United Arab Republic, Presidency of the Republic, National Planning Committee, *General Frame of the Five-Year Plan for Economic and Social Development, July 1960–June 1965* [Cairo, 1960], p. 121). Part of the divergence might be in the 1960 census category, "Personal Services n.e.c.," amounting to some 90,000 workers.

Line F. Residually derived as difference between A and E and total for services given in source referred to for lines B, C, and D, with allowance for 1960 defense estimate (see Table 6–2). Total is the same as that given in Table 2–9, line B–3 (see p. 33).

A. GENERAL GOVERNMENT

An evaluation of the changing structure of the government sector in Egypt involves a number of problems. On the financial side, the budget document itself is a mass of details from which it is difficult to extract meaningful totals; the expenditure categories shown there bear only a faint relationship to the desired economic and functional classifications. For the period before 1947–48, we have relied primarily on the major administrative classifications in the budget itself as a rough measure of the level and structure of government expenditure. From 1947–48, as we shall see, a far more satisfactory set of accounts is available.

The figures derived from this administrative classification are shown in Appendix Table VI–E–2 (page 381). As this table shows, from the late 1930's to 1946–47 there was a 150 percent increase in total government expenditures on goods and services (in current prices). Expenditures in areas which we have entitled "developmental" rose slightly less rapidly than did total expenditures, which in turn increased at a somewhat smaller rate than the growth in national income. While none of the available price indices can give a satisfactory deflator for these government expenditures, we may note in passing that the three indices which are available—the cost-of-living index, the retail price index, and the wholesale price index—all registered increases during this period roughly commensurate with the rise in government expenditures.[1]

Turning to the revenue side of the government accounts (see Appendix Table VI–E–1 [page 380]), throughout this period receipts rose more rapidly than expenditures, with the result that from 1939–40 to 1949–50 the government ran a cumulative budget surplus of some £E80 million. These continuing surpluses helped to alleviate (although they were far from eliminating) the inflationary pressures resulting from the extensive British military expenditures in the country during and after the war. As during the 1930's, the main source of the increase in government revenue was customs receipts, which, compared to 1938–39, had doubled by the end of the war and tripled by 1947–48.

There are two special problems with the employment statistics in the government sector. The first is that some workers—those in defense—were not included in the 1960 census (although they were included in the earlier censuses). We have tried to adjust for this by a rough estimate of employment in the military in 1960. Secondly, there might be some question as to where the line has been drawn between the supervisory authorities (e.g., the General Organization for Spinning and Weaving, or the Ministry of Agriculture) and the nationally owned producing units (e.g., nationalized companies, military factories). For our purposes, all of the first should be included with the government sector, while the second should not. In general, it seems that the censuses follow this breakdown, although employment in the military factories is probably not included at all. The figures in Table 6–2, though, should give a reasonably accurate picture of the role of the employment aspects of the government as a provider of services in the economy, exclusive of government enterprises.

In 1937 the government sector accounted for only 3.7 percent

---

[1] If these were the correct deflators, this would imply that in some sense, real government expenditures was constant; then the 80 percent increase in employment during this period (see below) might imply that there was a sharp reduction in nonwage expenditures of the government. In fact, a more likely explanation is that government money wage rates increased much less rapidly than the price indices, i.e., real wages in the government sector fell.

of total employment in the economy. The more detailed breakdown in Table 6-2 shows that nearly half of all government workers were in defense, justice, and police. While published figures are not complete in this regard, it seems that the employment in "developmental" aspects of the government—health, education, agriculture, industry, and communications—amounted to some 65,000 people, or just over 1 percent of total employment in the economy.

TABLE 6–2

EMPLOYMENT IN GENERAL GOVERNMENT

	1937	1947	1960
A. Education	37,350	70,580	168,520
B. Health	17,170	35,440	42,630
C. Defense	18,890	61,340	226,000
D. Justice and police	79,897	96,167	138,862
E. Other public administration	69,110	113,321	320,384
Total	222,417	376,848	896,396

SOURCES: *Line A.* 1937 and 1947: United Arab Republic, Department of Statistics and Census, *Population Census, 1947* (Cairo, 1954), p. 210; includes government, wakf, and community council education, as well as the Ministry of Education. 1960: *Population Census, 1960*, Vol. II (Cairo, 1963), p. 144; assumes employment in private education increased since 1947 in the same proportion as the number of private school students (i.e., 70.3 percent).

Line B. 1937 and 1947: *Population Census, 1947*, p. 206; includes employment in government, wakf, and community hospitals and clinics, as well as the Ministry of Health. 1960: *Population Census, 1960*, Vol. II, p. 144; assumes public component of health employment is as in 1947 (i.e., 76.3 percent).

Line C. 1937 and 1947: *Population Census, 1947*, p. 214; excludes workers for British army. 1960: Estimated on basis of wage payments to defense (pp. 118 and 141 in United Arab Republic, Presidency of the Republic, National Planning Committee, *General Frame of the Five-Year Plan for Economic and Social Development, July 1960– June 1965* [Cairo, 1960]), assuming average wage rates here equal to those in security and justice.

Line D. 1937 and 1947: *Population Census, 1947*, p. 218. 1960: *Population Census, 1960*, Vol. II, p. 144.

Line E. 1937 and 1947: *Population Census, 1947*, pp. 218 and 222; includes public councils (e.g., municipalities), other public administration (ministries), and other councils (wakfs). 1960: *Population Census, 1960*, Vol. II, "ministries and departments" (p. 144) plus non-Egyptian government servants (p. 85).

For 1937 and 1947, unemployed workers have been deducted in all categories.

During and immediately after the Second World War, employment in the government sector expanded quite rapidly, increasing by 20 percent during the decade between the two censuses. Out of an employment increase of some 800,000 in the whole economy during this decade, nearly 20 percent found work in the government sector. If we group defense, justice, and police together, we find that for employment as for expenditures, the major components of the government sector all grew at roughly the same rate. This expansion brought the employment share of the government sector in the whole economy to close to 6 percent.

From 1947, there is available a detailed restatement of government budgetary expenditures, cross-classified according to economic and functional categories. This study, the major results of which are presented in Appendix Tables VI–E–3 (pages 382–84) and VI–E–4 (pages 385–95), permits us to examine the changing role of the government sector in more detail, at least during the period covered by these accounts.[2] Perhaps we might start by referring forward to our examination in Chapter 9; as we indicate there, the share of current government purchases of goods and services in total output took three major jumps during the period covered by these detailed government accounts.[3] One of these increases—from 1951 to 1952—was simply the result of a sharp drop in gross national product, with government expenditures remaining roughly constant; in the other two cases, from 1947 to 1948 and from 1953–54 to 1955–56, the expansion in the government's share was the direct result of a sharp increase in public current expenditure. The net result of these changes was to raise the government's share in total output from 12 percent of GNP in 1947 to over 20 percent in 1956–57. We should like to examine the pattern of government spending to see if we can pinpoint the sectors responsible for these two rapid increases in the public sector's share of output; then, we should like to compare figures at the beginning and the end of this period, to see what overall changes have taken place in the structure of expenditures. (See Table 6–3.)

The first of these questions is relatively straightforward. The two sharp increases in government expenditure reflect the country's two military efforts, the Palestine campaign and the military build-up prior to Suez. The detailed figures indicate that over each of these intervals the increase in defense spending accounted for approximately 60 percent of the total rise in government expenditure. This pattern is strongly reminiscent of the pattern described for the British economy by Peacock and Wiseman.[4] In that study the authors argued that in periods of social turmoil, and most particularly during wartime, temporary and urgent needs for government expenditures result in sharp increases in taxation to levels which would previously have been considered excessive or intoler-

---

[2] The study was done by Rasheed Khalid of the United Nations, in conjunction with the Institute of National Planning in Cairo; we very much appreciate being permitted to use these data here.

[3] See Tables 9–1 (p. 216) and 9–2 (p. 217).

[4] A. T. Peacock and J. Wiseman, *The Growth of Public Expenditure in the United Kingdom* (Princeton: Princeton University Press, 1961), pp. 24–28 and Chart 1, p. 43.

able. After the need for these emergency expenditures subsides, tax rates may fall somewhat, but not to their earlier levels; instead, there is a "displacement effect," whereby the temporary expenditures are replaced by others of a more permanent nature. This line

TABLE 6–3

CURRENT GOVERNMENT EXPENDITURES, DEFENSE AND NONDEFENSE

(£E Million, Current Prices)

	Defense	Nondefense	Total	Share of Defense in Total (Percent)
1947–48*	8.1	50.6	58.7	13.8
1948–49	31.9	67.6	99.5	32.1
1949–50	33.7	71.6	105.3	32.0
1950–51	28.9	103.0	131.9	21.9
1951–52	41.4	108.0	149.4	27.7
1952–53	35.3	103.2	138.5	25.5
1953–54	37.8	109.9	147.7	25.6
1954–55	53.0	120.6	173.6	30.5
1955–56	82.0	137.7	219.7	37.3
1956–57	81.5	156.5	238.0	34.2

*Ten months only.
SOURCES: Appendix Tables VI–E–4 (pp. 385–95) and VI–E–6 (p. 399).

of reasoning has clear relevance to the Egyptian case. Judging from the one decade for which these detailed figures are available, the following modifications might be in order. First of all, defense expenditures have generally not fallen after reaching temporary peaks, but have stayed roughly constant for a while before moving on to the next surge upward. This means that while defense has clearly been a major force pushing the government's share of total output upward, there is no evidence of a true displacement effect— the substitution of other types of expenditures for defense between "wars"—at work here. Secondly, we shall see below that while revenues rose in keeping with expenditures during the earlier of these two growth periods, from 1953–54 to 1955–56 the major change in the government's financial position was rather a large increase in the deficit.[5] This suggests that rising defense expenditures can lead the way to higher total government spending both by making the public more used to paying higher taxes and by making the authorities more used to the idea of deficit finance.

For an overall look at the changing structure of government

───────────

[5] See Table 9–5 (p. 229).

expenditure during this period, we might concentrate our attention on the share of total current budgetary expenditures in each of the major functional categories (see Table 6–4). The increasing share

TABLE 6–4

DISTRIBUTION OF CURRENT BUDGETARY EXPENDITURES
(Percent of Total)

	1947–49	1955–57
Organs of state..........................	1.6	0.4
Fiscal administration.....................	3.0	2.3
General economic regulation..............	1.6	0.9
Conduct of foreign affairs................	1.0	0.7
Justice and police.......................	11.4	8.0
General research.........................	1.0	0.5
Defense.................................	26.3	39.7
Total, general services...............	45.9	52.5
Education...............................	9.5	12.2
Health..................................	6.0	3.2
Social security, special welfare services.....	5.2	4.3
Community services.....................	1.8	0.8
Tourism and culture.....................	0.4	0.6
Total, community and social serivces...	22.9	21.1
Agriculture and irrigation................	10.4	3.8
Mineral resources, construction, and manufacturing...................	2.0	2.4
Fuel and power.........................	1.9	8.9
Transport, storage, and communications....	16.4	11.1
Total, economic services..............	30.7	26.3
Unallocable.............................	0.4	0.0
Total...........................	100.0	100.0

NOTES: Figures are based on a simple average of the two first years and the two last years in Appendix Table VI–E–4 (pp. 385–95). Current expenditures include wages and salaries, rental of fixed assets, other current purchases of goods and services, and military construction and equipment.

of defense expenditures to which we have referred stands out clearly in this table. In the sector of community and social services, expenditures on education have grown more rapidly than the total, while the other components of this category, including health, have shown a relative decline. Perhaps the most surprising thing about the table is the decreasing share of so-called "economic services" in the total. It is true that these figures exclude government enterprises as well as expenditures in annexed budgets; still, we should have expected this sector to be among the faster growing components of the budget. This is primarily a reflection of the fact that current expenditures on agriculture and irrigation were roughly constant during this period, while the rest of the budget was growing rapidly. In the case of transport, storage, and communications, current expenditures rose by some 70 percent, but this was still considerably below the 150 percent increase in total current budgetary expenditures from 1947–49 to 1955–57.[6]

The closer one comes to the present, the more unmanageable Egyptian budgetary figures become. For one thing, closed accounts are not available since 1956–57, and we must rely on budgeted figures. Much more serious, however, has been the great multiplicity of budgets and annexed budgets, mixed together in changing proportions with current operating budgets (i.e., including gross turnover) of nationalized firms.[7] As we have indicated in the introduction to this study, we have not found it worthwhile to go through the monumental task of reclassifying and consolidating these figures. With some hesitation and only limited comment, we present the figures in Table 6–5, which may be as much as can be done at present to measure the changing structure of government expenditures in more recent years. The figures imply a roughly constant proportion of total expenditures devoted to defense, justice, and police; a marked rise in the importance of community and social services, particularly in the areas of education and health; and a continuing relative decline in economic services.[8] There are so many classification problems involved here that only in a few categories—general services and the components shown, health, education, tourism and culture, agriculture and irrigation— can these figures be considered as being at all comparable.

Let us return to look at the employment aspects of the government's activites during this period. Table 6–1 shows that from 1947 to 1960, employment in the government sector more than doubled, as some 500,000 workers were added to the government sector. Coming at a time when total employment in the economy

---

[6]The sharp increase in fuel and power is difficult to explain; it reflects one large purchase in 1956–57 in the category "other current goods and services," amounting to £E28.4 million. But for this one item, the drop in the share of economic services would have been substantially larger. In 1955–56 alone, for example, this share was 22.8 percent, compared to 30.7 percent in 1947–49.

[7]In recent years, particularly 1965–66, the budget has been very much improved in format.

[8]This decline is exaggerated by the removal of a number of governmental activities—notably, the railroads—from the regular budget and their inclusion in the business budget, which is not included in the figures in Table 6–5.

was growing rather slowly, the striking result was that over 40 percent of all new jobs in the economy during this period were in the government sector, exclusive of all government enterprises and nationalized firms.

TABLE 6–5

APPROXIMATE DISTRIBUTION OF
TOTAL GOVERNMENT EXPENDITURES

(Percent of Total)

	1956–57	*1963–64*
General research...................	0.5	1.5
Justice, police, and defense.........	31.9	28.9
Other general services..............	3.6	5.7
Total, general services..........	36.0	36.1
Education.......................	10.4	17.0
Health..........................	2.9	4.9
Tourism and culture...............	0.5	2.6
Other community services...........	24.5	23.2
Total, community and social services...........	38.3	47.7
Agriculture and irrigation...........	3.8	8.4
Other economic services............	19.6	3.3
Total, economic services.........	23.4	11.7
Public debt payments..............	2.2	3.5
Total......................	100.0	100.0
Total, £E million............	309.5	540.4

NOTES AND SOURCES: 1956–57 from Appendix Table VI–E–4 (pp. 385–95); includes total budgetary expenditures, current as well as capital and transfers. 1963–64: United Arab Republic, Ministry of the Treasury, *Statement by Dr. Abdel-Moneim el-Kaissouni on the Draft Budget of the U.A.R. for the Fiscal Year 1963–64* (Cairo, 1964), pp. 168–77. Includes all expenditures in services budget and by local administrations, but not business budget.

We started out this chapter with a question as to whether there is any evidence that the underemployment which we found in the agricultural sector was spreading into the services. With the exception of a few lines where specific services are rendered and can be counted (students taught or patients treated), it is not possible to measure productivity changes in the government sector. Traditional national income accounting evaluates output of the sector in terms of inputs, which means that the real product is assumed to change in proportion to employment, with labor productivity unchanged. This is obviously not of much help to us here. One might argue a priori that this large an increase in government employment was "clearly" excessive; casual empiricism might leave one convinced that there are large numbers of government workers who have nothing useful to do; one can even point to specific government policies, such as the rule that all college graduates (a not inconsiderable number of people) can always find employment in the government if they so desire. None of these are proofs, and no proofs can be offered, but there does seem to be a clear presumption that this expansion of employment in the government sector was in some sense excessive, that there was considerable overhiring and resulting underemployment of workers in this sector.

It would be interesting to attempt to evaluate this increase in government employment in terms of what it costs the economy, in real terms. There are two major components of this cost: the alternative output lost by hiring the worker here rather than somewhere else, and the increase in inflationary pressures which result from his moving onto the government payroll. Let us look at each of these in turn.

TABLE 6–6

GOVERNMENT WAGE RATES

	Index of Monthly Money Wage Rate of Government Workers 1954 = 100	Index of Monthly Real Wage Rate (Deflated by Cost-of-Living Index) 1954 = 100
1945	90.2	87.4
1946	87.5	86.5
1947	83.3	84.8
1948	89.3	90.2
1949	85.6	87.4
1950	104.2	100.6
1951	103.7	92.3
1952	93.5	83.8
1953	101.4	97.3
1954	100.0	100.0
1955	99.5	99.8
1956	107.9	105.6
1961	111.1	103.1

SOURCE: See Appendix Table II–B–11 (p. 315).

With regard to the first component, it is revealing to examine the developments in the field of government wage rates of this period. Converted to an index base, these figures are as shown in Table 6-6.

The fall in money wages in the early postwar years was a result of a small decline in the basic wage rate, accompanied by decreasing cost-of-living wage supplements; the period since 1951 has been characterized by a slow rise in average basic wages, offset in large part by falling cost-of-living allowances. The price deflator used here—the cost-of-living index—almost certainly understates the rise in prices during this period; the official wholesale price index rose by 40 percent from 1947 to 1961, compared to a rise of less than 10 percent in the cost-of-living index. It seems fair to conclude that money wage rates in the government sector have risen very little in the postwar period, at least up to 1960, while real wages have probably fallen somewhat. This is quite remarkable, particularly when we remember that this was the sector where over 40 percent of all new employment was located during these years. When we recall also that total employment during this period rose less rapidly than did population, whether we look at the whole economy or only at males aged 15 and above, it seems probable that alternative employment opportunities were quite limited; from the point of view of alternative production forgone in drawing these workers into the government sector, the real costs to the economy were probably minimal.

If alternative employment opportunities for these workers were negligible, we can think of domestic production outside the government as given. Yet the fact that workers are employed in the government will surely change the distribution of income, and may also affect the level of aggregate demand. Whether or not this will be so depends on the way the government finances its increase in expenditure; if taxes are raised enough to keep private demand constant in spite of the rise in government wage payments, no inflationary pressures would develop.[9] The fiscal position of the government is discussed at some length in the section dealing with savings in the economy, in Chapter 9. As we shall see there, a substantial part of the increase in government expenditures, particularly after 1953–54, was covered by deficit financing (see, for example, Table 9–5 [page 229]). Beyond this, the figures in Table 6–7 indicate that virtually all of the substantial increase in government debt outstanding from 1948 to 1952, and three quarters of the

---

[9]This argument is based on the proposition that with an unlimited supply of labor the balanced-budget multiplier that results from an expansion of government employment paid for out of increased tax revenues is not inflationary. This ignores any increases in other government purchases necessary to complement the expanded employment.

additional increase up to 1960, was obtained by loans from the Central Bank.

All these facts point to the conclusion that the expansion of employment in the government sector was financed in quite an expansionary way. To the extent that output responds in the simple Keynesian multiplier manner, this expansionary pressure might provide a useful stimulus to the economy. In Egypt, however, the range of goods whose production could be increased in response to rising demand is rather limited; this means that an increase in aggregate demand would result in heavy imports of commodities

TABLE 6–7

PUBLIC DEBT AND ITS DISTRIBUTION

(In £E Million)

	A	B	C
	Total Debt	Holdings of Debt by:	
End of:	Outstanding*	Central Bank	Commercial Banks†
1948...............	125.0	47.3	n.a.
1952...............	203.0	122.5	9.1
1960...............	406.0	276.6	52.1

*Figures refer to end of June, rather than end of December.
†Includes government-guaranteed securities, while other figures do not.
SOURCES: *Column A.* From *Annuaire Statistique, 1951–54*, p. 343; and National Bank of Egypt, *The Economy of the U.A.R. in the 1950's* (Cairo, 1963), p. 67; excludes agrarian reform bonds, and National Bank of Egypt and Bank Misr bonds. *Column B.* National Bank of Egypt, *Economic Bulletin*, various issues; includes treasury bills held as backing for note issues. *Column C.* National Bank of Egypt and Central Bank of Egypt, *Credit and Banking Developments*, various ssues.

with inelastic domestic supplies (food is the best example) and, failing that, pressures for substantial changes in internal relative and absolute prices. Clearly, the substantial deficit financing associated with the growth of employment in the government sector must have added significantly to the authorities' difficulties in seeking to achieve three interrelated goals: keeping the balance of payments in hand, controlling the level of domestic prices, and raising aggregate savings. The fact that they have been able to finance continuing and substantial balance-of-payments deficits has reduced the urgency of these problems somewhat. With foreign assets exhausted and liabilities increasing while a growing share of the economy has moved under direct government ownership, and hence is more responsive to socialist pressures to "improve the lot of the masses," these difficulties are likely to become more serious in the future.

In our discussion, we have treated an increase in consumer demand as a bad thing, on the assumption that in the short run the supply of consumer goods is fixed, so that any increase in demand would result in increased domestic inflationary pressure and/or growing balance-of-payments deficits. An alternative approach to this question by Little assumes that the capital stock can be used for the production of either capital or consumer goods;[10] then an increase in consumer demand, resulting perhaps from an increase in government employment paid for by deficit finance, would require that more of the given capital stock (or alternatively, a higher share of new investment) be allocated for the production of consumer goods. It is then possible, as Little has shown, to find the allocation of capital and labor between the two sectors which will maximize either the income or the rate of growth of the economy. His analysis is thorough and elegant, providing many interesting insights; its main weakness, for our purposes, lies in his concentration on conditions of equilibrium. The question he asks might be rephrased as follows: How much of the given capital stock (model I) or of new investment (model II) will have to be devoted to the production of consumer goods if the supply of these goods is to keep pace with rising demand? But if the supply of consumer goods (through the allocation of capital and labor) is not responsive to increased demand, the effect of expanding government employment paid for through deficit finance will simply be excess demand, with the undesirable results referred to in our discussion above.

B. COMMERCE

This is a mixed bag, taking in everything from the big export merchants to those engaged in "hawking and peddling (undefined)." Also included are other commercial activities such as financial institutions, insurance, and real estate; in 1960, these other groups together accounted for some 6 percent of employment in the sector, the remainder being in wholesale and retail trade proper. There are several sources of information which give us an idea as to the activities of this latter group. With regard to specific types of goods traded, in 1947 nearly 65 percent of all workers were engaged in the sale of food and food products. Another 14 percent were in a few small retail lines: haberdashery, peddling, and retail stores without specialty. The remainder were engaged in the trade of

---

[10]I. M. D. Little, "The Real Cost of Labor and the Choice between Consumption and Investment," *Quarterly Journal of Economics*, Vol. LXXV, No. 1 (February, 1961), pp. 1–15.

textiles, petroleum products, and a host of miscellaneous small lines. From the point of view of employment status, in 1960 67 percent of the workers in trade were self-employed and unpaid family workers.[11] The somewhat discredited industrial and commercial census tells the same story; in 1947, 76 percent of all commercial establishments engaged in trade employed no staff, while an additional 18 percent hired only one or two employees. These figures make it reasonable to characterize the commerce sector in Egypt as being concentrated (at least from an employment point of view) in a great many small-scale establishments, trading primarily in food and food products and other light consumer goods.

For reasons which we explained at the opening of this chapter, we should like to evaluate the change in labor productivity in this sector through time. It is not obvious just what concept of output is relevant for this purpose. It would not make much sense, for example, to use figures on real income earned in the sector (i.e., money income deflated by a cost-of-living index). More reasonable would be current money income deflated by an index of the price of the "products" of the sector (presumably a weighted average of retail and wholesale prices of all goods traded, including imports and exports). Alternatively, we might work with an index of the quantity of goods going through the trade channels. If the trade margin for each good is a constant percentage of the sales value of the good, these two approaches (deflated money income and an index of the quantity of goods traded) will follow the same pattern.[12]

For the decade 1937–47, no figures are available which would permit us to follow the deflated-income approach.[13] A rough com-

---

[11]Share of total Egyptians (i.e., excluding foreigners). All these figures are taken from the 1947 and 1960 population censuses.

[12]If p = price, q = quantity, and m = trade margin, then $\dfrac{\Sigma\, m_0 p_0 q_1}{\Sigma\, m_0 p_0\, q_0}$ is a quantity index using as weights value added per unit in the trade of each good in the base year. Alternatively, current money income in trade might be deflated by a price index, as follows:

$$\frac{\Sigma\, m_1 p_1 q_1}{\Sigma\, m_0 p_0 q_0} \times \frac{\Sigma\, m_1 p_0 q_1}{\Sigma\, m_1 p_1 q_1} = \frac{\Sigma\, m_1 p_0 q_1}{\Sigma\, m_0 p_0 q_0}$$

the same as the quantity index if the trade margin of each good remains unchanged.

[13]The only income estimate for this period, by Anis, is derived by multiplying a rough estimate of employment in the sector by a "reasonable guess" at wage rates; see M. A. Anis, "A Study of the National Income of Egypt," *L'Egypte Contemporaine*, Nos. 261–62 (November-December, 1950), pp. 806–7.

putation of the quantity of goods passing through the trading channels is possible, although the weighting only imperfectly approaches that suggested above; this indicates a rise in the quantity of goods traded of only 15 percent during the decade.[14] This leads us to conclude that the 34 percent increase in employment in commerce during this period (see Table 6-1) was out of proportion to the increase in services provided; expressed in another way, a fall in productivity per worker of some 14 percent seems indicated.[15]

During the following intercensal period the pattern of developments was quite different. On the one hand, employment was relatively stable, rising by less than 10 percent; real product, measured in the same way, rose by over 65 percent, implying an increase in output per worker of more than 50 percent. This means that in the postwar period the commerce sector has been able to handle a large increase in the quantity of goods traded with very little increase in employment in that sector.

In part, this increasing labor productivity can be found reflected in the employment statistics for the sector. Looking only at those engaged in trade (i.e., excluding finance, insurance, real estate, etc.), the proportion of the total who were self-employed fell from 74 percent in 1947 to 67 percent in 1960, implying some shift of workers from small family stores to larger establishments. Furthermore, the share of both women and young people fell, with their sum declining from 14.9 percent to 8.5 percent of total employment in trade. It is clear, though, that these shifts are small relative to the substantial increase in labor productivity over this period. Most probably, the main explanation for the developments during this period lay in the underutilization of capacity in this sector (specifically, underemployment of labor) which prevailed at the beginning of the period. After a modest overexpansion during the decade 1937–47, the sector has gone through a period of "growing to fit its skin." Here is no evidence of excessive expansion of employment.

This discussion helps to put in proper perspective the nationalizations which took place in the commerce sector in 1961. As we saw in Chapter 3, these put under full government ownership the whole

---

[14]This is a quantity index of goods traded. Weights are gross value of output in agriculture and industry, and total value of imports for 1947; these are applied to quantum indices of imports and of output in the two sectors. This formulation assumes that a constant proportion of total output goes through trade channels, which seems reasonable for this period.

[15]$(115/134) \times 100 = 86; 100 - 86 = 14.$

financial sector and all external trade, as well as a few major firms engaged in internal trade. The discussion here should make clear, though, that taking over a few of the largest firms in no sense implies that the commerce sector as a whole is in government hands. Of course, the nationalizations have had an impact on the sector out of all proportion to their share in employment. Government ownership of one large wholesaler permits the authorities to reach a large number of small retailers, controlling their supplies and influencing their prices. Furthermore, setting up a large chain of retail food stores—the so-called "cooperatives"—has had an important impact through the forces of competition on every neighborhood grocery store. The cooperatives have also provided a convenient channel through which the government can sell price-controlled commodities in short supply, such as Ramadan sweets, or (periodically) rice and sugar; in this way the government can be sure that the rationing takes place through longer queues rather than through higher prices. In spite of these facts, it is worth recalling that—at least from an employment point of view, and probably from an income standpoint as well—the overwhelming preponderance of internal trade is still in private hands.

C. TRANSPORT AND COMMUNICATIONS

This is a relatively small component of the total service sector, but its proportional growth has been quite high in recent years. Like commerce, it is made up of a number of rather diverse components. Perhaps the employment figures will be more meaningful if we distinguish between relatively modern, mechanized transport, on the one hand, and the traditional sector, including animal and cart transport, as well as porters, on the other.[16] The figures are as shown in Table 6–8. By far the largest employment increase, both in a proportional sense and as absolute increase, was in the "modern" sector. For this component, there is available a rough index of transport services provided in the economy, which indicates a rise in output of some 41 percent between 1937 and 1947.[17] This implies

---

[16]The "modern" sector includes transport by trains, trams, buses, automobiles, trucks, airplanes, and boats. The treatment of river navigation is debatable; in the figures shown, it is included with the modern sector, since the amount of capital per worker here is normally quite large.

[17]This is based on figures for passenger-kilometers and freight ton-kilometers for railways, paying passengers on trains, licenses issued for buses, trucks, and taxis, weighted by value added in 1950; the Suez Canal is excluded. See J. M. Crawford, *National Income Statistics*, mimeographed report to United Nations Technical Assistance Board, File No. TAA/173/20/06 (1955).

that in this area, as in the commerce sector, there was some decline (about 13 percent) in labor productivity during this period. It is impossible to say anything about the change in output (or, indeed, about the level of output) of the "traditional" transport sector. These figures make it seem likely, however, that to the extent that there was any excessive employment increase (i.e., rising numbers of underemployed workers) in the transport sector, it was primarily in the more mechanized, organized areas of the sector rather than in the numbers of people "walking the streets, ready to carry things" to which reference is usually made.

TABLE 6–8

EMPLOYMENT IN THE TRANSPORT SECTOR, 1937–47

	1937	1947	Percent Increase, 1937–47
"Modern" transport	82,361	131,196	59
"Traditional" transport	45,002	57,199	27
Communications and storage	11,548	14,940	29
Total	138,911	203,335	48

SOURCE: Population censuses.

The 1960 population census follows the international standard industrial classification, with complete figures available only at the two-digit level; therefore, we have to make some rough estimates to continue our former breakdown into mechanized and traditional transport. These figures, which are given in Table 6–9,

TABLE 6–9

EMPLOYMENT IN THE TRANSPORT SECTOR, 1947–60

	1947	1960	Percent Increase, 1947–60
"Modern" transport	131,196	166,600	27
"Traditional" transport	57,199	66,514	16
Communications and storage	14,940	27,096	81
Total	203,335	260,210	28

SOURCE: Population censuses.

indicate that in this period as well, employment in the more modern portions of the sector was expanding faster than in the nonmechanized portion, although the overall growth was slower and the differential not as great as in the earlier decade.

An evaluation of the services performed by the transport sector during this period presents a number of problems. In the first place, any estimates of real income earned or quantum indices of services provided are heavily influenced by the Suez Canal. This entity alone accounted for some 40 percent of value added in transport and communications in 1960, although less than 3 percent of the sector's employment was here. Clearly, the figures will be more meaningful from a productivity point of view if we treat the Canal separately. There is available a quantum index of services performed by the transport sector excluding the Canal, but it runs only to 1954.[18] Thereafter, we must rely on an estimated breakdown of income earned in the transport sector (to exclude the Suez Canal), deflated by changing transport unit costs. This is necessarily quite rough, but perhaps it can serve to give us a general idea of what the developments have been. These two approaches together indicate a 50 percent increase in "output" from 1947 to 1954, and perhaps a further 10 percent increase from 1954 to 1960, or a 60 percent increase over the whole period in the amount of services provided by the "modern" transport sector, implying an increase in labor productivity of some 30 percent.

In the case of the commerce sector, we have attributed the postwar increase in labor productivity primarily to the underutilization of capacity at the beginning of the period; in the case of transport the principal explanation lies in the substantial capital investment which took place during these years. Capital stock estimates have not been made, but some investment figures are available. According to one rough private estimate, investment in equipment for transport and communications amounted to £E53 million between 1947 and 1953, accounting for about 13 percent of total nonresidential gross investment for these years.[19] Official National Planning Committee figures are available for the years since 1952–53; the figures here are substantially higher, due partly to the inclusion of storage with transport and communications (including some small recorded increases in stocks); furthermore, these estimates

[18]This is the implicit index of National Planning Committee, Memo No. 1, specially prepared for the plan; see Appendix Table I–A–5 (pp. 281–85). The underlying statistics are not clear; for the largest component, road transport, the basis indicated is miles traveled in buses, trains, and taxis, but it is doubtful that there are adequate statistics on this. For the period of overlap with the index referred to in n. 17 above, however—1945 to 1951—the agreement is quite good, with Crawford's growth rate estimate being somewhat higher.

[19]S. H. Abdel Rahman, *A Survey of the Foreign Trade of Egypt in the Post-War Period, with Special Reference to Its Impact on the National Economy* (Ph.D. dissertation, Faculty of Commerce, Cairo University, 1959), Appendix C.

include installation costs and constructions in the sector, as well as machinery and equipment. Over the period 1953–54 to 1959–60, they indicate an investment in this sector of £E163 million, representing 20 percent of all investment during these years (once again excluding housing).[20] These figures make clear that there has been a significant reequipping of the transport sector in the postwar period. During the years 1947–55—the period for which detailed, reclassified import statistics are available — imports of transport equipment (excluding passenger cars) were as shown in Table 6–10. These figures suggest that a substantial portion of the capital

TABLE 6–10

AGGREGATE IMPORTS OF
TRANSPORT EQUIPMENT, 1947–55

(£E Million)

Railway and tramway equipment	14.6
Parts for same	2.0
Aviation and navigation equipment	12.2
Parts for same	6.2
Trucks and buses	10.9
Parts for same	19.3
Other vehicles and parts	1.6
Total	66.8

SOURCE: Unpublished study undertaken at the Social Research Center, American University at Cairo; see Appendix V–A–3 (pp. 344–53).

formation in the sector was gross but not net, in the sense that it was necessary to make up for the inadequate maintenance and shortage of parts during the war period; over 40 percent of the imports of transport equipment during this period consisted of spare parts. Investment figures cover too short a period to permit us to compute a stock figure, as we have done for manufacturing; it does seem likely, however, that there was a significant expansion of the capital stock in the transport sector during this period, making possible a substantial increase in the "real output" of the sector (quantity of services provided), in spite of the relatively small employment rise.

D. CONSTRUCTION

Ideally, we should like to break the construction sector into three parts and look at each one separately: residential housing,

---

[20]United Arab Republic, Department of Statistics and Census, *Ten Years of Revolution: Statistical Atlas* (Cairo, July, 1962), Table 11; see Appendix I–A–9 (p. 290).

other buildings (primarily government offices and factories), and all other construction work (transport facilities, dams and irrigation works, etc.). In practice, we can only make this breakdown in very rough terms, but it seems important to see which of these components was responsible for the very high rate of growth of output in this sector in recent years.[21]

In terms of employment, the great majority of the workers in the sector—over 80 percent in 1960 and close to 70 percent in earlier censuses—were engaged in the construction of buildings. Civilian construction had been sharply restricted during World War II, as the limited supply of materials was channeled primarily to the military authorities. In the immediate postwar years the sector expanded rapidly, with total production in the years 1948–50 attaining a level more than double that of 1945–47.[22] It is not clear what portion of this increase was in residential construction, as opposed to other types of buildings; it seems likely, though, that the main expansion was in the construction of houses and apartment buildings, to make up for the failure of housing to expand with the population and with increasing urbanization during the war years.[23] From 1949 to 1954, when this series of estimates stops, construction of buildings showed substantial year-to-year variations but no clear trend up or down.

The figures on construction activities other than building are less satisfactory. In the National Planning Committee memo referred to above (see note 18), there is a large category, construction connected with agriculture; this seems to have been estimated to be equal to government wage payments in certain irrigation projects. The extremely erratic behavior of this series, falling from £E13 million in 1948 down to £E3 million in 1950, and rising back to £E19 million in 1951, makes one suspicious of the figures; perhaps the fairest conclusion would be that there was a substantial amount

---

[21]In the period 1959–60 to 1962–63 the indicated growth rate of real product in this sector, 13.8 percent per annum, is exaggerated by inadequate adjustment for price increases; but even from 1952–53 to 1959–60, when this bias was probably not present, the 7.7 percent per annum growth rate in construction was the highest of any sector in the economy; see Table 3–2 (p. 45).

[22]This is shown in an index based on quantities of building materials used in the sector; see Appendix Table I–A–5, item 501 (p. 283).

[23]Abdel Rahman estimated that 81¼ percent of all private construction during this period was residential, but his justification for this assumption is extremely weak; see Abdel Rahman, *op. cit.*, Appendix B.

of work done on the irrigation system during this period;[24] if this work is considered as part of the construction sector, the construction of buildings accounts for barely half of total value added in the sector, although it still is by far the most important source of expansion in the sector.

During the years 1952–55, investment in housing accounted for one third of all capital formation in the country.[25] A substantial portion of this housing seems to have been in luxury apartments, which the authorities considered to be a misallocation of resources. In 1956, all construction or major alteration of buildings was made subject to license; the goal seems to have been to cut down on private investment in housing and to redirect the remaining funds into low-cost units. The first target was more fully met than the second; the total cost of authorized construction fell by over 25 percent from 1956 to 1957, while the average cost per room declined by less than 10 percent.[26] In 1958 the authorities took the further step of proclaiming a 20 percent reduction in rents of all buildings constructed after the revolution. At the same time, the government began a program of constructing low-cost popular housing. It is the anticipated expansion in this item which accounts for the substantial prospective increase in investment in housing during the planning period, as seen in Appendix Table I–A–9 (page 290), although reports from the Federation of Egyptian Industries indicate that this program is far behind schedule, with actual investments substantially lower than the planned levels.[27]

For the period since 1954, the major increases in output of the construction sector have come during two periods: 1956–58, when production grew by nearly 40 percent; and 1960–62, when the figures indicate a further rise of over 50 percent. This growth should be reflected in the data on capital formation in the various sectors (see Appendix Table I–A–9 [page 290]). For the earlier of these

---

[24]The length of canals and drains in the country (in kilometers) rose as follows:

1945	33,305
1950	35,238
1954	36,378

[25]See Appendix Table I–A–9 (p. 290).

[26]See Federation of Egyptian Industries, *Annuaire, 1957–58* (Cairo, 1958), p. 118; also P. K. O'Brien, *The Revolution in Egypt's Economic System, 1952–1965* (London: Oxford University Press, 1966).

[27]Federation of Industries in the United Arab Republic, *Yearbook* (Cairo, July, 1962), pp. 115–116.

two periods of growth, no such reflection appears. As we have seen, investment in housing reached a peak in 1955–56, declining somewhat thereafter;[28] neither in irrigation, in industry, nor in public services was there any significant expansion of investments during the period 1956–58. One possible explanation might involve the construction of military installations during this period of invasion and consequent intensification of military activity. Outside of this, the sharp increase in construction activity seems difficult to reconcile with the investment statistics.

During the planning period, since 1960, the rapid growth of the construction sector looks more plausible when compared with the investment data, although, as we have indicated, the growth rate is probably somewhat exaggerated. This increase was associated with the very rapid expansion of the industrial sector, along with heavy investments in transport, primarily railways and roads. Construction activity connected with the High Dam began to assume some importance during this period, although it was not the major source of growth in the sector at least through 1962–63 (see Appendix Table I–A–9 [page 290]).

On the whole, it seems that the construction sector has contributed in a healthy way to the overall growth of the economy. In the late 1940's the emphasis was on housing, to make good the accumulated shortages resulting from the war. When this construction shifted more toward luxury housing in the years after the revolution, the government took steps to channel resources into lower cost housing and other types of construction work more directly related to the development efforts. Although the real product figures for this sector look somewhat suspect, it seems clear that the increase in output was substantially higher than the 45 percent increase in employment in the sector between 1947 and 1960; it probably remains true that this sector has had a higher rate of growth of output than any other component of the national product.

E. PERSONAL AND OTHER SERVICES

Following the international standard industrial classification, the definition of "personal services" used in Egypt is a rather restrictive one; it excludes, for example, many professional services, such as medicine and law (which, in our breakdown in Table 6–1, are included under item E, "other services"). In 1947 the major com-

---

[28]See Appendix Table I–A–9 (p. 290).

ponents included in this sector were paid household servants (50 percent); tailoring (18 percent); hotels, bars, and restaurants (13 percent); and hairdressing (11 percent). The remainder were in such lines as clothes washing and ironing, shoe polishing, and entertainment. The pattern in 1960 was approximately the same, although domestic servants seem to have dropped somewhat, both relatively and absolutely.

For this sector the employment figures in Table 6–1 become more meaningful if we break the total down by age and sex, as shown in Table 6–11. Over the decade 1937–47, when the

TABLE 6–11

EMPLOYMENT IN PERSONAL SERVICES

	1937	1947	1960
Employment of males:			
Under 15......................	25,155	48,741	29,333
15 and over..................	229,108	285,246	367,748
Employment of females...........	72,436	139,821	169,946
Total employment..........	326,699	473,808	567,027

SOURCE: Population censuses.

largest expansion in the sector took place, less than 40 percent of the new jobs were held by men; nearly 50 percent of the increase in employment went to female workers, the remainder being young boys. The later period was quite different in this respect, with nearly 90 percent of all new jobs going to adult males. The marked expansion of employment here, most of which was in the category "personal services not elsewhere classified," seems to be a clear case of the spread of agricultural underemployment into the services. On the one hand, it is not uncommon for better-off Egyptians with a social conscience to employ more servants than they feel they need, in a conscious desire to help people who would otherwise either remain unemployed or fall back into the agricultural sector. Alongside this, there is substantial social pressure not to do any task oneself which one might hire a less skilled person to do; it is considered distinctly antisocial, almost immoral, for any person who owns a car not to pay someone to wash it regularly (and perhaps to drive it as well), or for a person of middle-class standing or above not to have constantly and immaculately shined shoes (not, of course, shined by himself); household tasks are highly specialized, so that cooks are generally not expected to clean house, while nannies and doormen are specialized—if not skilled—jobs. In short, the result of the general overpopulation of the country is that all pressures are aimed at finding new ways of absorbing more workers into personal services. Surely, most of these new workers—94,000 from 1947 to 1960, of whom nearly 90 percent were men—had little to add to the real value of the services performed in the economy during this period.

With regard to the category "other services," in the earlier censuses this is simply a residual figure. As such, no significance should be attached to the fluctuating level of employment in this group. We can form some idea of its composition from the figures for 1960, which are not derived residually. The major components are religious organizations, business services (including law), and recreation. In the earlier years, we have also included in this category the employment of Egyptians by the British forces in Egypt; this group reached 45,000 workers in 1947, accounting in large part for the high figure in that year. The category is of no particular analytical interest.

F. CONCLUSIONS

In this chapter, we examined the various components of the service sector, to see how each has developed over the past twenty-five years. We found evidence that in some of these areas, labor productivity has risen noticeably in the last decade; in others, specifically in the government and in personal services, no acceptable measure is available, but it seems likely that employment has expanded substantially more than the services which were provided. The figures in Tables 2–9 and 6–1 (pages 33 and 132) indicate that from 1947 to 1960, 80 percent of the increase in employment in the services and nearly 50 percent of the total employment increase in the whole economy was in these two areas.

In Chapter 2, we found that since the late 1930's, a high proportion of new job seekers have moved away from their traditional pursuits in agriculture, turning instead for employment to service lines, both in rural and in urban areas. We posed the question in that chapter as to whether this expansion of the services was primarily a demand or a supply phenomenon. This is a question which cannot be answered in any analytically precise way; for a potential employee to find a job, he must want to work at the going wage rate (the "supply side"), and an employer must be willing to hire him (the "demand side"). Still, the distinction does have some intuitive appeal. Perhaps we can rephrase it by asking whether the demand for the worker existed independently of the supply, or whether the employer took on the new worker "out of the kindness of his heart," to help him out, or to keep him from the ranks of the unemployed. The fact that over 80 percent of the expansion in employment in the services was in the government sector and in personal services makes this second, "supply-induced" expansion seem quite plausible.[29] The general picture is similar to that in many underdeveloped countries: A high and rising differential between agricultural and industrial wage rates draws people into the large provincial towns and major urban centers far in excess of the numbers that can be absorbed in a rapidly growing but relatively small industrial sector; a serious problem of extensive urban unemployment is avoided only because of the substantial increase in employment by the government, paid for to a significant extent by borrowing from the Central Bank. Thus the problem of urban unemployment is attenuated, but only at the cost of creating a new problem of excess aggregate demand. The impact of these growing demand pressures on the balance of payments, and on the levels of domestic savings and prices, will be among the recurrent themes in the remainder of this study.

[29]In the case of small-scale activities with a high degree of self-employment in areas of "traditional" transport and trade as well, it seem clear that supply creates its own demand (for workers).

International Trade

For many types of economic analysis, it is wise advice for an understanding of the whole economy to "keep your eye on the margin"; it is here that supply and demand configurations show themselves in determining commodity prices, that factors of production are allocated and their rates of return set. In a sense, the foreign trade of a country is one aspect of its margin, reflecting excess supplies and demands in commodity as well as factor markets. In earlier chapters, we indicated how developments in several specific sectors have spilled over here; now, we must take a more general look at Egypt's changing international economic situation.

A. BEFORE 1952

During the 1930's, Egypt's trade position showed a continuing merchandise deficit averaging close to £E1 million per year, virtually all of which was covered by net exports of specie. While full balance-of-payments estimates are not available for this period, it seems likely that invisibles and capital account items other than specie were relatively minor during this period.[1] This did not mean that there was perfect equilibrium every year; the merchandise account showed a surplus of £E4 million in 1935 and a deficit of

---

[1]Tadros indicates that by this period, many of the external assets accumulated during World War I had been repatriated, so that both foreign assets and external public debt were reduced. See H. Tadros, "The Balance of Payments," in Institut des Etudes Bancaires, *Série de Conférences Données durant la deuxième Année* (Cairo: Imprimerie Mondiale, 1956), pp. 6–7.

£E6 million in 1938, a swing equal to some 30 percent of imports during this period. Still, it seems fair to say that the balance of payments was not a serious problem. Customs duties were raised somewhat, both for increased revenue and for protective purposes; but except for this, trade was free of restrictions and controls.

During the war years, Egypt's trade situation was changed in a number of ways. On the one hand, shipping problems made it much more difficult to export, while rising needs for food at home for the British troops in the country brought about a reallocation of land from cotton primarily to wheat and a fall in food exports below the small figures attained in the 1930's. The result was that in spite of a general and substantial price rise, the average annual export value for 1940–44 was some 30 percent below the level for the preceding quinquennium. In the case of imports, on the other hand, the need to supply the troops was stronger than the problems of shipping restrictions; import values rose by some 20 percent over the same period, with the increases heavily concentrated in the categories of food, drink, and tobacco, and mineral fuels. During the war years, Egypt's merchandise deficit cumulated to some £E100 million. This figure was offset, however, by a massive inflow of funds to finance the British military expenditures; this has been estimated at £E550 million.[2] The result was that in spite of a large trade deficit, Egypt emerged from the war with sterling balances of approximately £440 million,[3] a sum equal to more than 80 percent of gross national product in 1945, and some ten times the (admittedly abnormally low) imports of that year. As we shall see, these balances were of major importance in covering the country's payments deficits up through the late 1950's, when they were finally exhausted.

In the years immediately after the war, imports into Egypt skyrocketed. Perhaps this phenomenon can best be highlighted by referring to Table 7–1. As this table shows, during the first three years after the war the rise in imports was equal to some 60 percent of the increase in GNP. Clearly, this was not a movement along a long-run import demand function but a rush to get onto this function after having been well below it as a result of the shortage of imports for nonmilitary purposes during the war. By 1948 the situation seems to have stabilized somewhat, with both average and marginal propensity to import just over 20 percent, and an income elasticity of demand for imports very close to one. The same picture can be seen with regard to imports of consumer goods; after being

---

[2] *Ibid.*
[3] National Bank of Egypt, *Economic Bulletin*, Vol. I, No. 1 (1948), p. 10.

artificially low at the war's end, these imports rose rapidly to approximately 14 percent of private consumption spending, staying close to that level through 1951. As we shall see, this was a period

TABLE 7–1

IMPORT PROPENSITIES IN THE EARLY POSTWAR PERIOD

	Income $Y*$ ($£E$ Million)	Imports $M†$ ($£E$ Million)	M/Y	$\Delta M/\Delta Y$	$E‡$
1945	552	60	0.11		
				0.61	5.6
1948	718	161	0.22		
				0.26	1.1
1951	1016	237	0.23		

	Consumption C ($£E$ Million)	Consumer Goods Imports Mc ($£E$ Million)	Mc/C	$\Delta Mc/\Delta C$	$E§$
1945	409	23	0.06		
				0.43	7.6
1948	521	71	0.14		
				0.14	1.0
1951	748	102	0.14		

*Gross national product at current market prices.
†Excluding gold.
‡Income elasticity of imports.
§Elasticity of consumer goods imports with respect to total consumer spending.
SOURCES: For income and total imports, see Appendix Tables I–A–2 (pp. 272–73) and V–A–3 (pp. 344–53). For total consumption expenditures, see Table 9–1 (p. 216). For consumer goods imports, see Appendix Table V–A–3 (pp. 344–53) and Table 7–7 (p. 171).

when imports, at least from the sterling area, were quite free of controls; full licensing was instituted for a brief period after Egypt left the sterling area in 1947, but this was soon found to be unnecessary and was abandoned. Thus, these relationships give us a free trade base with which we can compare the structure and level of imports after controls were instituted in 1952.

Turning to Egypt's sales abroad, for the last century the country's exports have been dominated by one product, cotton. The share of raw cotton in total exports of the country developed as follows:

1907–9	95 percent
1917–19	92
1927–29	81
1937–39	73
1947–49	80
1957–59	71
1963	54

This high dependence on one crop leaves Egypt's trade balance very much at the mercy of fluctuations both in supply and in demand for the product. From 1949 to 1950, when cotton prices rose sharply, the total value of Egyptian exports increased by nearly 30 percent; in 1961, when insects damaged a large part of the crop, total exports fell by 20 percent. In both cases the fluctuating earnings from cotton were larger in absolute terms than the variation of total exports. From a foreign trade point of view, Egypt clearly qualifies as an unstable, one-crop economy, although, as we have seen, the place of this commodity in the whole economy is perhaps smaller than in most countries for which this description is used.

In the early postwar years, Egyptian cotton exports were influenced by three factors. The first was a sharp rise in the price of cotton relative to other crops; as Chart 7–1 shows, the relative

CHART 7–1

AREA AND PRICE RATIOS OF COTTON AND OTHER CROPS

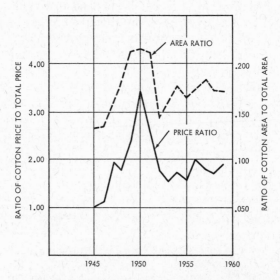

Notes and Sources: Data refer to ratio of a cotton price index to a Laspeyres price index of the 10 major other crops, and the ratio of cotton area to total area planted with these 11 crops. Area figures are lagged one year; i.e., 1945 shows price ratio for 1945 and area ratio for 1946. See *Annuaire Statistique*, various issues.

price of cotton more than tripled from 1945 to 1950. Even up to 1949, before the Korean boom, this relative price had risen by some 150 percent. Clearly, there was a strong inducement for farmers to shift as much of their land as possible into cotton. This is indeed reflected in the area figures, also shown in Chart 7–1. The result was that the average annual volume of cotton produced in 1948–50 was 50 percent above the 1945–47 average, and more than twice the level in the years 1942–44.

There has been some discussion in the literature as to whether Egyptian farmers are or are not sensitive to relative price changes. Stern has presented figures similar to those underlying Chart 7–1, and has concluded that "although it has not been possible to obtain a unique estimate in which one may have complete confidence, an elasticity coefficient somewhere between .40 and .60 may not be too wide of the mark."[4] This conclusion needs to be qualified somewhat, for two reasons. The first is that during most of the postwar period, there have been government controls on how much land is to be devoted to what crops.[5] It is true that these controls have not always been very effective; yet the fact that there were some years with no controls (e.g., 1950–51), while in other years there were changing limits on the amount of land that could legally be planted with cotton, means that his attempted measurement of the free price responsiveness of farmers is not so relevant to the present —or even postwar—situation. Furthermore, it may be worth pointing out that even in periods when the relative price of cotton was not abnormally high, cotton still yielded a substantially higher income per feddan, net of production costs, than most other field crops.[6] We argued in Chapter 4 that the necessity of maintaining a regular pattern of crop rotation puts an upper limit on the extent to which cotton can be substituted for other crops without destroying the fertility of the soil. It might be that a sharp increase in cotton prices would induce farmers to break their traditional rotation patterns, in the hope that the increased income from added cotton output at high current prices would outweigh the lower income from smaller yields in following years. The result would be a short-run measure

[4]R. M. Stern, "The Price Responsiveness of Egyptian Cotton Producers," *Kyklos,* Vol. XII, Fasc. 3 (1959), p. 383. Stern was criticizing an earlier article in the same journal which asserted that farmers in Egypt and the Sudan were not responsive to price changes; see R. S. Porter, "Comment," *Kyklos,* Vol. XI, Fasc. 2 (1958), pp. 231–43.

[5]Stern's "scatter" of arc elasticities, on which the quoted estimates are based, refer to the period 1899–1900 to 1937–38; he discusses the impact of instituting or eliminating controls in specific years during that period, but does not mention the growing importance of these controls in his discussion of the postwar period.

[6]See National Bank of Egypt, *Economic Bulletin,* Vol. XIV, No. 2 (1961), p. 190; also C. Issawi, *Egypt in Revolution: An Economic Analysis* (New York: Oxford University Press, 1963), p. 140.

of supply elasticity substantially larger than the longer run figure.[7] Stern's data, as well as the figures illustrated in Chart 7–1, make clear that Egyptian farmers do vary their planting in response to changing relative prices, although estimation of a specific measure of supply elasticity does not seem feasible. In any case the sharp rise in cotton prices, along with the relaxation and—for two years— removal of acreage controls, are primarily responsible for the large increase in cotton production during the period 1945–51. Domestic consumption of raw cotton for the production of yarn and cotton textiles rose little during this period, with the share of these uses in total raw cotton production falling from 20 percent to close to 15 percent. Furthermore, current production was supplemented by sales from the very large stocks accumulated during the war when exporting was difficult. In 1945 the carry-over of stock was equal to some 170 percent of the total crop of that year; by 1950, this inventory had been virtually eliminated. With cotton production nearly doubling and heavily supplemented by the drawing-down of accumulated stocks, at the same time that world cotton prices were tripling, Egypt's export receipts skyrocketd. Furthermore, the rough statistics which are available indicate that not only did cotton prices rise relative to those of other domestic crops; they also increased substantially relative to the price of Egypt's imports.[8] From 1945 to 1948, the terms of trade of the country improved by 80 percent, and at their peak in 1951 the relative price of the country's exports was nearly three times the level of 1945.

Before commenting on the full balance of payments during this period, perhaps we should say a word about the other components of the export list besides raw cotton. As we have indicated, the importance of this group rose from barely 5 percent of total exports at the turn of the century to over 40 percent in recent years. Table 7–2 gives a breakdown of the major components. In the early postwar years, noncotton exports were dominated by rice. This crop is a heavy user of water, and the area which could be devoted to it varied widely as a result of interyear differences in the height of the Nile flood; the average figures shown here conceal the large

---

[7]It might be noted in passing that Stern's supply elasticity measure is not comparable to the usual concept; his quantity component does not refer to cotton supply, or even to the area devoted to cotton production, but rather to the ratio of the cotton area to the area under other crops. A 1 percent increase in cotton area, for example, would result in a 1.4 percent increase in this measure.

[8]Import and export price indices are presented and discussed in Appendix Table V–A–7 (p. 363).

annual fluctuations in this item. Aside from rice, the only export categories of any significance were onions, and fuel and diesel oils. Manufactured textile products, particularly cotton yarn, were catapulted into the world market by the Korean boom. Other export categories were of minor importance during this period.

TABLE 7–2

EGYPTIAN EXPORTS, BY TYPES OF GOODS

(Average of Annual Figures, in £E Million)

	1937–39	1947–49	1957–59	1963
Raw materials (except cotton)	4.9	16.1	21.6	39.5
Food	2.2	14.4	16.5	34.6
Nonfood	2.7	1.7	5.2	4.9
Manufactured cotton products	1.3	1.7	11.1	27.2
Mineral fuels	0.4	1.5	4.0	20.1
Others, except raw cotton	2.8	5.5	10.6	19.0
Subtotal	9.5	24.8	47.3	105.8
Raw cotton	24.9	96.0	114.7	121.0
Total exports	34.4	120.8	162.0	226.8

SOURCE: Appendix Table V–A–3 (p. 000); data in *Annuaire Statistique, 1960–61*, pp. 370–71; and United Arab Republic, Ministry of the Treasury, *The Budget Report for the Fiscal Year July 1960–June 1961*, (Cairo, 1960), p. 136; Central Bank of Egypt, *Economic Review*, Vol. IV, No. 1 (1964), p. 102. Totals may not add due to rounding.

Let us turn to the full balance of payments of the country. The detailed annual figures are presented in Appendix Table V–C–1 (page 377); for our purposes the most important features of the period are brought out in Table 7–3, which shows the aggregate

TABLE 7–3

AGGREGATE BALANCE-OF-PAYMENTS FLOWS, 1946–51

(£E Million)

Trade deficit	−194.5
Export surplus of services	135.1
Balance on current account	− 59.4
Long-term capital outflow	− 34.1
To be financed	− 93.5
Reduction in sterling assets	−159.7
Increased holdings of foreign exchange and gold	86.4
Increase in other short-term liabilities	− 8.6
Net errors and omissions	− 11.6
Total financing	− 93.5

flows over the years 1946–51. The general picture is quite clear. In spite of the very substantial increase in exports to which we have referred, imports increased even more rapidly, so that over the years 1946–51 Egypt had a cumulative trade deficit of nearly £E200 million. A substantial part of this deficit was offset by the country's earnings from invisible exports, by far the most important component of which was expenditure in the country by the British army. As a result, the current account deficit was only £E60 million over these six years. As Table 7–3 shows, the sterling balances made available to the country and drawn upon during this period were large enough not only to cover this current account deficit, but also to finance a sizable private capital outflow, as well as permitting a substantial increase in the country's holdings of other foreign assets and gold.

It is perhaps generally accepted that the releasing of blocked sterling balances was quite liberal, "so liberal, in fact, as to put a severe strain on the British economy—and when the allowable releases were overdrawn, as by India in 1948–9, a new, more liberal agreement was promptly negotiated."[9] If this was true of the four countries within the sterling area whose balances were blocked, it seems to have been equally true of Egypt, in spite of her departure from the sterling area at the time of the abortive convertibility attempt in July, 1947. "The Egyptian negotiations left those Sterling Area countries whose balances had been officially blocked with little reason to believe that membership had yielded much, if any, advantage in their sterling balance treatment."[10] It is true that the fact that the balances could not be used for purchases from "American account" or "bilateral" countries (which included France) was a severe restriction; yet this had nothing to do with the blocking, which was concerned with purchases within the sterling area and, in the case of Egypt, from "transferable account" countries.[11] When Egypt left the sterling area in July, 1947, import and export licensing was extended to cover all trade with sterling area countries. "It was found, however, that very little of the released sterling was utilized. After further sums were released (at the beginning of 1948) controls were relaxed," and by March, 1948, "all restrictions were removed on goods imported from Scheduled countries (the "Sterling Area") and from countries accepting payment in transferable sterling, provided the goods were produced in that country."[12] This widespread freedom of trade was maintained throughout

---

[9]P. W. Bell, *The Sterling Area in the Postwar World* (Oxford: Clarendon Press, 1956), p. 25.

[10]*Ibid.*, p. 26.

[11]For a thorough discussion of this subject, see *ibid.*, chaps. ii–iii.

[12]National Bank of Egypt, *Economic Bulletin*, Vol. I, No. 1 (1948), p. 36.

this period, until drastic control measures forced themselves on the authorities in 1952.

B. 1952 AND THEREAFTER

1. Merchandise Trade

Since the end of 1951, Egypt's balance-of-payments situation has been fundamentally different in a number of ways. The export quantum index, which had doubled from 1945 to 1950, dropped by 30 percent in the following two years, growing only slowly thereafter so that the 1950 level was not reattained until 1960 (see Appendix Table V–A–9 [page 364]). With regard to the prices of traded commodities, the country was hit very hard by the sudden drop in the cotton price in 1952; since that year, the terms of trade of the country have remained fairly steady, some 40 percent below the peak level attained in 1951. With both export quantum and net

TABLE 7–4

INCOME TERMS OF TRADE

(Value of Exports in £E Million, Excluding Reexports
and Gold, Divided by Import Price Index, with
1938 = 100)

1948	46.4	1956	34.9
1949	44.8	1957	40.0
1950	56.4	1958	41.1
1951	57.5	1959	43.6
1952	34.3	1960	51.7
1953	33.8	1961	43.4
1954	35.2	1962	41.6
1955	34.5	1963	58.4

SOURCE: Appendix Tables V–A–4 (pp. 354–57), V–A–5 (p. 358), and V–A–7 (p. 363). B. Hansen and G. Marzouk, *Development and Economic Policy in the U.A.R. (Egypt)* (Amsterdam: North-Holland Publishing Co., 1965) have extended the official indices to 1960, as follows (1953 = 100): $Px = 113$; $Qx = 120$; $Pm = 92$; $Qm = 140$. Since 1960, we have assumed that the foreign price of Egypt's imports remained unchanged, but that devaluation raised the domestic price of these goods by 5 percent. This is applied in full to 1963 and to seven months of 1962.

barter terms of trade showing only slight upward trends, the income terms of trade of the country—the real quantity of imports which could be purchased from the proceeds of the country's exports—dropped by 40 percent from 1951 to 1952, and have risen only gradually since then; it seems probable that it was only in 1963 that they reattained the 1950–51 levels. It is true that real national income dropped as well from 1950–51 to 1952–53; yet this fall in real income seems to have been only about 10 percent, far smaller than the decrease in the real purchasing power (in terms of imports) of the country's exports. Clearly, there had to be some fundamental readjustments in the economy as a result of this sharp decrease in the country's capacity to import.

The figures in Table 7–4 become more revealing—one might say depressing—if they are put into a longer term historical context. Egypt's official import price index reaches back only to 1938; Issawi has suggested that we can get a measure of the price of the country's imports by looking at the price index of exports of British manufactured goods.[13] On this basis, the long-run income terms of trade comparable to the more recent figures in Table 7–4 are as shown in Table 7–5. These figures make it all too clear that there has been

TABLE 7–5

LONG-RUN DEVELOPMENTS IN THE
INCOME TERMS OF TRADE
(£E Million at 1938 Prices)

1903–7	38.4
1908–12	43.6
1913–17	37.7
1918–22	29.4
1923–27	41.9
1928–32	35.7
1933–37	36.3
1938–42	15.2
1943–47	16.4

SOURCE: C. Issawi, *Egypt in Revolution: An Economic Analysis* (New York: Oxford University Press, 1963), p. 28. In principle, these figures are fully comparable to those in Table 7–4.

no real long-run upward trend in the quantity of imports that Egypt could purchase with her commodity exports; the income terms of trade were virtually the same in 1957–59 as just before World War I or in the middle twenties. We are struck once again by the nature of the structural transformation which has taken place, for

---

[13]As we shall see in Appendix Tables V–A–7 and V–A–8 (p. 363), there are two alternative import price indices available with which we might deflate export values; since none of these seems inherently more reliable, and since (as we indicate in the Appendix) they all show roughly the same pattern, we have used Issawi's figures in the interest of convenience.

over this fifty-year period the real income of the country probably rose by close to 150 percent.[14]

With raw cotton continuing to dominate Egypt's exports, it is not surprising that the main source of the country's disappointing export performance can be traced back to this one crop. Let us turn for a moment to look at Egypt's place in the world cotton market. The salient features are brought out in Table 7–6. The main points to be noticed can be summarized briefly. While total world production of cotton rose by 50 percent in the twenty years from the late 1930's to the late 1950's, production of long-staple cotton, where nearly 70 percent of Egyptian production was concentrated in the 1930's, has stagnated. On the other hand, the market for extra-long staples has risen extremely rapidly. This is quite a specialized market, with the output going to such lines as automobile tires and shoelaces, as well as high-quality cotton textiles. Since Egypt produced some 70 percent of world output of extra-long-staple cotton in the 1930's, the rapid growth here has been a great boon to the country's exports. In view of these divergent trends in world demand, it is not surprising that there was a marked shift in Egypt from long- to extra-long-staple cotton. In spite of this shift, Egypt has not maintained her share of the extra-long-staple market; in recent years, her chief competition here has come from the Gezira area of the Sudan. With output from that area expected to expand further in the future, this competition is bound to intensify. Perhaps more significant is the fact that in virtually all of the major and fastest growing export markets for extra-long-staple cotton in the non-Communist world, the Sudan has now replaced Egypt as the dominant supplier. In 1962–63, the year after Egypt's disastrous crop failure, the Sudan's exports of extra-long-staple cotton were larger than Egypt's to West Germany, India, Italy, Japan, and the United Kingdom. Outside of the Communist bloc countries, only in France and the United States was Egypt still dominant; and in these two countries as well, the gap was closing.[15] This may well be partly a temporary phenomenon, resulting from the need to rebuild inventories after

---

[14]Aggregate real income may have risen by some 25 percent from pre-World War I to the late thirties, stayed unchanged from then to 1945, and approximately doubled from 1945 to 1960. See Hansen and Mead, *The National Income of the U.A.R. (Egypt), 1939–1962*, Memo No. 355 (Cairo: Institute of National Planning, July, 1963); and Appendix Tables I–A–5 (pp. 281–85) and I–A–8 (pp. 288–89).

[15]The picture is basically the same for 1963–64, although in this year United Arab Republic cotton recaptured the lead over the Sudan in the Indian market.

TABLE 7-6

WORLD COTTON PRODUCTION AND EGYPT'S PLACE IN IT

	1924-25 to 1928-29	1929-30 to 1933-34	1934-35 to 1938-39	1939-40 to 1944-45	1945-46 to 1951-52	1952-53 to 1957-58	1958-59 to 1960-61	1964-65†
Thousands of metric tons (annual averages):								
1. Total production..........	5,887	5,957	6,664	6,053	6,228	9,068	10,085	11,270
2. Egyptian share............	333	330	401	290	333	363	460	504
3. Long-staple*.............	n.a.	n.a.	664	n.a.	426	566	607	687
4. Egyptian share...........	n.a.	n.a.	274	n.a.	196	219	222	273
5. Extra-long-staple*.........	n.a.	n.a.	179	n.a.	209	268	413	451
6. Egyptian share............	n.a.	n.a.	126	n.a.	137	144	238	231
Percentages:								
7. Long-staple in total (3/1) ...			10.0		6.8	6.2	6.0	6.1
8. Extra-long-staple cotton in total (5/1).............			2.7		3.4	3.0	4.1	4.0
9. Egypt's share of long-staple cotton (4/3).........			41.3		46.0	38.7	36.6	39.7
10. Egypt's share of extra-long-staple cotton (6/5)...			70.4		65.6	53.7	57.9	51.2
11. Long-staple cotton in Egyptian production (4/2)....			68.3		58.9	60.3	48.3	54.2
12. Extra-long-staple cotton in Egyptian production (6/2)			31.4		41.1	39.7	51.7	45.8

*Excluding the USSR, mainland China, and eastern Europe.
†Preliminary.
SOURCE: International Cotton Advisory Committee, *Cotton—World Statistics* (Special Base Book Issue), Vol. XVI, Nos. 9–10, Part II (April, 1963); *ibid.* (Quarterly Bulletin), Vol. XIX, No. 3, Part II (October, 1965).

the 1961–62 crop failure, yet the seeking-out of new sources of supply by importers may well have resulted in a shift which it is difficult if not impossible to reverse.[16] These facts clearly do not present a very bright outlook. Egypt's cotton exports are concentrated in long staples, where world consumption today is at about the same level as in the 1930's, and in extra-long-staples, where she still produces more than 50 percent of world output, but where her southern neighbor has succeeded—at least temporarily—in displacing her from her dominant position in virtually all of the major markets of the non-Communist world.

While raw cotton continues to be the most important single item in the export list, Table 7–2 indicates that during the 1950's, and at an accelerated rate since then, other exports have made a growing contribution to the foreign exchange needs of the country. In the food category the most important item continues to be rice. Although there is no evidence to date of any lessening of the wide annual variations in supply—rice exports reached £E14.5 million in 1958 but were only £E1.9 million the following year—the greater stabilization of water flow resulting from the High Dam at Aswan should make possible a more regular and substantial production of this crop. Another hopeful sign is the rise in exports of cotton textiles; in recent years, this category has grown rapidly, with roughly 35 percent in the form of cotton piece goods, the rest as yarn. Egypt's concentration on higher quality long-staple cottons has permitted the country to establish a differentiated product in the world scramble for cotton textile markets, although import quotas in the United States and western Europe limit any increase in sales to these countries. Exports of mineral fuels have grown at an impressive rate in recent years, and although this is principally crude oil, in 1963 some 25 percent was refined in Egypt before export. It is true that the country is still a fairly sizable net importer of fuels, but this gap has been narrowing in recent years, and the country hopes to attain self-sufficiency in this area in the near future, in spite of increasing domestic fuel consumption.[17] Outside of these

---

[16]From 1960–61 to 1961–62 the increase in production of extra-long-staple cotton in the Sudan (94,000 metric tons) was larger than the concurrent fall in Egyptian output due to crop failure (89,000 metric tons). The Sudan did not maintain this high a level of output, but its share in this market has clearly been given a boost. See International Cotton Advisory Committee, *Cotton— World Statistics,* Vol. XVII, No. 3, Part II (October, 1963), p. 20.

[17]The phenomenon of substantial imports as well as exports of crude oil is due to the fact that the local production contains too low a portion of middle derivatives to be processed in Egyptian refineries. Efforts are under way to

(Continued on next page)

lines, Egypt has made some progress in trying to sell abroad the products of her manufacturing sector: cement, furniture, and artificial silks to the other Arab countries, automobile tires to Yugoslavia, and shoes to East Germany. While these and other similar exports are likely to grow in importance in coming years, it seems unrealistic to expect that for some time to come they will be more than a relatively minor supplement to the basic export list of cotton and cotton products, food and other raw materials, and perhaps petroleum.

With foreign exchange receipts rising only slowly at the same time that the development push was gaining momentum, considerable effort was devoted to the control of imports, in an attempt not only to hold down the aggregate level of imports but to change their composition in such a way as to restrict the import of "luxuries." It is quite a hopeless task to try to reclassify trade statistics so as to distinguish between essential and nonessential goods; wheat flour will be a luxury item if used for fancy pastries, a necessity if used for the poor man's bread; an automobile may be used only for pleasure outings, or it may be a business necessity. In Table 7–7, we have presented estimates of one trade breakdown by use, although the examples above should make clear that we cannot associate consumer goods with luxuries and capital goods with necessities. These figures indicate that the sharp drop in imports after the economy was "closed" in 1952 came primarily in the category of food, mainly wheat and flour. From 1948–50 to 1954–55, domestic production of wheat rose by 50 percent, as a result of the reallocation of land from cotton back to wheat, due in turn to both acreage control and the falling price of cotton, absolutely as well as relative to other crops. Other than this category, where agricultural policy was more important than commercial policy, the introduction of extensive trade controls in 1952 seems to have had little immediate impact on the structure of trade. In following years, however, the import needs for capital goods and intermediate products continued to grow rapidly; food requirements continued to rise with the population, and further land could not be spared from cotton without cutting the country's exports and raw cotton supplies for the do-

---

change this situation, making local refineries less dependent on imported crude. For a full discussion of the activities of this sector, see "Oil in the U.A.R.," in Central Bank of Egypt, *Economic Review,* Vol. IV, No. 1 (1964), pp. 9–19. To the extent that the problem concerns the relative demand in the domestic market for fuel oils and more highly refined gasoline, some help could be obtained from the tax structure, by taxing gasoline more lightly while increasing the rate of taxation of middle derivatives.

TABLE 7-7

EGYPTIAN IMPORTS, BY CATEGORIES OF USE

(Value Figures Are Annual Averages, in £E Million)

	1948–50		1954–55		1957–59		1961–63	
	Value	Percent	Value	Percent	Value	Percent	Value	Percent
Consumer goods..........	73.0	41.2	47.3	27.5	56.5	26.3	97.2	30.9
Food...................	32.0	18.1	10.0	5.8	34.4	16.0	66.6	21.2
Nonfood...............	41.0	23.2	37.3	21.7	22.1	10.3	30.6	9.7
Intermediate products...	72.7	41.1	82.9	48.2	91.9	42.7	103.1	32.8
Capital goods..........	28.9	16.3	38.1	22.1	44.6	20.7	80.2	25.5
Others.................	2.5	1.4	3.8	2.2	21.9	10.2	33.9	10.8
Total............	177.0	100.0	172.1	100.0	215.0	100.0	314.4	100.0

NOTE: We have tried to adjust earlier figures to fit the classification of 1961–63, which is taken directly from various issues of the Central Bank's *Economic Review*, and fairly detailed breakdown is available there. Capital goods includes only machinery and parts of all types, transport equipment and parts (including cars). and iron and steel structures. Food excludes beverages. Intermediate food products (e.g., raw sugar, cereals, and wheat flour) are all included with consumer goods. Intermediate products include fertilizers, iron and steel bars and sheets, wood and wood products, petroleum, and tobacco, among others. A footnote in the source of the 1961–63 data indicates that most of the category "others" is thought to consist of capital goods.

SOURCES: 1948–55: Appendix Table V–A–3 (pp. 344–53), adjusted; 1957–59: United Arab Republic, Ministry of the Treasury, *Budget Report for the Fiscal Year July 1960–June 1961*, (Cairo, 1960), pp. 142–45, adjusted; 1961–63: Central Bank of Egypt, *Economic Review*, Statistical Section, various issues.

mestic textile industry. The result was increasing stringency of trade controls, hitting most heavily on nonfood consumer goods such as watches, radios, sewing machines, and household appliances. Import substitution helped here, with the restraining of textile imports and the rising domestic supply of kerosene. The share of capital goods in total imports has increased substantially, particularly if we give much credence to the statement that most of the "other imports" should be included in this category;[18] they may have accounted for as much as a third of total imports in recent years.

TABLE 7–8

RECENT IMPORT PROPENSITIES

	Income Y (£E Million)	Imports M (£E Million)	M/Y	$\Delta M/\Delta Y$	E
1954..........	988	161	0.16		
				0.17	1.0
1960..........	1,414	232	0.16		
				0.36	2.2
1962..........	1,614	303	0.19		

	Consumption C (£E Million)	Consumer Goods Imports Mc (£E Million)	Mc/C	$\Delta Mc/\Delta C$	E
1954..........	697	49	0.07		
				0.02	0.3
1960..........	1,064	58	0.05		
				0.32	5.9
1962..........	1,164	90	0.08		

NOTES AND SOURCES: See Table 7–1. The 1962 import figures are influenced by the 25 percent currency devaluation which took place in May of that year. We might point out as well that the concept of import propensities takes on a rather different meaning in the context of strict government control over all foreign trade.

A comparison of Tables 7–1 and 7–8 indicates that the combination of increasing trade controls and increasing domestic food supplies lowered the import propensities in the economy quite substantially. From 1954 to 1960, imports rose at approximately the same rate as national income. Since 1960, by contrast, imports have been growing considerably more rapidly, with consumer goods playing a major role; from 1960 to 1962, the increase in consumer goods imports provided over 40 percent of the total increase in private consumption. The fact that virtually all of this increase was in the form of wheat and flour, most of which was provided through

---

[18]Central Bank of Egypt, *Economic Review*, Vol. IV, No. 1 (1964), p. 101.

American aid, tells us very little about what the level of consumer goods imports would have been in the absence of this aid. We shall return to this question below.

Egypt's trade pattern sustained a pronounced shift in geographical distribution during the 1950's, reflecting in large part the political crises through which the country went. Already in 1954 the balance had begun to shift away from the sterling area and toward western Europe, particularly France, Germany, and Italy; the Communist bloc accounted for less than 10 percent of the country's trade in that year. During the following three years, Egypt's trade with the bloc grew steadily, receiving the greatest boost from the Suez crisis of 1956, when many of Egypt's traditional markets to the West were closed and assets blocked. As we shall see below, Egypt's trade statistics, based on returns from the customs administration, consistently understate the value of the country's trade with eastern Europe; a somewhat more reliable picture can be obtained by referring to the full current account of the balance of payments, derived from Central Exchange Control statistics.[19] These figures indicate mounting deficits with the West, as exports dropped sharply while imports fell more slowly. It was during this period that the Communist bloc countries, particularly the USSR, moved in as substantial buyers of Egypt's exports; the share of Egypt's total current receipts coming from sales to eastern Europe rose from 10 percent in 1954 to 36 percent in 1957, with a slight decline since then (see Table 7-9).

There were two major and interrelated components to the policies which the government followed in attempting to deal with these disparate developments, both aggregate and regional, in the country's foreign trade. The first amounted, in effect, to a partial devaluation of the currency; the second was the growing reliance on bilateral agreements. It is not necessary for our purposes to trace in detail the various techniques which were used to alter the effective exchange rate of the country.[20] Export accounts, as well as their successor, the import entitlement system, were basically equivalent to a combination of import duties and export subsidies; in 1955, these complex arrangements were replaced by the explicit use of import taxes and export subsidies, later supplemented by a

[19]See pp. 180–84 below.
[20]For a detailed presentation of these techniques, see B. Hansen and G. Marzouk, *Development and Economic Policy in the U.A.R. (Egypt)* (Amsterdam: North-Holland Publishing Co., 1965), chap. vii, sec. 7.3; also I. H. El Isawy, *The Development of the U.A.R.'s Foreign Exchange Policy*, Memo No. 452 (Cairo: Institute of National Planning, June, 1964).

TABLE 7-9

EGYPT'S REGIONAL BALANCE OF PAYMENTS, CURRENT ACCOUNT

	1948*		1954		1957		1963	
	Receipts	*Payments*	*Receipts*	*Payments*	*Receipts*	*Payments*	*Receipts*	*Payments*
Millions of pounds:								
American monetary area	4.5†	12.4†	16.6	19.6	11.7	12.6	33.2	124.5
Sterling area, total	71.6	60.0	71.7	54.5	26.1	20.4	65.0	72.9
(United Kingdom)	(41.8)	(36.6)	(47.5)	(38.8)	(15.6)	(6.9)	(46.0)	(51.5)
Europe:								
Western	29.7	45.1	81.0	100.3	57.9	86.2	86.6	115.9
Eastern	16.5	13.8	21.6	18.3	85.2	84.4	110.6	120.8
Middle East	20.8	41.6	16.3	17.7	33.4	38.0	34.9	26.6
Others			15.0	8.2	22.9	26.8	33.5	26.0
Total	143.1	172.9	222.2	218.6	237.2	268.4	363.8	486.7
Percent of Total:								
American monetary area	3.1	7.2	7.5	9.0	4.9	4.7	9.1	25.6
Sterling area, total	50.0	34.7	32.3	24.9	11.0	7.6	17.9	15.0
(United Kingdom)	(29.2)	(21.2)	(21.4)	(17.8)	(6.6)	(2.6)	(12.6)	(10.6)
Europe:								
Western	20.8	26.1	36.5	45.9	24.4	32.1	23.8	23.8
Eastern	11.5	8.0	9.7	8.4	35.9	31.4	30.4	24.8
Middle East	14.5	24.1	7.3	8.1	14.1	14.2	9.6	5.5
Others			6.8	3.8	9.7	10.0	9.2	5.3
Total	100.0	100.0	100.0	100.0	100.0	100.0	100.0	100.0

*Balance of trade only.
†United States only.
SOURCE: National Bank of Egypt, *Economic Bulletin*, Vol. III, No. 1 (1950), pp. 29–30; Vol. VIII, No. 2 (1955), pp. 98–99; Vol. XI, No. 2 (1958), pp. 146–47; Central Bank of Egypt, *Economic Review*, Vol. IV, No. 2 (1964), pp. 144–45. Totals may not add due to rounding.

variable premium on foreign exchange earnings from exports. The goal of all these policies was not only to halt the deterioration in the overall trade balance, but to use what amounted in effect to multiple exchange rates to encourage exports and discourage imports involving convertible currencies, as well as discriminating against nonessental imports in favor of capital goods and other "necessities."[21] All of these special regulations were finally swept away in 1961 and 1962, when foreign trade was brought fully and directly into the hands of government enterprises (in July, 1961), and variable premiums were eliminated in favor of a new, unified exchange rate of $2.30 per pound, applicable to all transactions except Suez Canal charges and Egyptian dealings with the International Monetary Fund. While this change represents a 19 percent devaluation in the par value of the Egyptian pound, this devaluation was in effect accomplished gradually over the course of the 1950's, so that the impact of the new semiofficial par value in 1962 on the average exchange rate at which trade was effected was minimal. The unification of exchange rates should have had some differential impact, with countries which has previously been discriminated against (i.e., hard-currency countries such as the United States) finding purchases from Egypt more expensive and sales to Egypt somewhat easier. The unification of effective rates had already been generally achieved in 1961, however, while the continuing foreign exchange shortage means that the increased ease of selling is only relative to other foreign countries; the general discrimination in favor of domestic producers remains. This had formerly been expressed as a premium that had to be paid over and above the official exchange rate to purchase foreign currency for imports; now, it is "built in" to the official exchange rate. Except for the differential impact on countries and commodities specially favored or discriminated against before 1962, the effect of the change was relatively minor.[22]

---

[21]For example, at the end of 1959 the system was as follows: "Proceeds in convertible currencies from exports of raw cotton and a few other items received a variable premium, while most other export proceeds in convertible currencies received a fixed premium of 17.5 per cent. Most receipts in convertible currencies from invisibles received a premium of 27.5 per cent. Payments in convertible currencies for all imports and most invisibles were subject to a premium of 27.5 per cent, but half the premium collected for imports of capital goods, raw materials, and foodstuffs was refunded." Hansen and Marzouk, *op. cit.*, p. 197.

[22]Of course, the price of some imported goods did rise somewhat, although not nearly in proportion to the change in par value. Beyond this, the base for ad valorem duties has increased by 25 percent.

In a sense, a continuing payments deficit per se implies an over-valued exchange rate; the question might be asked whether a further devaluation of the Egyptian pound would eliminate the country's external deficit. In international trade theory, the answer to this question depends on a large number of complex variables such as world price elasticity of demand for the country's exports, and domestic import and savings propensities. In the Egyptian case the analysis is considerably simplified by two facts: the price inelasticity of demand for imports, and the price inelasticity of the supply of the major export. The first results from the fact that Egyptian imports have generally been restricted in recent years to three categories: foodstuffs, intermediate inputs to the manufacturing sector, and capital goods. For foods the government's price stabilization and subsidy program would probably prevent any domestic price increase from taking place; for the other two, it seems implausible to expect demand by the nationalized industries to be much influenced by price increases. On the export side, we have seen that there is only limited scope for increasing the area devoted to cotton. This means that potential gains from devaluation are largely confined to other exports for which there might be both elastic world demand and elastic domestic supply. Surely, there are some such commodities; yet the scope for improvement along these lines seems quite limited.[23]

If a variable degree of currency devaluation was one characteristic of Egypt's trade situation since the revolution, a second important characteristic was growing bilateralism. In part, this was a natural result of the increased dealings with the Communist bloc, with consequent need to seek a balance not only in total trade but in component parts. By the end of the 1950's, Egypt's foreign commercial relations were governed by a large network of bilateral trade and payments agreements, covering their trade not only with the Communists bloc nations but also with a number of western countries. Generally, these agreements stated that each country would permit trade (i.e., freely issue import and export licenses) up to some specified value, from a detailed list of commodities; debits and credits would be from a special account set up for this purpose; trade ceilings and swing credits were generally specified; the debtor country was given a limited period (typically six months to one year) in which to settle balances above the credit ceiling,

---

[23] An additional limitation results from the substantial import content of output, particularly in some potential export lines such as the manufacture of tires.

after which time payment could be demanded in convertible currency. It is difficult to specify how much trade took place under these agreements, since not all commodities were included in the accompanying list; what we can say is that in 1959, 80 percent of Egypt's total trade was with countries with which she had such payments agreements.[24]

This trend toward bilateralism is difficult to evaluate, since it is so closely bound up with the shift in trade away from the West to the Communist bloc. It may well be that the bilateral agreements were desired in and of themselves by the Egyptians, perhaps in the belief that they "provided a means of importing without foreign exchange payment";[25] It seems more likely, however, that the first concern was to establish trading relations with the Communist countries, because this was a large potential market for exports which Egypt was having a hard time selling in the open market, and because of the possibility of purchasing strategic goods there which she could not buy from the West. Trade with the eastern bloc was what the Egyptians wanted; bilateralism was a natural concomitant, since virtually all foreign trade of Communist countries is carried out on a strictly bilateral basis. One anticipated benefit from the bilateral agreements must have been highly desirable for the Egyptians: They hoped that it would assure them a dependable and substantial market for their major export. The story is now familiar of Egypt's cotton exported under agreement to Czechoslovakia and reappearing in the market of western Europe to compete with the rest of the crop;[26] yet at the time the agreements were negotiated, there was every hope that this would be a net addition to the demand for Egyptian cotton, an addition which was more dependable in quantity and price than existing markets.[27]

Discussion of the advantages and disadvantages of trade organized so as to be balanced on a bilateral basis with each trading

---

[24]For a listing and description of the agreements in force on April 20, 1959, see National Bank of Egypt, *Economic Bulletin*, Vol. XII, No. 2 (1959), pp. 179–87.

[25]R. F. Mikesell and J. N. Behrman, *Financing Free World Trade with the Sino-Soviet Bloc*, Princeton Studies in International Finance, No. 8 (Princeton: Princeton University Press, 1958), p. 98.

[26]This episode remains one based on unverified rumor, which is not to deny that it is probably true; for a listing of journalistic and commercial rumor sources, see R. L. Allen, *Middle Eastern Economic Relations with the Soviet Union, Eastern Europe and Mainland China* (Charlottesville: University of Virginia Press, 1958), p. 22.

[27]There was a clause in the agreements specifically precluding reexport.

partner generally starts from the presumption that it will succeed. If that is so, it is a straightforward proposition that if we enforce bilateral balance with each trading partner, the gains from trade of the country will be lower than under multilateral trading agreements. One way of expressing this is to say that the necessity of maintaining bilateral balance prevents the country from buying in the cheapest market and selling where prices are highest. Evaluation of bilateralism in Egypt is more complex. On the one hand, as we have indicated, it was largely a by-product of increasing trade with the Communist bloc, and cannot be evaluated apart from that shift, with all the economic and political factors involved. With regard to the trade with the West, it seems that the impact of the bilateral agreements on actual trade flows has been minimal, and that the main factor in evaluating these agreements for Egypt has been the accompanying swing credits; at the end of July, 1960, the latest date for which detailed figures have been published, Egypt's net indebtedness to the five western European countries with which she had such agreements in the clearing accounts set up under the agreements amounted to £E26.5 million.[28] The inefficiencies resulting from any trade distortions due to bilateralism are probably more than offset by this effective capital inflow.

2. Invisible Current Items

In the immediate postwar years, Egypt's balance-of-payments position was considerably strengthened by her substantial invisible exports, particularly in the form of expenditures in the country by British military forces. This item fell sharply after the revolution and disappeared entirely in 1955, when the last British troops were withdrawn from the country. During the early 1950's, toll receipts from the Suez Canal amounted to £E25–30 million; but since a large part of this was remitted overseas as dividends and retained earnings, the net benefit to the country's balance of payments was less than half that figure, representing local expenditures of the company, both current and capital, an annual payment to the Egyptian government, plus any increase in the company's monetary assets retained within the country.[29] After the nationalization, the

---

[28]National Bank of Egypt, *Economic Bulletin*, Vol. XIII, Nos. 3–4 (1960), p. 300. This figure includes a debt of £E14.8 million to Italy, arising largely from a special agreement for the financing of wheat imports.

[29]Prenationalization finances of the Suez Canal Company and their impact on the Egyptian economy are discussed in detail in United Nations, *Economic Developments in the Middle East, 1955–56* (New York, 1957), pp. 101–5; and National Bank of Egypt, *Economic Bulletin*, Vol. IX, No. 3 (1956), pp. 223–27.

situation was strikingly different; the full toll receipts remained in Egypt, with the exception of the compensation payments to former stockholders, amounting to £E4 million per year during the years 1959-63, £E3 million in 1964, and none thereafter.[30] Gross receipts from tolls have more than doubled since their prenationalization levels, reflecting a very rapid increase in the number and size of ships using the canal;[31] by 1963 the gross receipts amounted to over £E70 million, nearly 20 percent of Egypt's total current receipts.

A second invisible export item which grew in importance during this period was tourism. There is a substantial discrepancy between the estimates of foreign exchange receipts from this source made by the Exchange Control authorities, on the one hand, and the Tourist Administration, on the other. There are three main differences between these two estimates: The Tourist Administration's definition includes all visitors staying up to a year, including foreign experts and students, compared to a six-month cutoff for the Central Exchange Control authorities; furthermore, the Central Exchange Control figures exclude from this category all transactions of less than £E100, thereby leaving out a substantial number of tourist transfers.[32] Finally, since one set of estimates refers to tourist expenditures while the other concerns currency exchanged through official channels, an additional and major source of divergence is the purchase of Egyptian currency in the black market, both inside and outside Egypt, by foreign tourists.

The Tourist Administration estimates for 1962 are shown in Table 7-10. Estimates from this source for earlier years were higher, reaching £E23 million in 1961, but the reduction in 1962 may well reflect the introduction of more realistic estimating procedures by this organization.[33] This is clearly a field where Egypt has a great comparative advantage; the hotel-building spree of the past few years and the extensive promotional efforts, in Europe as well as the United States, attest to the country's desire to exploit this advantage. Administrative blunders such as overbooked hotels and stranded Nile cruises are particularly damaging in this area where

---

[30]For details of the settlement, see National Bank of Egypt, *Economic Bulletin*, Vol. XI, No. 2 (1958), pp. 186-87.

[31]Comparing 1963 with 1955, the number of ships passing through the canal rose by 30 percent, while total tonnage rose by 80 percent.

[32]These figures are discussed in National Bank of Egypt, *Economic Bulletin*, Vol. XIV, No. 2 (1961), p. 205, and Vol. XVI, Nos. 1-2 (1963), pp. 68-69. If the Tourist Administration's estimates are correct, the remaining tourism expenditures enter the balance of payments in the two categories "shipping" and "other receipts," both of which are quite large.

[33]The number of visitors increased from 1961 to 1962, but estimates of both average length of stay and average expenditure per day fell.

public relations are of such crucial importance, but these should become rarer as the Tourist Administration gains in experience and sensitivity in managing its growing domain. A political settlement making the crossing of borders in the area less onerous would add measurably to the country's receipts from tourism; but even failing this, Egypt has many attributes which will undoubtedly continue to draw tourists in increasing numbers from Europe and the United States as well as from the rest of Africa and the Arab world.

TABLE 7–10

Tourism in the United Arab Republic, 1962

Tourist Groups	Number of Tourists	Average Length of Stay per Tourist (Nights)	Average Daily Spending per Tourist (£E)	Total Receipts (£E000)
Arabs..................	116,112	17.0	2.7	5,355
Europeans:				
Germans.............	15,957	14.8	5.2	1,419
British..............	20,531	9.0	6.0	1,113
Greeks..............	12,646	20.0	6.0	1,514
Italians.............	9,734	20.5	6.0	1,195
Others..............	28,412	16.8	6.5	2,866
Total.............	87,280	15.5	6.0	8,107
Americans:				
United States........	33,920	7.3	7.9	1,989
Others..............	6,427	8.3	8.0	428
Total.............	40,347	7.5	7.9	2,417
Others...............	47,441	11.6	3.0	1,701
Total.............	291,180	14.3	4.1	17,580

Source: National Bank of Egypt, *Economic Bulletin*, Vol. XVI, Nos. 1–2 (1963), p. 70.

3. A Statistical Detour

Before turning to the balance-of-payments estimates, it is useful to examine the relationship between the various trade statistics and to attempt to assess their inclusiveness. Basically, there are two sets of trade data: the estimates of the Customs Administration and the figures of the Central Exchange Control. It is quite natural that these two should diverge somewhat, as a result of such factors as different timing of receiving the goods and incurring a debt for them, and differing valuation of specific commodities by the two authorities. Comparative figures from the two sources over the past ten years are given in Table 7–11. These aggregative figures do not reveal any clear or systematic bias toward undercounting in

TABLE 7–11

IMPORT AND EXPORT STATISTICS

(£E Million)

	Imports		Exports	
	Customs	Central Exchange Control	Customs	Central Exchange Control
1954...................	161.4	150.7	138.3	139.8
1955...................	183.2	190.3	138.4	133.1
1956...................	181.3	192.3	132.9	129.9
1957...................	182.6	217.5	171.6	166.0
1958...................	240.2	214.0	166.3	161.0
1959...................	222.2	235.3	160.5	164.3
1960...................	232.5	255.2	197.8	200.2
1961...................	243.8	237.8	168.9	161.3
1962...................	302.9	290.0	158.3	142.8
1963...................	398.4	402.6*	226.8	228.8*
Total.............	2,348.5	2,385.7	1,659.8	1,627.2

*Including transit trade.
SOURCE: National Bank of Egypt, *Economic Bulletin*, Vol. XIII, No. 2 (1960), p. 138; Central Bank of Egypt, *Economic Review*, Vol. III, No. 2 (1963), p. 153; Vol. IV, Nos. 1 and 2 (1964), pp. 20 and 135.

either series. On the export side the discrepancy between the two sets of figures has consistently been relatively minor; on the import side the Central Exchange Control figures were generally larger from 1955 to 1960, but smaller in the following two years. When we turn to the more detailed breakdown in Table 7–12, a striking systematic divergence emerges; the Central Exchange Control's estimates of Egypt's imports from the USSR are consistently and significantly above those of the Customs Administration, while the Central Exchange Control has a relative underestimate of the value of Egypt's exports to Czechoslovakia.

Before giving our interpretation of these figures, let us turn to some other relevant considerations. One might be suspicious that Egypt's trade and payments estimates are incomplete on two counts. The first concerns imports of capital goods financed by credit facilities from the Communist bloc, while the second is in the area of strategic goods imports. Several of the early balance-of-payments estimates of the newly formed Central Bank refer to the first of these questions; at the time of the 1962 estimates, the 1961 figures were revised "by adding the value of equipment imported under foreign loans (and not previously recorded) to the debit side of the current account as well as to the credit side of the capital account."[34]

[34]Central Bank of Egypt, *Economic Review*, Vol. III, No. 2 (1963), p. 151.

This adjustment consisted of an increase in reported imports from
the USSR of £E12 million, and from East Germany of £E10.8

TABLE 7–12

IMPORT AND EXPORT STATISTICS, EASTERN EUROPE

(£E Million)

	Imports		Exports	
	Customs	Central Exchange Control	Customs	Central Exchange Control
Eastern Europe:				
1956	27.2	36.2	44.7	34.3
1957	50.1	69.3	74.2	77.6
1958	79.5	74.7	75.2	66.5
1959	64.1	71.2	74.8	75.2
1960	58.6	62.1	86.9	78.8
1961	60.8	78.7	73.1	67.9
1962	70.1	83.6	61.2	54.6
1963	70.9	109.5	99.6	96.2
Total	481.3	585.3	589.7	551.1
USSR:				
1956	7.9	11.7	5.6	4.7
1957	18.6	27.2	31.3	33.0
1958	31.7	31.6	28.6	27.3
1959	26.8	34.8	28.3	28.7
1960	22.8	22.7	30.9	31.1
1961	27.6	38.9	25.4	25.9
1962	24.6	41.8	24.1	23.4
1963	21.3	57.9	44.2	47.2
Total	181.3	266.6	218.4	221.3
Czechoslovakia:				
1956	3.8	6.4	20.8	9.2
1957	6.3	8.8	14.6	10.5
1958	10.1	11.3	15.0	11.5
1959	8.1	8.5	16.2	13.5
1960	8.0	9.3	12.9	8.0
1961	6.0	8.1	23.8	15.4
1962	10.2	7.3	12.6	8.6
1963	11.0	9.5	22.1	13.9
Total	63.5	69.2	138.0	90.6

SOURCE: National Bank of Egypt, *Economic Bulletin*, and Central Bank of Egypt, *Economic Review*, various issues. Eastern Europe includes Austria, Bulgaria, Czechoslovakia, East Germany, Greece, Hungary, Poland, Rumania, the USSR, and Yugoslavia.

million. In commenting further on these adjustments, the Central
Bank says that "it is to be pointed out again that recorded payments
for imports within the framework of foreign loans have been in-

cluded and 1961 figures adjusted accordingly,"[35] but also mentions "payments for recorded imports, which may not necessarily cover all imported capital equipment . . . ."[36] These comments, made in 1963, make it seem likely that while the coverage of the balance of payments was improved in 1961, there still remained some capital goods imports not included. By the following year, the Central Bank's discussion of the balance-of-payments estimates says that "payments for imports . . . cover imports financed through long and short-term loans and credits . . . ."[37] This seems to imply that any remaining lack of coverage was removed in the 1963 estimates.

The final fact to be brought into the picture here is that there is a substantial item in the current account of the balance of payments, government expenditures not elsewhere included (n.e.i.). There is no detailed cross-clarification of the current account country by country, but the discussion of the 1961 figure in the text indicates that out of a total expenditure in this category of £E30.9 million in that year, £E15 million was spent in eastern Europe, including £E7.3 million in Czechoslovakia.[38]

With all these parts of the picture before us, it is clear that possibilities open to the authorities for "adjusting" the balance-of-payments picture are numerous. One can leave out the imports as well as the capital inflow (foreign credits), thereby understating the increase in foreign liabilities; one can leave out the imports and undervalue the offsetting exports, thereby giving a true measure of the capital position but understating both sides of the current account; or one can include the imports, but under a different heading, which means that the current account as a whole is accurate. It seems likely that Egypt has used all three of these devices. For our present purposes the most serious of these is the first, which

[35]*Ibid.*, p. 158.
[36]*Ibid.*, p. 152.
[37]*Ibid.*, Vol. IV, No. 2 (1964), p. 135.
[38]*Ibid.*, Vol. II, No. 1 (1962), p. 22. The year 1961 was not a representative year in this regard; total government expenditures and expenditures in eastern Europe developed as follows (in £E million):

	Total	Eastern Europe
1957	16.9	7.8
1958	21.7	5.7
1959	27.9	11.6
1960	25.3	8.9
1961	30.9	15.0
1962	28.4	13.3
1963	28.3	6.4
1964	36.8	7.3

leaves out both the import and the increasing liability. It is impossible for us to estimate the extent of this omission. One possible and plausible assumption is that imports of strategic and capital goods, to the extent that they were matched either by current exports or by payments in hard currency, were treated in a consistent way in the balance of payments, either by understating both import and export values, or by including both, perhaps with the imports listed in a different category. This means that imports of these types financed by credits would not appear in the balance of payments, thereby leading to some understatement of the change in foreign indebtedness using balance-of-payments data alone. As we have seen, the comprehensiveness of the estimates has been improving in recent years, although the official discussions of these changes refer only to capital goods financed by credits, not strategic goods. If this treatment which we have described is the one actually used, as we suspect, then, for consistency, the authorities may also have excluded from the balance of payments exports to repay credits not counted originally.[39]

4. The Capital Account

With this background, let us turn to an examination of the full balance-of-payments figures and the way in which the current account deficits have been financed. Once again, we have summarized the detailed figures shown in the Appendix into major aggregates (see Table 7-13). As the table shows, invisible net exports have continued to grow, but the trade deficit has expanded far more rapidly, so the current account deficit has mushroomed to reach £E123 million in 1963 alone. There have been striking changes in the methods of financing this growing deficit. Up to 1958, Egypt relied almost exclusively on her supply of foreign assets. The main component here continued to be sterling, although other foreign assets played a significant role, including those accumulated in the early postwar period, when more blocked sterling was released to Egypt than was needed for current transactions. During 1959, sterling assets continued to help finance the payments

---

[39]The higher Central Exchange Control figures for imports from the USSR are intriguing. Following the line of reasoning in the text, it may be that these were imports of capital or strategic goods (hence not included in the Customs Administration statistics) which were matched by current payments (hence included in the balance of payments). Still, the apparently inconsistent treatment of the USSR and Czechoslovakia in this regard is puzzling.

deficit, although at a decreasing rate; by 1960, these were virtually exhausted. Other foreign exchange holdings continued to provide some assistance; but by 1962, these too were at rock bottom. The burden of finance was gradually shifted so as to rely almost entirely, by 1963, on foreign loans and grants.

TABLE 7–13

AGGREGATE BALANCE-OF-PAYMENTS FLOWS, 1952–58 AND 1959–63
(£E Million)

	1952–58	*1959–63*
Trade deficit...........................	−329.8	−523.5
Services...............................	153.8	170.1
Balance on current account..............	−176.0	−353.4
Long-term capital and aid (net)...........	2.9	298.1
(U.S. counterpart funds)..............	(4.7)	(195.7)
Compensations........................	− 5.3	− 67.3
To be financed..................	−178.4	−122.6
Reduction in sterling assets..............	−128.1⎱	− 86.3
Holdings of foreign exchange and gold.....	− 41.3⎰	
Other short-term liabilities..............	− 12.9	− 50.4
Net errors and omissions................	3.8	14.1
Total financing.....................	−178.4	−122.6

If we add to the current account deficit Egypt's compensation payments resulting from the Nile waters agreement and the nationalizations, these figures imply that between 1959 and 1963, Egypt had to find foreign exchange amounting to some £E420 million over and above her current export receipts. There are three possible sources for obtaining this foreign exchange: from foreign aid grants, from foreign loans, and from the use of foreign assets held at the beginning of the period. For present purposes, it seems best to treat sales of U.S. surplus commodities to Egypt in exchange for local currency as grants rather than loans; aside from this, Egypt's receipts of foreign grants have consisted primarily of funds to cover specific technical assistance projects and have been relatively minor in the aggregate.[40] The detailed figures of Table 7–14 provide a starting point for an estimate of the breakdown between the other two categories. These figures can be summarized as shown in Table

[40]The United Nations has estimated that from 1954 through May, 1960, some 3 percent of total aid from the Communist bloc to all underdeveloped countries was in grant form, the rest as credits. See United Nations, *International Economic Assistance to the Less Developed Countries,* (New York, 1961), pp. 51–52.

TABLE 7–14

FOREIGN ASSETS AND LIABILITIES OF THE BANKING SYSTEM, 1958–63

(£E Million; Year-End Figures)

	1958	1959	1960	1961	1962	1963
I. Foreign assets:						
A. Central Bank, total......	141.0	127.3	130.8	104.5	105.8	95.2
Gold................	60.6	60.6	60.6	60.6	60.6	60.6
Foreign exchange and securities..........	62.9	45.3	31.3	10.0	10.4	5.5
Payments agreements (debit).............	17.5	21.4	38.9	33.9	34.8	29.1
B. Commercial banks, total..	26.6	36.5	26.6	31.6	28.5	30.4
Due from banks abroad	21.8	29.4	21.4	28.4	24.8	27.2
In foreign currencies..	13.8	22.5	15.5	22.0	18.4	19.0
In £E..............	8.0	6.9	6.0	6.4	6.4	8.2
Other assets..........	4.8	7.1	5.2	3.2	3.7	3.2
C. Total foreign assets......	167.6	163.8	157.4	136.1	134.3	125.6
II. Foreign liabilities:						
A. Central Bank, total......	81.5	94.8	108.9	108.5	143.9	143.9
Payments agreements (credit).............	68.5	82.7	88.6	87.3	106.3	99.9
Net IMF position......	13.0	12.1	18.3	17.6	37.6	44.0
Other liabilities........	n.a.	n.a.	2.0	3.6	n.a.	n.a.
B. Commercial banks, total..	4.3	8.0	5.5	11.3	34.6	29.2
Due to banks abroad...	0.4	7.4	5.3	11.1	23.1	18.8
In foreign currencies..	0.4	0.6	0.4	4.1	13.2	5.7
In £E..............	3.9	6.8	4.9	7.0	9.9	13.1
Other liabilities........	0.0	0.6	0.2	0.2	11.5	10.4
C. Total foreign liabilities...	85.8	102.8	114.4	119.8	178.5	173.1
III. Net foreign assets:						
A. Central Bank..........	59.5	32.5	21.9	−4.0	−38.1	−48.7
B. Commercial banks.......	22.3	28.5	21.1	20.3	− 6.1	1.2
C. Total..................	81.8	61.0	43.0	16.3	−44.2	−47.5

SOURCES: International Monetary Fund, *International Financial Statistics*, January, 1965, p. 292; Central Bank of Egypt, *Economic Bulletin*, Vol. I, No. 2 (1961), p. 233; Vol. II, No. 1 (1962), p. 26; Vol. III, No. 4 (1963), p. 453; Vol. IV, No. 1 (1964), p. 90. We have followed the Egyptian practice of treating the net IMF position as a liability rather than a reduction in assets, as the IMF does. Aside from this, our figures imply a slightly higher figure than the IMF's for Central Bank external assets at the beginning of the period, and a slightly lower figure at the end.

7–15. In rough approximation, these figures imply that during this period, Egypt reduced her external assets by £E46 million, increased her international indebtedness by £E180 million, and financed the remainder of her deficit through foreign grants.[41]

This estimate of the increase in Egypt's external debt is sur-

---

[41]This assumes that the residual item consisted entirely of increasing liabilities.

TABLE 7-15

(£E Million)

Total to be financed (1958-63 inclusive).............	£420
Financing:	
U.S. counterpart funds......................... £195	
Central Bank:	
Decrease in assets............................ 46	
Increase in liabilities:	
To IMF.................................. 31	
To clearing accounts....................... 31	
Commercial banks, net............................ 21	
Other decrease in assets, increase in liabilities, and	
technical assistance grants (net)............. 96	
Total financing.................................	£420

prisingly low. It should be clear from the discussion above that this figure understates the actual increase in indebtedness to the extent that strategic and capital goods imports covered by foreign credits do not appear in the balance-of-payments statistics. It is interesting to attempt to compare this figure with such limited and highly selective information as is available concerning foreign loans which the country has received. One important component of this concerns credit facilities from the Communist bloc countries. This is an area where accurate information is particularly lacking, relying all too often only on press releases, which frequently do not specify whether the commitment was finalized or not, and which sometimes mention no figures. As an indication of the problems involved here, we present in Table 7-16 three recent United Nations estimates of Communist bloc commitments to the United Arab Republic. In large part, these divergencies can be explained simply by changing estimates as to when a given agreement was finalized; did

TABLE 7-16

COMMITMENTS OF BILATERAL ECONOMIC ASSISTANCE FROM COMMUNIST
BLOC COUNTRIES TO THE UAR

($ Million)

	Total, 1954 to Start of First Annual Figure Shown	1958	1959	1960	1961	1962
I..............	8	241	122	225		
II..............	333		160	298	6	
III..............	357			15	302	26

SOURCES: All from United Nations publications, as follows: (I) *International Flow of Long-Term Capital and Official Donations, 1951-59* (New York, 1960), p. 34; (II) *International Flow of Long-Term Capital and Official Donations, 1959-61* (New York, 1962), p. 27; (III) *World Economic Survey, 1963*, Part I: *Trade and Development: Trends, Needs, and Policies* (New York, 1964), p. 273.

the $225 million Russian credit to finance the second stage of the
High Dam enter into force when it was first signed, in August,
1960, or when it was later confirmed in 1961? For our purposes these
technicalities are irrelevant. The major credit facilities from eastern
Europe which the author has been able to identify during the
period 1958–63 were as shown in Table 7–17. The most recent of
the United Nations estimates in Table 7–16 shows a total of $700
million, indicating that while this list is not complete, it probably
includes the most important transactions.

TABLE 7–17

	Million Rubles	$ Million*	£E Million*
USSR:			
A. Industrialization	700	175.0	60.9
B. High Dam, first stage	400	100.0	34.8
C. High Dam, second stage	900	225.0	78.3
Total	2,000	500.0	174.0
Others, for industrialization:			
East Germany		27.3	9.5
Czechoslovakia		26.4	9.2
Hungary		16.9	5.9
Yugoslavia		20.1	7.0
Others		18.1	6.3
Total		608.8	211.9

*All conversions made at official exchange rates.

Once a credit facility has been offered, a number of steps follow.
A specific contract is proposed, then negotiated, then concluded;
thereafter, and with a lag of undetermined length, the imports are
actually received in the country. Repayment is generally in equal
annual installments over twelve years, starting one year after the
delivery of all equipment specified in the contract for a specific
project. It should be clear that for our purposes the increase in indebtedness is only "registered" at the time imports are received.
There are no current figures on the actual rate of utilization of these
Communist bloc credit facilities.[42] The first two Russian agreements
were signed in 1958, the industrialization agreement in January, the

---

[42]Discussing credits from all Communist bloc countries to developing market
economies as a whole, a recent United Nations study concluded that "according to a rough estimate, the total disbursements of economic grants and credits
to the developing countries between 1954 and 1962 were within the range of
one-quarter to one-third of total commitments." Figures specified for India and
Ceylon over the period from 1956 to 1962–63 show a ratio of utilization to
commitments of 28 percent and 36 percent, respectively. United Nations,
*World Economic Survey, 1963, Part I: Trade and Development: Trends, Needs,
and Policies* (New York, 1964), pp. 274–75.

first High Dam agreement in December; the second High Dam agreement was finalized in late 1960 or 1961. Each of these agreements specifies that the credit facilities are to be used within four years. The General Organization for the Implementation of the Five-Year Industrial Plan reported that as of March, 1961, the situation on its share of the Soviet credits was as follows:[43]

	£E Million
Contracts concluded	26.5
Contracts under negotiation	8.0
Contracts proposed	20.8
Unutilized	5.6
Total	60.9

As of the same date, some £E21.1 million of the £E37.9 million of credit facilities from the other Communist countries had been committed to specific projects. While it may well be that as the time limit of these agreements expired, there was a rush to negotiate specific contracts for the remaining credits, it seems quite plausible that a substantial share of the imports financed by these credits still had not reached Egypt by the end of 1963. In the case of the first-stage High Dam credits, the negotiation of contracts was probably more straightforward, although there is still the likelihood that some of the imports did not arrive in Egypt until 1964 or even later. Since the second stage in the construction process did not start until mid-1964, it is most likely that none of these credits had been drawn on as of the end of 1963. All in all, it seems likely that from the end of 1958 through 1963, Egypt's increase in indebtedness to the Communist countries for nonmilitary purposes probably did not surpass £E100 million, and may have been closer to £E80 million. As we indicated, all of these are credits to be repaid over twelve years, at 2½ percent interest.

If we add one final identifiable capital inflow, the International Bank's loan to the Suez Canal Authority, we find that we have a tentative identification of the country's pattern of increase in indebtedness, from 1958 through 1963, as follows:

	£E Million
Commercial banks, short-term liabilities	21
Liabilities to IMF	31
Liabilities to clearing accounts	31
Liabilities to IBRD	19
Credit facilites from Communist bloc used	80
	182

---

[43] S. El-Naggan, *Foreign Aid to the United Arab Republic*, Memo No. 382 (Cairo, Institute of National Planning, December, 1963), p. 43.

As we have indicated, the balance-of-payments estimates probably understate the value of actual net imports to some extent, primarily due to their noninclusion of certain capital goods imports as well as strategic goods financed by Communist bloc credits; with regard to the former, these probably have to do primarily with equipment for the High Dam, and a figure of £E15–25 million may provide the right order of magnitude. A rough estimate of the total increase in external liabilities through 1963, for nonstrategic imports, might be close to £E200 million, with the difference between this total and that above accounted for by commercial credits from western Europe, the United States, and Japan, as well as by a heavier use of the credit facilities from the Communist bloc.

With regard to credits for military goods, estimates have ranged widely and can only be considered as giving rough orders of magnitude. As of 1958, Egypt may have received some $250 million in credit for arms from the USSR and Czechoslovakia.[43a] Whether all those credits have been drawn upon, and whether more recent arms deliveries were made under the original credits or new ones received since then, is anybody's guess. The terms have reportedly specified repayment in cotton over a period of seven to ten years. This would mean that credits drawn on for the original arms purchase in 1955 would have been fully repaid by now, unless there has been some easement of terms.[44] There seems to be no feasible way, on the basis of currently available materials, to estimate Egypt's current external indebtedness due to credits for military goods.

5. Concluding Comments

If we look back at the Egyptian balance-of-payments situation in the postwar period, perhaps the feature which stands out most clearly is the continuing and growing deficit on current account. From the war's end to 1951, these deficits were no particular cause for concern. Current receipts nearly tripled from 1946 to 1951, while the net barter terms of trade shifted sharply in Egypt's favor. Cur-

---

[43a]See Council for Economic and Industry Research, Inc., *Foreign Assistance Activities of the Communist Bloc and Their Implications for the United States*, Study No. 8, U.S. Senate, Special Committee to Study the Foreign Aid Program (Washington, D.C.: U.S. Government Printing Office, July, 1957), p. 724.

[44]"Exchanging for good Egyptian cotton arms which were generally obsolete for the Russians (although certainly not for the Egyptians, with different potential adversaries) was very good business for the Russians; in fact, they claimed that the whole transaction was purely a commercial one. See Allen, *op. cit.*, p. 52.

rent deficits were small and were easily covered by drawing on accumulated sterling assets. Since 1951, the situation has been quite different. The income terms of trade of the country fell by 40 percent from 1951 to 1952, largely as a result of the collapse of the Korean cotton boom; it was only in 1963 that the income terms of trade reattained their 1951 level. In the meantime, however, a number of other changes have taken place in the rest of the balance of payments. Net receipts from invisible exports rose from 8 percent of merchandise exports in 1952 to 22 percent of a much larger total in 1963. This has been supplemented, since 1959, by large-scale

TABLE 7–18

REAL IMPORT CAPACITY OF SELECTED BALANCE-OF-PAYMENTS ITEMS

	Merchandise Exports	Net Exports of Services	Grants and Long-Term Capital Inflow	Total	Index (1948 = 100)
1948........	46.4	8.6	− 2.8	52.2	100.0
1949........	44.8	8.8	− 1.5	52.1	99.8
1950........	56.4	7.2	− 1.2	62.4	119.5
1951........	57.5	7.1	− 1.3	63.3	121.3
1952........	34.3	2.8	− 0.4	36.7	70.3
1953........	33.8	5.5	− 0.1	39.2	75.1
1954........	35.2	3.7	− 0.1	38.8	74.3
1955........	34.5	5.8	0.6	40.9	78.4
1956........	34.9	7.3	0.5	42.7	81.8
1957........	40.0	4.8	0.0	44.8	85.8
1958........	41.1	8.2	− 1.0	48.3	92.5
1959........	43.6	9.9	3.2	56.7	108.6
1960........	51.7	8.5	3.0	63.2	121.1
1961........	43.4	6.3	9.2	58.9	112.9
1962........	41.6	7.8	21.2	70.6	135.3
1963........	58.4	13.1	24.1	95.6	183.2

NOTES: For each category, receipts (in £E million, at current prices) have been deflated by an import price index, with 1938 = 100; thus, each flow measures the real quantity of imports that could be financed from this source, expressed in 1938 prices. The first column, therefore, is simply the income terms of trade of the country. Since 1960, when no import price index is available, we have assumed that the foreign price of Egypt's imports remained unchanged; however, we assume that the devaluation increased the domestic price of these goods by 5 percent. This is applied in full for 1963 and for seven months of 1962. Thus the deflator used is as follows (1938 = 100):

$$1960 = 369.5$$
$$1961 = 369.5$$
$$1962 = 380.3$$
$$1963 = 388.0$$

foreign aid and long-term loans. The result is that Egypt's capacity to finance commodity imports from current sources, grants, and long-term loans increased quite rapidly. One measure of the extent of this increase is shown in Table 7–18. It is difficult to know what base year to adopt for purposes of comparison here; both 1951, the peak of the boom, and 1952, the trough of the following downturn, are rather misleading. We have chosen to refer back to 1948 as the base year of our index. The figures in the table imply that after the Korean boom and the succeeding downturn, it was only in 1958–59 that the level of the late forties was reattained. Thereafter, the capacity to finance imports grew at an average rate of 14.6 percent per annum.[45] The fact that in spite of this rapid expansion the overall balance of payments has remained substantially in deficit is an indication of the strains put on the balance of payments by an active effort to boost the growth rate of the economy. In principle, the country should eventually reach a stage where it is less dependent on imports, being able to produce at home a higher portion of the intermediate and final goods needed for domestic uses; as we have indicated, however, we can find little evidence that this stage is fast approaching in Egypt.

The question arises as to whether Egypt's external situation is a sustainable one. How serious a problem is her growing external debt? The answer, it seems to us, is that while one can hardly look with equanimity on such a large debt outstanding, with a considerable portion of it falling due in the near future or subject to immediate call, this is not nearly so serious a problem as the fact that the current account deficit in the balance of payments shows no sign of declining and, in fact, has continued to rise; with foreign exchange reserves virtually exhausted, these deficits must be financed by ever-increasing foreign borrowing. Current account deficits are presently running at well over £E100 million a year; and while additional credit facilities already negotiated with the Communist bloc will undoubtedly cover a substantial part of these deficits, it seems clear that there will remain a residual, probably a substantial residual, which will have to be financed by borrowing from the West. Coming on top of her already heavy short-term indebtedness, this will surely cause serious problems for Egypt. We suspect that in the near future the authorities will be forced to reduce sharply the current account deficits of the country, perhaps to one third to one half of the 1963–64 levels. Surely, it is not realistic to expect that the foreign sector will be able to continue to provide a massive escape valve for excess demand, as it has over the past two decades, particularly since the advent of comprehensive planning in 1960.

---

[45]The expansion of grants and long-term loans is responsible for nearly half this increase; yet, even excluding these items, the real import capacity grew at 7.7 percent from 1958 to 1963, still quite an impressive rate.

The Financial System, Money, and Prices

A. FINANCIAL INSTITUTIONS

Our concern in this chapter is with the interaction between the financial system and the level and structure of demand in the economy. The discussion of Chapter 6 indicated that a substantial part of the expansion of government expenditures was financed by borrowing from the Central Bank; we should like now to examine the total pattern of bank lending, to see how this interacted with the balance of payments to influence both the level of production and prices in the economy. We shall start by presenting a brief summary picture of the financial system of the country. Our comments touch on three institutions or groups: the Central Bank, the commercial banks, and other financial institutions.

Until the creation of the Central Bank of Egypt in 1960, central banking functions—to the extent that they were undertaken at all—were in the hands of the National Bank of Egypt. This institution had for many years enjoyed the sole right of note issue, as well as acting as banker to the government; it was privately owned, however, and accepted deposits from anyone, while doing a small amount of business in commercial loans and advances. In 1951 the bank was given further control over the monetary situation, in exchange for a greater governmental voice in the operation of the bank. The most important change introduced at that time was the bank's authorization to require that commercial banks hold a portion of their reserves as deposits at the National Bank. In return, the National Bank agreed to refrain from undertaking small commercial transactions, although it retained the right to make commercial loans to the private sector, if it felt this to be in the public interest.[1] Perhaps the main contribution of the National Bank during the 1950's was in facilitating the seasonal ebb and flow of credit by the commercial banks, particularly in the financing of the cotton crop. As Issawi points out, the commercial banks came to depend on the National Bank to finance their peak seasonal needs; in 1959, for example, loans to commercial banks rose from zero in August to £E31.1 million in December, falling to £E5.1 million by the following August.[2]

In 1960 a new institution, the Central Bank of Egypt, was established; the National Bank remained, but as a purely commercial bank, with smaller deposits than Bank Misr, one of its former controllees. The Central Bank took over the liabilities which were within its area of responsibility—notes issued, government accounts, commercial bank reserves, clearing accounts of payments agreements—along with their counterpart assets, as well as the main office building and a large part of the head office staff of the National Bank. Of course, all of the control features were also transferred, including the authorization to undertake open-market operations. This had been extended to the National Bank in 1957, but the limited capital market made it an empty privilege, then as now.

With regard to commercial banking in Egypt, the National Bank's discussion of the situation in 1952 gives a fair picture of the nature of the banks up to the start of the nationalizations in 1956.[3] In 1952, there were 24 commercial banks operating in Egypt, of which 12 were registered outside Egypt, while most of the rest had clear foreign control or ownership; Issawi indicates that there was only one, Bank Misr, plus the National Bank itself, which was not "mainly foreign owned and still largely managed by foreigners or members of minority groups."[4] The degree of concentration of business may be seen from the fact that in 1952 the six largest banks accounted for 78 percent of all advances and 85 percent of deposits;

[1]See National Bank of Egypt, *Economic Bulletin*, Vol. III No. 2 (1950), pp. 80–85; also C. Issawi, *Egypt in Revolution: An Economic Analysis* (New York: Oxford University Press, 1963), pp. 266–69.

[2]*Ibid.*, p. 267.

[3]National Bank of Egypt, "Commercial Banks in Egypt," *Economic Bulletin*, Vol. V, No. 1 (1952), pp. 22–30. The following figures exclude the National Bank itself.

[4]Issawi, *op. cit.*, p. 249.

the corresponding shares of the largest two banks (Bank Misr and Barclays Bank, D. C. and O.) were 46 percent and 56 percent, respectively. At that time, 11 of the 24 were members of the Clearing House; the remaining 13 accounted for only 7 percent of total deposits.

The changing position of the commercial banks after 1956 had three aspects: sequestration, Egyptianization, and finally full nationalization. These three aspects were intertwined, and all moved forward together until the final law of 1961, whereby commercial banks as well as insurance companies and other specialized financial institutions were all brought fully under government ownership.

The presentation of aggregate balance sheets of commercial banks is of recent origin in Egypt. Until 1950, monetary analysts concentrated on figures of currency outstanding, plus check clearances through the two major clearinghouses. It was only in 1951 that estimates were made of the total value of bank deposits, first restricted to the eleven clearing banks, but later (in 1952) extended to all commercial banks in the country. The Central Bank has recently published revised and detailed money supply estimates for the period since 1952; we have extended this series back to 1947, using data for clearing banks alone. Before that, the only estimate we have seen of the level of deposits in commercial banks is a private one, for 1939. The resulting figures are presented in Appendix Table VI–A–1 (pages 372–75), with summary data for selected years in Table 8–2 (page 197).

TABLE 8–1

DISTRIBUTION OF CREDIT OUTSTANDING, BY
TYPES OF BANK, END OF 1961

£E Million

Central Bank	17.4
Commercial banks	258.4
Agricultural and Cooperative Credit Bank	41.4
Industrial Bank	9.2
Real estate banks	23.4
Total	349.8

SOURCE: Central Bank of Egypt, *Credit and Banking Developments, January 1961–June 1962* (Cairo, 1962), p. 22. These figures exclude virtually all loans to the government; see Appendix Table VI–C–2 (p. 377).

There are a number of other financial institutions operating in Egypt. The relative importance of these organizations in the Egyptian credit structure may be seen from Table 8–1. In 1961, 93 percent of the loans of the Agricultural and Cooperative Credit Bank were to cooperatives, principally to finance the purchase of fertilizers and insecticides.[5] By far the largest part of the bank's funds came directly from the commercial banks and the Central Bank. With regard to the mortgage (real estate) banks, the majority of their credits were in long-term loans, secured by buildings; roughly half of their funds were from capital and reserves, with relatively small amounts of borrowing from the banking system. In 1961, some 65 percent of the Industrial Bank's loans were to corporations under the control of public organizations. "Borrowings from the Central Bank, in addition to bonds issued by the [Industrial] Bank and acquired by the Central Bank, represented at the end of June 1962 about 76.1 percent of the total balance sheet of the Bank."[6] These figures make clear that while these specialized institutions have a significant role to play in the Egyptian credit structure—their loans account for some 20 percent of the total credits of the financial system to the private sector—this role is primarily one of channeling funds of the commercial and Central banks to meet specific needs in the economy. Instead of acting as intermediaries between savers and investors, they intermediate between banks and investors. The banks' funds may or may not result from concurrent savings in the economy; in the case of the Central Bank, there is every reason to believe they do not. The importance of these institutions would seem to be that they change the pattern, and perhaps also the level, of lendings by the commercial banks—and more significantly, the Central Bank—to the rest of the economy.

B. THE MONEY SUPPLY

With this brief institutional background, let us turn our attention to the level and composition of the money supply (see Table 8-2). The decline in the relative importance of deposits is surprising; a priori, we should expect the opposite trend as the country becomes more developed and more sophisticated in its financial dealings. The fall in this ratio in Egypt might be attributed to a number of factors. Perhaps the most important is the declining role in the economy of foreigners, the heaviest users of the banks, and the converse growth in importance of the Egyptian middle class, who

---

[5]These and all the following data in this paragraph are taken from the informative publication of the Central Bank of Egypt, *Credit and Banking Developments, January 1961–June 1962* (Cairo, 1962), pp. 2–23.

[6]*Ibid.*, p. 16.

generally do not have the habit of keeping their money in banks. Beyond this, we might mention the growing fear of confiscation of assets. This factor has probably been of particular importance since the banking system was nationalized in 1961; consistent use of a bank account now gives the government a complete and immediate accounting of all one's financial transactions, with the further possibility of checking on a given transaction (e.g., a large payment) before it is authorized. In this context, it is perhaps not surprising that bank deposits have declined in relative importance. As Table 8-2 shows, there has been a marked change in the composition

TABLE 8-2

THE MONEY SUPPLY AND ITS COMPONENTS

(£E Million)

End of:	Currency Outside Banks	Private Demand Deposits	Quasi-money	Total Deposits	Total Money Supply	Ratio, Deposits to Money Supply
1939	31.6	n.a.	n.a.	65.0	96.6	0.67
1947	141.1	176.8	19.1	195.9	337.0	0.58
1954	187.0	152.9	59.0	211.9	398.9	0.53
1964	417.2	199.2	179.3	378.5	795.7	0.48

SOURCE: *Annuaire Statistique, 1960–61* (Cairo, 1962), p. 353; C. Issawi, *Egypt in Revolution: An Economic Analysis* (New York: Oxford University Press, 1963), p. 251; Appendix Table VI-A-1 (pp. 372-75). The 1939 figure exaggerates the level of deposits somewhat by including deposits in foreign branches of the National Bank; presumably, these are small. As the notes in the Appendix indicate, the 1947 figures refer only to clearing banks; inclusion of remaining institutions would push deposits up somewhat and currency outside all banks down somewhat. Quasi-money, which is included in total money supply, refers to time and savings deposits. All figures exclude interbank and governmental deposits.

of these deposits in the past fifteen years, with time deposits growing very rapidly while demand deposits have generally stagnated.[7]

The question arises as to whether the rising share of currency in the money supply is a good or bad thing. It is often argued that if savings are deposited in banks rather than held as currency, they are more amenable to government control to assure that they are used productively. We have argued elsewhere that this line of reasoning has a number of different aspects to it, most of which

---

[7] The National Bank has often argued in its publications that the usage of these time deposits in Egypt is such that they should be included in the money supply; see, for example, National Bank of Egypt, *Economic Bulletin*, Vol. XIV, No. 1 (1961), p. 27. We feel that this argument is correct; concentration on demand deposits and currency alone would substantially understate the true growth in means of payment in recent years.

are fallacious.[8] Admittedly, there is the possibility that the availability and use of a commercial bank would lead an income recipient to consume less; alternatively, it might induce him to invest less, i.e., lead him to hold more of his savings in the form of financial or monetary assets. Neither of these arguments seems convincing, at least in the Egyptian context. Failing these, it seems that the monetary authorities might be indifferent as to the specific form—currency or deposits—in which people chose to hold their money. In fact, we could carry this argument one step further. In Egypt the main difference between these two forms of money holding would seem to lie in their impact on the liquidity of the commercial banks. The main source of increase in the money supply over the past decade has been government borrowing from the Central Bank; if the resulting new money is deposited by its recipient in a commercial bank, it provides the basis for a possible additional expansion of the money supply, adding further to the expansionary pressures resulting from the deficit. This increase in bank liquidity could be offset by monetary policy, but this is not always easy to achieve, particularly where the change is substantial. What we are saying is simply that a lower share of bank deposits in total money supply results in a lower money multiplier and hence a smaller expansionary effect of the government deficit. In an inflationary context, the decline in this share makes the Egyptian authorities' task easier.

In Egypt, as in all countries of the world, there are three major factors influencing the level of the money supply: the banking system, the government, and the foreign sector. In Egypt, only the Central Bank can issue currency; in this situation, we can measure the impact of the government on the money supply by examining its relationship with the banking system. A balanced government budget does not affect the level of the money supply, nor does a deficit financed by borrowing outside the banks. The introduction of the foreign sector complicates the picture somewhat. If a country has a deficit in the current account of its balance of payments which is financed by a net decrease in external assets of the banking system, the money supply in the country will fall by an amount equal to the current account deficit (unless offset by other factors in the economy); if a similar deficit is paid for by a capital inflow outside the banking system, no such fall will result. Pulling together

---

[8]"Savings, Investment, and the Analysis of Growth," *Economic Development and Cultural Change*, Vol. XII, No. 1 (October, 1963).

these various strands, we see that if the government runs a deficit, borrowing from the Central Bank to finance this, it will exert an expansionary pressure on the economy. If this pressure results in increased imports which are paid for by drawing down Central Bank reserves, the original impact on the money supply of the government deficit is correspondingly offset. From the point of view of its impact on the money supply, it is as if the government had borrowed foreign currency from the Central Bank and used it to buy imports, with no domestic monetary effects. If, on the other hand, the resulting imports had been offset by capital inflows outside the banking system, the situation would be different. The excess demand for commodities would have flowed abroad, as in the first case, but now the money supply would have risen by an amount equal to the government deficit.

With this brief discussion as background, let us turn to an examination of the level of the money supply in Egypt. The detailed annual figures are presented in Appendix Table VI–A–1 (pages 372–75), with data for selected years shown in Table 8–3. Looking first at the period from 1948 to 1960, perhaps the most striking thing is the very slow rate of increase in the money supply. Total loans outstanding of the banking system—to the private sector, the specialized institutions, and the government—rose from £E150 million at the end of 1948 to nearly £E700 million at the end of 1960; yet this increased lending of nearly £E550 million was accompanied by a rise in the money supply of only some 20 percent of that figure. Fully two thirds of the new lending was offset by decreases in net external assets of the banking system.

The phenomenon of excess demand expressing itself in a balance-of-payments deficit, which in turn tempers the increase in the money supply, is a familiar one in developing countries. The thing which sets Egypt apart in this regard is the very great extent to which this has taken place. The result is illustrated in a striking way in Table 8–4. This increase of nearly 50 percent in the income velocity of money is puzzling. In a "standard, textbook case" for underdeveloped countries, we might expect to find a high rate of bank lending, both to the private sector and to the government, as the major expansionary force in the economy. If this force surpasses the capacity of the economy to increase output, there would be pressures on both internal prices and the balance of payments; with both of these under government control, the economy might develop a measure of suppressed inflation, which might show up

TABLE 8–3

The Money Supply and Its Determinants, Selected Years
(£E Million, End-of-Year Figures)

	1948	1955	1956	1958	1960	1963
Money supply:						
I. Net currency circulation outside banks	154.8	185.3	226.6	206.9	219.8	345.0
II. Private demand deposits	195.2	154.7	170.5	177.9	185.0	170.7
III. Private time and savings deposits	23.5	66.0	59.2	70.1	80.1	173.2
Total	373.5	406.0	456.3	454.9	484.9	688.9
Factors affecting the money supply:						
I. Liabilities:						
A. Post Office Savings Bank deposits	29.8	27.2	26.6	34.8	40.6	59.2
B. Governmental deposits	53.2	35.3	36.2	61.2	77.4	81.1
C. Other deposits	0.0	19.2	19.7	52.8	121.4	192.8
1. Clearing and other accounts	(0.0)	(19.0)	(14.3)	(36.3)	(49.1)	(47.3)
2. U.S. counterpart funds deposits	(0.0)	(0.0)	(0.0)	(5.8)	(53.8)	(101.5)
3. IMF account	(0.0)	(0.2)	(5.4)	(10.7)	(18.5)	(44.0)
Total	83.0	81.7	82.5	148.8	239.4	333.1
II. Assets:						
A. Net foreign assets	346.2	221.9	180.2	137.6	112.4	54.9
B. Claims on private sector	85.4	160.2	175.3	217.4	255.8	317.1
C. Claims on specialized banks and other entities	6.0	11.1	17.9	54.7	89.3	109.8
D. Claims on government	58.2	136.2	217.8	251.8	350.6	613.4
1. Securities	(6.3)	(26.6)	(33.1)	(43.7)	(111.6)	(539.3)
2. Treasury bills	(12.7)	(71.0)	(146.0)	(160.0)	(185.0)	
3. Counterpart of subsidiary notes and coins	(9.4)	(11.4)	(12.1)	(13.3)	(13.4)	(14.9)
4. Post Office Savings Bank deposits	(29.8)	(27.2)	(26.6)	(34.8)	(40.6)	(59.2)
Total	495.8	529.4	591.2	661.5	808.1	1,095.2
III. Balancing items	−39.3	−41.7	−52.4	−57.8	−83.8	−73.2

Notes and Sources: See Appendix Table VI–A–1 (pp. 372–75).

(among other ways) in a *decrease* in the ratio of income to money.[9] Egypt seems to fit all these characteristics except the last one. How does it happen that instead of falling, the ratio of income to money has risen so sharply in Egypt? Superficially, the answer is quite simple; as we have seen, two thirds of the increase in bank lending was offset by a reduction in net external assets of the banking system. Yet this fact calls into question the earlier step in this chain which says that large-scale bank lending was the major expansionary force in the economy, because of its impact on aggregate demand. Is the expansionary force a result of the increased bank lending per se, without regard to the resulting change in the money supply?

TABLE 8–4

RELATIVE GROWTH OF MONEY AND INCOME

(£E Million)

	Money Supply M	Income Y	Income Velocity Y/M
1939.............	97	194	2.00
1948.............	374	773	2.07
1955.............	406	1,072	2.64
1956.............	456	1,125	2.47
1958.............	455	1,256	2.76
1960.............	485	1,467	3.02

SOURCE: Table 8–2, and Appendix Tables I–A–1 (pp. 270–71), I–A–2 (pp. 272–73), I–A–7 (pp. 272–75), and VI–A–1 (p. 287).

M refers to year-end figures, and includes time and savings deposits. Y is gross national product at current market prices; the figures for 1939 and 1948 are averages of the year shown and the following one, while the other figures refer to the fiscal years of which the indicated year end is the midpoint.

In the simple Keynesian theory of income determination, an autonomous change such as an increase in government spending with taxes held constant would result in a multiple increase in income, the multiplier being equal to $\dfrac{1}{mpm + mps}$.[10] It would also result in an increase in imports equal to the original autonomous shift times $\dfrac{mpm}{mpm + mps}$, with a corresponding fall in the domestic

---

[9] If there was any increase in the degree of monetization of the economy—the share of a given output which was marketed—this also would result in a fall in income velocity of money (if we include nonmarketed output in income, as we should). Changes of this type were negligible in Egypt during this period.

[10] mpm = marginal propensity to import; mps = marginal propensity to save.

money supply.[11] To the extent that mpm is large relative to mps, the final and overall increase in the money supply resulting from the government deficit and ensuing expenditure changes will be small, in the limit approaching zero. But the multiple increase in income remains; this is a function not of the relative size of mpm and mps, but of the absolute size of their sum.

If we are not happy with this application of the Keynesian model to a country like Egypt, we might take a different tack by emphasizing the effect of bank lending on domestic productive capacity. Let us exaggerate actual differences and say that there are three types of bank loans: those which finance the payment of debts abroad, such as compensation payments for the nationalizations, with no impact on the domestic economy;[12] those which finance projects with a high import content, which (presumably) result in an increase in domestic productive capacity but with little increase in domestic demand; and those which result in expenditures with a low import content (e.g., government wage payments), resulting in a multiple expansion of domestic demand and (in some cases) in domestic productive capacity as well. We can make a connection between bank lending and the level of income in the country by concentrating on the increase in aggregate demand from the third type of loan; alternatively, we might emphasize the supply side, saying that the increase in productive capacity financed by bank lending makes possible an increase in output, with the actual level of production adjusting more or less automatically to the productive capacity of the economy. This is not an either-or proposition; both factors may have some role to play. Whichever of these lines we choose to emphasize, the important thing to notice is that both ignore the level of the money supply as an important variable in its own right. Both assume that income can rise substantially without being seriously constrained by the failure of the money supply to increase apace; in these oversimplified formulations, they both imply that money does not matter.

The actual developments in Egypt make it tempting to say that these models provide a reasonably accurate framework of analysis, and indeed (in Egypt, at least!) money does matter very little. If the level of income can double over a period when the money supply rose by only 30 percent, as was the case from 1948 to 1960,

---

[11]Assuming the external deficit is financed by drawing down foreign assets of the banking system.

[12]This would be true whether or not the concurrent loan from the Central Bank to the government were specifically designated for the payment of compensations.

does this not indicate rather persuasively that the failure of the money supply to grow more rapidly was not a serious constraint on the growth of income? This line of reasoning might be countered in either of two ways. The first would be to say that the demand for money is an important and functionally stable variable, but that there were identifiable forces at work in the economy shifting the function, so that, in effect, this large increase in velocity was a desired one; the second would be to say that the economy was off its money demand schedule, and that this was a significant factor in keeping the rate of growth from being even higher. Let us see if we can find evidence to support either of these two lines.

One logical reason for expecting a fall in the demand for money would be an increasing rate of inflation; however, as we shall see in Section C below, prices in Egypt have been remarkably stable. A more relevant consideration concerns income distribution; with greater equality of income in 1960 than in 1948, the asset demand for money per pound of income may have been smaller in the later year. Nationalizations may have provided an additional explanation; public enterprises generally have the right to fall back on government funds, permitting them to economize on cash holdings, while economies of scale in cash needs of larger production units may have had some importance as well.[13] Yet, in 1960 the major nationalizations were still to come. Portfolio balance theory suggests that a rising rate of return on alternative assets may have induced people to shift out of money; yet the range of alternative financial assets is quite limited in Egypt. Perhaps more significant has been the shift away from all financial assets to commodities such as carpets, jewelry, and antiques. This type of shift may have been important not primarily as a hedge against inflation but as an attempt to invest in assets whose value is, on the one hand, not so obvious to government officials and, at the same time, not so directly dependent on the decisions of the government. The demonetization of all notes of large denomination in early 1957 may have had an important psychological impact here.[14] Beyond this, there was probably a substantial amount of capital flight during the 1950's, as people

---

[13] See J. Tobin, "The Interest-Elasticity of the Transactions Demand for Cash," *Review of Economics and Statistics*, Vol. XXXVIII, No. 3 (August, 1956), p. 246.

[14] There was an announced period of one month prior to the terminal date in 1957 when all £E50 and £E100 notes could be exchanged in the banks for notes of smaller denomination; but for people with large cash hoards, conversion could mean questions and perhaps confiscation. In fact, this was generally not the case in 1957, but people may have been awakened to the danger of its happening.

attempted to substitute foreign investments and deposits for domestic money holdings. On the whole, there are a number of reasons to believe that the demand for money—particularly the asset demand for domestic money—may have fallen rather sharply during this period. If this is the full explanation of the 50 percent increase in income velocity of money, it suggests that the asset demand for money comprised over 30 percent of the total money supply outstanding in Egypt in the late 1940's, a surprisingly high level for a country at her stage of development.

An alternative explanation of this increase in the income velocity of money centers on the possibility that the country may have been off its money demand schedule, either at the beginning or the end of the period, or both. Egypt may well have found herself at the end of World War II in a highly liquid position, as a result of expenditures by the British unmatched by taxation in Egypt, at a time when the supply of commodities for consumption purposes was restricted by military priorities.[15] Still, the country had gone through three and a half years of rapidly increasing production and relatively free imports between the war's end and the end of 1948, when our period of comparison starts. Table 9–1 (page 216) indicates that the domestic savings rate in the economy was extremely low in 1946 and 1947, but by 1948 had risen sharply to a level equal to or even above what has since been a long-run normal level. Furthermore, Table 8–4 indicates that the income velocity in 1948 was slightly above that in 1939.[16] All these facts suggest that there was no excessive liquidity in the economy at the start of the period. Is there any evidence that a disparity developed during the period between supply and demand for money, perhaps exercising thereby a restraining force on the growth of income? This is a puzzling proposition when looked at more closely. It might be taken to imply that a person has enough income to make a certain expenditure, but not enough cash for this purpose. But since income always provides cash in equal amount,[17] this line of reasoning is

---

[15]We are here using the term "liquidity" in the sense of the ratio of monetary assets in the hands of the public to current money income, not with reference to the external assets of the country.

[16]Outside of the one private estimate for 1939, money supply figures are not available before 1947; the comparable income velocity of money in that year was 1.92; it seems likely that it was even lower in 1945, although this is impossible to document.

[17]Unless it is income in kind; this can be in the form of either goods or services which the income recipient wants to consume himself (in which case there is no need for cash) or things he wants to sell or trade (in which case they might best be considered not as income but as inventories).

not convincing. A second possibility would arise if consumers had difficulties in converting previous savings invested in financial assets into money, either because they decided to keep their asset in a more liquid form or because they wanted to reduce these assets by dissaving. In view of the limited range of alternative financial assets, this consideration hardly seems relevant to the Egyptian case. Alternatively, we might mean that for a given level of income of the economy as a whole, producers need a certain amount of money as working capital to finance current levels of production. This implies that the real bottleneck is a shortage of bank lending, perhaps reflected (although for institutional reasons, not necessarily) in a rise in interest rates. In Egypt, however, we have seen that the slow increase in the money supply was in no sense a result of low levels of bank lending; on the contrary, bank credit expanded quite rapidly throughout the 1950's. On the whole, we can see no reason to believe that the slow rate of growth of the money supply exercised any restraining force on the rate of growth of the economy.

There remains one more comment to make before passing on to more recent years. For the period 1948–58, as well as each of the subperiods within it shown in Table 8–3, the fall in external assets of the banking system was larger than the current account deficit of the balance of payments; over the whole ten-year period, the excess amounted to £E68 million. This means that the reduction in external assets fully covered the balance-of-payments current account deficit, besides making possible a net capital outflow from the country—with a concomitant fall in the domestic money supply—of £E68 million. After 1958, a new factor was introduced into the picture, namely, compensation payments for nationalized property. If these payments are added to the current account deficit, the payment needs of the country during the three years 1958–60 (£104.8 million) were somewhat larger than the reduction in net external assets of the banking system (£E93.8 million).

During the final period covered by our data, 1961–63, payment needs (for current account deficits plus compensation payments) rose markedly, to £E321 million; the banking system was able to cover barely 40 percent of this amount through decreased assets and increased liabilities (£E130 million). When combined with an increased rate of bank lending, particularly to the public sector— government borrowing from the banking system amounted to £E150 million in 1963 alone—we find that the money supply began to grow at a much faster rate, averaging about 12 percent a year during these three years. Up-to-date income estimates are not available, but figures for 1961 and 1962 indicate a slight fall in the income velocity of money, reversing the trend of the prior twenty years. During 1964 the money supply again rose quite sharply, increasing by more than 15 percent during the course of the year. The economy has clearly been under substantially greater expansionary pressure during the 1960's than in the previous decade. One reason for this is simply that the magnitude of government borrowing from the banking system has grown much more rapidly. Aside from this, the changing method of financing the current account deficit in the balance of payments has also had a role to play. We have already pointed to the fact that one result was a much more rapid rate of increase in the money supply. An alternative way to approach this question is to concentrate not on the rate of growth of the money supply, but on the impact of credit on aggregate demand. A bank loan, whether to the government or to the private sector, generally results in an immediate increase in expenditures, partly for domestic goods, partly for imports; this rise in expenditures may result in a multiple increase in domestic demand, depending on the composition of the expenditures and the marginal savings rate (i.e., on the multiplier) relevant to the specific expenditure change. The important thing for present purposes is that if there is a payments deficit which is not covered by changes in net external assets of the banking system, it must be matched by some other type of capital inflow; where private external assets are negligible,[18] this means that the nonfinancial sectors of the economy have received additional loans from outside the country. It is because it implies a higher total amount of credit extended to spending units in the country, rather than because of its impact on the money supply per se, that the payments deficit is more expansionary when financed by a private capital inflow than when it is offset by a fall in external assets of the banking system.

C. PRICES

An analysis of price changes in Egypt is seriously hampered by weaknesses of the underlying statistical data. The basic price indices are presented and discussed in some detail in Appendix Table VI–F–1 (pages 400–01). Suffice it to point out here that they

---

[18]Or at least (as in Egypt) unavailable for domestic purchases or imports, since holding them is illegal for citizens.

suffer from two major defects: They are weighted by output volume in 1939; and they generally refer to official, controlled prices rather than actual market prices. Such independent checks as we have, generally dealing with specific sectors in the economy and referring only to the period up through 1960, imply that while the official aggregate indices do understate the price increase somewhat, the divergence is probably not too large.[19]

Let us look, then, at the pattern of price developments since 1939, as indicated in the official statistics. These show a steady and marked price rise during the war years, reaching a level in 1945 some three times the 1939 figure. The following period, until 1949, was one of moderate decline of prices. This is remarkable, in view of the large unsatisfied demand which existed at the close of the war; the virtual lack of foreign trade controls and large supply of foreign exchange, along with the rapid expansion of domestic production, were the major factors permitting prices to remain stable, and even fall somewhat. The following period, lasting to 1954, covers the sharp rise and subsequent fall of prices associated with the Korean War; at the peak, in 1951, the wholesale price index had risen to about 125 percent of the 1949 level.[20] Since the rise was larger than the subsequent decline, prices ended up the cycle some 10 percent above the 1949 level. The years 1956 and 1957 saw great political and economic turmoil, when prices rose by 20 percent; since that time, the indices indicate a rather remarkable stability.

---

[19]See pages 211 and 212 below. There is one commodity group where there has consistently been a substantial divergence between official and market prices; this is in meats, which are officially controlled, but where official prices have been regularly and openly ignored. With this exception, officials and individuals with whom we discussed this question agreed that the divergencies were generally quite small, at least through 1960.

[20]The National Bank has made an interesting study of the cause of the price increase from August, 1949, to December, 1951, i.e., covering the impact of currency devaluation (along with sterling in September, 1949) and the Korean boom. The results are shown in the following price indices for various commodity groups, using August, 1949 = 100.

	June, 1950	December, 1951
Domestically produced and consumed articles:		
Under price control.............	98	103
Noncontrolled.................	112	118
Imported goods:		
Under price control.............	105	105
Noncontrolled.................	100	134
Exports........................	148	200

SOURCE: National Bank of Egypt, *Economic Bulletin*, Vol. V, No. 1 (1952), pp. 9–15.

Over the whole period from 1949 to 1960, the wholesale price index rose by less than 35 percent, or an average rate of only 2.7 percent per year. How should we explain this slow rate of increase? There are a number of components to the answer. The first is clearly the price controls. The National Bank indicates that in early 1952, articles with weighting equal to one third of the total in the wholesale price index were subject to government control; "the government fixes prices and bears loses should procurement costs be higher."[21] The detailed figures in note 20 above indicate that there was a significantly lower rate of price increase for controlled articles. Since that time, the number of commodities subject to price control has expanded substantially; there are still a large number of commodities whose prices are not quoted on the official price list, but many of these are under the direct control of the Ministry of Industry. By 1963 the government set the price for virtually all manufactured goods, all exported and imported goods, and some basic foodstuffs.[22] Of course, price controls do not necessarily mean constant prices; this is generally only the case for the basic foodstuffs, where the government pays the market price[23] and sells at its own fixed price, subsidizing (as in wheat) or taxing (as in sugar) for the difference. For Ramadan sweets, the goal is to break even on the group as a whole, making profits on some (e.g., cashews) and sustaining losses on others (e.g., almonds). For manufactured goods, prices are generally on a straight cost-plus basis: direct costs plus overhead costs, allocated on the assumption of full-capacity operation, plus a "profit" markup. This markup seems to depend on a number of factors: the degree of risk involved,[24] the rate of capital turnover, and some appraisal as to whether the good is a luxury or a necessity. Clearly, this does not imply constant prices (if raw material prices change, for example), although every effort has been exerted in recent years to keep prices from rising; in 1962 the Minister of Industry gave an order that no price of any industrial good be increased without his personal approval. In the case of imports, these are subsidized (to bring their prices down to the low home level) if they are necessities, taxed if they compete with home-produced goods, and priced on a straight cost-plus basis (i.e.,

---

[21]National Bank of Egypt, *Economic Bulletin*, Vol. V, No. 1 (1952), p. 11.

[22]Our discussion of price controls is based on interviews with a number of officials in the ministries of Supply and Industry, in the spring of 1963.

[23]These are either world prices (for imports) or their appraisal of cost-plus prices (for domestic products).

[24]The main risk mentioned here was that people might not like the product, surely a strange reason for raising the price.

an allowance for importer and retailer) if they are neither of these. Again, in this last case, there is no implication that prices are constant.

If government controls were one reason for relative price stability during the 1950's, a second reason was the possibility of running balance-of-payments deficits. One way of indicating the~~ the importance of this factor is that over the decade of the 1950's, domestic "absorption" of commodities averaged about 2 percent higher than domestic production. An additional consideration was the respectably high rate of increase in real output. Appendix Tables I-A-6 (page 286) and I-A-8 (pages 288-89) indicate that over the whole period from 1945 to 1960, gross national income at constant prices rose to an average annual compound rate of nearly 4.3 percent.

Since 1960, one reads numerous press releases (in western newspapers) and hears increasing numbers of complaints (from Egyptians as well as foreigners) that prices have been rising sharply. The latest official price indices which we have seen, which run through 1964, give only limited indication of general price increases; in some major categories (e.g., industrial products) the index fell from 1960 to 1964. We have no independent checks of the price indices since 1960; we suspect, however, that divergencies are beginning to expand between actual facts and official figures, that the near stability of the indices is purely a statistical phenomenon. All the factors we enumerated above were still operative, and on an expanded scale: price controls had been extended in scope, the balance-of-payments current account deficits had grown to over 6 percent of domestic production, the growth rate of real income was close to 6 percent. If, in spite of all these facts, there were still price increases, we might ascribe them to two factors: rising costs, due to lower efficiency in production, increased supervisory and administrative expenses, and higher wage rates; and a level of aggregate demand growing even faster than the rising supply of goods and services from domestic output and net imports.

The question arises as to what difference it makes whether or not Egypt really is undergoing substantial inflation. Would a price rise of 10 or 20 percent per annum spell disaster for the Egyptian economy? This is a subject which has been debated at great length, both in theory and with reference to specific countries. The main components of the answer concern questions of income distribution and resulting changes in the allocation of output (including the investment rate), as well as the impact of the rise in domestic prices on the balance of payments. On the first of these points, one should ask what component of final expenditure ends up getting squeezed, in real terms. Beyond this, if the investment share rises (and even if it does not), does the inflation result in a misallocation of investment which more than offsets the higher level? In Egypt, where the major source of inflationary pressures has come from an attempted rapid expansion of investment, effected primarily by public corporations intent on meeting their targets as set out in the five-year plan, it seems entirely possible that some forced savings will result; and misallocation of investment as a result of inflation (as distinct from misallocation resulting from bad planning or politics) seems unlikely to be a serious problem.[25] With regard to the balance of payments, domestic inflation is analytically equivalent to a currency appreciation with stable domestic prices. We argued in Chapter 7 that an exchange rate depreciation would do very little to help Egypt's balance of payments. This clearly does not imply, however, that the country could face what amounts to an appreciation with equanimity; there is always a danger of pricing one's exports out of the world market.

Our final concern in this chapter has to do with developments in relative prices. There are at least two sets of relative prices which are of interest to us: between capital goods and consumer goods, and between manufactured and agricultural consumer goods. Unfortunately, there are virtually no data to tell us what has happened to the relative price of capital goods. A large part of the capital goods is imported, and so might have been reflected in the import price index; but the National Bank despaired of obtaining any satisfactory measure of these prices and left them out of its index entirely. If we are content to look at either export until value indices or domestic wholesale prices of electrical and nonelectrical machinery in the United States, the United Kingdom, and Germany, the indices show price increases from 1953 to 1960 ranging from 5 to 30 percent; over this same period the Egyptian wholesale price index, which is weighted by 1939 values and therefore refers primarily to consumer goods, rose by 18 percent.[26] This is not particularly helpful, but perhaps it is as much as we can do at present.

---

[25]On the other hand, it is true that excess demand and resulting inflationary pressures may make good planning more difficult.

[26]See B. Balassa, "Recent Developments in the Competitiveness of American Industry," in United States Congress, Joint Economic Committee, *Factors Affecting the United States Balance of Payments* (Washington, D.C.: U.S. Government Printing Office, December, 1962), p. 44; for United Arab Republic price indices, see Appendix Table VI–F–1 (p. 400–401).

The other part to this question, concerning the relative prices of foodstuffs and manufactured consumer goods, is altogether more interesting. The basic fact from which we might start is that over the decade 1952–53 to 1962–63, real output of the agricultural sector rose by less than 30 percent, while production in the manufacturing sector doubled. If all of the output of both sectors had been in consumer goods, this differential growth rate would have had to be "justified," either by different income elasticities of demand, by offsetting adjustments in the composition of foreign trade, or by changes in relative prices. If we had annual figures on real income and consumption per capita, food and nonfood, plus information on the relative prices of these two commodity groups,

TABLE 8–5

PRICE INDICES FOR AGRICULTURAL AND INDUSTRIAL PRODUCTION

(1954 = 100)

	Food Prices				Industrial Prices		
	A	B	C	D	E	F	G
1945	68			99			
1946	70			98			
1947	71		92	91		84	77
1948	80		92	91		100	
1949	78		89	92		92	
1950	85	96	97	100		103	
1951	118	117	103	108		121	
1952	92	97	100	106		117	
1953	98	99	102	99	95	104	
1954	100	100	100	100	100	100	100
1955	104	100	103	101	103	101	
1956	106	101	113	103	107	113	
1957	104	103	119	109	113	126	
1958	102	102	121	109	117	121	
1959	101	104	119	110	121	122	
1960			118	110		124	111

NOTES: (A) Prices of all field crops except cotton; (B) prices of total agricultural output, except cotton; (C) wholesale price index, food subindex; (D) retail price index (food, fuel, and soap to 1956; food only thereafter); (E) implicit price deflator; (F) wholesale price index, industrial products subindex; and (G) our computed index.

SOURCES: A and B: Total agricultural output and total field crops, in current and constant prices, 1950–1960, from United Arab Republic, Department of Statistics and Census, *National Income from the Agricultural Sector for the Years 1958–60* (Cairo, n.d.). From this are deducted estimates of current- and constant-price value of cotton output, using current values and price deflators in *Annuaire Statistique*; the resulting series yields an implicit deflator. For 1945–50 a similar procedure was followed from the memo by el Imam (M. M. el Imam, *A Production Function for Egyptian Agriculture, 1913–1955*, Memo No. 259 [Cairo: Institute of National Planning, December, 1962]). C, D, and F are from mimeographed publications of the Department of Statistics and Census. E: Income from industry, from United Arab Republic, Department of Statistics and Census, *Ten Years of Revolution: Statistical Atlas* (Cairo, July, 1962), Table 9, is combined with the National Bank's index of industrial production (*Economic Bulletin*, various issues) to yield an implicit price deflator. G: This is a price index we have computed, using as weights value added in 1960, as shown in the 1960 census of industrial production. Nonalcoholic beverages were excluded, as no data were found; except for that, each industrial sector which, at a three-digit level, accounted for as much as 1 percent of industrial value added, was included.

we should be able to estimate income and price elasticities of demand for each commodity group. Unfortunately, this seems to be far beyond the data available in Egypt. We have followed a more pedestrian approach, going first to the conclusion and asking whether there has indeed been a change in relative prices of manufactured consumer goods and foodstuffs. Several different sets of data on this subject are presented in Table 8–5. These indicate no clear shift one way or another in these relative prices; for both

TABLE 8–6

CURRENT VALUES OF APPARENT CONSUMPTION,
BY MAJOR COMMODITY GROUPS

(£E Million)

	1950	1954	1960
Total agricultural output	473	416	556
Less: Value of cotton output	214	97	152
Value of food output, ex-farm	260	319	404
Value added in food processing	21	15	29
Value of food output, including processing	281	334	433
Food imports	38	11	33
Exports	10	6	21
Net imports	27	5	12
Apparent consumption, food	308	339	445
Domestic output of manufactured (nonfood) consumer goods	120	151	241
Exports	1	2	20
Imports	49	39	25
Net imports	48	37	5
Apparent consumption, nonfood	168	188	246
Apparent commodity consumption, total	476	527	691
Share of food in total	0.65	0.64	0.64

NOTES AND SOURCES: This table is very rough and is designed to indicate orders of magnitude. Food here excludes beverages and tobacco. In the nonfood component, we have used total value of output, as shown in the censuses of industrial production, of ISIC 21, 22, 23, 26, 28, and 30, and value added in 24. Perhaps we should point out that all consumption of services is excluded in this presentation. Totals may not add due to rounding.

groups of commodities, if we set 1954 = 100, prices may have been in the range of 80–90 in 1947, and 110–125 in 1960.[27]

If relative prices of these major commodity groups remained

---

[27]The fact that these somewhat (although not entirely) independent sectoral estimates show roughly the same pattern as the subindices of the wholesale price index increases our confidence in that index. We should point out that the industrial price indices measure not only manufactured consumer goods but the total output of the industrial sector; Table 5–4 (p.111) indicates that in 1960, roughly two thirds of industrial value added was in consumer goods lines, either for the local market or for export.

unchanged, we can look at current-value figures on production and trade, to see how the unbalanced growth rate in production to which we referred above was converted into balanced growth in consumption. The first thing to notice is that we cannot identify agricultural output with food production; as Table 8–6 shows, there was a marked shift away from cotton toward food production in the early 1950's, so that the output of food rose substantially faster than did total agricultural output. Secondly, it is clear that in large measure the adjustment has taken place through the foreign trade sector. This shows up most distinctly as a fall in the net imports of manufactured consumer goods, rather than as a rise in food imports, although (at least in the later period) both factors were at work. These crude figures give no indication that rising incomes were causing a shift in the composition of the consumption basket.

D. CONCLUDING COMMENTS

During the 1950's, total loans outstanding of the Central and commercial banks rose by over 250 percent, with nearly half the increase going to the government sector. We might normally expect the result of this rapid credit expansion to be a high rate of inflation in the country. In fact, the price increase averaged a modest 2.7 percent per annum. The main explanation for this relatively slow rate of price increase is that a substantial portion of the expansionary pressures resulting from the new bank lending was channeled overseas. For most of this period, the banks were able to finance the resulting current account deficits by drawing on their external assets. One way of looking at this was that total assets of the banking system—domestic credit outstanding plus net foreign assets—rose at only 3.5 percent per annum during the decade. The result was that in spite of a very rapid domestic credit expansion, the money supply increased only slowly; the income velocity of money rose by 50 percent. One can advance reasons for believing that this was accompanied by a downward shift in the demand for money as a function of income, although the extent of this shift cannot be measured unless we assume that the economy was always on its demand function. We have found no evidence to support the idea that the rate of growth of the money supply was in any sense too slow.

Since 1960, the inflationary pressures in the economy have increased, partly because domestic credit expansion has continued to grow, but also because the method of financing the current account deficit in the balance of payments has changed; with 60 percent of this now covered by/borrowing outside the banking system, the result has been a much more rapid increase in the money supply. Another aspect of this is that figures on domestic credit expansion now substantially understate the total of new loans received by spending units in the economy. Once again, the price inflation which we might expect to result has been converted largely into balance-of-payments deficits, but these deficits have risen from some 2 percent of domestic product during the 1950's to close to 7 percent in 1962 and 1963. We saw in Chapter 7 that Egypt is likely to have increasing difficulties in financing such large deficits. If the country is forced to cut down on her supply of net imports, it will no longer be possible to have credit expansion of over 10 percent a year as well as relatively stable prices, as has been the case in the 1960's; the excess demand in the economy will be turned inward, with a resulting sharp increase in domestic inflationary pressures. Surely, this three-way tug-of-war between demand, prices, and the balance of payments is going to be a growing problem in the future.

9

Consumption, Investment, and Savings

A. ALLOCATION OF OUTPUT[1]

In approaching the question of how the product of the economy was allocated among different uses, we are faced with a number of data problems. For the past decade, there are available official estimates of total capital formation in the economy, based primarily on figures of capital goods imports. We feel that these figures are reasonably reliable; they include both private and public capital formation, with no breakdown available. Before 1952, on the other hand, we must rely on private estimates of capital formation.[2] Like the later figures, these are based primarily on the value of capital goods imports; however, these estimates use a substantially lower markup, intended to cover only trade and transport margins.

---

[1]This subject has been discussed, and alternative figures have been presented, in B. Hansen *The National Outlay of the U.A.R. (Egypt), 1937–39 and 1945–1962–63*, Memo No. 377 (Cairo: Institute of National Planning, December 8, 1963); B. Hansen, *Savings in the U.A.R. (Egypt), 1938–39 and 1945–46–62–63*, Memo No. 551 (Cairo: Institute of National Planning, March, 1965); B. Hansen and G. Marzouk, *Development and Economic Policy in the U.A.R. (Egypt)* (Amsterdam: North-Holland Publishing Co., 1965), Tables A.4 and A.5, pp. 321–22.

[2]S. H. Abdel Rahman, *A Survey of the Foreign Trade of Egypt in the Post-War Period, with Special Reference to Its Impact on the National Economy* (Ph.D. dissertation, Faculty of Commerce, Cairo University, 1959), Appendix C.

TABLE 9–1

ALLOCATION OF OUTPUT, 1945–52

(£E Million, Current Prices)

	1945	1946	1947	1948	1949	1950	1951	1952
Gross national product	552	535	578	718	829	952	1,016	920
Net imports of goods and services	− 45	19	20	4	− 9	11	15	53
Total resources available	507	554	598	722	820	963	1,031	973
Allocation:								
Gross investment	31	48	64	101	109	111	142	128
Fixed capital	34	50	65	95	115	119	130	128
Recorded stock changes	− 3	− 2	− 1	6	− 6	− 8	12	0
Public consumption	67	68	71	100	105	132	141	144
Private consumption	409	438	463	521	606	720	748	701
Share in GNP:								
Net imports	− 8.2	3.6	3.5	0.6	− 1.1	1.2	1.5	5.8
Gross investment	5.6	9.0	11.1	14.1	13.1	11.7	14.0	13.9
Public consumption	12.1	12.7	12.3	13.9	12.7	13.9	13.9	15.7
Private consumption	74.1	81.9	80.1	72.6	73.1	75.6	73.6	76.2
Domestic savings	13.8	5.4	7.6	13.5	14.2	10.5	12.5	8.1

NOTES AND SOURCES: *GNP:* S. H. Abdel Rahman's estimates, at market prices; see Appendix Table I–A–2 (pp. 272–73). *Net imports:* Current account surplus (–) or deficit; see Appendix Table V–C–1 (pp. 366–69). *Fixed capital formation:* Abdel Rahman's estimate, increased by 22.75 percent; see text. *Stock changes:* Official estimates of the National Planning Committee, Memo 40A, converted from constant prices to current prices by an index of cotton prices; see B. Hansen, *The National Outlay of the U.A.R. Egypt, 1937–39 and 1945—1962–63,* Memo No. 377 (Cairo: Institute of National Planning, December 8, 1963), pp. 4 and 10. *Public consumption:* For 1947–52, Appendix Table VI–E–6 (p. 399); for 1948–49 to 1950–51 the fiscal year ran from March 1–February 28, so fiscal 1948–49 has been used as an estimate for calendar 1948, etc. Thereafter, when the calendar year ran from July 1–June 30, the average of two two fiscal years was used. For 1947–48 the fiscal year covered only ten months (May 1, 1947, to February 28, 1948); in our estimate for calendar 1947, we have raised this by 20 percent. For 1945 and 1946, we have extrapolated backwards the 1947 estimates on the basis of UN estimates of government wages and salaries; see United Nations, Department of Economics and Social Affairs, *The Development of Manufacturing Industry in Egypt, Israel, and Turkey* (New York, 1958), p. 92. Private consumption is a residual. In the last section of the table (share in GNP), consumption share plus investment share minus net imports should equal 100; divergencies are due to rounding. Domestic savings is the difference between investment and net imports.

TABLE 9–2

ALLOCATION OF OUTPUT, 1952–53 TO 1962–63
(£E Million, Current Prices)

	1952–53	1953–54	1954–55	1955–56	1956–57	1957–58	1958–59	1959–60	1960–61	1961–62	1962–63
Gross national product	905	963	1,014	1,072	1,125	1,195	1,256	1,372	1,467	1,550	1,679
Net imports of goods and services	31	2	15	33	32	26	28	40	48	85	120
Total resources available	936	965	1,029	1,105	1,157	1,221	1,284	1,412	1,515	1,635	1,799
Allocation:											
Gross investment	119	132	146	172	151	165	181	171	229	248	307
Fixed capital	116	123	134	160	150	150	180	184	225	258	289
Recorded stock changes	3	9	12	12	1	15	1	−13	4	−10	18
Public consumption	138	148	174	220	238	n.a.	n.a.	187	211	260	290
Private consumption	679	685	709	713	768	n.a.	n.a.	1,054	1,075	1,127	1,202
Share in GNP:											
Net imports	3.4	0.2	1.5	3.1	2.8	2.2	2.2	2.9	3.3	5.5	7.1
Gross investment	13.1	13.7	14.4	16.0	13.4	13.8	14.4	12.5	15.6	16.0	18.3
Public consumption	15.2	15.4	17.2	20.5	21.2	n.a.	n.a.	13.6	14.4	16.8	17.3
Private consumption	75.0	71.1	69.9	66.5	68.3	n.a.	n.a.	76.8	73.3	72.7	71.6
Domestic savings	9.7	13.5	12.9	12.9	10.6	11.6	12.2	9.6	12.3	10.5	11.2

NOTES AND SOURCES: *GNP:* B. Hansen and D. Mead, *The National Income of the U.A.R. (Egypt), 1939–1962,* Memo No. 355 (Cairo: Institute of National Planning, July, 1963), p. 21, and more recent unpublished estimates. As for Table 9–1. For each of 1959–60 and 1960–61 the figure has been raised by £E10 million to account for imported equipment for the High Dam not recorded in the official balance-of-payments estimates; see B. Hansen, *The National Outlay of the U.A.R. (Egypt), 1937–30 and 1945—1962–63,* Memo No. 377 (Cairo: Institute of National Planning, December 8, 1963), p. 12. *Fixed capital formation and stock changes: Ibid.,* pp. 5 and 12. *Public consumption, 1952–53—1956–57:* Appendix Table VI–E–6 (p. 399); *1959–60—1962–63:* Hansen, *op. cit.,* pp. 5 and 12. Private consumption is a residual. Figures for 1962–63 are preliminary.

In Table 9–1, we have adjusted the earlier figures upward, chaining the two series together for 1952–53.[3]

A further problem concerns the level of government expenditures. As we saw in Chapter 6, there has recently been completed a detailed reclassification of Egyptian governmental receipts and expenditures, giving an economic and functional cross-classification of all expenditures included in the ordinary budget.[4] The main problems with this study, from the present point of view, are as follows:

1. A few public enterprises—notably the railroads, the post office, and telephone and telegraph—are included in the estimates.

2. The data cover only the ordinary budget, leaving aside all annexed budgets; these became ever more numerous and significant during the 1950's.

3. The period covered is shorter than we should have hoped. Specifically, closed accounts of the budget have been published only through 1956–57, so the reclassification stops with that year. Thereafter, we must rely on other sources, perhaps yielding inconsistent estimates.

As we explain in the Appendix, we have made our own estimates and adjustments in an attempt to overcome the first two of these weaknesses;[5] the third presents a more serious problem. For the period since 1959–60, the Ministry of Planning has made estimates of current consumption in the government sector, but there is reason to believe that these are not comparable with the earlier series. We shall use both series as they stand, without adjustment, realizing that this probably implies a downward bias in the share of public consumption in the years since 1959–60 (relative to the earlier period), with an equal upward bias in the private consumption share.[6] As in all such tables, private consumption is derived residually.

---

[3]This involves increasing the figures for 1952 and earlier by 22.75 percent. This might be compared with the ratio of the two markups: 87.3 percent for the Planning Committee, 40.0 percent for Abdel Rahman; 187.3/140.0 = 1.338.

[4]See p. 135 and Appendix VI–E–4 (pp. 385–95).

[5]See Appendix Table VI–E–6 (p. 399).

[6]Working with *budgeted* figures (not actual expenditures) for current government expenditures (presumably from the ordinary budget, excluding interest payments, price subsidies, railways and petroleum authorities, and "developmental" expenditures), Hansen, estimated a current expenditure increase from 1956–57 to 1959–60 of 6 percent, compared to an expenditure decrease of 20 percent indicated by the figures in Table 9–2; if the budgeted figures give an accurate measure of expenditure trends during the interim period, then, for

What do these figures show? In the case of investment, we find that after a marked increase in the immediate postwar years, and with the exception of a brief period in the mid-1950's, the investment rate has generally remained in the range of 12–14 percent through 1959–60, with no discernible trend either upward or downward.[7] During the planning period, by contrast, the investment rate has risen quite markedly, reaching over 18 percent in the preliminary estimates for 1962–63. Clearly, the planning effort has had a major impact here.

The other side of this increase in the rate of investment has been the growing deficit in the balance of payments. A current account deficit makes it possible for a country either to consume a larger amount, given its level of production and rate of investment, or to maintain its rate of consumption but increase the rate of capital formation, or some combination of these two. It is impossible to say precisely how the net imports have been divided between consumption and investment. In order to do this, we should need to know what the allocation of output would have been if domestic production had remained unchanged while net imports had been zero. One imperfect indicator of the uses to which the excess imports have been put is the domestic savings ratio. If this ratio had been relatively stable for some time before the expansion of current account deficits, we might want to assume that in the absence of higher deficits the ratio would have continued unchanged. Then, if in the aggregate the increased imports were used to make possible a higher rate of consumption, public or private, the savings rate would fall; if they were devoted to investment, this rate would stay constant. This is an imperfect indication, since even in the absence of the deficit the allocation of output may have been changing. If the government decided independently to push up the investment rate, then, in the absence of aid, the consumption share would fall; foreign loans or grants would then make it possible to avoid this decline in the consumption

---

a comparable series, we should adjust the public consumption estimates for 1956–57 and earlier in Tables 9–1 and 9–2 downward by 25 percent, or the figures for 1959–60 and thereafter upward by 35 percent. Hopefully, this question can be cleared up when more complete data are made available for the later period. In the meantime, we have left the original figures unadjusted, recognizing the probable bias introduced in this way. See Hansen, *The National Outlay,* pp. 5 and 12.

[7] There is no obvious explanation for the unusually high investment share in 1955–56; figures in Appendix Table I–A–9 (p. 290) indicate that the largest part of the increase in investment was in the industrial sector.

share, keeping the savings rate constant; this would mean that the net imports of goods and services were being used to raise consumption above the level it would otherwise have reached. We can never know "what would have been" in the absence of aid; the assumption that otherwise proportional shares in output (and hence the domestic savings rate) would have remained constant must remain nothing more than an assumption.

Our estimates of domestic savings are derived as the difference between gross capital formation and the balance-of-payments current account deficit. Both of these series suffer from statistical weaknesses which make them less reliable on a year-to-year basis than for looking at longer term trends. The balance-of-payments figures are derived from payments data, which may well diverge in timing from actual receipts and shipments of goods and services; in the case of investment, we have only very limited information on stock changes.[8] These two factors help to explain the wide annual fluctuations in the domestic savings rate shown in Tables 9–1 and 9–2. Leaving aside these year-to-year variations, one would be hard pressed to say that there has been any clear long-run trend either upward or downward in the savings ratio. In view of the roughness of the statistics, it would seem fairest to say that after rising from a very low level in the immediate postwar years, it has shown no long-run change, even during the planning period, averaging close to 12 percent of gross national product, but with wide annual fluctuations around this level. This implies that relative to a situation with no payments deficit but where the share of output going to different uses remained constant (which, as we have indicated, may not be the proper standard of comparison), all the net increase in goods and services available as a result of the growing import surplus has been devoted to capital formation. Alternatively, and in the same restricted sense, it means that a higher investment rate has been achieved only because the country has run mounting import surpluses.

A constant savings rate implies a constant relationship between total consumption and income; there have been rather clear shifts, however, in the breakdown of this total as between private and public consumption. During the late 1940's the public consumption share in total output remained in the range of 12–14 percent; thereafter, it rose unsteadily to reach a level in 1955–57 of over 20 per-

---

[8]These two points are emphasized by Hansen in *The National Outlay*, pp. 3–4 and Tables I–III.

cent of total output. It is most unfortunate that more recent figures are not available on a comparable basis. Later aggregate figures of government expenditure from another source imply a sharp drop in the government's share to 1959–60, although, as we have indicated, this drop is almost certainly exaggerated by noncomparability of these estimates.[9] If interim budgeted expenditure figures give us a rough measure for adjusting the two series, the government's share in 1962–63 may have been some 10 percent above the level of 1956–57, after having declined somewhat, then risen rapidly during the early years of the plan.

The estimates in the tables of the private consumption share are disturbingly erratic. We have already pointed to a number of problems and weaknesses in the underlying figures; since private consumption is derived residually, errors in any of the other series will be reflected here, in the same way that they show up in the estimates of the savings rate. In fact, the estimate of the level of private consumption is even weaker than that of domestic savings, since it involves not only investment and net imports (which alone can tell us the level of savings), but also the size of the total product, as well as current government expenditures. In short, it is a residual dependent on all the other series in the tables. With these qualifications as background, perhaps the following generalizations may be tentatively advanced.

There were two periods covered by the tables when private consumption share was abnormally high. The first was in the immediate postwar years, when it presumably can be explained by a rush to make up for wartime shortages of consumer goods; domestic savings fell to an abnormally low level. The second period, which is less pronounced, covers the Korean boom, as well as the following slump and the revolution of July, 1952. One possible explanation for this period is as follows. From 1949 to 1951, prices rose by some 20 percent, after having been stable or even falling from the end of the war up to 1949. The lower savings rate and higher consumption may well have been in response to these inflationary conditions. But what of 1952, when prices were beginning to fall? Here, one might point to the high level of net imports, perhaps ordered either by ultimate consumers or by traders in the expectation that the boom conditions of 1951 would continue, but in actual fact resulting in a substantial (and unrecorded) increase

---

[9] See n. 6 above.

in stocks.[10] With the exception of these two periods, the share of private consumption in total output has shown a rather clear downward trend.[11] During the planning period itself, it is clear that there has been a marked shift away from private and toward public consumption.

During the period 1957–59 a series of household expenditure surveys were undertaken, which give us some indication of the pattern of consumption expenditure in Egypt. We shall mention here only one aspect of this study, the share of "own produce" in consumption spending. For all rural households, the figures are as shown in Table 9–3. Virtually all of the consumption of own produce was concentrated in two crops, wheat and maize; for these

TABLE 9–3

SHARE OF OWN PRODUCE IN TOTAL FOOD
CONSUMPTION, RURAL HOUSEHOLDS,
BY SIZE OF HOUSEHOLD

Number of People in Household	Percent Own Produce in Total Food Consumption
1	3
2	9
3	10
4	12
5	15
6	18
7	17
8	19
9	21
10 and above	26
All rural households	18

SOURCE: United Arab Republic, Central Statistical Committee, *Household Sample Budget Survey in the Egyptian Region, 1958–1959* (Cairo, April, 1961), pp. 256–57 (in Arabic).

two alone, the share of own produce in total usage rose from 12 percent for one-person households to nearly 70 percent for the largest units; the average for all rural households included in the sample was 48 percent. For all urban families taken together, the

---

[10]If this is the case, it gives us additional reason for saying that the restrictive commercial policy of the revolutionary government may not have played as large a role in the dramatic improvement in the balance of the payments after 1952 as one might believe; see also p. 170.

[11]Let us recall that there is probably an upward bias, which may amount to as much as five or six percentage points, in the private consumption share for 1959–60 and thereafter.

corresponding figures were 25 percent of wheat and maize but only 1 percent of total food consumption, from own production.[12] Official national income estimates for the agricultural sector in Egypt are based primarily on output data (area times yield) and hence do include autoconsumption. By making some crude assumptions as to the distribution of income between rural and urban areas as well as the raw wheat content of both flour and maize, we can estimate the share of agricultural output which is consumed by its producer at between 4 and 5 percent, a surprisingly low level for a country with such a poor and yet predominant agricultural sector.[13]

If we accept at face value the figures shown in Tables 9-1 and 9-2, and ignore any possible changes in relative prices within the economy, we can use them to examine what has happened to average real consumption per capita. The results, expressed in index form are shown in Table 9-4. These are figures which clearly do not "speak for themselves." One type of critic of the regime—sometimes characterized by foreign aid givers—might say that the 25 percent increase in real per capita consumption over the past nine years (looking at the unadjusted figures) proves that the regime is not doing its share in contributing to the development effort, but is devoting too large a share of increases in output to consumption rather than investment purposes. A different type of critic would say that the fact that per capita consumption is little or no higher today than it was twelve years ago proves that Arab Socialism is a failure, perhaps with the additional twist that this is proof that only private enterprise can "do the job." Neither of these criticisms is convincing as it stands. The second is the easier to answer. The peak year of the Korean boom is an uninteresting base year for comparison. Presumably, if we now had a "Vietnamese boom" (God forbid), real consumption would again be given a substantial boost. Aside from this, income distribution has become a great deal more equal in the past decade, so that although the average level may be the same now as in 1951, surely there has been an improvement in the lot of the lower 75 percent of the population.[14]

---

[12]Wheat is shown separately from flour and bread; for urban households, most grain consumption was in these more refined forms.

[13]The assumptions used are that 40 percent of wheat and maize output are consumed in rural areas, the rest in urban areas; 45 percent of rural and 7 percent of urban consumption of maize and wheat (making allowance for the wheat and maize content of flour and bread) is autoconsumption. This is compared to gross agricultural output, excluding clover.

[14]Although, as we have seen, certain groups at the bottom end of the income scale may be worse off.

If the peak year of the boom is not a fair base for comparison, it might be argued that starting from the bottom of a downturn is more justifiable, since it gives an indication of how much consumption can in fact be squeezed, permitting the largest possible share

TABLE 9–4

REAL PER CAPITA PRIVATE CONSUMPTION

(Index, 1953–54 = 100)

1945	= 88		1957–58 = n.a.	
1946	= 100 } 100		1958–59 = n.a.	
1947	= 99		1959–60 = 124	
			1960–61 = 122 } 123	
1948	= 109 } 110		1961–62 = 121	
1949	= 111		1962–63 = 127	
1950	= 121		Adjusted figures:	
1951	= 123 } 120		1959–60 = 116	
1952	= 115		1960–61 = 112 } 113	
			1961–62 = 110	
1952–53 =	109		1962–63 = 115	
1953–54 =	100			
1954–55 =	99 } 100			
1955–56 =	96			
1956–57 =	99			

NOTES AND SOURCES: This table is based on real national income estimates (Appendix Tables I–A–6 [p. 286] and I–A–8 [pp. 288–89]), share of consumption in money income (Tables 9–1 and 9–2), and annual population figures, assuming constant geometric growth rates between censuses. For the adjusted figures, public consumption has been adjusted upward for these years by 35 percent; see p. 218, n. 6.

of output to be devoted to capital formation. Once we get above some minimal subsistence income, the problems of restraining consumption are partly political, partly administrative. From both points of view, the situation was far different in 1959–60, when the economy was booming, from what it was in 1953–54, when the recent halving of the cotton price had brought severe hardships to large segments of the economy. On the whole, we feel that the question of whether consumption in Egypt has grown "too fast" is far too complex an issue to be settled simply by reference to figures such as those in Table 9–4. For one thing, we might want to ask whether it would have been administratively feasible to hold the level of consumption below the actual level. Here, it seems that the answer is clearly positive. After the nationalizations, industrial wage rates have been permitted to rise substantially faster than in earlier years; it would have been administratively feasible to avoid these wage increases. Alternatively, a small rise in the controlled price of basic foodstuffs could have been used as a means of lowering the real value of a given money wage. To give a third example, the agricultural sector might have been taxed by raising the price of fertilizers or insecticides. The fact that it would have been feasible to restrain consumption in these ways does not necessarily imply that it would have been wise to do so. The third example given above is clearest here; a higher price of fertilizers may well have resulted in lower fertilizer usage and hence lower output. The same principle is equally valid for the first two cases, if lower real wages result in lower initiative or labor efficiency.[15] These considerations cannot be taken lightly in a setting where a significant part of the increase in wage rates has taken the form of profit-sharing schemes, designed specifically to provide incentives for the workers to be more effective and efficient in their jobs.[16]

Recent theoretical models of aid dependence developed within the Agency for International Development of the United States government help us to see the significance of these relationships.[17] One of the points emphasized by these models is that if a country is eventually to make a successful transition away from dependence on foreign aid, it must increase domestic savings sufficiently to cover domestic capital formation. A necessary condition for this development to take place is that the marginal savings rate exceed the target investment rate;[18] this target investment rate, in turn, is equal to the product of the marginal capital–output ratio and the target rate of growth of output. With target growth rates of 6–7 percent and a capital output ratio in the range 2.5–3 in Egypt, it is

[15]We leave aside as irrelevant the possibility that it might result in lower labor supply.

[16]The fact that higher wages result in higher output does not in itself prove that the higher wages are justified; if consumption rises by more than output, then, from the point of view of the planner, one of whose primary concerns is maximizing investment, the game may not be worth the candle. In this case, it takes a wise man—one willing to assert the nature of the "proper" community welfare function—to choose whether the country should forgo consumption of 100 to permit additional investment of 25. For example, assume a closed economy where investment adjusts to equal savings, and where the marginal propensity to consume of laborers is one; suppose an increase in laborers' wages of 100 causes them to work harder, so that output goes up by 75; then an increase in consumption of 100 is made possible by a rise in total output of 75 and a fall of investment (with resources switched to producing consumer goods) of 25.

[17]See, for example, H. B. Chenery and A. M. Strout, *Foreign Assistance and Economic Development*, Draft of AID Discussion Paper No. 7 (Washington, D.C., April 22, 1965).

[18]Leaving aside the special case where the average savings rate is already high.

clear that the present savings ratios in the neighborhood of 12 per-cent—both marginal and average—are far from meeting this test. This implies that unless at some point there is a substantial increase in the domestic savings rate, there is no prospect of eliminating the dependence on capital inflow, in the form of aid and long-term loans, without suffering a serious drop in the rate of growth of output.

If we agree that at some time in the future the savings rate will have to be raised if dependence on foreign capital is to be over-come, is there not a case to be made for postponing this as long as possible, on the ground that at a later date, when incomes are higher, the country will be better able to spare a larger portion of its output for investment purposes? The very asking of this question implies, however, that in the meantime additional foreign grants and loans will be available to cover the continuing balance-of-pay-ments deficit; as we saw in Chapter 7, this is far from clear. With many credit lines extended to the limit and aid givers becoming restive at best, Egypt may well find she is forced to close this gap, if not by increasing savings, then by cutting investment and hence the growth rate.

It might be argued that what is required is not a cut in con-sumption, but simply its stabilization, on a per capita basis. This is true in the aggregate but is not at all easy to implement in prac-tice. For example, one way which has been proposed to hold real private consumption down is to reduce the government's food price-subsidy program. If decreases in real consumption achieved in this way were just adequate to offset increases in consumption in other sectors, resulting perhaps from increasing real wage rates for industrial or government workers, it would appear from aggregate figures that consumption per capita had remained constant. Clearly, though, this would be only a statistical phenomenon, with some people better off and others absolutely, not just relatively, worse off. If we are to rely on methods which only operate to restrict in-creases in consumption without causing a fall in real income of any major group within the economy, it may well be that the in-creases in the marginal savings rate would have to come about much more slowly. This might mean, for example, that *increases* in wage rates would be sharply limited or ruled out for industrial as well as government workers; that, as much as possible, the pricing of agricultural output as well as inputs be adjusted so that increases in consumption per capita—and not just on an overall average basis—will be restrained. If there is to be any absolute reduction in real consumption of specific sectors, this might best be concentrated in groups most able to bear it, either through the tax system or by raising the prices of domestically produced luxury-type consumer durables, such as washing machines and refrigerators. These and similar moves may be the least—and perhaps the most—that foreign creditors and aid givers can expect as a clear sign that the Egyptian authorities are aware of the seriousness of their "savings gap" and are at least moving in the right direction toward solving it.

Recent reports from Egypt suggest that in the last half of 1965 and early 1966 a number of steps have in fact been taken in just this direction.[19] Prices of a number of domestically produced goods such as automobiles, major kitchen appliances, and television sets have been increased by an average of 25 percent, with the additional income going to the Treasury; tax rates have been raised for the higher income brackets; government current expenditures as well as government financing of construction projects have been reduced. These measures are expected to improve the net savings position of the government by some £E100 million in 1965-66, and by £E150 million in fiscal 1967. Beyond this, there are a number of indications that the high rate of investment during the first five-year plan will give way to a period of consolidation, when the emphasis will be on more efficient utilization of existing resources, along with the elimination of certain specific bottlenecks, such as the construction industry. All of this is highly encouraging; surely, with a period of consolidation and readjustment, the Egyptian economy should be in a position to continue to move ahead, but perhaps on a firmer basis.

B. SOURCES OF SAVINGS

In this section we should like to examine the various sources and patterns of savings in the economy. There are several aspects to this subject which are of interest to us here. Perhaps the major ones concern the importance of the different components relative to total savings in the economy, the relationship between savings and investment within the different sectors, and the specific forms in which savings are accumulated and excess investments financed.

---

[19]The following discussion is based primarily on press releases and on discussions with Egyptian government officials in September, 1965. See *New York Times*, Paris Edition, "African Business Review," February 7, 1966, p. 1; *International Financial News Survey*, Vol. XVII, No. 50 December 17, 1965), pp. 453-54.

Aside from the basic statistical sources and official commentaries on them (in the *Economic Bulletin* of the National Bank of Egypt, for example), a number of specific studies have been undertaken in this area, upon which we shall draw liberally.[20]

Historically, the process of financing capital formation in Egypt has been quite simple and straightforward. The government undertook rather modest amounts of investment in the construction of buildings, roads, and irrigation facilities; for the most part, these were financed either out of current budget surpluses or by drawing on funds accumulated through earlier surpluses. In the case of private investment, there have been two major sources of funds: retained corporate profits, and income of wealthy land owners, who used their "agricultural surplus" to finance increasing stocks in commerce as well as plant and equipment in manufacturing. While the largest part of the industrial sector was organized in corporate form, the shares were generally closely controlled by a select group. When new stocks were issued, holders of outstanding shares were given first preference, which usually meant that none were sold to outsiders. Dividends were often distributed in the form of additional shares, to capitalize accumulated reserves and to reduce the computed profit rate, thereby avoiding charges of exploitation and excessive profits.[21] Admittedly, this picture is exaggerated and oversimplified. Surely, there were some sales of securities to the general public and some long-term lending for the finance of capital formation by financial institutions, particularly Bank Misr, drawing on funds deposited in the bank by small savers. Yet it seems fair to say that the role of these markets and institutions was relatively minor in providing intermediation between savers and investors.

During the 1950's, these simple patterns began to change in a number of ways. By far the most important concerns the changing role of the government. Table 9–5 is quite revealing in this regard.

---

[20]Perhaps the most important are the following: S. Amin, "Financing Investment in the Egyptian Region of the UAR," *L'Egypte Contemporaine*, No. 297 (July, 1959), pp. 5–29 (in French); G. Marzouk, "Monetary and Financial Analysis in the Egyptian Region," *ibid.*, No. 300 (April, 1960), pp. 5–25; A. Hosni, *Financing Capital Formation in the U.A.R.* Memo No. 211 (Cairo: Institute of National Planning, 1962); Hansen and Marzouk, *op. cit.* chap. viii; P. K. O'Brien, *The Revolution in Egypt's Economic System, 1952–1965* (London: Oxford University Press, 1966), chap. vii; and a number of Planning Committee studies and memoranda discussed in this last source.

[21]These and other similar points are discussed in some detail in A. A. el Gritly, "The Structure of Modern Industry in Egypt, "*L'Egypte Contemporaine*, Nos. 241–42 (November-December, 1947), pp. 380–417. See also Amin, *op. cit.*, p. 6.

TABLE 9-5

GOVERNMENT SAVINGS AND INVESTMENT

(£E Million)

	Receipts from Taxes, Fees, and Charges	Transfer Payments and Subsidies	Current Net Revenue in Budget	Current Expenditure in Budget	Public Savings in Budget	Government Capital Formation		
						Ordinary Budget		Annexed Budgets
						Total	Social Over-head Capital	
	(1)	(2)	(3)	(4)	(5)	(6)	(7)	(8)
1947-48	81.2	18.1	63.1	56.7	6.4	7.2	3.1	0.0
1948-49	113.2	24.6	88.6	96.8	− 8.2	10.1	6.0	0.0
1949-50	124.9	23.9	101.0	101.8	− 0.8	47.4	31.7	0.0
1950-51	159.4	26.9	132.5	127.9	4.6	27.0	5.0	0.0
1951-52	163.5	32.0	131.5	144.7	−13.2	24.5	6.4	0.0
1952-53	163.6	35.4	128.2	134.0	− 5.8	13.9	3.1	0.2
1953-54	171.5	27.7	143.8	143.0	0.8	8.6	4.7	20.2
1954-55	176.9	30.2	146.7	167.0	−20.3	9.8	4.6	31.4
1955-56	198.4	33.9	164.5	204.8	−40.3	19.3	8.4	46.2
1956-57	179.7	40.4	139.3	228.7	−89.4	10.7	6.1	39.1

SOURCES: Cols. 1, 2, 6, and 7: Appendix Tables VI-E-3 (pp. 382-84) and VI-E-4 (pp. 385-95). Col. 3: col. 1 − col. 2. Col. 4: Appendix VI-E-6 (p. 399). Col. 5: col. 3 −col. 4. Col. 8: Appendix Table VI-E-5 (pp. 396-98).

All figures in this table exclude both receipts and expenditures of public enterprises.

Social overhead capital includes all community and social services, agriculture, and irrigation.

It shows that over the period covered by these detailed estimates, there was little or no increase in investment expenditure within the budget, either on social overhead capital or as directly productive investment. The most significant developments came rather from the sharp increase in current government expenditures, resulting in substantial government dissaving, along with the undertaking of substantial capital expenditure by public administrative units with annexed budgets. There are a number of statistical qualifications which are discussed in the Appendix tables on which Table 9–5 is based; the figures on capital formation, in particular, look suspiciously erratic. In general, though, this picture of rising current budgetary deficits along with increasing capital formation by independent authorities seems well documented. How was this excess of public investment financed? Table 6–7 (page 142) tells a large part of the story: From the end of 1952 through 1960, the government debt outstanding rose by more than £E200 million, with the majority of these new loans coming from the Central Bank.[22]

Outside of the government, it is tempting to compare savings with capital formation within each sector, concluding that if the two are close to each other, autofinancing has been of major importance. This conclusion does not necessarily follow; it is quite possible that the saving was being done by one group, while others in that same sector were carrying out capital formation. We might believe, for example, that some members of the household sector used their current savings to accumulate bank deposits, while other households—or perhaps even the same ones—borrowed from banks to finance the construction of housing. In this case the savings of the sector might equal its investment, but it would be misleading

---

[22]These figures by themselves do not tell us where in the rest of the economy the level of savings was rising to offset the decrease in public savings and the increase in capital formation in annexed budgets. In part, this can be located in the insurance and pension program for government staff; by June, 1960, this program had built up a reserve of £E65 million, although not all of his had been matched by current savings. The government itself put up half the funds, accounting for part of the indicated government dissaving in Table 9–5. See Hansen and Marzouk, *op. cit.*, pp. 216–19. Aside from this, the figures in Table 9–2 suggest that there may have been some temporary decline in domestic savings during this period, while the balance-of-payments deficit remained at close to £E30 million per year. It is clear that this is an area where the data leave much to be desired. Particularly in the area of public savings in the budget, several widely divergent estimates have been made; see *ibid.*, Table 8.7, and our Appendix Table I–A–4, Part VI (p. 277). These alternative estimates suggest that the figures in Table 9–5 may overstate the degree of government dissaving.

to say that this construction was autofinanced. One way to avoid this difficulty is to look at the changes in the full balance sheet (including physical and financial assets as well as liabilities) of each sector during a given period and then attempt to associate changes in specific assets and liabilities. This type of analysis is hazardous at best, relying on a specific set of behavioral assumptions. We might believe, for example, that corporations generally do not save except in order to carry out specific investment projects; if this is so, then, by comparing corporate retained earnings with their investment, we could get a measure of the extent to which this group relied on autofinancing. Using a number of such behavioral assumptions, not all of which are made explicit, Hosni has concluded that in 1958, over 65 percent of fixed capital formation in the private section—households and private enterprises—was autofinanced.[23] Hosni's behavioral assumptions are generally plausible, although alternative explanations are quite possible as well; on the whole, it seems likely that during this period somewhere between 50 and 75 percent of private capital formation was financed out of current savings of the investor, with the rest coming from sale of securities, bank loans, and reduction of financial asset holdings, probably in that order of importance.

Developments since the beginning of the planning period in 1960 are more difficult to evaluate. On the one hand, virtually all of manufacturing and finance and a large part of commerce are under direct government ownership and control; on the other hand, the absence of any final government accounts means that we must rely on a number of indirect and not very satisfactory indicators, such as budgeted figures on expenditures and receipts, and the level of lending by the banks. We have already indicated that the domestic savings ratio was probably roughly constant, so that the increased rate of investment was matched by a growing balance-of-payments deficit. With regard to domestic savings, Hansen has estimated, on the basis of as yet unpublished figures, that the government's current expenditures have been, on the average, somewhat higher than the budgetary current net income; this means that public savings in the budget have been, on the average, negative.[24] Private savings in the form of compulsory social insurance payments have ac-

---

[23]Hosni, *op. cit.*, pp. 12–27. See also Marzouk, *op. cit.*; and Appendix Table I–A–4 (pp. 276–80).

[24]This excludes social insurance payments, which are outside the budget proper, and which we treat here as private savings. See Hansen, *Savings in the U.A.R.*, Table 2; and Hansen and Marzouk, *op. cit.*, Table 8.7.

counted for over 20 percent of total domestic savings during the planning period; perhaps another 30 percent can be identified as gross profits of nationalized firms, all of which were "retained" (at least within the enlarged government sector) for capital formation. The remaining 50 percent represents the savings of households, as well as all enterprises still remaining in private hands. A portion of this private saving was used directly for investment by the saver: in the construction of housing, in increasing stocks of commodities in private commercial concerns, in private capital formation in agriculture. There was, however, a significant amount of private saving held in the form of financial assets; during the first three years of the plan, the public's holdings of money and quasi-money rose by £E155 million, a figure equal to over 25 percent of gross domestic savings during this period.[25]

Once again, we have oversimplified the actual developments somewhat, leaving aside a number of relatively minor financial flows; yet we feel that in the main the picture we have given of the savings-investment relationship is an accurate one. In broad outlines the picture is still remarkably simple. Investment in the private sector is relatively small and is generally self-financed out of income and savings of the investor.[26] Public capital formation is partially offset by profits of nationalized firms; for the rest, it is financed by private savings, both voluntary and compulsory, along with a substantial reliance on foreign savings in the form of a rising balance-of-payments deficit. In these circumstances, the role of the financial institutions as channels for activating the savings of the economy and allocating them among various investment projects is of only limited significance.

---

[25] This figure includes money holdings of nationalized firms and hence cannot be compared directly with the level of savings in the private sector excluding these enterprises. It is interesting to note that over 60 percent of this increase was in the form of currency holdings. For this type of asset accumulation, it is not very meaningful to say that the financial system provided the means for transferring funds from savers to investors.

[26] Hansen's estimate for 1962–63 is that gross investment in the private sector constituted less than 10 percent of total domestic capital formation; see his *Savings in the U.A.R.*, p. 11.

Planning

A. BACKGROUND OF THE PLAN

By the time of the revolution in 1952, Egypt had already experienced two five-year plans. The first covered the years 1935–39, the second 1946–47 to 1950–51. Both were simply a list of public works projects, to be financed primarily from current budgetary revenues, supplemented by drawings on the State Reserve Fund, the accumulation of earlier budgetary surpluses.[1] After the revolution, the approach of the authorities to the question of planning went through several stages.[2] During the early years—roughly 1953–55—planning was taken to mean thorough project analysis, with the emphasis on cost and demand studies. In time, though, the authorities became concerned—perhaps in part under the stimulus of foreign experts with planning models to sell—that while this work was important, it was too partial and micro-oriented to give the information which was needed for optimization. The years 1956–59 were exciting and interesting ones for Egyptian planners; there was intensive work on a number of different aggregative planning models,

---

[1]United Kingdom, Department of Overseas Trade, *Economic Conditions in Egypt*, July, 1935, pp. 8–9; United Kingdom, Overseas Economic Survey, *Egypt*, November, 1947, pp. 3–4, and October, 1951, pp. 23–24. See also p. 50 above.

[2]This discussion follows closely that of N. A. Deif, *Some Uses of Economic Accounting in Planning Economic Development of the U.A.R.*, Memo No. 210 (Cairo: Institute of National Planning, September, 1962).

with a stream of foreign experts visiting the country to confer, suggest, and criticize. Of these, none was more influential—at least among the planners themselves—than Ragnar Frisch. Frisch stayed in Egypt for several extended periods; under his guidance, there developed a small group of capable Egyptian economists who were familiar in a working way with the most sophisticated and advanced planning methodology which had been developed at that time.[3]

While Frisch's work was perhaps the most important in the sense that its development and attempted estimation were carried the farthest, there was also considerable experimentation with alternative planning models.[4] In addition to these aggregative studies, there was an almost endless number of memos written within the National Planning Committee[5] on planning problems and techniques in specific areas or sectors: employment and labor, the government and the budget, exports and the balance of payments.[6] An additional product of this period was a two-year transitional plan for the years 1958 and 1959.[7] Although this was never implemented, the preparation of it in 1957 provided useful experience for the later work on the five-year plan. Finally, there was a massive frontal attack on the problem of data availability. The primary visible output of this work was a highly detailed set of national accounts for the year 1954, including an 83 × 83 input-output table and commodity balance data showing sources and uses of approximately three hundred specific commodities. Probably more important than this set of accounts, though, was the fact that this same group of

---

[3]Perhaps the best sources of information on Frisch's early work in Egypt are the mimeographed *Current Notes* which he wrote while working at the National Planning Committee.

[4]Two of these have been given an able reformulation and critical appraisal in a recent study by el Imam, incidentally performing the additional service of making this work available in English. See M. M. el Imam, *Models Used in Drafting the 20-Year Plan (1959–1978)*. Memo No. 255 (Cairo: Institute of National Planning, December, 1962). The original studies which el Imam was discussing were in National Planning Committee Memo No. 71 (by Drs. A. F. Sherif, N. A. Deif, and A. A. Meguid) and Memo No. 75 (M. Ibrahim).

[5]The words "Committee" and "Commission" are used interchangeably in the title of this organization; the official title, of course, is in Arabic and has been translated both ways. This group has been, since 1957, the primary planning body in the country, first directly within the Presidency and later as technical secretariat of the newly formed Ministry of Planning.

[6]A complete listing of these memos up through early 1960 is given in Annex IV of the French version of the five-year plan; for some reason, this Annex was omitted from the English translation.

[7]This was published in an early memo—No. 62, 1957—of the National Planning Committee.

planners gained a remarkable "feel" for the basic data. In the course of preparing these 1954 estimates, they were forced to compare and reconcile a number of different sources of data on just about every aspect of the economy.[8] N. A. Deif, one of the most able of this group, emphasized the importance of this work when he said that "only a person who knows the limitations of utilized information can know the limitations of conclusions based on it."[9]

In view of the sharp break which we discuss below between the various planning models experimented with during this period and the plan itself, we have not found it important in our study to explore and evaluate these models in any great detail. In fact, it may well be another ten years or more before the Egyptian data can be developed to a point where they can be relied on for use in an optimizing decision model. Even then, there will remain formidable theoretical problems, such as the choice of appropriate social discount rates, not to mention the political problems of inducing jealous ministers to bow to the convincing logic of the computer. In short, there is little prospect that these theoretical studies of planning methodology will bear much more fruit in the next five years than they have in the last five. Still, we feel that the exercise has been important and worth pursuing. This is true partly because it is only in this way that these tools can be developed to the stage where they will give useful answers. Even more important, we feel, is the fact that these theoretical studies have helped to focus attention on the right questions: How fast should one try to push the economy to grow? In what specific directions? What are the major constraints and obstacles which will have to be overcome? While the planning models have not so far succeeded in providing operational answers to these questions, still, by concentrating attention on them, they have forced the economists to struggle with these central questions rather than ignoring them. To give one specific example, Frisch devoted a great deal of analysis and discussion to the question of how large an investment push the economy could sustain, given a constraint of permissible foreign indebtedness. We feel that he was not successful in developing an operational way of answering this question; yet by focusing attention on this relationship, awakening the authorities to its importance, he performed a real service; there are still all too many people in posi-

---

[8]These studies are reported in remarkable detail in National Planning Committee Memo No. 55 (bis), August, 1958, Parts 1–4.

[9]Deif, op. cit., p. 29.

tions of importance in Egypt who do not think in these terms.[10] If the planners have not provided the answers to the questions asked of them, it is not because they have been wasting their time on irrelevancies, but because the answers are complex.

With a considerable period of advanced and intensive work on planning techniques behind them, the people of the National Planning Committee were eminently qualified to take a major role in the preparation of the five-year plan. In fact, their role in the actual construction of the plan was relatively limited. The place where this shows up most clearly concerns the choice of a target rate of growth of output. While in its preliminary studies the Planning Committee had worked primarily with growth rates in the range of 3–4 percent per annum, for the actual plan it was instructed on highest authority to adopt the target of doubling national income in ten years, implying an average annual growth rate of 7.2 percent per annum. The task of drawing up a national plan within the framework of an aggregate growth rate more than double that which had previously been thought of as feasible must have been discouraging and frustrating in the extreme.

The procedures whereby the plan itself was drawn up have been discussed in some detail by Hansen and Marzouk, and we have drawn heavily on their discussion.[11] Once the overall target growth rate had been set, broad sectoral output figures were estimated, using rough guesses of demand elasticities, along with projections of government requirements. To these broad figures were applied sectoral capital–output ratios, giving a preliminary estimate of investment needs, by sectors. These were then passed on to the ministries, which were asked to present detailed figures on individual investment projects within the specified total. The result was that there was considerable scope for variation from ministry to ministry with regard to both proficiency of evaluation and criteria of choice. The National Planning Committee attempted to bring some coordination of techniques and approaches here, but without much success.

Perhaps the basic characteristic of both the plan itself and the economy during the planning period has been a concentration on the control of the level and structure of investment, with relatively

---

[10]See, for example, the quotation from the former Minister of Industry on page 51 above.

[11]Hansen and Marzouk, *Development and Economic Policy in the U.A.R. (Egypt)* (Amsterdam: North-Holland Publishing Co., 1965), chap. xi, sec. 11.2, especially pp. 303–4.

little centralized attention to detailed production decisions. This means that the core of the development plan is a list of specific investment projects to be undertaken during the five-year period. Discussing the evaluation procedures used for appraising these projects, S. H. Abdel Rahman, the Secretary General of the Planning Committee during the period when the plan was being drawn up, makes the following comments:

> Each of these projects in the planning stage was examined against the totality of industrial production, not as existed then, but as generally expected during the implementation stage. Using the techniques of input-output analysis and interflow tables, both direct and indirect effects of each project could be ascertained. . . .
> Linear programming techniques, if properly formulated, indicate relative weight to each project based on the given preference criteria.[12]

These remarks, along with numerous similar ones by a wide range of writers, suggest that preference criteria *were* given, that linear programming techniques *were* used in this appraisal process. Such was not the case. It would be more accurate to say that there were some attempts by the Planning Committee to evaluate the actual projects put forward by the various ministries in this way, but this exercise was quite divorced from the process of choosing the specific investment projects to be included in the plan.

Discussions of planning techniques in Egypt also often suggest that use has been made of analysis in terms of material balances. This approach, which is at the core of Soviet-type planning techniques, centers around an analysis of the quantity available (from domestic production and imports) and the distribution (among intermediate and various final uses) of a large number of rather narrowly defined commodities. In fact, as we have indicated, commodity balance data were drawn up for 1954 for some three hundred commodity groups; these data form the basis for the 1954 input-output table. Less detailed estimates were also made for 1959, fiscal 1960, and fiscal 1965 (with the latter figures being the plan targets).[13] The figures for 1959 and fiscal 1960 were based on

---

[12]S. H. Abdel Rahman, *Comprehensive Economic Planning in the U.A.R.*, Memo No. 238 (Cairo: Institute of National Planning, September, 1962), p. 23.

[13]See National Planning Committee Memo No. 36 (November, 1959); and United Arab Republic, Presidency of the Republic, National Planning Committee, *General Frame of the Five-Year Plan for Economic and Social Development, July 1960–June 1965* (Cairo, 1960), pp. 57–76. Hereafter, this is referred to as the *General Frame;* all page references are to the English edition.

a much less extensive data effort than those of 1954; time was short, the plan had to be produced in a hurry. The actual planning procedures used as described above suggest that the 1964–65 target figures on commodity balances were in large measure irrelevant to the choice of investment projects to be included in the plan; resource needs simply were not specified in great enough detail at the time the investment plan was being drawn up to provide detailed guidance on specific projects. Some efforts were made to present and analyze the expected results of the investment program in terms of commodity balances, but these did not result in any significant alterations in the investment projects as proposed by the ministries.[14]

B. THE PLAN

The basic planning document which emerged from this work is entitled *General Frame of the Five-Year Plan for Economic and Social Development, July 1960–June 1965;* it was printed in English, French, and Arabic, and was designed to be the blueprint for the economy during the period July, 1960–June, 1965. The introductory chapter sets this five-year span within the rough context of a ten-year period, with the overall goal of doubling national income during the decade. Although there are some inconsistencies between the first half of the plan and the last, in general it is an extremely detailed piece of work, with far more information than one expects to find in such a document.[15] This publication has been supplemented by annual plans, printed only in Arabic and for more limited distribution, giving a specific statement of the plan one year at a time, along with a brief report on the performance of the preceding years. It has been a mark of the difficulty of implementing the overall plan that these annual statements have often not been completed until well into the period they were designed to cover, in one case not until the fiscal year was nearly over. In the following comments, we shall concentrate primarily on the major features of the overall five-year plan itself.

[14]The five-year plan itself includes an estimate that during the final year of the plan, inventories would increase by £E117.6 million. Presumably, this is the result of the type of analysis discussed above, reflecting the imbalances found by the Planning Committee in the investment program, as presented by the ministries, and as included in the plan itself; see *General Frame*, pp. 204–5.

[15]One should realize that most of the estimates for the base year of the plan, 1959–60, were completed before that year was more than half finished and, as such, should be considered only as tentative guesses as to how things would turn out—but guesses by generally well-informed people.

Perhaps we should start with aggregate output and its sectoral breakdown. The main features of the planned growth of income are shown in Table 10-1. Looking first at the period 1959-60 to 1964-65, perhaps the most striking characteristic is the overwhelming importance of the industrial sector, accounting for over 50 percent of the planned increase in income over this period. If we add to this the optimistic target increase in agricultural income, we find that nearly 75 percent of the total growth was expected to come from these two commodity-producing sectors. In the service sectors, by contrast, the anticipated growth was relatively modest, averaging only 4.4 percent per annum during this period. These planned patterns of development would result in a structural transformation whereby the share of the industrial sector would increase from 21 to 28 percent of total income, with the largest part of this shift being not at the expense of agriculture—the "standard case" of structural transformation—but rather of services.

The last column in the table permits us to compare these target growth rates with estimated achievements over the first three years of the plan.[16] In the agricultural sector the results have been most disappointing; it seems clear that planning has made little or no change in the slow rate of increase of agricultural output of earlier years. In the industrial sector, growth rates have fallen substantially short of the planned targets, but have been quite impressive all the same.[16a] The main difference between planned and actual achievements, however, has been in the services, where, instead of an anticipated low growth rate, the actual increase has been quite high. The resulting structural transformation has followed the more familiar pattern, whereby both services and industry have increased their relative importance at the expense of agriculture. The planners may have felt that the service sector as a whole was somewhat overextended in the base year of the plan, with very little expansion needed, in spite of rapid growth in the

[16]Figures have recently been released reporting on real growth rates over the full five-year period. We have not used these figures here since we have not been able to evaluate their reliability. If they are correct, they would not change the overall picture presented above in any basic way. Agriculture's average annual growth rate would rise to 3.3 percent, industry's would fall slightly, to 8.9 percent, and the overall indicated growth rate would be 6.5 percent. Transport and communications is reported to have grown at 11.1 percent, reflecting the rapid expansion of receipts from the Suez Canal. The other sectors in Table 10-1 are not explicitly shown in the published breakdown (see n. 18, p. 53).

[16a]As we have indicated, in both the industrial sector and construction, growth rates are somewhat exaggerated by inadequate deflation for price changes; see notes to Appendix Table I-A-8 (pp. 288-89).

TABLE 10-1

ACTUAL AND TARGET INCOME LEVELS, BY SECTORS

(£E Million, Constant Prices)

	1959–60	1964–65	1969–70	Implied Annual Compound Growth Rates		Estimated Actual Growth Rates, 1959–60 to 1962–63
				1959–60 to 1964–65	1964–65 to 1969–70	
Agriculture	400	512	627	5.1	4.1	1.7
Industry	273	540	802	14.6	8.2	9.4
Construction	52	51	75	− 0.5	8.0	14.5
Subtotal, commodity sectors	725	1,103	1,504	8.7	6.4	5.3
Trade and finance	127	162	265	5.0	10.4	
Basic development sectors:						
Transportation and communications	97	117		3.8		
Housing	73	84		2.9		
Public utilities	7	9		5.2		
Security, justice, defense	51	61		3.6		
Public administration	33	45		6.4		
Subtotal, basic development	261	316	435	3.9	6.6	
Other services:						
Education	52	67		5.2		
Health	11	15		6.4		
Social and religious	4	6		8.4		
Culture and recreation	13	18		6.7		
Personal services	89	108		3.9		
Subtotal, other services	169	214	360	4.8	11.0	
Subtotal, all services	557	692	1,060	4.4	8.9	7.0
Grand total	1,282	1,795	2,564	7.0	7.4	5.9

SOURCE: United Arab Republic, National Planning Committee, *General Frame of the Five-Year Plan for Economic and Social Development, July 1960–June 1965* (Cairo, 1960), pp. 11 and 43; and Table 3–2 (p. 45). The total refers to gross national product at market price but excluding customs duties. The rather odd breakdown, calling public administration a "basic development sector" while education is in "other services," for example, is taken from the plan.

commodity-producing sectors; if that is the case, the actual developments would have increased the sectoral imbalances in the economy.

It is interesting to notice what a different configuration was anticipated, as of 1959, for the second planning period, from 1964–65 to 1969–70. During this period, expansion of the services was expected to play a major role, while both agriculture and industry were expected to slow their rate of expansion. The revised second five-year plan, currently in its final stages of preparation, will need to be substantially modified to take account of actual developments during the first planning period.

Turning to investment outlay under the plan, the sectoral structure of investment has few surprises, corresponding roughly to the pattern of income change outlined above. The implied sectoral capital output ratios are shown in Table 10–2. In view of our rough

TABLE 10–2

IMPLIED INCREMENTAL CAPITAL-OUTPUT
RATIOS,

1959–60 TO 1964–65

Agriculture	3.00
Industry, total	1.57
Mining and manufacturing	1.30
Electricity	11.84
Total economy	2.95

NOTES AND SOURCE: United Arab Republic, National Planning Committee, *General Frame of the Five-Year Plan for Economic and Social Development, July 1960–June 1965* (Cairo, 1960), pp. 23, 43, and 45. The table shows the ratio of gross investments during the planning period, excluding land and stock changes, to the increase in gross value added from the base year to the final year of the plan.

estimates of the average capital-output ratio in industry, which we found to be in the range 2.1–2.4,[17] these figures seem unduly optimistic for the industrial sector, although heavy planned investment in transport, communications, and storage, as well as such heavy capital users as housing and the High Dam, raised the overall average appropriately close to the traditional level of 3.0 (which was presumably assumed to hold for the agricultural sector).[18]

---

[17]See Table 5–7 (p. 115).

[18]An earlier study of this relationship in Egypt, working with balance sheets and income statements of 160 industrial and commercial companies, yielded an average capital-output ratio of 1.9; see National Bank of Egypt, *Economic Bulletin*, Vol. IX, No. 4 (1956), pp. 320–14.

Perhaps more interesting than the sectoral allocation of investment is its overall level, particularly when examined relative to aggregate income. Excluding land but including stock changes, the planned figure was £E1,636.4 million, a total equal to just over 20 percent of planned income during the period.[19] The plan is highly optimistic about the supply of savings to match these investments; in fact, by the final year of the plan, domestic savings were expected to exceed planned investment by some £E40 million, making it possible for the country to start repaying its external debt. This massive increase in domestic savings was supposed to appear in all major sectors of the economy: in retained corporate profits, which were presumed to double; in the current account of the government, with a planned surplus of £E90 million; and—perhaps most surprising—in household savings, which were expected to rise to £E80 million, exclusive of life and social insurance installments; this would imply a marginal savings rate in households of 16 percent, compared to an average savings rate of this group in 1959–60 of barely 3 percent.[20] Such high marginal savings rates may not be impossible prima facie; but with little or no discussion as to how private savings were to be increased in this way, and little or no determination to use the government budget to generate public savings, it is not surprising that these plans have gone awry.[21]

In the area of foreign trade, the planning targets for exports were quite reasonable, both in the aggregate and in various specific commodity groups; in fact, by 1964 the target levels for exports had already been surpassed.[22] In the case of imports, on the other

---

[19]Assuming income grows steadily at 7 percent each year over the five-year period.

[20]*General Frame*, pp. 196–97, and Appendix Table I–A–4, Part III (p. 277). The plan targets would have resulted in a rise in the average savings rate of households to 6.1 percent by 1964–65.

[21]Savings targets in the plan are discussed in more detail in P. K. O'Brien, *The Revolution in Egypt's Economics System, 1952–1965* (London: Oxford University Press, 1966), pp. 92–94; and Hansen and Marzouk, *op. cit.*, sec. 11.3. The discussion in Hansen and Marzouk centers around the proposition that out of total investment of £E1,636 million, £E540 million was to be matched by foreign savings, the rest from domestic sources; this leads them to suggest that *relative to the plan figures*, domestic savings were *higher* than the target level, foreign savings lower. We have been unable to locate this breakdown between foreign and domestic savings in the plan itself; surely, it is a nonsensical one, particularly when we recall that in the final year of the plan a current account *surplus of* £E40 million was anticipated.

[22]Planned exports for 1964–65 were £E229.3 million; actual exports in calendar year 1964 had reached £E234.4 million.

hand, the plan was widely unrealistic in expecting that import substitution would work rapidly enough to reduce the level of imports in 1964–65 to some 6 percent *below* the level in the base year. In actual fact, from 1959 to 1964 (calendar years) the value of imports *rose* by over 80 percent. The main divergencies here reflect the failure of the agricultural sector to grow as planned, resulting in a heavy dependence on imported foodstuffs, as well as a rise in the need for imported intermediate products, providing a substantial share of the inputs to the growing industrial sector.[23]

C. PLAN IMPLEMENTATION

The discussion in Section A above suggests that the primary concern of the authorities has been the control of investment; operating decisions on levels of employment, output, and quality of product have generally been made at the enterprise level.[24] Perhaps this focus of attention helps us to understand the divergence between target and actual output figures during the early years of the plan. As we have indicated above, the manufacturing sector—where output is perhaps most responsive to the level of investment—has grown at a high rate, although still below the target growth rate. In agriculture, on the other hand, investment is mainly of a long-term, low-yielding nature, and current output increases are perhaps more dependent on the introduction of new technology than on new capital equipment. In the services, finally, where employment and income vary quite independently of capital formation, the planning approach which concentrates on the control of investment, with relatively little attention paid to changes in aggregate demand, has most clearly led to difficulties. As we saw in Chapter 9, there is evidence that the authorities are becoming increasingly aware of this aspect of the problem and are using price, wage, and tax policies as tools of control in a way they had not before envisaged.

The authorities' task in controlling investment was somewhat simplified by the fact that a large portion of total capital formation was undertaken within the public sector. The precise breakdown between public and private investment is not given for the

---

[23]Compare *General Frame*, pp. 86–87; and Central Bank of Egypt, *Economic Review*, Vol. IV, No. 1 (1964), p. 20, and Vol. V, No. 2 (1965), p. 145; see also pp. 109–10 above.

[24]For further discussion on this point, see Hansen and Marzouk, *op. cit.*, sec. 10.2.

full plan period; in the base year of the plan, some 86 percent of total capital formation was in either government administration (40 percent) or government enterprises. The first two annual plans indicate that approximately 80 percent of all capital formation in those two years was to be in the public sector. The control of private investment was effected primarily through import licensing, supported by the control of credit made available through the financial system. With regard to public sector investment, there was some question as to the division of authority between the Ministry of Planning, the Ministry of the Treasury, the various ministries in charge of the specific area in which a project falls (e.g., industry or agriculture), and the financial system. The picture here has been a constantly altering one, reflecting changes in both the organizational structure of the government and the influence of the individuals in the various posts. Until 1964 the ministries of Planning and the Treasury were, in many respects, merged; each had its own technical staff, but one man served as minister for the two areas. Since that time, there has been a growing separation of the two ministries; by the end of the first planning period, the situation which had emerged was that the Ministry of Planning was responsible for setting the overall targets for the five-year period, while the Treasury determined the timing of specific projects within this period. This means that the annual state budget, including the "business budget" (for public enterprises) as well as the public administration sector, had become, in effect, the annual plan for the economy. Organizational charts can never give an accurate picture of where fundamental decisions are in fact being made; it seems clear, though, that through its authority to determine the level and content of the investment program in any given year, along with the use of tax policy for the control of aggregate demand, the Ministry of the Treasury now plays a growing and central role in the control of the economy.

Turning to the position of the financial system, there has been considerable discussion as to the functions of nationalized banks in a centrally planned economy. Once again, the picture has been an evolving one; the latest step in this process was taken in the early months of 1964. At that time, all commercial banks were merged into five major enterprises, each of which was responsible for all banking operations with the public sector in specified areas of the economy. For example, all banking business of the textile industry was to be concentrated in the hands of Bank Misr, while all other companies supervised by the Ministry of Industry, as well as those in the field of petroleum, were to deal with the Bank of Alexandria. The explanation for this reorganization, as outlined by the Central Bank, was to make it possible "to supervise through the banking system the activities of the productive units, and to make sure that they work and develop according to the overall development plan as well as to make a proper assessment of the implementation of the plan in the financial field."[25] With regard to the financing of capital formation, the policy of the financial system seems to be to provide whatever support is necessary for the implementation of the plan. With regard to loans relating to current production, such as the provision of working capital or lending to finance inventory accumulation, normal banking standards have continued to apply. As we have indicated, enterprises were given considerable freedom to vary their production plans in response to changing market forces. Within the given constraints (particularly concerning pricing and investment), firms were expected to behave as profit-maximizers; whether or not they could get bank loans depended to a large extent on whether the banks felt they were successful in this regard.

D. CONCLUDING COMMENTS

With real income during the planning period rising at an annual rate of 5–6 percent a year, while population has been growing at 2.5–3 percent, it is clear that the country has been making very impressive progress. The question might be asked as to whether this throws any light on the earlier debate as to the proper target growth rate for the plan. Specifically, it might be argued that the achievement of such high growth rates proves that the planners were unduly pessimistic and conservative in thinking in terms of a target growth rate of 3 percent per annum for the first five years of the plan. The problem with this line of reasoning is that the planners were thinking in terms of a growth rate which could be sustained over a twenty-year period. It seems clear that in Egypt the place where a higher growth rate shows up most sharply—in effect, the real constraint on growth—is in the balance of payments. It may be that Egypt will continue to find ways to finance massive deficits, by loans and grants from East and West (including such potential new donors as France), or that Arab brotherhood will

---

[25]Central Bank of Egypt, *Economic Review,* Vol. IV, No. 2 (1964), p. 163. This publication presents a good summary of the 1964 reorganization.

bear fruits in the form of loans from oil-rich states; if so, the low-grow-rate proponents will indeed have been proved overly conservative. There is surely a risk, though, that new financing will not be forthcoming; in that case, there may well be an impending crisis which would involve not only a slower growth rate but a sharp cutback in production in many existing enterprises which rely on imports for current production needs and spare parts.

How long can these payments deficits be expected to last? Or to express the question differently, over how long a period must foreign financing be found if current high growth rates are to be sustained? There are two necessary and interdependent conditions for the elimination of Egypt's balance-of-payments deficit. The first, which we discussed at some length in Chapter 9, is that the amount of savings which people are willing to undertake domestically must increase to the point where these savings are equal to the amount of investment necessary to sustain the growth rate. The second is that, concurrently with this increased willingness to save, there must be a change in the structure of production and demand which will close the gap in the current account of the balance of payments. This might be an integral part of the increased savings rate (if more domestic saving means a lower demand for imports or for goods which could be exported); or it might simply come at the same time (if oil is discovered in exportable quantities, if domestically produced goods are more successful in replacing imports or in entering the world market as exports). These are the major problems facing the Egyptian economy at the present time. As we pointed out in Chapter 9, all indications are that the authorities have been paying increasing attention to these problems in recent months. Perhaps it is significant that at the time of this writing (April, 1966), the details of the second five-year plan have not yet been made public, although ten months of the new planning period have elapsed; this suggests that the reappraisal of the economic potential of the country is still in progress. It will be most interesting to see what picture emerges in the second plan.

The Growth of the Economy in Perspective

From the late nineteenth century into the 1930's, the growth of the Egyptian economy can be broadly characterized by proportional expansion all around. This in no sense implies stagnation; aggregate output grew considerably throughout this period, the population and labor force doubled in size, export receipts more than quadrupled from the 1890's to the 1920's; technology in agriculture improved considerably. Yet the basic characteristics of the economy remained quite unchanged. Of these, the most fundamental was the overwhelming predominance of the agricultural sector. Industry was rudimentary, centered around simple processing of agricultural products (e.g., grain milling, cotton ginning). The services were closely tied in to agriculture, particularly in such areas as commerce and finance. Income estimates are not available during this period, but the population censuses show the share of the agricultural sector in total employment virtually stable at 70 percent from the turn of the century through the 1930's.[1]

Within this agricultural sector, the strictly limited supply of cultivable land was a dominating feature; other inputs, on the other hand—labor, fertilizers, irrigation facilities—grew rapidly; multiple cropping gained widespread acceptance, as did new higher yielding strains of seeds. The result was an increase in agricultural output of some 30 percent from pre-World War I levels to the peak year

---

[1]See Appendix Table II–B–1 (p. 304).

ot the 1930's. With population growing more rapidly, however, average food consumption per capita declined by 10–15 percent over this period. In short, increasingly intensive land utilization made it possible to sustain a large and constant percentage of the steady population growth, although with some decline in living standards. The extent and manner in which these workers were absorbed into the production process is a separate question, which we discussed at some length in earlier chapters. Surely, the marginal productivity of additional workers declined markedly during this period. Whether or not it actually reached zero is for present purposes not of primary importance; what does seem clear is that by the 1930's the prospects of providing either income or useful employment for ever-expanding numbers of agricultural workers were dim indeed.

We see no reason to believe that a fundamental and dramatic change took place in the agricultural sector during the 1930's; specifically, we should not like to argue that during this period the sector reached its limit in absorptive capacity. Whether or not the marginal productivity of additional workers was zero, surely the sector was capable of absorbing more people, by spreading the existing work as well as the existing food supply among more individuals. The implied reduction in living standards might then have been at least partially offset by improvements in technology, which may or may not have been labor-using. In short, we should argue that the structural transformation began when it did, not primarily because the agricultural sector could absorb no more people and they were pushed out of the sector, but because conditions outside of agriculture changed in such a way as to make it possible for increasing numbers of people to find jobs in other sectors.

The primary change here came with the war. As we have seen, employment in the services expanded by over 40 percent during the decade 1937–47; the government sector accounted for nearly one third of this expansion, while personal services, transport, and commerce all showed a considerable increase. Shipping problems gave a natural monopoly to local producers of manufactured goods; industrial employment rose by 50 percent over this decade. During the six years after the war's end the domestic economy remained generally buoyant, first as a result of pent-up demand growing out of the wartime scarcities, then in response to highly favorable developments in the export markets. In a number of industries, wartime shipping restrictions were replaced by rising tariff protection.

Capital goods and raw material imports, on the other hand, were freely available, at least from the sterling area; the rapid rise in foreign exchange receipts eliminated any serious balance-of-payments problem for the country. The result was that the economy went through a period of thirteen years (1939–51) of virtually uninterrupted expansionary pressures. This was followed by a sharp economic downturn and a political revolution. Since then, the structural transformation of the economy has continued, but (at least up to 1960) at a much slower rate; furthermore, since 1952, the natural forces of the market have been largely replaced by a conscious government policy as the prime mover of the structural transformation which has taken place.

Looking at the period since the 1930's as a whole, this transformation has had several different aspects. One of these concerned the distribution of income, as between rich and poor as well as between Egyptians and foreigners. This is an area in which empirical data are extremely weak, and we must rely on fragments of information. The population censuses show a decline in the number of foreigners in Egypt from 203,761 in 1947 to 143,312 in 1960; the numbers for 1937 were substantially higher.[2] If average real income per capita in the whole economy had remained constant from 1937 to 1960 while 100,000 foreigners left the country, and assuming that average income per capita of foreigners was twenty times that of Egyptian nationals, the implication would be that average income per capita of Egyptians had risen by some 16 percent over this period. The departure of foreigners does not necessarily and by itself result in higher income for Egyptians; it simply means that the statistical measure, average income per capita of all residents of the country, can be a misleading indicator of the welfare of citizens of the country.

A second aspect of income redistribution concerns the breakdown between rich and poor Egyptians. Here the primary development which comes to mind concerns the land reforms. Our discussion in Chapter 4 suggests that a substantial redistribution has taken place, particularly as between large and medium-scale farms. Beyond this, the measures undertaken in July, 1961, sharply limited both income and asset holdings of wealthy Egyptians. On the

---

[2] These figures refer to people who were born in Egypt but were subjects of other countries, as well as non-Egyptians born abroad but in the country at the time of the census. The first of these two categories alone declined from 182,617 in 1937 to 145,912 in 1947; comparable figures for the second category are not available to us for 1937.

whole, it is clear that a major step has been taken toward greater equality of income distribution in the country.

This income redistribution is significant in a number of respects, aside from its direct effects on the welfare of the populace. For one thing, as we shall see below, it may have had some impact on the composition of consumer demand. Beyond this, the departure of foreigners, whether they be managers or skilled artisans, surely did have an impact on output and productivity. The capital outflow associated with their departure added to the balance-of-payments pressures of the country. Finally, and perhaps most significantly, the income redistribution which took place within the country was associated with a loss of political influence of the wealthy few who previously had dominated the economic policy of the government. In this respect, income redistribution was a sine qua non for the other aspects of structural transformation, at least during the past decade, when the government has played the leading role in this process.

A second aspect of the structural change which has taken place in Egypt since the 1930's concerns the relative importance of the various industrial sectors. Here the major change has centered around the rapid expansion of the services; one way of expressing this is that from 1937 to 1960, over 60 percent of all new jobs created were in the services. The industrial sector grew at quite a rapid rate, but starting from such a small base, its impact on employment and income were only just beginning to reach significant proportions by the late 1950's. During the first five-year plan the industrial sector was expected to provide over half the increase in income and 35 percent of the expansion in employment in the whole economy; although the sector has clearly fallen considerably short of these targets, it has nonetheless reached the point where its contribution on both fronts during the 1960's has been of major significance. Even during the planning period, however, income earned in the services has grown at a more rapid rate than the commodity-producing sectors.[3]

The third type of structural change which has taken place during the past three decades is in the distribution of output among various categories of final use. This is clearly closely related to the changing sectoral distribution of income and employment discussed above. If the manufacturing sector is to grow at a consistently high rate, there must be a considerable amount of investment in

---

[3]This is largely a result of the slow rate of growth of agriculture.

industry; the rapid expansion of the government sector is reflected directly in both aspects of structural change. There are two levels on which we can approach this interrelationship. The first concerns the major aggregates of private consumption, public consumption, and investment; here, the primary question is whether the levels of savings and taxes in the economy are adequate to free enough resources for the desired level of government spending and capital formation. The evidence from the balance of payments, with its persistent current account deficits in spite of continuing attempts to reduce or eliminate them, suggests that the answer is negative. One way of expressing this is that the rising share of investment and public consumption in final uses of output was a direct counterpart of the shift in center of gravity out of agriculture and toward industry and the services; this increase in investment and government spending, in turn, resulted in considerable excess demand, which spilled abroad through the current account deficits in the balance of payments.

We have spoken as if a high rate of investment is directly associated with the shift in sectoral distribution of output during this period. This need not necessarily have been the case; a high rate of investment might have been channeled predominantly into agriculture, aiming at a high rate of growth of output without this type of sectoral change. In fact, though, during the 1950's, 85 percent of gross capital formation was in industry and the services.[4] It seems clear that the structural transformation which took place, particularly in the case of rapid expansion of the industrial sector, would have been impossible without a high rate of capital formation, although it is equally clear that a high rate of capital formation could have taken place without any such transformation if the investment had been concentrated primarily in agriculture.

So far, we have approached the interrelationship between these two types of structural change at an aggregative level; there might also arise questions concerning the more detailed composition of the major components of final demand. For example, expansion of personal services cannot get very far out of line with expansion of the food supply without causing imbalances at a microlevel. Clearly, the major consideration here is income elasticity of demand for specific consumption groups; the analysis is made more difficult, however, by changes in income distribution to which we have referred, taking place at the same time that average income per

---

[4]See Appendix Table I–A–9 (p. 290).

capita was rising. Perhaps this consideration helps to explain our findings in Chapters 8 and 9 that although real consumption per capita may have risen by 15–20 percent from 1954 to 1960, the share of food in total commodity consumption remained virtually unchanged.

If the income elasticity of demand is the major determinant of the requirements for balanced growth, the resulting pattern can be modified in two important ways. The first concerns relative prices of different goods and services. This particular aspect has not been of major significance in Egypt, at least up to the mid-1960's; the emphasis has been on price stability, with prices of a wide range of basic consumer goods held constant by government action, while market forces held wages of unskilled workers in the area of personal services virtually unchanged. Since 1965, by contrast, increasing attention has been paid to the manipulation of relative prices; this has taken the form of a sharp increase in the price of manufactured consumer goods, particularly consumer durables. Such a shift is clearly desirable from an equity point of view, if we think of the price increase as the equivalent of a turnover tax; it may be quite reasonable from the point of view of costs, in terms of foreign exchange. Yet one should point out that the substitution effect here works in the direction of increased demand for foodstuffs; these have a low average import content, but with inelastic domestic supply the marginal import content may be close to one. Raising the price of manufactured consumer goods may be an effective and equitable way of reducing aggregate demand; it may not be an effective way of reducing the average import content of consumption spending.[5]

Aside from changes in relative prices, the other consideration which softens the requirement of strictly balanced growth of production among the various components of consumer demand concerns foreign trade. A large amount of trade, even if it is balanced, gives a country substantial flexibility as between the structure of production and consumption; in 1960, Egypt's current receipts from abroad amounted to over 20 percent of gross national products. Beyond this, the country consistently had a deficit in the current account of the balance of payments; this amounted to only 1.7 percent of GNP in 1960, but rose to over 7 percent in 1962 and has

---

[5]This would not be so to the extent that demand is shifted to goods with elastic domestic supply and low import content; but there are not many goods of this type. Textiles would seem to qualify, although here there might be an offsetting reduction in exports.

remained very high since then. Of course, even this large a margin of flexibility does not rule out the possibility that certain specific goods or services might be in unexportable excess supply, in spite of aggregate excess demand in the economy; on the whole, though, this does not seem to have been a serious problem.[6]

So far in this chapter, our concern has been to explore the nature of the structural transformation which has taken place in the Egyptian economy over the past three decades. The next point which we should like to emphasize is the close relationship between this structural change and the growth in output of the economy. We have already referred to the employment aspects of this change; of the 2.1 million new jobs for men created between 1937 and 1960, nearly 75 percent were in the services and in industry.[7] Turning to the income side, Appendix Tables I–A–6 (page 286) and I–A–8 (pages 288–89) suggest that from 1945 to 1960, gross national product at constant prices grew at an average annual rate of 4 percent; this was achieved in spite of the fact that the agricultural sector grew at less than 1.7 percent per annum on the average over this same period. Another way of expressing this is that the agricultural sector accounted for only some 14 percent of the increase in aggregate real income over this fifteen-year period, although over 40 percent of national income was earned in this sector in 1945. Even taking account of population growth, which may have averaged close to 2 percent per annum during these years,[8] the conclusion stands out that the rate of growth of real income has been quite impressive, and has been heavily dependent

---

[6]We might refer again here to the curious item in the five-year plan indicating that in the year 1964–65, inventories would rise by £E117.6 million; this apparently reflects the skepticism on the part of the Ministry of Planning that even if production targets were achieved, the resulting output could either be absorbed at home or exported. See United Arab Republic, Presidency of the Republic, National Planning Committee, *General Frame of the Five-Year Plan for Economic and Social Development, July 1960–June 1965* (Cairo, 1960), pp. 204–5; and p. 238 above. In fact, this problem seems to have been relatively minor.

The ideas discussed in the preceding paragraphs will be familiar to those who are used to thinking in terms of an input-output model; our reasoning could easily be expressed in terms of such a model, which is closed in terms of consumer demand and open internationally, but with some allowance for the impact of price changes on the structure of final demand.

[7]The corresponding figure for total employment—men, women, and children— is 81 percent; as we indicated in Chapter 2, however, the figures on employment of women, particularly in agriculture, are highly questionable.

[8]The population growth rate was lower at the beginning and higher at the end of this period.

on the structural transformation of the economy which we have discussed above.

The question might be asked as to whether this growth in output is truly real, rather than simply a statistical phenomenon. In the case of many of the services, real output is measured by inputs; if productivity changes, either up or down, this may be quite an imperfect measure. Our discussion in Chapter 6 suggests that this challenge is only relevant to the government sector and personal services; these two components, which are grouped together under the heading "other services" in the income figures, account for only 17 percent of the overall increase in real income from 1945 to 1960. Even if there is some exaggeration in real growth here, its importance in the aggregate is small.

A similar challenge might be made against the industrial sector; if the prices of domestically produced manufactured goods are substantially above world prices, the rapid growth of this sector is too heavily weighted in the whole economy. This consideration was of growing importance during the 1950's; particularly since the intensive industrialization program associated with the start of the first industrial plan in 1958, many new industries have been established producing goods at costs well above world prices. At least up through 1960, however, we feel that this factor was not important enough to alter the basic picture of continuing and significant growth in aggregate output, closely tied in with the structural changes taking place in the economy.

A further question concerns whether the actual growth path which the economy has followed was the only feasible one for the country. Our approach to this question stems from our analysis of the agricultural sector; with factor proportions in this sector so unfavorable to labor, with heavy capital inputs and relatively advanced productive techniques already in use, it seems unrealistic to expect substantial and continuing increases in agricultural output. If this is so, it suggests that the aggregate growth of the economy will necessarily be heavily dependent on manufacturing industry and the services. A number of important questions remain: What will be the relative emphasis on these two major categories in the expansion of output? At what rate can the two together be pushed? What will be the detailed composition of the growth pattern within each of these two broad categories? These are important questions, on which one might find much to criticize the Egyptians; but with regard to the overall pattern of growth in the economy, relying on a joint and rapid expansion of these two sectors, we can find little to criticize; in fact, we see no real alternative.

A third question which might be raised is whether the growth path followed over the past three decades is a viable and sustainable one for the future. Here, perhaps the most important part of the answer centers around the relationship between growth and structural change, on the one hand, and the balance of payments, on the other. Our discussion above suggests that foreign trade has had a major role to play in making possible this continuing growth. From an aggregative point of view, the fact that the country had more goods and services available for final use than its current output made it easier to devote more resources to investment and government spending, both of which played a major role in the growth and transformation of the economy. At a more detailed level, imbalances between the structure of production and final demand could be handled by exports and imports. The fact that net imports were positive meant that consumer demand could be permitted to rise more rapidly; that is, it could be adjusted upward toward the supply of those commodities whose production was rising more rapidly, rather than being held back to the rate of growth of more slowly rising commodities, such as food.

In the future, there is every prospect that the country will be forced to curtail sharply her balance-of-payments deficits. Will this mean a correspondingly sharp fall in aggregate growth rates? Not necessarily; but if this is to be avoided, at the microlevel, increasing attention will need to be paid to balancing supply and demand of specific commodities, by more careful planning as well as more active use of the price system. At a macrolevel, the overriding need will be to hold the level of aggregate demand down to equality with the quantity of goods and services the economy can produce. Aggregate demand is made up of three major components: private consumption, government consumption, and investment; if we are to reduce their sum while sustaining the high growth rate of output, the need is clearly for a further fall in the already reduced share of private consumption in total output. Beyond this, the rapid relative expansion of the government sector which has taken place in the last two decades surely will not continue in the future; more likely, it will maintain its current share of total output and employment, thereby putting a greater burden on other sectors to sustain a high rate of aggregate growth on both fronts. On the whole, we see no reason to believe that the present situation in the Egyptian economy is basically unhealthy; we do not feel that there are significant portions of current output, the end point (for the moment) of the past growth process, which are deadweight loss and which need to be eliminated from the economy. On the other hand, it seems clear that the economy will not be able to continue to grow in the same way in the future, i.e., based on an ever-expanding service sector along with an expansion of manufacturing output approaching 10 percent per year. Surely, the present policy of concentrating more attention on using the existing capital stock more efficiently rather than building new factories head over heels makes a great deal of sense. Beyond this, there are important gains to be made by higher productivity in agriculture—for example, by improving yields of maize, and by taking advantage of the new flexibility in cropping patterns which will result from the completion of the High Dam at Aswan. In short, what we are suggesting is that perhaps the economy has gone through as much structural transformation as it can manage at present; what is needed is another period of proportional expansion all around, similar to the first thirty years of the twentieth century, except that now, precisely as a result of the transformation which has taken place in the meantime, growth will be of quite a different character, and hopefully at a substantially higher rate than during the earlier period of proportional growth.

STATISTICAL APPENDIX

TABLE OF CONTENTS

*The numbering of these tables is designed to follow in a general way the
outline in Table 10 of *A System of National Economic Accounts and Historical
Data* (Economic Growth Center at Yale University).

Appendix T

National Income and Product Estimates: General Discussion

There is a long history of national income estimates in Egypt, going back to 1922, when M. I. G. Lévi estimated the income of the country to be £ E301 million.[1] This figure was immediately attacked with the charge that it was close to 100 percent too high (i.e., that the correct figure was nearer to £ E150 million), while others offered additional evidence to support Lévi.[2] The debate has been carefully summarized by M. A. Anis, who came to the predictable conclusion that the best estimate was somewhere in the middle, probably in the range £ E200–250 million.[3] The wide margin of error rests in large measure on the weakness of the basic statistical data, making it virtually impossible to improve much on them now. There have also been a number of detailed studies of particular sectors which either include or can be used to derive estimates of value added in these specific sectors. Aside from these, the next major study of the aggregate income of the country was that

---

[1] M. I. G. Lévi, "L'Augmentation des Revenus de L'Etat: Possibilités et Moyen d'y Parvenir," *L'Egypte Contemporaine*, No. 68 (December, 1922), pp. 596–617.

[2] J. Baxter, "Notes on the Estimate of the National Income of Egypt, 1921–22," along with Lévi's reply, *L'Egypte Contemporaine*, No. 73 (May, 1923), pp. 405–69; J. I. Craig, "Notes on the National Income of Egypt," *L'Egypte Contemporaine*, No. 76 (January, 1924), pp. 1–9.

[3] M. A. Anis, "A Study of the National Income of Egypt," Appendix I, "History of Estimates," *L'Egypte Contemporaine*, Nos. 261–62 (November-December, 1950), pp. 849–70.

of Anis.[4] Originally presented as a doctoral dissertation at the University of London, this work first covered the years 1937–45, but was later extended to include one additional year, 1950. The estimates are presented following three different approaches: income by factor shares, output by industrial origin, and output by final use. Anis makes clear that these three estimates are not independent and hence provide no real means of cross-checking the different totals. The third of these approaches is in fact quite useless; capital formation is taken as a residual, while personal consumption is estimated by multiplying rough estimates of the quantity of each commodity used for consumption purposes by "average annual retail prices quoted at Cairo official markets. Out of the various varieties quoted the main variety has been chosen."[5]

In spite of very extensive discussion—the original journal article covered 265 pages—it is not easy to glean from text or table notes just how individual figures were derived. In some sectors (industry, for example), annual employment data have been applied to value added in a base year, adjusting for changes in wholesale prices of output of the sector; in the services, employment data have been combined with rough estimates of wage rates, in some cases with a fixed markup to cover the nonwage component. On the distributive shares side, the weakest element is profits. "The method of estimate consisted of adding up incomes from different sources in the Cairo Area as representing about 50 percent of the taxable capacity of the whole country."[6] All in all, the figures give only a rough idea of the order of magnitude of gross national product. The figures, along with more detailed notes, are given in Appendix Table I–A–1 (pages 270–71).

The next major contribution to the study of Egypt's income was contained in the doctoral dissertation of S. H. Abdel Rahman.[7] This estimate, which covered the years 1945–54, was designed to provide a comparable series with that of Anis. Abdel Rahman presents value added at market prices, while Anis' figures are at factor cost, so that direct comparison of individual sectors is not possible, although total indirect tax and subsidy figures make possible the presentation of a continuous series for the aggregates. The figures were estimated only from the output point of view. The results are shown in Appendix Table I–A–2 (pages 272–73).

Official interest in the preparation of national accounts dates from the mid-1950's, when the Statistical and Census Department of the Ministry of Finance and Economy undertook the task of making estimates of the income of the country. After some preliminary work on the year 1948, detailed estimates were made of the national income of the country in 1953, following both sectoral value added and distributive shares

---

[4] *Ibid.*, pp. 651–924; and "The National Income of Egypt, 1950," *L'Egypte Contemporaine*, No. 271 (January, 1953), pp. 19–30.

[5] Anis, *op. cit.*, 1950, p. 817.

[6] Anis, *op. cit.*, 1953, p. 23.

[7] S. H. Abdel Rahman, *A Survey of the Foreign Trade of Egypt in the Post-War Period, with Special Reference to Its Impact on the National Economy* (Ph.D. dissertation, Faculty of Commerce, University of Cairo, 1959).

approaches.[8] This estimate was later extended back to 1950 and forward to 1954 by the Statistical and Census Department. More recently, this department has made further estimates covering 1957–60, which purport to be comparable to the earlier series.[9] For the earlier years, these estimates were based heavily on an analysis of profit and loss statements of a small number of companies, along with data taken from tax returns.[10] In later years, when the basic data have become a great deal more complete, experimentation with different classifications and methods of estimation means that the series is not easy to use as its stands. The estimates have also been presented at constant (1954) prices, but the methods of deflation used are implausible for the period 1950–53[11] and rather weak for the later years. During this later period, all services are deflated by the official cost-of-living index; trade is deflated by the price of 16 commodities,[12] construction by the price of building materials. Mining and manufacturing are more satisfactorily handled, being deflated by the price of 28 major products, while in agriculture the figures are from the competent study of the Department of Statistics and Census evaluating both inputs and outputs at constant 1954 prices.[13] With the

[8]The results were published in Republic of Egypt, Ministry of Finance and Economy, Statistical and Census Department, *National Income of Egypt for 1953: "Official Estimate"* (Cairo, 1955).

[9]Current and constant price series for 1950–58 were published in United Arab Republic, Central Statistical Committee, *Basic Statistics*, June, 1962 (in English), pp. 231–32. More detailed figures and a description of methods of estimation for 1957 and 1958 are given in two mimeographed studies of the Department of Statistics and Census, *Estimates of National Income in the U.A.R. (Egypt) for the Years 1957 and 1958* and *Methods of Estimation of National Income in the U.A.R. (Egypt), 1957 and 1958* (Cairo, 1962) (both in Arabic). For 1959 and 1960 figures at current and constant prices, see Central Bank of Egypt, *Economic Review*, Vol. IV, Nos. 3–4 (1964), pp. 278–87.

[10]For a careful and critical appraisal of these estimates, see J. M. Crawford, *National Income Statistics*, mimeographed report to United Nations Technical Assistance Board, File No. TAA/173/20/06 (1955).

[11]The original estimates were first published in *Annuaire Statistique, 1951–54* (Cairo, 1956), p. 305; the adjusted ones in *Annuaire Statistique, 1954–56* (Cairo, 1959), p. 313. The footnotes to the adjusted figures indicate that they had been reestimated on new bases, and changes coming from price variations were excluded by taking as base wholesale prices of 1950 (although these are later presented in a 1954-base series). Comparing the two series, the sixteen sectors of the economy can be broken into three groups: (*a*) eight sectors where there was no change; the two sets of figures are identical; (*b*) four sectors where the 1950–52 figures are identical, but the 1953 revised estimates are multiplied by a factor 1.117; (*c*) four sectors where all figures were multiplied by a factor which varied from sector to sector, but was the same within each sector for all four years, 1950–53. With the exception of agriculture, where revised current and constant price estimates are used, the earlier of these estimates are now called the current price estimates, the adjusted figures the constant price estimates (see, for example, the references in n. 9 above).

[12]And a strange group they are: fresh fish, salted fish, coffee, tea, wood, iron bars, steel, skins, pepper, coal, paper, nickel, lead, zinc, tin, iron sheets.

[13]United Arab Republic, Department of Statistics and Census, *National Income from the Agricultural Sector for the Years 1958–1960* (Cairo, n.d.) (in Arabic).

passage of time and the accumulation of experience the figures should improve, although constantly changing personnel seems to be a continuing problem. We have made no use of the figures in our study and have not reproduced them here.

The next major step in the development of national accounts in Egypt came with the important work in this area by the National Planning Committee. In the first instance, this was centered around the year 1954; for that year, there is available a most impressive abundance of data on many different aspects of the economy. The most basic work of this intensive data-gathering effort was in the form of commodity flow studies; for each of some 300 commodities, estimates were made of the quantity and value of output, as well as the costs of production, broken down among intermediate inputs (specified among the same 300 commodities) and different components of value added. A circular was sent to all government departments, asking them to specify how much of each of these 300 commodities they had used during the year; special studies were made in the area of capital formation. A great deal of effort was expended to make sure that the data were consistent and comprehensive.[14] The outcome was that all necessary data were at hand for estimating income, output, and expenditure, at least in the commodity-producing sectors of the economy. The services were clearly on much shakier grounds, although for some, such as commerce, the commodity statistics—which (in principle) tell the value of a commodity when it is sold by the producer as well as when it is bought by the user—were of great help in making the estimates. For others, such as household services, the data have always involved a large measure of guesswork.

As for the visible output of this study, there are three major components. The first is the commodity balance tables; these give figures for 73 commodity groups on sources (domestic production and imports) and uses (public consumption, private consumption, capital formation, exports, and intermediate uses). These are similar in format to those for 1959–60 and 1964–65 in Section III of the five-year plan.[15] The second product of this work was an 83 × 83 input-output table of the economy. This is more precisely an interflow table, since, besides the intermediate relationships of the input-output table, it also specifies final uses of the output of each sector, as well as value added, both broken down by their different components. This table has twice been condensed, first

---

[14]See National Planning Committee, Memo No. 55 (bis) (August, 1958), Parts 1–4. This memo is filled with cases where different estimates of the same total are compared, divergencies explored, and the proper figures used for the problem at hand.

[15]United Arab Republic, Presidency of the Republic, National Planning Committee, *General Frame of the Five-Year Plan for Economic and Social Development, July 1960–June 1965* (Cairo, 1960), sec. III, pp. 53–78. As we shall see, the statistical basis for these later estimates was far less complete.

to a 33 × 33 level, and finally to specify only seven sectors. The 7 × 7 interflow table is shown in Table I–A–3 (pages 274–75).[16]

Finally, this same basic set of data has been drawn upon to present estimates of national income and product for the country. The methodology (although not detailed statistical sources) is given in National Planning Committee Memo No. 74, while the figures themselves are given in Memo No. 95. We have reclassified and reorganized the data in the latter of these memos in such a way as to make them conform as closely as possible to the standard format used by the Economic Growth Center at Yale University.[17] The resulting figures appear in Appendix I–A–4 (pages 276–80).

One of the uses to which this set of data was put by the planners was to extend its backward through time by applying indices of physical output or, failing that, inputs or employment, to give an estimate of the pattern of change of real product at constant prices over the period 1945–54. The figures and detailed sources of this study are presented in Appendix Table I–A–5 (page 000). There are some conceptual differences between the 1954 figures in this study and those presented in Memo No. 95; for example, Appendix Table I–A–5 excludes government services as well as the income of household servants. Aside from these conceptual differences, the two estimates are very similar and, for most sectors, identical.[18]

We have made several adjustments in these figures in order to bring them to a total of gross national product, as this is normally defined.[19] The first of these is to add an estimate of government wage payments; these figures are presented and explained in Appendix Table II–B–11 (page 315). Secondly, in the agricultural sector the original figures in the memo were computed on the basis of an *output* index; due to a changing pattern of inputs to agriculture (particularly fertilizers), this is not a satisfactory indicator of changes in real value added in the sector. We therefore preferred to use the figures in a recent study by the Department of Statistics and Census,[20] which computed both output and in-

---

[16]The 33 x 33 table as well as the 7 x 7 one are published in G. E. Eleish, "The Applicability and Utilization of the Input-Output Model in a Developing Economy: The Case of Egypt Examined," in T. Barna (ed.), *Structural Interdependence and Economic Development* (New York: St. Martin's Press, 1963) (reprinted as Institute of National Planning Memo No. 168 [March 31, 1962]).

[17]See Yale University, Economic Growth Center, *A System of National Economic Accounts and Historical Data* (New Haven, n.d.).

[18]For a discussion of apparent divergencies in agriculture, see the notes to Appendix Table I–A–3 (p. 274).

[19]In the remainder of this Appendix, we have drawn heavily on a memo written jointly by the author and Bent Hansen, entitled *The National Income of the U.A.R. (Egypt), 1939–1962*, Memo No. 355 (Cairo: Institute of National Planning, July, 1963).

[20]United Arab Republic, Department of Statistics and Census, *National Income from the Agricultural Sector for the Years 1958–1960* (Cairo, n.d.) (in Arabic).

puts in constant 1954 prices. These figures are not available before 1950; before that, we have been forced to use the implied output index in the NPC memo figures. As a result, and to the extent that there was a marked increase in fertilizer consumption in the immediate postwar years, our figures overstate the increase in real value added in agriculture from 1945–50.

As a third adjustment, we have included an estimate of value added in household services. In the absence of other information, we have assumed these to be unchanged (in real terms) throughout the period, at a level of £E17 million.[21] Finally, since the figures refer to domestic product, we have added net factor returns from abroad. The adjusted figures are given in Appendix Table I–A–6 (page 286).

With the methods here applied in calculating the real domestic product, regard has not been paid to effects on real national income from changes in the terms of trade. The gains and losses in connection with changes in the terms of trade may be calculated in many different ways. Here, we chose the following method. For each year, exports and imports were estimated in terms of 1954 prices; this was done through deflating the current price figures by the export and import price indices of the National Bank of Egypt.[22] In this way, we arrived at a hypothetical surplus (deficit) on the balance of trade which would have ruled, ceteris paribus, if the prices of export and import commodities had been the same as in 1954. The difference between this hypothetical surplus and the actual surplus is what the country could have spent extra abroad without deteriorating its net debt position toward the rest of the world if, ceteris paribus, the 1954 prices had been ruling in that particular year. This difference is then taken to be the loss from terms-of-trade shifts in the particular year compared with 1954; to express it in terms of 1954 prices, it was deflated by the import price index.[23] Given the definition of gains (losses) from terms-of-trade changes, the estimates are defective for at least two reasons: They do not take invisibles into account, and the import price index only comprises a limited number of import goods (machinery and equipment are, for instance, not included). For 1945–54, we were unable to form an opinion about the development of the prices for invisibles.

For the period since 1954, it was the National Planning Committee's original intention to bring the figures up to date and keep them current on the basis of continuing commodity studies which perhaps would not be as detailed as those for 1954, but would still cover all the major areas of the economy; in fact, fairly extensive data for 1955 and 1956 were collected at the same time that the 1954 work was done. This process turned out to be too time-consuming, and the pressing problems of draw-

---

[21]This is the estimate for 1954 given in NPC Memo No. 95.

[22]See Appendix Table V–A–7 (p. 363).

[23]We have actually calculated the gains and losses from terms of trade on two other definitions also. The results differ somewhat, but agree on the main features, namely, the big shifts in 1947–48 and during the years 1950–52.

ing up the plan itself pushed the interim income estimates into the background. Efforts in this area were concentrated in presenting a set of accounts similar to those of 1954 for the base year of the plan, 1959–60.[24] It is clear that these accounts are substantially less reliable than the earlier figures. They were done quickly, perhaps in three to four months. More important, they were completed before the period they covered was over; reporting on the economy during the period July, 1959–June, 1960, they were made during the early months of 1960. This means that they were estimates by informed people of what the national income and product would turn out to be, rather than a report on what had actually taken place. It is in this light that the later figures which have been reorganized and presented in Appendix Table I–A–4 (pages 276–80) must be interpreted.

In 1963 the National Planning Committee published a series of national income estimates covering the period 1952–53 to 1962–63.[25] There has been no published discussion as to how these estimates were derived, but they agree with the figures for the 1959–60 in the Plan Frame, as well as the figures for 1954 in Memo No. 95 and Memo 1.[26] It seems likely that they are based largely on the same type of selective commodity studies which underlay the 1959–60 figures. This means that we cannot expect them to be as precise as the 1954 figures. Still, the figures are plausible; and in working with them, we have found no reason to doubt that they present a generally accurate picture, at least through 1959–60. The figures are presented in Appendix Table I–A–7 (page 287).

We have taken these figures as a starting point for constant price estimates of national income over the period 1952–53 to 1959–60; since that year, the Ministry of Planning has itself made constant price estimates, permitting us to bring the table up through 1962–63. These figures, which are expressed in terms of 1954 prices (to make them comparable from this point of view with those in Appendix Table I–A–6 [page 286]) are given in Appendix Table I–A–8 (pages 288–89); the notes to the latter table explain the precise methods used in deriving these estimates.

---

[24]There is an interesting memo, No. 36, which presents for 1959 (calendar year) detailed commodity balance data similar to those which played such an important role in the 1954 accounts. This was done at the time it was anticipated that calendar 1959 might be the base year of the plan. As in the case of the 1959–60 figures in the plan itself, these rested on a much less thorough data-gathering effort than the 1954 accounts; but the study indicates that there was a continuing effort to bring the accounts up to date following this approach, even on the basis of more limited information.

[25]This was published in United Arab Republic, Department of Statistics and Census, *Ten Years of Revolution: Statistical Atlas* (Cairo, July, 1962), Table 9, "Estimates of National Income by Economic Activities."

[26]That is to say, they can be reconciled with them in large measure, once we adjust for differing treatment of such things as government wage payments and customs duties. For a detailed comparison of the 1954 figures, see Hansen and Mead, *op. cit.*, pp. 4–5.

TABLE 1-A-1

Gross National Product, 1937–50

(£E Million, Current Prices)

	1937	1938	1939	1940	1941	1942	1943	1944	1945	1950
I. Income by factor shares:										
A. Rent:										
Land[a]	35	35	35	39	38	47	63	73	90	130
Buildings[b]	13	13	13	13	14	15	15	16	16	40
B. Profits and interest:										
Agricultural[c]	23	23	23	23	33	60	58	76	79	100
Nonagricultural[d]	38	39	40	50	59	81	96	112	123	230
C. Salaries and wages[e]	52	53	53	63	85	118	147	172	185	325
D. Government income[f]	6	6	6	7	10	11	11	13	11	20
E. Undistributed profits	...	...	...	...	...	7	7	13	13	10
F. Gross domestic income (at factor)[g]	167	169	170	195	239	339	397	475	517	855
II. Output:[h]										
A. Agriculture	80	80	81	82	92	130	157	187	217	374
B. Manufacturing	13	13	13	17	26	37	46	57	54	105
C. Commerce (trade and finance)	11	11	11	16	23	33	42	52	50	150
D. Transport	5	5	6	9	10	14	16	17	15	115
E. Professions	15	16	17	21	26	35	41	47	50	35
F. Service of persons	8	8	8	9	10	12	15	16	16	
G. Public services	9	9	9	10	11	15	21	26	31	
H. Rent of dwellings	12	12	12	12	12	13	13	13	13	40
I. Other services	9	9	9	12	17	25	32	38	42	46
J. Gross domestic product (at factor)[g]	163	163	166	188	227	314	383	453	488	865

III. Expenditure:[i]

A. Personal consumption	143	148	146	167	228	271	292	326	650
B. Government and local authorities (current)	26	27	27	32	41	57	64	80	178
C. Capital formation	13	8	33	51	76	78	132	122	113
D. Gross domestic expenditure (at market)	182	183	206	250	345	406	488	528	941
E. Subsidies[j]	3	3	3	3	3	6	5	10	12
F. Less indirect taxes[k]	-19	-18	-18	-20	-22	-22	-29	-36	-93
G. Gross domestic expenditure (at factor)[l]	165 / 166	168	191	233	326	390	464	502	860

[a] Average rent times arable land.

[b] From house tax; makes some allowance for maintenance and repairs. Rent of public buildings excluded.

[c] Including livestock. Value added in agriculture less land rent and wage payments.

[d] Includes professional earnings.

[e] Includes allowances in kind.

[f] Trading profits of public enterprises.

[g] We have entitled these totals gross rather than net, as Anis does, since in no sector other than buildings has he been able to make any allowance for the using-up of the capital stock.

[h] Detailed notes on output cannot be very precise; as we indicate in the discussion, there is a heavy reliance on employment figures, supplemented either by wages per worker or by value added per worker. Since annual employment figures are either weak or nonexistent, there must have been a heavy reliance on interpolation.

[i] See discussion on page 264 above; these figures are most imprecise.

[j] Payments made by government toward cost of goods and services bought by the public.

[k] The main items are customs duties and tobacco and cigarette duties.

[l] The average of the other two approaches, which Anis feels gives the best single estimate.

SOURCES: M. A. Anis, "A Study of the National Income of Egypt," *L'Egypt Contemporaine*, Nos. 261–62 (November–December, 1950), pp. 651–924; and "The National Income of Egypt, 1950," *L'Egypt Contemporaine*, No. 271 (January, 1953), pp. 19–30.

TABLE I–A–2

GROSS NATIONAL PRODUCT, 1945–54

(£E Million, Current Prices)

	1945	1946	1947	1948	1949	1950	1951	1952	1953	1954
A. Government[a]	58.5	59.8	58.9	64.0	74.1	90.3	109.9	122.4	123.3	136.2
B. Private sector:										
1. Agriculture[b]	215.6	189.8	203.4	246.9	316.8	361.7	348.3	269.2	272.7	309.6
2. Cotton ginning and pressing[c]	1.4	1.9	1.6	1.7	2.1	2.0	2.0	2.8	2.0	2.1
3. Mining, quarrying, and salines[d]	6.9	6.6	7.0	9.8	11.8	13.7	13.2	14.5	14.7	11.8
4. Manufacturing[e]	33.7	34.5	34.9	46.6	46.7	53.4	65.7	63.6	60.7	63.3
5. Building and construction (private and public)[f]	11.3	14.5	17.4	23.0	30.0	28.6	30.8	29.5	26.8	27.6
6. Electricity, gas, and water[g]	2.0	2.2	2.6	3.1	3.5	4.1	4.4	4.8	5.1	5.5
7. Commerce, storage, and transportation[h]	124.5	135.0	154.6	213.6	235.3	282.2	318.4	289.8	250.0	244.8
8. Banking and real estate[i]	6.4	6.5	6.9	7.4	7.6	8.5	8.9	9.3	9.6	10.5
9. Insurance[i]	1.0	1.0	1.0	1.3	1.7	2.0	1.8	2.0	2.3	2.2
10. Services[j]	49.7	51.7	54.7	61.2	62.9	68.3	73.8	74.3	76.5	79.9
11. Ownership of dwelling[k]	35.9	37.2	38.4	40.8	43.5	45.3	47.7	49.6	53.1	55.8
C. Gross domestic product (at market)	546.9	540.7	581.4	719.4	836.0	960.1	1,024.9	931.8	898.8	949.3
D. Rest of the world[l]	-4.9	-5.3	-3.0	-1.1	-6.9	-8.3	-9.0	-12.1	-11.1	-13.1
E. Gross national product (at market)	551.8	535.4	578.4	718.3	829.1	951.8	1,015.9	919.7	887.7	936.2

F. Plus subsidies[m]	2.7	5.5	4.8	8.9	10.5	9.7	15.3	15.9	10.6	4.8
G. Less indirect taxes[n]	−37.5	−48.2	−59.1	−66.8	−76.7	−89.8	−115.4	−99.9	−106.6	−108.9
H. Gross national product (at factor)	517.0	492.7	524.1	660.4	762.9	871.7	915.8	835.7	791.7	832.1
I. Gross domestic product (at factor)	512.1	498.0	527.1	661.5	769.8	880.0	924.8	847.8	802.8	845.3

[a] From government budgets. It was attempted to make them net of depreciation. Includes value added in enterprises as well as wages and salaries in general government.

[b] Official estimates of the Ministry of Agriculture.

[c] Value added per cantar times quantity handled.

[d] Based on analysis of values, costs, and quantities of major commodities.

[e] A quantity index times the wholesale price index gives an idea of the value of gross output; this is multiplied by the value of output in 1950 to give a gross value of output series. Inputs are handled in the same way; the difference between the two series measures value added. The figures are generally gross of depreciation.

[f] Rough estimates based on materials used.

[g] Value added (from 1954 census of industrial production) times output index; prices have remained constant.

[h] Weak figures based on a study of trade margins in internal and external trade. Excise taxes and customs duties are included here.

[i] From company reports.

[j] Professional and household servants' income from employment, and estimated wage rates, assuming that the latter change with the cost-of-living index. Other services: 1954 employment (from census of establishments) times wage rates (200 percent of that for services in survey of wages and working hours), traced back in proportion to commodity production.

[k] Fixed percentage of total rental income (from tax data).

[l] From balance-of-payments data.

[m] Includes only wheat subsidies.

[n] The main items are customs duties and tobacco and cigarette dues.

SOURCE: S. H. Abdel Rahman, *A Survey of the Foreign Trade of Egypt in the Post-War Period, with Special Reference to Its Impact on the National Economy* (Ph.D. dissertation, Faculty of Commerce, Cairo University, 1959). As in the case of Anis' figures, these data are in between being gross and net of depreciation; once again, we have called them gross, since depreciation deductions have been limited.

TABLE I–A–3

An Input-Output Table for the Egyptian Economy for the Year 1954

(£E Thousand)

	(1)	(2)	(3)	(4)	(5)	(6)	(7)
				Purchasing Sector			
Producing Sector	Agricul-ture	Electricity and Petrol	Industry and Mines	Transpor-tation and Commu-nication	Suez Canal	Construc-tion	Services
1. Agriculture............	47,481		205,790				92
2. Electricity and petrol..	2,824	2,098	9,181	6,120	262	1,226	4,787
3. Industry and mines....	11,222	10,016	190,785	3,337	217	17,861	11,351
4. Transportation and communication.....	1,103	1,555	6,850	1,656	823	1,378	29,146
5. Suez Canal..........				18			
6. Construction.........	21	63	38	131			3,004
7. Services.............	148,734	4,404	77,220	6,897	2,039	8,798	28,659
8. Imports.............	16,500	5,352	43,518	7,342	461	10,233	7,313
9. Total input.........	227,885	23,488	533,442	25,501	3,802	39,496	84,352
10. Value added.........	172,929	14,678	138,252	60,664	27,627	31,815	470,209
11. Total output.........	400,814	38,166	671,694	86,165	31,429	71,311	554,561

Source: G. E. Eleish, "The Applicability and Utilization of the Input-Output Model in a Developing Economy: The Case of Egypt Examined", paper presented to the International Conference on Input-Output Techniques, Geneva, September 11–15, 1961, reprinted as Institute of National Planning Memo No. 168, (March 31, 1962), and in T. Barna (ed.), *Structural Interdependence and Economic Development* (New York: St. Martin's Press, 1963). This paper also presents the 33 x 33 table. These figures differ in a number of ways from those in Appendix Table I–A–4. The value of household servants is placed at £E38.7 million here, only £E17 million there; the foreign trade figures diverge somewhat, particularly in the case of imports, presumably because the input-output table relies exclusively on exchange control data, while in Memo No. 95 (which underlies Appendix Table I–A–4), some use was made of customs data as well; the estimates of stock changes do not agree. For the rest, divergencies exist for each figure, but they are negligible. The low value added and high intermediate purchases from services in agriculture come from treatment of property ownership (including land) as a separate activity, so that rental payments are considered as an intermediate purchase. To correct for this, we could shift into the agricultural sector the rental value of agricultural land, either excluding or including value added in agricultural real estate companies (some of whose income is derived from other sources, but with inadequate detail to separate agricultural from nonagricultural components). The first procedure (excluding these companies, as was done in National Planning Committee Memo No. 95) shows value added in agriculture of £E231,415,000, while including them (as was done in National Planning Committee Memo No. 1) yields a figure of £E296,369,000. This item has been the source of much disagreement about these accounts.

(8)	(9)	(10)	(11)	Purchasing Sector (12)	(13)	(14)	(15)	(16)
Total Intermediate Consumption	Capital Formation (Private Sector)	Change in Stocks	Household Consumption	Government Consumption	Capital Formation (Government)	Exports	Total Final Demand	Gross Production
253,363		27,619	113,612	3,051		3,169	147,451	400,814
26,498		43	7,187	3,591		847	11,668	38,166
244,789	9,304	13,429	299,909	22,914	1,447	106,760	426,905	671,694
42,511			31,997	5,277		6,380	43,654	86,165
18						31,411	31,411	31,429
3,257	43,171		2	2,344	22,537		68,054	71,311
276,751	7,100		216,767	12,607	333	41,003	277,810	554,561
90,779	24,604	198	48,964	7,277	1,062		82,105	172,884
937,966	84,179	14,431	718,438	57,061	25,379	189,570	1,089,058	2,027,024
916,174			38,717	99,218			137,935	1,054,109
1,854,140	84,179	14,431	757,155	156,279	25,379	189,570	1,226,993	3,081,133

TABLE I–A–4

INTEGRATED NATIONAL ACCOUNTS, 1954 AND 1959–60

(£E Million)

			1954	*1959–60*
I.	Expenditure on gross national product:			
	A. 1.1	Private consumption expenditure............	726.5	991.0
	B.	Government administration consumption expenditure...............................	156.6	213.2
	1.2	Goods and services purchased..............	57.2	69.9
	1.3	Services, direct...........................	99.4	143.3
	C.	Gross capital formation.......................	118.5	203.9
	1.4	Business sector...........................	73.4	103.7
		a) Machinery.............................	37.6	
		b) Various industrial goods.................	3.4	
		c) Buildings and public works..............	32.4	
	1.5	Government administration................	24.9	80.1
		a) Machinery.............................	1.0	
		b) Various industrial goods.................	1.6	
		c) Buildings and public works..............	22.3	
	1.6	Households (housing)......................	10.8	9.0
	1.7	Stock changes............................	9.4	11.1
	D.	Foreign sector:		
	1.8	Exports of goods and services..............	196.6	235.0
	1.9	Less imports of goods and services..........	201.3	247.6
		Expenditure on gross domestic product.......	996.8	1,395.5
	E. 1.10	Net factor income from abroad............	−12.9	0.4
		Expenditure on gross national product......	984.0	1,395.9
	F. 1.11	Statistical discrepancy.....................	13.0	−75.0
		Gross national income at market price......	997.0	1,320.9
II.	Distribution of gross national income:			
	A.	Payments by producing units to individuals........	746.8	1,045.9
	2.1	Wages and salaries........................	365.2	570.3
		a) Business sector.........................	248.8	411.0
		b) Government administration..............	99.4	143.3
		c) Households............................	17.0	16.0
	2.2	Net interest payments.....................	0.3	4.0
	2.3	Net distributed profits, organized sector......	1.0	6.4
	2.4	Profits of nonorganized sector, distributed.....	378.7	449.9
	2.5	Business transfer payments.................	1.6	15.3
	B.	Gross retained earnings:		
	2.6	Organized busines sector...................	42.1	37.7
	2.7	Retained earnings of nonorganized business sector.............................	32.7	25.6
	C.	Payments by producing units to government:		
	2.8	Direct taxes..............................	55.3	51.5
	2.9	Customs duties...........................	86.7	95.6
	2.10	Other indirect taxes.......................	28.9	88.8
	2.11	Government business sector, transferred to administration......................	30.3	66.6
	D.	Less:		
	2.12	Production subsidies.......................	19.0	81.2
	2.13	Interest on public debt....................	6.7	7.1
	2.14	Interest on consumer debt.................	0.0	2.5
	E.	Gross national income at market.................	997.0	1,320.9

TABLE I–A–4—Continued

		1954	1959–60
III. Receipts and expenditures of households and nonprofit institutions:			
A. Payments by producing units to individuals		746.8	1,045.9
3.1	Wages	365.2	570.3
3.2	Net interest	0.3	4.0
3.3	Distributed profits, organized sector	1.0	6.4
3.4	Distributed profits, nonorganized sector	378.7	449.9
3.5	Business transfer payments	1.9	15.3
Less:			
3.6	Interest on consumer debt	0.0	2.5
B. Current transfers from general government:			
3.7	Social security benefits	1.0	2.7
3.8	Other transfers	14.5	13.2
C. 3.9	Current transfers from ROW	8.5	22.9
	Personal income	770.8	1,082.2
D. 3.10	Private consumption expenditure	726.5	991.0
E. Payments to government:			
3.11	Taxes	10.4	28.7
3.12	Social security payments	5.8	17.1
F. 3.13	Transfers to ROW	10.2	10.9
	Total expenditures	752.9	1,047.7
3.14	Savings	17.9	34.5
	Total expenditures and savings	770.8	1,082.2
IV. Government administration revenue and current expenditures:			
A. Payments by producing units to government:			
4.1	Direct taxes	55.3	51.5
4.2	Customs duties	86.7	95.6
4.3	Other indirect taxes	28.9	88.8
4.4	Government business sector profits transferred to general administration	30.3	66.6
B. Payments by households to government:			
4.5	Taxes	10.4	28.7
4.6	Social security payments	5.8	17.1
C. 4.7	Less net interest on government debt	5.7	7.1
	Total revenues	211.7	341.2
D. Government expenditure on goods and services:			
4.8	Goods and services	57.2	69.9
4.9	Direct services (wages)	99.4	143.3
E. 4.10	Subsidies to business sector	9.7	10.3
F. Current transfers to households:			
4.11	Social security benefits	1.0	2.7
4.12	Others	14.5	13.2
G. 4.13	Current transfers to ROW	9.4	27.9
	Total current expenditure	191.2	267.3
4.14	Savings of general administration	20.5	73.9
	Total expenditure and savings	211.7	341.2
V. External account:			
A. Exports of goods and services:			
5.1	Commodity exports	144.1	168.8
5.2	Invisible exports	52.5	89.1
B. Factor incomes from abroad:			
5.3	Interest	2.6	3.0
5.4	Profits	2.5	0.5

(Continued on next page)

TABLE I–A–4—Continued

			1954	1959–60
C.	5.5	Current transfers from abroad	24.4	11.2
		Total current receipts	226.1	272.6
D.		Imports of goods and services:		
	5.6	Commodity imports	164.5	229.2
	5.7	Invisible imports	36.8	57.2
E.		Factor incomes paid to abroad:		
	5.8	Interest	1.8	2.6
	5.9	Profits	16.1	0.5
F.	5.10	Current transfers to abroad	12.2	6.0
		Total current expenditures	231.4	295.5
G.	5.11	Minus current account deficit	5.3	22.9
		Expenditures and deficit	226.1	272.6
VI.		Gross domestic capital formation and savings:		
A.		Gross domestic capital formation:		
	6.1	Government administration	24.9	80.1
	6.2	Business sector	73.4	103.7
	6.3	Stock changes	9.4	11.1
	6.4	Households	10.8	9.0
		Total domestic capital formation	118.5	203.9
B.		Gross retained income:		
	6.5	Organized business sector	42.1	37.7
	6.6	Nonorganized business sector	32.7	25.6
C.	6.7	Household savings	17.9	34.5
D.	6.8	General government savings	20.5	73.9
E.	6.9	Current account deficit	5.3	22.9
F.	6.10	Statistical discrepancy	0.0	9.3
		Total domestic savings	118.5	203.9

NOTES: *1954:* All references are to United Arab Republic, National Planning Committee, *Egyptian National Accounts, 1954*, Memo No. 95 (Cairo, December, 1958).

1.1: Table 24/12. Includes wages of household servants, as well as consumption of goods and services.

1.2 and 1.3. Table 24/15. 1.3 includes both wages and salaries (line 64) and the government's share in the insurance fund (line 65).

1.4. Table 24/9. Includes both organized and unorganized sectors.

1.5. Table 24/16.

1.6. Table 24/13.

1.7. Table 24/9. Also broken down by major commodity groups.

1.8. See 5.1 and 5.2.

1.9. See 5.6 and 5.7.

1.10. Table 24/19.

2.1. (a) Table 24/6. (b) Table 24/15. In the accounts in Memo No. 95, social insurance installments of workers in the business sector are handled through the appropriation accounts of households (i.e., included in wage payments and then paid into the fund by households); for workers in public administration, on the other hand, they are paid by the government directly to the fund on behalf of the workers (see Table 24/21, line 65). We add them in to make all go through the household sector. (c) Table 24/12, line 64.

2.2. Table 24/21, line 63; interest receipts of households.

2.3. Table 24/7, line 61.

2.4. Table 24/12, line 93 minus line 94. We treat profits of this sector used for investment purposes as retained earnings within the sector rather than savings of households.

2.5. Table 24/7, line 66.

2.6. Table 24/7, line 92, minus surplus of social security, now transferred to government administration, and net receipts of insurance companies, here treated as household savings.

2.7. Table 24/8, line 94; see 2.4 above.

2.8. Table 24/21, line 67.

2.9. Table 24/21, line 68.

2.10. Table 24/21, line 69.

2.11. Table 24/7, line 62.

TABLE I–A–4—Continued

2.12. Table 24/21, lines 73 and 74. Includes both production and capital subsidies.
2.13. Table 24/21, line 63.
2.14. Table 24/21, line 63.

3.1–3.5. See 2.1–2.5.
3.6. See 2.14.
3.7. Table 24/21, line 66.
3.8. Table 24/21, lines 66 and 79.
3.9. Table 24/21, line 76. ROW refers to Rest of the World.
3.10. See 1.1.
3.11. Table 24/21, line 67.
3.12. Table 24/21, line 65.
3.13. Table 24/21, line 76.

4.1–4.4. See 2.8–2.11.
4.5–4.6 See 3.11–3.12.
4.7. Table 24/21, line 63; payments less receipts.
4.8–4.9. See 1.2–1.3.
4.10. Table 24/21, line 73.
4.11–4.12. See 3.7–3.8.
4.13. Table 24/21, lines 75 and 77.

5.1. Table 24/19, line 5 (R1).
5.2 Table 24/19, line 5 (R2), plus Table 24/12, line 76.
5.3. Table 24/19, line 63.
5.4. Table 24/19, line 61.
5.5. Table 24/6, line 76.
5.6. Table 24/19, line 5 (F1).
5.7. Table 24/19, line 5 (F2), plus Table 24/12, line 76, and Table 24/15, lines 75 and 77.
5.8. Table 24/19, line 63.
5.9. Table 24/19, line 61.
5.10. Table 24/6, line 76.

6.1–6.4. See 1.4–1.7.
6.5–6.6. See 2.6–2.7.
6.7. See 3.14.
6.8. See 4.14.
6.9. See 5.14.

1959–60: All references are to United Arab Republic, Presidency of the Republic, National Planning Committee, *General Frame of the Five-Year Plan for Economic and Social Development, July 1960–June 1965* (Cairo, 1960) (English edition).

1.1. P. 196. Includes expenditures on household servants (wage payments). Data in Sections 2 and 3 of the *Plan Frame* imply a consumption figure of £1,010 million.
1.2–1.3. P. 141. This is nearly the same as the total derived by adding the public component of value added and production requirements in sec. II, pp. 43–48, but does not agree with the figures on p. 204 or p. 216.
1.4. P. 204. Out of total capital formation in the business sector, including stock changes (£114.8 million), £95.3 million was stated to be in the government business sector (p. 161).
1.5. P. 204 or p. 141.
1.6. P. 204.
1.7. P. 57. Total capital formation shown here agrees with sum of 1.4–1.6.
1.8–1.9. P. 243.
1.10. (5.3 plus 5.4) minus (5.8 plus 5.9).

2.1. (a) P. 216; includes social insurance payments. (b) See 1.1 plus 1.2. (c) P. 196.
2.2. P. 197; total household interest receipts.
2.3. P. 197; net coupons of joint stock companies paid to households, plus remunerations of members of boards of directors. See also p. 199.
2.4. Pp. 218–19; profits transferred from noncorporate business sector to household sector.
2.5. Pp. 199–217. Includes life insurance compensations, other business compensations, donations, and bad debts to household sector.
2.6. P. 229. Includes private companies in which the Economic Organization participates (£3 million) and other joint stock companies (£34.7 million). Increases in the social insurance reserve are treated as government savings, along with profits of the government business sector, while savings through other types of insurance are treated as being in the household sector.
2.7. P. 229.
2.8–2.10. P. 218. "Other indirect taxes" includes excise duties on domestic goods, other miscellaneous fees and duties, and other miscellaneous payments to public administration, from production, appropriation, and capital accounts.

(Continued on next page)

TABLE I–A–4—Continued

2.11. P. 229. Includes amounts used by government businesses to finance their own capital ormation (£32.3 million), as well as amounts transferred to government administration.

2.12. P. 216. Includes production subsidies (£10.3 million) as well as capital subsidy by public administration to government business sector.

2.13–2.14. P. 216.

3.1–3.5. See 2.1–2.5.

3.6. See 2.14.

3.7. Pp. 199 or 216–17.

3.8. P. 216. Includes government pensions, subsidies to individuals and nonprofit organizations, and miscellaneous compensations.

3.9. P. 219 or p. 241; see also 3.13 below.

3.10. See 1.1.

3.11. Pp. 241–42. Includes direct and indirect taxes, miscellaneous fees and duties, various payments (including capital payments) to public administration, and estate taxes and inheritance fees.

3.12. Pp. 216–17. We have included payments by businesses and government on behalf of individuals with wages, and here as expenditures.

3.13. P. 218. This and 3.9 are both very puzzling items in the accounts; both receipts and expenditures are listed for the household sector, and the reference in the text (p. 200) is quite confusing. Perhaps the most plausible explanation is that the receipts item represents expenditures by tourists in the country as well as transfer payments, while payments similarly includes expenditures of Egyptian travelers abroad as well as transfers.

4.1–4.4. See 2.8–2.11. *NB:* 4.4 includes all profits of public enterprise, even if these were in fact used for capital formation within the enterprise.

4.5–4.6. See 3.11–3.12.

4.7. See 2.13.

4.8–4.9. See 1.2–1.3.

4.10. P. 216 production subsidies.

4.11–4.12. See 3.7–3.8.

4.13. P. 218. See also comments for 3.13. It seems quite probable that here as well, this includes current expenditures overseas. It is not possible to separate the expenditure component from the transfer component.

5.1. P. 85. Excludes customs duties.

5.2. Difference between total exports (p. 243) and commodity exports (5.1), plus that portion of miscellaneous revenues credited to households (£22.9 million) (p. 219).

5.3–5.4. P. 243.

5.5. Miscellaneous revenues from ROW credited to business sector. Some of these may be invisible exports; for consistency with 1954 (when the category was referred to as transfers), it is included here rather than under 5.2 above.

5.6. P. 87.

5.7. Difference between total imports (p. 243) and commodity imports (5.6), plus that portion of miscellaneous imports debited to households and public administration (p. 218).

5.8–5.9. P. 243.

5.10. Miscellaneous expenditures or transfers abroad by business sector; see 5.5 (p. 218).

6.1–6.4. See 1.4–1.7.

6.5–6.6. See 2.6–2.7.

6.7. See 3.14.

6.8. See 4.14.

6.9. See 5.11.

TABLE I-A-5

VALUE ADDED, BY SECTORS, 1945–54

(£E Thousand, Constant 1954 Prices)

		1945	1946	1947	1948	1949	1950	1951	1952	1953	1954
0	Agriculture	261,294	259,861	257,841	283,480	280,471	261,118	245,103	281,665	270,175	296,369
1	Mining and quarrying	4,962	4,613	5,049	7,051	8,705	10,185	9,923	10,011	9,923	8,705
2	Electricity	1,976	2,032	2,120	2,209	2,407	2,605	2,289	2,974	3,334	3,695
3	Basic industries:										
301	Rubber	87	146	203	218	237	320	412	368	325	484
302	Basic chemicals	10,448	9,728	10,345	11,066	9,368	7,823	5,301	5,816	4,941	5,147
303	Vegetable and animal oils	4,526	5,572	5,708	4,789	6,614	7,655	7,155	5,958	6,707	7,127
304	Medicinal preparations	104	129	153	199	242	227	211	224	236	306
305	Cosmetics and drugs	11	57	99	71	39	54	68	82	92	354
306	Dyestuffs and paints	87	97	102	155	208	223	232	218	198	484
307	Matches	97	113	144	178	208	257	272	257	257	257
308	Other chemicals	505	499	486	480	474	486	499	598	698	623
309	Oil refining	5,098	4,805	5,000	7,060	8,923	8,825	9,021	9,216	9,021	9,805
310	Cement	966	1,324	1,434	1,710	1,986	2,290	2,538	2,596	2,428	2,758
311	Basic minerals				...	850	2,106	2,413	3,668	4,031	4,270
312	Mineral products	2,517	3,256	3,997	4,736	5,427	6,168	7,858	7,414	5,121	4,934
313	Repair of electrical machinery	2,668	3,515	4,361	4,016	3,672	3,954	4,236	4,048	3,828	3,138
314	Repair of nonelectrical machinery	1,302	922	542	1,030	1,465	1,410	1,302	1,193	1,030	4,544
315	Repair of transportation means	458	348	238	290	339	370	400	335	269	440
	Total, basic industries	28,874	30,512	32,812	35,998	40,042	42,168	40,918	40,491	39,982	44,671

(Continued on next page)

TABLE I–A–5—Continued

	1945	1946	1947	1948	1949	1950	1951	1952	1953	1954
4 Other industries:										
401 Ginning and pressing...	1,484	1,727	1,816	2,548	2,481	2,437	2,304	2,835	2,015	2,215
402 Slaughtering and meat packing...	2,371	2,663	3,032	3,339	3,323	3,294	3,255	2,961	3,382	4,859
403 Milk products...	7,117	5,780	7,944	8,164	11,211	10,898	9,095	9,374	10,397	11,630
404 Fruit packing and preservation...	154	197	241	269	295	394	491	443	1,003	1,145
405 Fish conservation ...	116	116	116	116	116	116	116	116	116	116
406 Grain milling ...	3,758	3,180	3,469	3,552	3,676	3,841	4,130	4,047	4,089	4,130
407 Bread baking ...	6,558	5,621	5,706	6,387	7,069	9,197	10,049	9,624	8,516	8,516
408 Sugar...	7,058	7,911	8,763	9,426	10,232	10,943	10,327	9,947	9,759	12,411
409 Chocolates and sweets..	193	213	232	187	140	224	351	220	369	251
410 Diverse foods...	295	813	1,329	1,452	1,551	1,673	1,772	1,575	1,378	2,461
412 Tobacco...	5,556	5,556	5,438	6,667	6,374	6,199	6,024	5,732	5,848	5,848
413 Spinning and weaving..	7,898	8,202	8,962	10,328	12,000	12,000	12,759	13,062	14,430	15,189
414 Ready-made clothes...	3,963	3,885	3,807	3,807	3,807	2,690	3,535	3,652	3,730	3,885
415 Wood...	116	129	139	180	217	281	342	322	301	339
416 Furniture...	1,154	1,197	1,239	1,966	2,650	2,778	2,864	3,035	3,163	4,274
417 Building materials...	939	930	1,007	1,776	1,886	2,036	1,651	1,500	2,184	1,868
418 Agricultural tools...	498	498	498	498	498	498	498	498	498	593
419 Paper and paper products...	198	245	285	338	385	432	472	583	688	583
420 Printing and publishing	1,511	1,943	2,376	2,499	2,592	2,653	2,684	2,653	2,592	3,085
421 Nonmetallic minerals..	433	592	751	831	900	1,037	1,173	1,071	968	1,139
422 Shoe and leather products...	329	207	184	172	161	172	184	344	504	573
423 Leather tanning...	497	497	497	507	550	561	575	600	761	543
424 Other...	2,523	2,489	2,451	2,532	2,599	2,905	3,211	3,210	3,206	3,034
Total, other industries...	55,205	55,112	60,813	68,131	75,323	77,740	78,571	78,092	80,417	89,183

5 Building and construction:										
501 Buildings	8,361	8,361	8,959	15,808	16,788	18,118	14,694	13,348	19,432	16,662
502 Roads and paths	214	255	258	316	354	336	374	393	381	479
503 Railroad construction	6	3	584	. . . . .	75	12	77	26	. . . . .	29
504 River transportation	112	144	155	171	182	155	326	299	203	203
505 Construction connected with irrigation and agriculture	10,077	12,332	13,960	13,766	6,674	3,016	19,993	15,603	15,781	14,930
506 Construction in agricultural sector	722	722	722	722	722	722	722	722	722	722
Total, building and construction	19,492	21,817	24,638	30,783	24,795	22,359	36,186	30,391	36,519	33,025
6 Transport and communications:										
601 Storage	975	976	1,187	1,229	1,377	1,229	1,018	895	1,169	1,066
602 Transport by railroad	7,524	7,000	6,017	6,780	7,074	7,552	8,186	8,213	8,967	9,187
603 Transport by road	16,858	19,987	22,920	26,441	30,274	34,107	36,963	37,237	38,058	39,114
604 Transport by sea	3,893	3,893	3,893	3,893	4,333	4,057	4,111	3,729	3,893	3,893
605 Transport by river	1,529	897	1,223	753	1,351	1,483	602	723	1,762	752
606 Transport by air	129	145	184	201	377	594	720	636	552	681
607 Transport by mail	1,950	1,873	1,796	1,703	1,625	1,548	1,591	1,621	1,644	1,707
608 Telephone and telegraph	2,601	2,703	2,809	2,912	3,018	3,121	3,448	3,586	3,770	3,940
609 Radio broadcast	261	271	281	292	303	313	345	360	378	395
Total, transport and communications	35,720	37,744	40,310	44,204	49,732	54,103	56,984	57,003	60,193	60,736
7 Suez Canal	2,430	5,606	5,799	17,148	22,312	24,190	23,831	23,997	26,261	27,614
8 Real estate ownership	49,571	51,041	52,510	55,526	58,852	62,177	65,116	68,287	73,391	77,335
9 Money and brokerage:										
901 Commercial banks	3,405	3,720	3,733	4,515	4,586	5,834	6,875	5,855	6,205	6,979
902 Insurance companies	555	555	651	751	861	1,004	1,108	1,256	1,399	1,604

(Continued on next page)

TABLE I–A–5—Continued

	1945	1946	1947	1948	1949	1950	1951	1952	1953	1954
903 Other financial institutions	2,564	2,564	2,564	2,564	2,564	2,564	2,564	2,564	2,564	2,564
904 Stock exchange	.....	6	7	8	9	9	10	12	13	13
Total, money and brokerage	6,530	6,845	6,455	7,838	8,020	9,411	10,557	9,687	10,181	11,160
10 Commerce	115,270	135,058	140,240	160,805	181,858	100,789	198,447	182,921	171,029	177,064
11 Other services:										
110 Water and public utilities	4,149	4,290	4,360	4,641	4,852	5,133	5,485	5,766	5,977	7,033
111 Health services	2,385	2,478	2,555	2,603	2,689	2,791	3,004	2,697	3,011	3,189
112 Sports and entertainment	2,291	2,440	2,600	2,755	2,921	3,097	3,284	3,479	3,687	3,910
113 Personal services	22,808	23,811	24,882	25,985	27,089	28,259	29,463	30,734	32,072	33,443
114 Education	2,109	2,268	2,428	2,727	3,025	3,363	3,701	3,701	3,742	3,980
115 Legal services	1,252	1,513	1,773	2,034	2,295	2,557	4,747	5,790	5,633	5,216
116 Other services	14,537	14,721	14,937	15,166	15,395	15,654	13,998	13,519	14,271	15,297
Total, services	49,530	51,522	53,534	55,911	58,266	60,853	63,682	65,686	68,393	72,067
Grand total	630,854	661,762	682,621	769,144	810,791	827,707	831,606	851,204	849,800	901,624

NOTES:

0. Index based on output figures from Ministry of Agriculture.

1. Output index of S. H. Abdel Rahman (see Table IV–A–3 [p. 338]).

2. Production figures, major companies.

301, 304–6, 308, 312–15. SWWH.
302. Output of fertilizers, caustic soda, match acid.
303. Cottonseed oil output.
307. Output.
309. Output index.
310. Output index of S. H. Abdel Rahman, *A Survey of the Foreign Trade of Egypt in the Post-War Period, with Special Reference to Its Impact on the National Economy* (Ph.D. dissertation, Faculty of Commerce, Cairo University, 1959).
311. Output.

404, 409-10, 414-16, 410-22. SWWH.
401, 411, 413. Output index of Abdel Rahman, *op. cit.*
402. Slaughterings.
403. Output estimates of Ministry of Agriculture.
405, 417. Assumed constant throughout.
406. Output.
407. Consumption.
408. National Bank of Egypt output estimates.
412. Imports, from customs figures.
417. Output.
423. Output.
424. SWWH. Includes upholstery, spectacles, watches, jewelry, buttons, etc.

501. Building materials used.
502. Government expenditures.
503. Materials used in new installations.
504. Government expenditures.
505. Private as well as governmental irrigation and agricultural construction; based on estimates of wages paid, and other expenditures.
506. Assumed constant.

601. Unclear.
602. Passengers and freight carried.
603. Miles traveled in buses, trams, taxis.
604. Receipts.
605-8. Special studies by National Planning Committee Memo No. 5 (May, 1958).
609. Output.

7. Receipts of company.

8. Rental values less repair costs.

901. Checks canceled.
902. Not clear.
903. Assumed constant.
904. Minor, estimated roughly.

10. Trade margins were computed for each of forty-four commodity groups and then applied to output figures of each group. Imported goods were all treated together as one group.

110. Output.
111-13, 115-16. Employment.
114. Number of students.

SOURCES: These detailed figures as well as the sources were published in National Planning Committee Memo No. 22, specially prepared for the plan (November, 1959). As we indicate in our introductory discussion, they are derived by applying indices to 1954 value-added figures. The indices used are explained above. Where employment figures were used, these were often taken from the survey of wages and working hours (listed as SWWH above). As we shall see in the discussion of this study in connection with Appendix Tables II–B–5 to II–B–8 (pp. 307–13), these are far from satisfactory figures. This should make us most cautious about their use.

TABLE I–A–6

GROSS NATIONAL INCOME AND PRODUCT, 1945–54
(£E Million, at Constant 1954 Prices)

Year	Agriculture	Industry and Electricity	Construction	Transport and Communications (Including Suez Canal)	Housing (Ownership of Real Estate)	Commerce and Finance	Other Services Including Government	Total: Gross Domestic Product at 1954 Market Prices	+ Net Factor Income from Abroad	Gross National Product at 1954 Market Prices	Net Gains or Losses (−) from Terms of Trade Changes	Real Gross National Income at 1954 Prices (Including Terms of Trade Effects)
1945	303	91	19	38	50	122	117	740	− 8	732	−38	694
1946	302	92	22	43	51	142	121	773	− 9	764	−40	724
1947	299	101	25	46	53	147	126	797	− 5	792	−45	747
1948	328	113	31	61	56	169	133	891	− 3	888	31	919
1949	325	126	25	72	59	190	145	942	− 9	933	10	943
1950	303	133	22	78	62	210	157	965	−11	954	68	1,022
1951	304	132	36	81	65	209	167	994	−13	981	113	1,094
1952	334	132	30	81	68	193	181	1,019	−12	1,007	9	1,016
1953	315	134	37	86	73	181	178	1,004	−11	993	−25	968
1954	312	146	33	88	77	188	192	1,036	−13	1,023	0	1,023

AVERAGE ANNUAL COMPOUND GROWTH RATE

Year	Agriculture	Industry and Electricity	Construction	Transport and Communications	Housing	Commerce and Finance	Other Services Including Government	Gross Domestic Product		Gross National Product		Real Gross National Income
1945–51	0.0	6.4	11.3	13.5	4.5	9.4	6.1	5.0		5.0		7.9
1951–54	0.9	3.4	−2.9	2.8	5.8	−3.5	4.8	1.4		1.4		−2.2
1945–54	0.3	5.4	6.3	9.8	4.9	4.9	5.7	3.8		3.8		4.4

NOTES AND SOURCES: This table, which is discussed in Appendix I, is identical with Table 4 of B. Hansen and D. Mead, *The National Income of the U.A.R. (Egypt), 1939–1962*, Memo No. 355 (Cairo: Institute of National Planning, July, 1963), except that revised estimates of government wage payments have been used. These figures are presented and discussed in Appendix Table II–B–11 (p. 315).

TABLE I-A-7

GROSS NATIONAL INCOME AND PRODUCT, 1952–53 TO 1962–63

(£E Million, Current Prices)

Year	Agriculture	Industry and Electricity	Construction	Transport and Communications	Housing	Commerce and Finance	Other Services	Subtotal	Agriculture, Alternative Estimate	Customs Duties	GNP at Market Price
1952–53.........	252	127	25	54	59	72	217	806	275	76	905
1953–54.........	262	140	27	55	56	75	232	847	295	83	963
1954–55.........	301	155	26	58	62	83	235	920	315	80	1,014
1955–56.........	312	170	27	62	65	92	237	965	339	80	1,072
1956–57.........	374	192	32	58	67	101	243	1,067	365	67	1,125
1957–58.........	381	218	38	65	68	109	247	1,126	370	80	1,195
1958–59.........	364	240	43	72	70	116	252	1,157	381	82	1,256
1959–60.........	405	269	47	92	73	131	272	1,289	407	81	1,372
1960–61.........	403	297	44	102	74	147	297	1,364	...	...	1,467
1961–62.........	441	344	99	114	78	155	325	1,556	...	...	1,550
1962–63.........	469	376	91	124	78	177	319	1,634	...	...	1,679

NOTES AND SOURCES: United Arab Republic, Department of Statistics and Census, *Ten Years of Revolution: Statistical Atlas* (Cairo, July, 1962), Table 9. The alternative estimates for agriculture are from United Arab Republic, Department of Statistics and Census, *National Income from the Agricultural Sector for the Years 1958–1960* (Cairo, n.d.) (in Arabic), p. 21. For the last three years the sectoral figures are a mixture of current and constant prices, final and preliminary estimates, and projections; the totals in the final column are revised estimates of the National Planning Committee, at current prices.

TABLE I-A-8

GROSS NATIONAL INCOME AND PRODUCT, 1952–53 TO 1962–63

(£E Million, Constant Prices of 1954)

Year	Agriculture	Industry and Electricity	Construction	Transport and Communications	Housing	Commerce and Finance		Other Services	Gross National Product		Gains from Terms-of-Trade Change	Gross National Income	
						I	II		I	II		I	II
1952–53	325	140	25	54	54	170	142	217	990	962	+ 8	998	970
1953–54	315	143	27	55	56	161	158	232	989	986	0	989	986
1954–55	318	152	26	58	62	164	163	235	1,015	1,014	+ 8	1,023	1,022
1955–56	329	163	25	62	65	174	165	237	1,055	1,046	+10	1,065	1,056
1956–57	339	174	28	58	67	175	151	236	1,077	1,053	+17	1,094	1,070
1957–58	355	190	33	62	68	193	167	240	1,141	1,115	+14	1,155	1,129
1958–59	376	202	38	69	70	209	172	245	1,209	1,172	+17	1,226	1,189
1959–60	392	213	42	88	73	217	184	259	1,284	1,251	+26	1,310	1,277
1960–61	390	239	39	97	74	227	197	289	1,355	1,325	+30	1,385	1,355
1961–62	361	262	55	111	76	233	198	289	1,387	1,352	+30	1,417	1,382
1962–63	412	279	63	121	78	280	211	302	1,535	1,466	+20	1,555	1,486

AVERAGE ANNUAL COMPOUND GROWTH RATE

	Agriculture	Industry and Electricity	Construction	Transport and Communications	Housing	Commerce and Finance		Other Services	Gross National Product			Gross National Income	
						I	II		I	II		I	II
1952–53 to 1959–60	2.7	6.2	7.7	7.2	3.1	3.5	3.8	2.5	3.8	3.8		4.0	4.0
1959–60 to 1962–63	1.7	9.4	14.5	11.2	2.2	8.9	4.7	5.3	6.2	5.5		5.9	5.2

NOTES AND SOURCES: This table is taken directly from B. Hansen and D. Mead, *The National Income of the U.A.R. (Egypt), 1939–1962*, Memo No. 355 (Cairo: Institute of National Planning, July, 1963), Table 8, except that it is expressed in 1954 prices rather than in terms of 1953–54 prices, as that table is. For all sectors for the period since 1959–60, the Ministry of Planning has made estimates of output at constant prices, which are used here (chained to our 1959–60 figures). These are believed to be an accurate statement of changes in real output for all sectors except industry and construction, where published figures are probably inadequately deflated for price changes, and hence result in some exaggeration of true growth rates. For the period 1952–53 to 1959–60 the following techniques were used to measure changes in real output:

Agriculture. Here, we have used the Department of Statistics and Census estimate, whereby all output as well as all inputs are valued at 1954 prices. See United Arab Republic, *National Income from the Agricultural Sector for the Years 1958–1960* (Cairo, n.d.) (in Arabic), p. 24.

Industry and electricity. In this sector, we have used an output index spliced together from two different sources of information. For 1952–59 the industrial production index of the National Bank of Egypt was used (see Appendix Table IV–A–1 [p. 336] for a discussion of this index); from 1959 to 1960, we used the value added for enterprises engaging ten persons and more in industry as shown by the production census, adjusted by the wholesale price subindex for industrial products. Quite apart from the different nature of the two sources of information used, the following biases should be noticed: (a) In the index of the NBE, input figures (employment and/or use of raw materials) are in certain cases used as substitutes for output figures. Productivity changes are in this way disregarded, and this means, in all probability, a downward bias. (b) The index of the NBE does not include certain new products and industries established during the second half of the fifties. This means probably grown more slowly than enterprises with ten or more persons, although little information is available about establishments with less than 10 persons. An attempt has been made to estimate a maximum limit for the bias implied here. Under certain reasonable assumptions, it was found that this bias might amount at most to 11 percentage units out of an increase of about 70 percent from 1952 to 1960. See B. Hansen and G. Marzouk, *Development and Economic Policy in the U.A.R. (Egypt)* (Amsterdam: North-Holland Publishing Co., 1965), chap. v, sec. 2.1. Although there is here a clear upward bias, it does not seem to disturb the results in a major way. With these oppositely directed biases in force, it is difficult to say whether the industrial production index is biased upward or downward in general.

Construction. Here, we have deflated the sectoral income at current prices by a simple average of the official wholesale price subindex for building materials and an index of average weekly wages for all workers. If productivity has increased, a downward bias is introduced. Most probably, productivity has actually increased in construction due to a shift toward industrial buildings and construction.

Transport and communications. Sectoral income is deflated by a crude index comprising Suez Canal toll rates and railway fares.

Commerce and finance. Two alternative methods are used. (I) The real contribution is assumed to be proportional to the flow of commodities. On this assumption the change in real income (at market price) from commerce and finance is set equal to the rate of increase of real income from agriculture and industry plus real imports with addition of customs duties in proportion to those of 1953–54. (II) The sectoral income at current prices including all customs duties is deflated by a simple average of the wholesale and retail price index.

Housing. The level of rents is taken to have been unchanged during the period. Actually, rents have been kept unchanged by the rent controls, but since an increasing part of the existing stock of houses consists of new houses built at a higher level of costs than the prewar houses, and since the income from housing is estimated on the basis of the rental value of the houses (as assessed in connection with the building taxation), an upward bias in the real estimates is introduced here.

Other services. This sector includes government administration, domestic services, and other services. Concerning the government, there may here be an upward bias in the estimate of government wages and salaries itself. This is due to the fact that from 1957–58 and onward, only budget *estimates* exist, and these tend usually to exaggerate expenditures. Also, it should be remembered that some government wages and salaries are simply a form of unemployment benefits. Whether this has increased during the period is difficult to say; in the beginning of the period, there were large payments clearly of this type to former employees with the British military forces. Concerning the deflator chosen, government wages and salaries have, in principle, been unchanged during the whole period. (Since closed accounts have not been available since 1956–57, it has not been possible to extend the estimates in Appendix Table II–B–11 [p. 315]; it seems likely that a slowdown in the usual automatic upgrading of civil servants may have resulted in a temporary fall in average wage rates of government employees). However, since from 1956 the government's payments to the pension funds corresponding to 10 percent of government wages and salaries are included in the government sector income, we have taken the increase in government wage level to be 10 percent from 1952–53 to 1959–60. For domestic and other services, little is known about the wage level and its development. There may be a tendency for such wages to increase in conformance with wage rates for agricultural laborers (which may have experienced a 10 percent increase in wages during the fifties). For the sector as a whole, we assumed that the wage level has increased by 3 percent in 1956–57 and by a further 2 percent in 1958–59 (the pension scheme was only gradually extended to comprise all government employees), and this was used as a deflator.

TABLE I-A-9

GROSS INVESTMENT BY SECTORS, 1952–53 TO 1962–63

(£E Million)

	1952–53	1953–54	1954–55	1955–56	1956–57	1957–58	1958–59	1959–60	1960–61	1961–62	1962–63
Agriculture and land reclamation	6.9	5.5	6.0	8.7	12.5	14.5	16.3	16.7	20.7	31.8	27.1
Irrigation and drainage	6.8	9.3	9.3	9.3	7.1	6.7	8.5	8.6	12.2	22.3	37.6
High Dam	...	...	...	0.5	0.4	0.5	1.2	4.2	8.5	10.3	12.5
Industry	29.5	27.2	33.6	49.2	31.1	35.6	47.8	49.3	67.0	99.9	113.9
Electricity	5.8	11.3	7.3	9.5	9.3	7.7	6.7	6.2	5.5	13.0	26.7
Transport, communications, and storage	19.1	19.2	23.6	24.5	15.5	23.5	27.0	30.0	67.2	71.1	59.4
Suez Canal	...	...	...	...	4.0	5.0	6.0	5.8	5.9	11.2	8.0
Housing	37.7	46.0	50.0	52.0	50.0	48.0	40.0	31.1	18.2	42.1	46.1
Public utilities	2.9	2.7	4.6	5.1	6.4	7.7	10.4	7.5	7.7	13.8	16.1
Education services	4.1	5.0	5.1	6.0	6.5	7.3	8.2	7.8	6.7	11.4	11.2
Health services	1.3	1.4	1.5	1.5	1.6	1.7	1.8	1.2	0.5	3.3	5.6
Social services	0.5	0.5	0.5	0.5	0.6	0.6	0.6	0.9	1.1	1.3	1.7
Other services	4.0	4.3	4.7	5.3	6.0	6.6	6.9	2.1	3.6	23.4	32.6
Total	118.6	132.4	146.2	172.1	151.0	165.4	181.4	171.4	224.8	354.9	398.5

NOTES AND SOURCES: United Arab Republic, Department of Statistics and Census, *Ten Years of Revolution: Statistical Atlas* (Cairo, July, 1962), Table 11. The figures for industry and electricity are based on import statistics; for the rest, we have not been able to determine the sources of these figures. Storage includes a limited amount of stock changes. The figures for 1961–62 and 1962–63 are prospective; revised totals for the last three years are as follows (in £E million):

1960–61..................229
1961–62..................248
1962–63..................307 (provisional)

For industry and electricity, comparable figures for earlier years are as follows:

1942–43..............	4.7
1943–44..............	1.8
1944–45..............	3.3
1945–46..............	6.6
1946–47..............	14.8
1947–48..............	20.0
1948–49..............	30.7
1949–50..............	33.3
1950–51..............	35.7
1951–52..............	39.3

These are from mimeographed tables of the National Planning Committee, and are derived by applying an 87.3 percent markup to CIF value of imported industrial machinery and equipment.

TABLE I–A–10

GROSS VALUE ADDED PER WORKER, BY SECTORS

(£E per Year, at 1954 Prices)

	1947	1960
Agriculture	73.4	88.5
Industry and electricity	171.5	293.1
Services, total	168.5	237.2
Commerce	130.0	186.7
Transport and communications	227.7	357.7
Construction	223.2	257.9
All others	105.4	171.7

SOURCES: Appendix Tables I–A–5 (pp. 281-85) and I–A–8 (pp. 288-89); text Tables 2–9 (p. 33) and 6–1 (p. 132). Employment figures include men, women, and children. Customs receipts have been excluded from the commerce sector. The transport sector is dominated by the Suez Canal, which in 1960 accounted for 3 percent of employment and 40 percent of income in the sector. The figures for construction are surprisingly high and might lead us to question the income figures in this sector; the 15 percent increase in real value added per worker here over thirteen years seems plausible, however.

Appendix II

Population and Labor

TABLE II–A–1

TOTAL POPULATION, BY REGION

(In Thousands)

	1882	1897	1907	1917	1927	1927*	1937	1947	1960
Cairo	398.7	589.6	678.4	790.9	1,064.6	1,070.8	1,309.7	2,075.9	3,348.8
Alexandria	232.6	315.8	353.8	444.6	573.1	600.1	709.7	949.4	1,516.2
Port Said	20.4	50.2	61.3	91.1	129.8	101.0	119.0	164.6	245.3
Ismailia						65.3	90.7	177.1	284.1
Suez	10.9	17.2	18.3	31.0	40.5	40.5	49.7	107.2	203.6
Damietta	34.0	31.5	29.4	31.0	34.9	170.5	205.7	258.9	388.0
Dakahlia	591.5	742.5	876.2	986.6	1,080.7	1,088.0	1,229.8	1,457.5	2,014.9
Sharkia	443.7	728.3	856.0	955.5	1,016.9	1,063.7	1,164.3	1,352.3	1,819.8
Kalyubia	271.2	396.5	464.2	528.6	558.9	582.9	638.3	716.5	988.1
Kafr-el-Sheikh						484.3	551.0	682.9	973.0
Gharbia	922.6	1,296.7	1,484.8	1,659.3	1,792.0	1,091.9	1,156.6	1,298.2	1,715.2
Munufia	654.8	862.2	970.6	1,072.6	1,105.2	1,062.9	1,114.4	1,124.9	1,348.0
Behera	394.7	628.9	765.1	892.2	977.0	949.9	1,037.7	1,214.1	1,685.7
Giza	265.4	378.9	437.0	524.4	591.4	593.0	696.4	845.3	1,336.4
Beni-Suef	216.0	309.3	372.4	452.9	508.2	602.4	665.3	727.1	859.8

Fayum	218.9	371.0	441.6	507.6	554.0	554.0	602.1	669.7	839.2
Mena	304.6	521.6	653.2	763.9	839.7	1,026.2	1,133.1	1,268.0	1,560.3
Asyut	555.9	758.1	876.6	981.2	1,078.6	797.9	896.5	1,035.6	1,329.6
Suhag (Girga)	517.1	683.7	793.7	864.7	968.4	968.4	1,118.4	1,283.5	1,578.9
Qena	473.3	703.5	770.1	838.8	902.2	902.2	1,017.6	1,106.3	1,351.4
Aswan	141.9	206.0	232.8	253.3	267.4	267.4	305.1	290.8	385.4
Red Sea	2.4	2.1	1.6	4.7	5.2	5.2	9.9	15.9	25.5
Southern Desert	21.5	24.3	26.8	25.9	25.4	25.4	29.1	32.5	33.9
Western Desert	9.3	12.2	18.6	11.9	49.0	49.0	52.6	74.8	103.5
Sinai	4.2	4.8	7.4	5.4	15.1	15.1	18.0	37.7	49.8
Subtotal	6,705.8	9,634.8	11,190.0	12,718.3	14,177.9	14,177.9	15,920.7	18,966.8	25,984.1
Nomads (estimated)	98.2	79.8	97.4	32.7	40.0	40.0	12.0	55.1	101.2
Total	6,804.0	9,714.5	11,287.4	12,750.9	14,217.9	14,217.9	15,932.7	19,021.8	26,085.3

NOTES AND SOURCES: Earlier years (1882–1927) from United Arab Republic, Department of Statistics and Census, *Population Census, 1947* (Cairo, 1954), pp. 46–49; later years (1927*-60), from United Arab Republic, Department of Statistics and Census, *Census of Population, 1960*, (Cairo, 1963), Vol. II, pp. 1–3. There have been numerous changes in succeeding censuses in the geographical boundaries of each province; these are discussed in some detail in J. L. Abu-Lughod, "Urbanization in Egypt: Present State and Future Prospects," *Economic Development and Cultural Change*, Vol. XIII, No. 3 (April, 1965), pp. 313–43. The 1947 census included a table showing population in each province and governorate, based on 1947 boundaries, and going back all the way to the first census in 1882; the first five years in the table are from that source. The 1960 census had a similar table based on 1960 boundaries, but going back only to 1927; this is the source of the last four columns. The year 1927 is included in each series, for comparative purposes.

TABLE II–A–2

Population, by Age and Sex
(In Thousands)

Age	1907			1917			1927		
	Male	Female	Total	Male	Female	Total	Male	Female	Total
Under 5	866.8	909.6	1,776.4	858.4	895.8	1,754.2	994.5	1,036.2	2,030.7
5– 9	796.8	768.8	1,565.6	904.0	897.1	1,801.1	937.4	922.0	1,859.4
10–14	671.4	523.3	1,194.7	1,401.9	1,178.8	2,580.7	860.5	719.9	1,579.9
15–19	528.7	418.6	947.3				680.1	614.7	1,294.8
20–24	816.5	918.2	1,734.7	938.6	1,040.4	1,979.0	522.7	577.3	1,100.0
25–29							573.5	652.6	1,226.2
30–39	739.4	757.2	1,496.6	849.5	873.2	1,722.7	988.7	1,013.5	2,001.2
40–49	509.4	514.9	1,024.3	572.5	569.7	1,142.2	662.0	654.5	1,316.4
50–59				375.1	376.9	752.0	391.3	409.5	800.8
60–69				228.6	262.4	491.0	244.6	274.3	519.0
70–79	687.6	762.7	1,450.3	138.5	141.4	279.9	120.4	138.0	258.4
80–89				55.0	71.7	126.7	46.9	64.4	111.4
90 and over				20.9	26.5	47.4	18.0	22.2	40.3
Unstated				25.4	15.0	40.4	18.3	21.1	39.4
Total	5,616.6	5,573.3	11,189.9	6,368.4	6,348.9	12,717.3	7,058.1	7,119.8	14,177.9

Age:	1937			1947			1960		
	Male	Female	Total	Male	Female	Total	Male	Female	Total
Under 1	244.5	245.7	490.2	257.9	249.8	507.7	383.4	369.2	752.6
1– 4	777.4	840.0	1,617.4	1,021.7	1,055.5	2,077.1	1,728.1	1,651.5	3,379.6
5– 9	1,107.9	1,101.0	2,208.8	1,208.9	1,191.2	2,400.1	1,971.9	1,827.1	3,799.0
10–14	1,030.9	878.2	1,909.1	1,142.3	1,071.2	2,213.5	1,651.4	1,527.2	3,178.6
15–19	713.2	633.1	1,346.3	984.0	917.4	1,901.5	1,114.1	1,040.3	2,154.4
20–24	539.7	565.2	1,104.8	677.8	706.2	1,383.9	921.1	874.2	1,795.3
25–29	616.7	692.9	1,309.6	685.7	786.5	1,472.3	859.8	1,054.3	1,914.1
30–34	557.9	634.5	1,192.4	620.1	689.5	1,309.6	806.9	844.1	1,651.0
35–39	600.4	540.6	1,141.1	659.2	653.6	1,312.9	847.4	879.2	1,726.6
40–44	474.8	472.2	947.0	569.1	566.2	1,135.3	660.7	614.2	1,274.9
45–49	345.1	313.2	658.3	428.5	415.2	843.7	567.2	577.1	1,144.3
50–54	330.3	335.5	665.8	421.2	448.5	869.7	493.8	503.6	997.4
55–59	144.7	134.3	279.0	171.1	173.1	344.2	322.9	315.4	638.3
60–64	274.0	304.1	578.1	252.0	298.8	550.8	320.8	353.9	674.7
65–69				83.8	82.1	165.9	163.9	169.5	333.4
70–74	191.1	244.4	435.4	107.8	136.7	244.5	133.5	167.7	301.3
75 and over				75.5	100.2	175.8	120.9	147.2	268.0
Unstated	18.2	19.2	37.4	25.1	33.3	58.4	0.2	0.5	0.7
Total	7,966.7	7,954.0	15,920.7	9,391.7	9,575.0	18,966.8	13,068.0	12,916.1	25,984.1

Source: Population censuses. All figures exclude nomads. For a discussion of misreporting of ages, see text, p. 24.

TABLE II–A–3

Urban and Rural Population

	Urban	Rural	Total
1927	3,770,825	10,407,039	14,177,864
1937	4,436,106	11,484,588	15,920,694
1947	6,262,302	12,704,465	18,966,767
1960	9,863,703	16,120,398	25,984,101

NOTES AND SOURCES: The breakdown used here is based on administrative distinctions; the urban population includes all people counted in the five major urban governorates (Cairo, Alexandria, Port Said, Ismailia, and Suez), capitals of all other governorates as well as markaz (roughly, country or district) capitals. This distinction is first used explicitly in United Arab Republic, Department of Statistics and Census, *Population Census, 1960* (Cairo, 1963), Vol. II, from which these figures are taken (p. 3). The census also gives cross-classifications following this breakdown by governorate, age and sex, occupation, economic activity, employment status, and educational, marital, and health status. All figures exclude nomads.

TABLE II–A–4

NUMBER OF STUDENTS, BY LEVEL OF INSTRUCTION, 1897–98 TO 1948–49

	1897–98	1907–08	1912–13	1921–22	1927–28	1936–37	1948–49
Elementary (kuttab)*........	2,924	175,515	232,423	342,820	592,001	1,024,242	1,069,382
Preparatory†...............	n.a.	24,279	38,731	29,702	43,174	53,581	64,927
Primary...................	7,282	62,630	86,778	96,364	131,134	130,453	256,388
Secondary................	611	5,567	9,697	15,442	27,109	39,677	90,353
Commercial...............	n.a.	332	1,909	2,351	4,243	2,770	10,477
Agricultural..............	n.a.	n.a.	427	523	497	1,643	3,312
Teacher training..........	n.a.	959	1,927	2,536	12,226	3,344	6,448
Higher education..........	n.a.	n.a.	n.a.	2,282	5,562	9,371	26,740
Technical and trade schools..	n.a.	n.a.	n.a.	4,652	7,352	17,409	23,694
Others (including n.a.)......	n.a.	19,663	22,887	14,999	18,225	21,801	44,799
Total...............	n.a.	288,945	394,779	511,671	802,517	1,270,551	1,596,520

*Includes only students in schools inspected by the government; the rapid expansion registered here reflects growing governmental inspection and (in most cases) subsidizing of these schools, which were originally set up and run by the mosques.

†Includes kindergarten, higher elementary, and mixed preparatory-primary.

SOURCES: All figures are from United Arab Republic, Department of Statistics and Census, *Statistique Scolaire*; and *Annuaire Statistique*, various issues.

TABLE II-A-5

Number of Students, by Level of Instruction, 1953-54 to 1961-62

	1953-54	1954-55	1955-56	1956-57	1957-58	1958-59	1959-60	1960-61	1961-62
Nursery	.....	9,963	13,397	7,429	7,225	7,347	8,418	8,268	9,553
Primary	1,392,741	1,580,089	1,860,942	1,975,874	2,086,704	2,286,067	2,452,377	2,610,169	2,754,566
Special schools	8,828	3,170	9,761	11,176	7,861	6,297	6,025	6,277	6,317
Advanced preparatory schools	2,988	5,867	8,551	5,660	1,793	.....	.....	.....	.....
General practical preparatory	.....	.....	.....	.....	1,161	1,250	1,774	2,095	2,270
General preparatory	348,574	346,376	328,470	318,243	278,224	247,792	249,129	253,737	300,853
General secondary	92,062	106,095	107,612	109,153	109,395	115,608	120,767	132,161	124,607
Industrial preparatory	2,127	2,723	5,804	8,736	13,736	15,895	18,033	22,197	24,574
Multipurpose preparatory	.....	.....	.....	.....	.....	623	603	461	354
Commercial preparatory	181	225	539	1,551	3,747	5,190	5,716	5,593	6,038
Agricultural preparatory	952	1,356	1,875	2,638	4,837	6,687	7,729	8,727	8,937
Technical preparatory for girls	.....	.....	.....	.....	498	1,358	1,919	2,355	2,165
Industrial secondary	9,007	6,846	7,192	9,719	11,594	13,735	15,722	19,968	22,626
Technical secondary for girls	.....	.....	.....	.....	.....	.....	.....	.....	317
Multipurpose secondary	.....	.....	.....	.....	.....	100	168	270	270
Commercial secondary	4,381	4,511	7,431	10,763	16,886	22,497	28,130	36,226	39,775
Agricultural secondary	2,302	2,669	3,738	4,370	6,119	7,443	9,001	10,533	11,049
Domestic secondary	3,148	3,616	4,112	4,586	5,636	6,237	7,326	8,363	7,278
General teacher training	17,540	19,032	21,641	21,385	18,162	11,505	9,604	12,414	12,546
Rural teacher training	587	628	719	1,628	2,452	3,622	3,728	5,021	7,479
Supplementary training	433	453	447	486	384	156	.....	.....	.....
Special training	3,084	2,741	2,870	1,954	753	158	.....	.....	.....
Special training, French	1,992	2,181	2,127	2,074	1,897	1,574	1,214	783	329
Primary physical training	272	.....	751	1,004	1,129	965	883	970	980
Higher institutes	5,285	6,522	7,059	7,371	9,699	11,269	13,605	19,897	22,711
Foreign schools and institutes	86,358	86,835	96,314	90,883	92,504	95,089	93,834	94,625	91,728
Total	1,982,842	2,191,898	2,491,352	2,596,683	2,682,396	2,868,464	3,055,705	3,264,110	3,457,322
Universities	51,681	56,180	59,550	64,211	73,144	77,170	83,141	86,980	91,908
Grand total	2,034,523	2,248,078	2,550,902	2,660,894	2,755,540	2,945,634	3,138,846	3,351,090	3,548,960

SOURCE: United Arab Republic, Ministry of Education, Department of Statistics, *Comparative Statistics of Education from 1953-54 to 1961-62* (Cairo, 1961), pp. 10-16. This publication also gives a careful summary explanation of the Egyptian educational ladder.

TABLE II–A–6

ILLITERACY

	Total Persons Aged 10 and Over	Persons Not Able to Read and Write Aged 10 and Over	Illiteracy Rate		
			Total	Male	Female
1907........	7,848,024	7,277,303	92.7	87.0	98.6
1917........	9,161,944	8,357,461	91.2	84.8	97.7
1927........	10,268,404	8,816,601	85.9	76.1	95.6
1937........	11,603,488	9,885,300	85.2	76.6	93.9
1947........	13,489,946	10,407,972	77.2	66.1	88.2
1960........	17,914,323	12,587,686	70.3	56.6	83.8

NOTE: Total excludes nomads and those for whom literacy is not stated. These figures count as literate those able to read but not write, totaling 130,748 in 1960.

SOURCE: UNESCO, *Progress of Literacy in Various Countries*, Monographs on Fundamental Education, No. VI (Paris, 1935), pp. 83–84; and population censuses.

TABLE II–A–7

TOTAL POPULATION, BIRTH AND DEATH RATES: ANNUAL ESTIMATES, 1917–60

	Total Population Estimate for July 1 (Thousands)	Live Birth Rate	Death Rate (Excluding Stillbirths)	Rate of Natural Increase	Deaths under One Year (Percent of Live Births)	Stillbirths (Percent of Total Births)
1917.....	12,795	40.1	29.4	10.8	n.a.	12.1
1918.....	12,936	38.9	39.6	− 0.7	n.a.	12.6
1919.....	13,078	37.7	29.4	8.4	12.8	11.5
1920.....	13,222	42.2	28.0	14.3	13.7	11.7
1921.....	13,368	41.8	25.0	16.8	13.3	12.2
1922.....	13,515	43.1	25.1	18.0	14.0	11.4
1923.....	13,663	43.1	25.8	17.3	14.3	10.2
1924.....	13,813	43.8	24.9	18.9	15.0	9.3
1925.....	13,965	43.5	26.5	17.1	15.5	8.8
1926.....	14,119	44.2	26.7	17.4	14.6	8.2
1927.....	14,276	44.0	25.2	18.8	15.2	8.1
1928.....	14,438	43.6	26.3	17.3	15.1	7.9
1929.....	14,602	44.2	27.6	16.6	15.9	7.4
1930.....	14,767	45.4	24.9	20.6	15.1	7.5
1931.....	14,935	44.5	26.6	17.9	16.0	7.3
1932.....	15,104	42.5	28.5	14.0	17.4	7.6
1933.....	15,275	43.8	27.5	16.2	16.2	7.4
1934.....	15,449	42.2	27.8	14.4	16.6	7.3
1935.....	15,624	41.3	26.4	14.9	16.1	7.1
1936.....	15,801	44.2	28.8	15.3	16.4	7.6
1937.....	16,008	43.4	27.1	16.2	16.5	7.8
1938.....	16,395	43.2	26.3	16.9	16.3	7.3
1939.....	16,588	42.0	25.9	16.1	16.1	7.7
1940.....	16,887	41.3	26.3	15.0	16.2	7.7
1941.....	17,190	40.4	25.7	14.8	15.0	7.3
1942.....	17,499	37.6	28.3	9.4	16.8	7.2
1943.....	17,814	38.7	27.7	11.1	16.0	7.3
1944.....	18,134	39.8	26.0	13.8	15.2	7.6
1945.....	18,460	42.7	27.7	14.9	15.3	7.7
1946.....	18,792	41.2	25.0	16.2	14.1	7.0
1947.....	19,068	43.8	21.4	22.3	12.7	7.1
1948.....	19,533	42.6	20.4	22.2	13.9	6.9
1949.....	20,010	41.5	20.5	21.0	13.5	7.0
1950.....	20,498	44.1	19.0	25.1	13.0	6.9
1951.....	20,998	44.5	19.2	25.3	12.9	7.9
1952.....	21,510	45.1	17.7	27.4	12.7	7.9
1953.....	22,035	42.4	19.5	22.9	14.6	8.4
1954.....	22,573	42.4	17.8	24.6	13.8	8.2
1955.....	23,124	40.1	17.5	22.6	13.6	8.5
1956.....	23,688	40.5	15.3	24.2	12.4	8.4
1957.....	24,266	37.7	17.7	20.0	13.0	7.7
1958.....	24,858	39.8	16.5	23.3	11.2	7.7
1959.....	25,465	42.4	16.1	26.3	10.9	7.5
1960.....	26,085	42.7	16.8	25.9	10.9	7.9

NOTES AND SOURCES: United Arab Republic, Department of Statistics and Census, *Vital Statistics*, various issues. Annual estimates of total population assume constant growth rates between censuses. For a discussion of these figures see pp. 21–24 of text.

TABLE II–A–8

DECLARED CASES OF SELECTED INFECTIOUS DISEASES

	1927	1937	1947	1954	1957
Plague	78	73	15	0	0
Typhus	794	2,084	173	168	469
Yellow fever	n.a.	1	170	0	1
Typhoid	2,362	5,209	4,601	12,111	14,339
Scarlet fever	72	57	10	10	41
Diphtheria	2,453	1,847	1,809	1,217	1,325
Measles	3,995	1,502	6,886	6,416	17,059
Pulmonary tuberculosis	n.a.	5,007	6,523	7,161	5,403
Other tuberculosis	n.a.	n.a.	94	560	543

SOURCE: *Annuaire Statistique*, various issues. The main weakness of these figures is in the area of tuberculosis, which is far more common than these figures indicate.

TABLE II–A–9

MAJOR CAUSES OF DEATHS

	1928	1950	1957
Infectious and parasitic diseases	10,004	7,253	7,920
Heart diseases	3,166	7,180	13,803
Bronchitis	8,487	14,810	19,493
Other respiratory diseases	12,435	7,348	8,977
Gastroenteritis and colitis	39,220	70,615	87,656
Infant diseases	10,489	23,988	20,573
Senility	10,137	19,911	20,170
All others	25,948	33,518	33,878
Grand total	119,886	184,623	212,470

SOURCE: *Annuaire Statistique*, various issues.

TABLE II–A–10

PER CAPITA CONSUMPTION, CALORIES PER DAY

	1934–35 to 1938–39	1948–49 to 1950–51	1951–52 to 1953–54	1954–55 to 1956–57	1957–58 to 1959–60	1960–61
Cereals	1,752	1,686	1,662	1,824	1,788	1,769
Potatoes and other starchy food	11	21	18	19	20	27
Sugars and syrups	136	152	168	173	170	149
Pulse, seeds, and nuts	218	118	106	105	105	119
Fruits and vegetables	71	99	141	163	151	163
Meat	29	46	49	54	52	47
Eggs	7	3	4	4	5	5
Fish	5	15	13	19	19	20
Milk and cheese	92	147	111	116	103	103
Fats and oils	129	85	85	97	117	126
Total	2,450	2,372	2,357	2,570	2,530	2,530

SOURCES: United Nations Food and Agriculture Organization, *Yearbook of Food and Agricultural Statistics*, Vol. IX, Part 1: *Production* (Rome, 1956), p. 207; and Vol. XVI, Part 1 (Rome, 1963), p. 252.

TABLE II–B–1

EMPLOYMENT, BY INDUSTRIAL SECTOR

(In Thousands)

	1907	*1917*	*1927*	*1937*	*1947*	*1960*
Agriculture........	2,343.0	2,932.4	3,539.0	4,019.6	4,074.7	4,406.4
Mining and quarrying...	4.0	3.0	10.0	10.7	12.9	21.1
Manufacturing.....	281.0	361.0	422.0	345.4	553.0	713.1
Electricity, gas, and water...	n.s.	5.0	23.0	21.0	22.6	36.8
Construction.......	95.0	60.0	86.0	116.5	111.7	158.9
Commerce........	161.0	324.0	459.0	436.1	587.5	641.4
Transport, storage, and communications......	101.0	151.0	196.0	137.1	201.6	260.2
Other services......	448.0	473.0	514.0	696.3	1,046.4	1,595.3
Total.........	3,433.0	4,309.4	5,249.0	5,782.7	6,610.4	7,833.2

SOURCES: *1907–27:* Population censuses. For the years 1937–60, see notes to text Table 2–9 (p. 33). Agriculture includes forestry, hunting, and fishing, but excludes nomads and female agricultural laborers inferred from schedules.

TABLE II–B–2

EMPLOYMENT BY INDUSTRIAL SECTOR, ADULT MALES

(In Thousands)

	1937	*1947*	*1960*
Agriculture..................	2,975.8	3,139.0	3,560.0
Mining and quarrying........	10.4	12.4	20.6
Manufacturing...............	319.6	501.6	694.9
Construction.................	113.4	108.3	156.0
Commerce...................	375.5	503.1	586.9
Transport, storage, and communications........	133.3	195.1	255.5
Other services...............	529.1	786.2	1,319.8
Total...................	4,457.1	5,245.7	6,593.7

SOURCES: Population censuses, adjusted as explained in notes to Tables 2–9 (p. 33) and 2–10 (p. 37). Manufacturing includes electricity, gas and water.

APPENDIX II–B–3

ESTIMATES OF EMPLOYMENT IN MANUFACTURING, 1954

In making our estimate of industrial employment for 1954, we have relied on the census of establishments. This census is designed to cover all productive establishments; employees of the Department of Statistics and Census inquire (in principle, at least) at every apartment or office in every building in the country, asking if any productive work goes on there, and, if so, what its general nature is and how many people are engaged in the work. The results of these censuses, which were taken every three years from 1942 to 1960, have been used as the frame for numerous other surveys, such as the census of industrial production (which returns yearly to all industrial establishments with 10 or more workers) and the early surveys of wages and working hours (which returned every six months to a rotating 25 percent sample of industrial establishments of all sizes) to get more detailed information on specific questions. We have used the 1954 and 1960 censuses of establishments to give a measure of employment changes in each two-digit industry of the manufacturing sector; these rates of increase were then applied to the employment figures shown in the 1960 population census (once again, at a two-digit level) to give a measure of 1954 employment which is roughly comparable to that shown in the population censuses (see text Table 5–4 [p. 111]). As an indication of the relative degree of coverage of the two censuses, the 1960 population census reported total employment (ISIC 2 and 3) of 713,100, while the census of establishments for that year indicated 521,769. If these figures were complete and comparable, the difference would represent employment outside of establishments, i.e., out of doors; in fact, statistical differences of one kind or another probably account for most of the discrepancy. Results of the census of establishments are published only in highly aggregative form in the *Annuaire Statistique*, although more detailed figures are available within the Department of Statistics and Census.

TABLE II–B–4

WORKING STATUS OF POPULATION

(In Thousands)

	1927	1937	1947	1960
Employer..........................	1,109.5	796.4	794.8	576.4
Self-employed.....................	587.9	1,328.1	1,619.6	1,752.1
Employees:				
Directors and subdirectors.........			2.3	
Employees.....................			265.6	
Laborers and artisans............			2,452.9	
Wives helping their husbands*.....			89.6⎫	
Relatives helping their chiefs*......			1,274.9⎬	1,440.9
Domestic servants*..............			197.5	
Total employees.................	3,521.4	3,886.2	4,282.8	5,315.4†
Total economically active...........	5,218.8	6,010.7	6,697.2	7,643.9
Unemployed......................	25.9	23.1	35.4	174.9

*In principle, this excludes domestic work in own house, which was listed separately.

†Includes 3,850,661 paid employees and 23,827 unpaid workers other than family members.

SOURCE: Population censuses. Figures include Egyptians as well as foreigners aged 5 and above, except 1960, which is for age 6 and above. The figures on unemployment cannot be taken seriously. There may have been some change in the demarcation between the first two categories between 1927 and 1937, accounting for the shift indicated here.

TABLE II-B-5

INDUSTRIAL WAGE RATES, 1938

Group of Industry	Number of Establishments	Average Daily Wages in Piasters					Daily Working Hours	Days of Work per Month
		Girls	Boys	Women	Men	Average		
Food industries............	1,728	2.97	2.79	5.45	9.85	9.41	9.34	24.2
Textile and clothing.......	2,203	2.48	1.44	5.24	6.63	6.06	9.77	25.0
Construction of buildings...	1,638	2.00	1.54	3.75	8.25	7.13	8.95	24.0
Machines, tools, and precious metals....	454	.....	1.64	.....	11.22	10.44	9.04	24.0
Chemical industries........	136	.....	3.12	9.25	10.58	9.98	8.85	24.0
Contracting	47	.....	2.61	12.57	12.37	12.23	9.05	23.0
Other industries...........	435	2.75	2.19	7.19	10.37	9.49	8.58	23.1
Total.............	6,641	2.52	1.73	5.54	8.40	7.76	9.50	24.0

SOURCE: M. A. Anis, "A Study of the National Income of Egypt," L'Egypte Contemporaine, Nos. 261–62 (November–December, 1950), p. 803. Anis indicates that these data are taken from an inquiry of the Ministry of Commerce and Industry in 1938. Questionnaires were sent to 6,641 establishments, employing 86,807 workers (out of a total of 92,021 establishments and 138,675 workers, according to the 1937 industrial and commercial census); replies were received from only 1,100 establishments, but "as they were distributed among various parts of the country, the sample may be considered as fairly representative." Establishments with less than three employees were excluded. Wage rates are based on average payments to total staff, excluding only the owner; i.e., they include laborers as well as clerical and administrative workers.

TABLE II–B–6

AVERAGE WEEKLY INDUSTRIAL WAGE RATES, 1942–49

(In Piasters)

Industries:	July, 1942	Jan., 1943	Jan., 1944	Jan., 1945	Jan., 1946	Jan., 1947	Jan., 1948	Jan., 1949
Connected with vegetable foods	79	76	101	109	122	119	118	122
Connected with animal foods	72	98	80	92	102	138	112	120
Connected with drinks	92	83	119	128	122	122	119	126
Tobacco	85	100	98	88	110	144	124	145
Extraction of fats and oils	106	101	90	151	121	128	113	129
Chemical industries	83	91	101	115	129	130	138	153
Paper and paper articles	80	56	100	72	79	120	117	104
Printing, bookbinding	110	107	96	138	139	153	209	184
Rubber	89	85	107	88	144	89	137	151
Jewelry, scientific instruments	82	79	97	124	150	140	155	140
Leather and furs (including shoes)	79	77	92	124	127	111	122	116
Textiles	90	62	77	90	99	132	117	117
Clothing	69	60	78	89	93	96	101	106
Construction materials	73	73	101	134	120	141	154	156
Metallurgy and metal manufacturing	99	77	89	99	115	120	121	127

Machines and machine tools	107	82	90	122	119	158	131	137
Woodworking	78	74	91	105	108	119	126	126
Transport means	144	143	157	196	198	214	235	239
Mineral fuel	206	188		247		434		
Weighted average, manufacturing	89	75	91	108	114	128	127	129
Power, heat, water irrigation	112	111	139	155	156	161	152	170
Hairdressing, beautifying, cleaning clothes	78	50	62	80	97	79	105	125
Contractors of buildings	100	89	116	147	132	140	168	128
Roads and bridges	97	25	56	167	191	161	170	243
Contractors of public works	93	105	113	136	121		245	172
Mines	136	139	146	167	210	328	233	419
Quarries	78	63	92	105	166	152	161	144
Salines	102	90	115	164	187	137	138	277
Other	69	77	89	87	93	93	112	82
Various	94	125	77	142	151	115	172	109
General total	95	82	98	120	123	134	139	144

NOTES AND SOURCES: See p. 312.

TABLE II–B–7

AVERAGE WEEKLY INDUSTRIAL WAGE RATES, 1949–63

(In Piasters)

	July, 1949	Jan., 1950	Jan., 1951	Jan., 1952	Jan., 1953	Jan., 1954	Jan., 1955	Jan., 1956	July, 1957	July, 1958	Jan., 1959	Jan., 1960	July, 1961	Jan., 1962	Jan., 1963
01 Agriculture (ginning and pressing)	192	193	200	222	159	116	130	138	184	182	153	151	*	*	*
12 Metal mining	150	143	121	120	181	225		230	252	240	260	236	281	250	281
13 Crude petroleum and natural gas	519	489	458	787	733	780	676	703	874	813	993	950	957	1,059	852
14 Stone quarrying, clay, and sand	88	148	178	204	229	85	130	122	218	130	138	126	204	203	234
20 Food manufactures	121	129	132	164	152	158	161	173	188	185	172	167	178	172	195
21 Beverage	142	134	174	176	191	207	230	221	219	247	265	246	246	242	298
22 Tobacco	183	134	197	199	204	169	127	208	235	247	236	239	236	242	274
23 Manufacturing of textiles	100	120	147	170	181	195	206	204	212	217	219	210	215	205	228
24 Manufacturing of footwear and wearing apparel	113	112	127	135	138	221	196	205	247	241	262	269	238	239	231
25 Wood and cork except furniture	112	126	138	149	146	165	162	158	154	152	157	159	173	170	187
26 Furniture and fixtures	140	137	160	158	159	162	173	184	187	181	191	201	193	191	206
27 Paper and paper products	116	103	114	122	142	153	158	249	179	159	165	148	153	151	201
28 Printing, publishing, etc.	162	160	166	203	195	202	204	214	220	220	221	220	278	254	274
29 Leather and its products, except shoes	138	163	195	167	181	187	187	185	215	218	210	222	226	216	225

30 Rubber products	147	143	181	175	184	182	210	203	229	257	260	233	248	230	239
31 Chemicals and chemical products	156	139	173	177	162	164	168	162	193	200	204	191	225	217	264
32 Manufacturing of petroleum and coal	513		468	646	694	603	191	680	678	669	680	679	728	683	641
33 Manufacturing of nonmetallic minerals	159	156	182	186	196	187	199	212	211	215	230	251	233	233	248
34 Basic metals	81	92	210	158	239	178	214	293	329	315	316	299	323	310	347
35 Metal products	140	135	144	153	154	172	157	226	212	205	217	208	182	183	200
36 Nonelectrical machinery	139	149	167	161	227	204	252	251	281	259	250	220	214	217	233
37 Electrical machinery	147	148	155	193	194	197	197	250	209	235	235	227	241	223	257
38 Transport equipment	227	272	418	463	274	311	362	371	301	343	274	355	309	322	343
39 Miscellaneous manufacturing	161	131	144	155	153	161	155	185	178	175	164	213	147	150	169
Weighted average, manufacturing	130	134	166	176	186	193	195	213	217	221	219	218	221	214	236
4 Construction	67	121	144	122	135	170	209	180	196	n.a.	214	241	219	226	257
5 Electricity, gas, and steam	217	236	271	218	285	233	335	375	405	378	385	400	380	399	395
6 Commerce													298	293	321
7 Transport	280	271	479	322	368	398	318	416	351	340	348	337	327	328	348
8 Personal services	102	108	129	126	135	185	189	207	192	211	213	236	193	195	211
General total	146	149	189	199	182	224	219	238	232	237	233	232	237	229	254

*Included with category 23 during these years.

NOTES AND SOURCES: See p. 312.

TABLE II–B–8

INCREASE IN INDICATED WAGE RATES COINCIDENT WITH CHANGE
IN COVERAGE OF SURVEY OF WAGES AND WORKING HOURS

Average Weekly Wage Rate
(in Piasters)

		(1) Average, July, 1952, and January, 1953	(2) Average, July, 1953, and January, 1954	Ratio, (2)/(1)
20	Food....................	155	165	1.06
21	Beverages................	122	186	1.52
22	Tobacco.................	202	200	0.99
23	Textiles.................	165	202	1.22
24	Clothing.................	138	209	1.51
25	Wood...................	147	167	1.14
26	Furniture...............	159	178	1.12
27	Paper...................	127	157	1.24
28	Printing.................	185	201	1.09
29	Leather.................	174	197	1.13
30	Rubber.................	184	184	1.00
31	Chemicals...............	170	155	0.91
32	Petroleum, coal..........	751	629	0.84
33	Nonmetallic minerals......	190	175	0.92
34	Basic metals.............	238	157	0.66
35	Metal products...........	154	161	1.05
36	Nonelectrical machinery....	184	195	1.06
37	Electrical machinery.......	184	199	1.08
38	Transport equipment......	283	254	0.90
39	Miscellaneous manu- facturing.............	157	141	0.90

NOTES AND SOURCES FOR TABLES II–B–6, II–B–7, and II–B–8: All figures in these tables through 1961 except the weighted averages for manufacturing are taken from the regular publication of United Arab Republic, Department of Statistics and Census, *Survey of Wages and Working Hours*. Figures for 1962 and 1963 are from United Arab Republic, Department of Statistics and Census, *Statistical Yearbook, 1964* (Cairo, 1965) (in Arabic), pp. 132–38, but are based on the same survey. In principle, this survey is published twice yearly, covering the first week of January and July of each year, but it has occasionally been omitted, as in January of 1957 and 1958.

There have been three basic changes since the start of this study in July, 1942. The first was the change in classification, in July, 1949, to adopt ISIC; this is relatively minor in importance, although it makes it impossible to present one continuous series. The second change was the gradual expansion of coverage into areas such as personal services and transport, which were not included in the original survey; this also is not serious for our purposes, since we concentrate our attention on manufacturing, and here there have been no significant changes in inclusions. The third and by far the most important change has been in the sample techniques in the survey. Before July, 1953, the approach used was as follows: All enterprises listed in the triennial census of establishments were divided into four groups, as nearly as possible equal in size, both in the aggregate and in each detailed industrial sector. All the establishments in one of these four groups were covered in the survey of wages and working hours of January, 1944, for example; all in the second group in July, 1944, etc.; so that in principle, each establishment was revisited every two years. As of July, 1953, this procedure was replaced by a complete survey of all establishments with ten or more workers. The shift from a 25 percent sample to full coverage should not affect the comparability of the results, but exclusion of all smaller establishments is more serious. To check on the importance of this factor, we have examined the extent to which reported wage rates rose from just before to just after this change in coverage. The results, which are shown in Table II–B–8, indicate that in only four sectors (at a two-digit level) was this change in coverage associated with an increase in reported wage rates of as much as 15 percent; and three of these—beverages, clothing, and paper—are relatively minor in importance, at least when weighted by 1954 employment in firms with ten or more employees. The remaining sector is textiles; the 22 percent increase in reported wage rates in this sector does introduce some upward bias into the index, and hence causes some exaggeration in the increase in wage rates in industry reported in Table 5–8 (p. 116).

The figures before July, 1949, include clerical and administrative workers as well as laborers; thereafter, they are restricted to laborers. Before 1953, only cash wages were reported (including overtime, before taxes); after 1953, wages in kind were also included; these amount to only about two percent of the total. See United Nations, Department of Economics and Social Affairs, *The Development of Manufacturing Industry in Egypt, Israel, and Turkey* (New York, 1958), p. 119. The original sources include a three-digit breakdown as well.

Reported averages for the whole industrial sector in the original publications are simply total wages paid divided by total employment in covered enterprises. We have recomputed these averages for the manufacturing sector, using as weights for 1942–49 employment in each sector as shown by the 1947 population census, and for 1949–60 employment in 1954 as shown in the 1954 census of industrial production (which covered all firms with ten or more employees).

TABLE II–B–9

AVERAGE DAILY MONEY WAGE OF PAID AGRICULTURAL LABORERS

(In Millièmes)

	Men	Women	Boys
1937–40	30	20	15
1943	63	39	30
1945	93	57	46
1950	116	n.a.	n.a.
1959	110–140	n.a.	60–70

SOURCE: *1937–40, 1943, and 1945:* Studies by Fellah Department, Ministry of Social Affairs, quoted in M. Anis, "A Study of the National Income of Egypt," *L'Egypte Contemporaine,* Nos. 261–62 (November-December, 1950), pp. 752–53. Anis says that the data are based to a large extent on the judgement of social workers; field work was not large, but the material was collected from various parts of the country and different periods of the year. There is no reason to doubt that the figures present a reasonably accurate general picture.

1950: United Nations, Department of Economics and Social Affairs, *The Development of Manufacturing Industry in Egypt, Israel, and Turkey* (New York, 1958), p. 120.

1959: United Arab Republic, Ministry of Agriculture, *Monthly Bulletin of Agricultural Economics and Statistics,* March, 1962 (in Arabic), pp. 39–42; for detailed figures see text Table 4–24 (p. 95). Aside from these figures, we may cite rough earlier estimates discussed in B. Hansen, *Marginal Productivity Wage Theory and Subsistence Wage Theory in Egyptian Agriculture,* Memo No. 547 (Cairo: Institute of National Planning, March, 1965), pp. 39–41; see also United Kingdom, Department of Overseas Trade, *Report on the Economic and Financial Situation of Egypt for 1919* (London, Cmd. 843, 1920) p. 10. These references indicate that daily wage rates for men may have been in the range of 35–45 millièmes immediately before World War I, higher than in the late 1930's.

TABLE II–B–10

Average Monthly Wage Rates of Government Employees, by Grade

(£E per Month)

	1	2	3	4	5	6	7	8	9
1945	81.4	64.8	50.4	37.8	26.6	16.3	13.1	8.2	5.8
1946	81.6	64.2	50.1	37.7	25.4	16.1	12.9	8.3	5.5
1947	79.5	62.8	48.8	37.4	25.3	16.0	12.8	8.4	5.4
1948	78.6	61.0	47.1	34.7	23.4	15.7	12.3	8.3	5.4
1949	75.1	59.8	46.9	34.9	23.2	15.6	12.2	8.2	5.3
1950	76.4	60.2	47.5	35.6	24.2	16.0	12.3	8.2	5.5
1951	78.0	62.7	47.8	36.7	26.1	15.8	12.1	8.3	5.5
1952	80.8	63.8	48.9	38.9	26.9	16.1	12.5	8.4	5.3
1953	79.4	63.4	49.4	38.3	27.2	16.3	12.6	8.5	5.6
1954	80.1	64.8	49.4	38.3	25.7	16.8	12.9	8.9	6.0
1955	79.3	64.1	48.1	37.1	25.8	16.5	12.9	8.9	6.0
1956	84.0	67.6	49.5		26.7	17.5	13.7	9.4	6.3
1961	87.5	72.5	55.0	40.0	30.0	20.0	14.5	11.5	7.5
Number of employees, 1961	1,268	2,641	7,814	19,259	26,715	51,044	43,036	75,073	7,757

Notes and Sources: These data are taken from the annual publication of United Arab Republic, Department of Statistics and Census, *Survey of Employees of the Egyptian Government and Public Enterprises*; the figures refer to cash wages, excluding cost-of-living bonuses, of general government employees (excluding public enterprises).

TABLE II–B–11

Government Wage Rates and Wage Payments

	1945	1946	1947	1948	1949	1950	1951	1952	1953	1954	1955	1956
1. Government wage payments, excluding cost-of-living bonuses (£E000)	34,239	35,190	36,140	40,453	45,934	52,306	57,861	58,700	62,298	73,537	84,527	94,633
2. Cost-of-living bonuses (£E000)	11,201	10,636	9,702	13,026	13,420	30,504	31,623	33,133	31,143	28,969	29,200	29,993
3. Wages, including cost-of-living bonuses (£E000)	45,440	45,826	45,842	53,479	59,354	82,810	89,484	91,833	93,441	102,506	113,727	124,626
4. Ratio, cost-of-living bonuses to wages	0.327	0.302	0.268	0.322	0.292	0.583	0.547	0.564	0.499	0.393	0.345	0.316
5. Average wage rate, excluding cost-of-living bonuses (£E/month)	14.7	14.5	14.2	14.6	14.3	14.2	14.5	12.9	14.6	15.5	16.0	17.7
6. Average wage rate, including cost-of-living bonuses (£E/month)	19.5	18.9	18.0	19.3	18.5	22.5	22.4	20.2	21.9	21.6	21.5	23.3
7. Same index, 1954 = 100	90.2	87.5	83.3	89.3	85.6	104.2	103.7	93.5	101.4	100.0	99.5	107.9
8. Total wage payments, 1954 rates (£E100)	50,376	52,372	55,032	59,886	69,338	79,472	86,291	98,217	92,150	102,506	114,298	115,501
9. Real wage rate	87.4	86.5	84.8	90.2	87.4	100.6	92.3	83.8	97.3	100.0	99.8	105.6

NOTES AND SOURCES: This table presents revised and more detailed estimates of the figures in Table 3 of B. Hansen and D. Mead, *The National Income of the U.A.R. (Egypt), 1939–1962*, Memo No. 355 (Cairo: Institute of National Planning, July, 1963). Rows 1 and 2 for the years 1947–56 are from Appendix Table VI–E–4 (pp. 385–95); before 1951, the fiscal year was March 1–February 28; fiscal 1947–48 is used for calendar 1947, etc. Thereafter, when the fiscal year was changed to run from July 1 to June 30, we used the average of the fiscal year estimates. For 1945 and 1946, we extrapolated the 1947 figure backward, using estimates of nonmilitary government wage payments in United Nations, Department of Economics and Social Affairs, *The Development of Manufacturing Industry in Egypt, Israel, and Turkey* (New York, 1958), p. 92. Row 5 shows simply total monthly wage payments divided by employees in all nine cadres; it reflects, therefore, both changing wage rates in each cadre and a changing distribution of workers among cadres. Row 6 = (1 + row 4) × (row 5). Row 8 = row 3 ÷ row 7 × 100. In row 9, we have divided row 7 by the cost-of-living index, using 1954 = 100.

Appendix III

Agriculture

TABLE III–A–1

INDICES OF AGRICULTURAL OUTPUT

(1953 = 100)

	National Bank of Egypt	Department of Statistics and Census	Food and Agriculture Organization,* Old Series	Food and Agriculture Organization,* New Series	National Planning Committee Memo No. 1	Income from Agriculture
1935–39....	102.0	91.7	83.7			
1945.......	87.7	n.a.			96.7	
1946.......	90.8	n.a.			96.2	
1947.......	94.9	n.a.			95.4	
1948.......	110.2	101.8	94.6		104.9	
1949.......	108.1	100.0	95.4		103.8	
1950.......	104.0	96.3	94.6		96.6	96.3
1951.......	98.9	92.7	92.1		90.7	97.0
1952.......	108.1	100.9	99.6	102.0	104.2	104.6
1953.......	100.0	100.0	100.4	97.8	100.0	100.0
1954.......	112.2	110.1	110.5	108.4	109.7	106.3
1955.......	111.2	108.3	107.1	109.5		109.0
1956.......	110.2	111.9		113.7		111.1
1957.......	123.4	119.3		123.3		116.4
1958.......	125.5	120.2		123.3		120.9
1959.......	130.6	124.8		127.5		123.2
1960.......		128.4		130.7		127.4
1961.......		112.8				
1962.......		139.4				
1963.......		154.1				

*Agricultural years; 1953 refers to 1953–54, etc. We have set the average of 1952–53 and 1953–54 equal to 100.

NOTES AND SOURCES: See p. 320.

TABLE III–A–2

INDEX NUMBERS OF AGRICULTURAL OUTPUT: MAJOR COMMODITY GROUPS

(1953 = 100)

	Fibers	Cereals	Pulses	Oil Grains	Other Crops	Vegetables	Fruits	Animal Products	Total Food Production	FAO Food Production
1935–39	126.6	88.5	137.0	109.8	69.9	58.8	46.5	84.0	84.0	
1948	124.0	94.7	131.5	108.7	88.8	88.8	61.9	105.0	96.6	
1949	125.3	90.3	139.7	105.4	83.2	82.3	64.6	105.0	94.1	
1950	120.3	86.7	98.6	105.4	82.5	70.6	63.7	107.6	91.6	
1951	113.9	83.2	108.2	103.2	83.9	75.9	80.0	110.9	92.4	
1952	141.8	77.9	109.6	127.4	88.8	95.3	96.3	102.5	91.6	96.1
1953	100.0	100.0	100.0	100.0	100.0	100.0	100.0	100.0	100.0	103.9
1954	108.9	113.3	115.1	106.5	117.5	113.5	98.1	110.1	110.9	115.1
1955	105.1	109.7	121.9	105.4	119.6	117.6	105.1	107.6	110.1	118.4
1956	102.5	117.7	102.7	105.4	117.5	124.7	88.8	117.6	115.1	126.3
1957	127.8	115.0	121.9	121.9	125.9	131.8	106.5	117.6	117.6	129.6
1958	143.0	104.4	117.8	132.9	125.9	144.1	112.6	119.3	115.1	127.4
1959	145.6	112.4	104.1	134.0	137.1	171.8	107.0	121.8	120.2	133.0
1960	154.4	115.9	135.6	140.7	137.8	178.2	113.5	117.6	122.7	138.5
1961	109.9	105.3	76.7	95.6	133.6	187.1	103.7	120.2	114.3	130.7
1962	151.9	137.2	147.9	141.8	146.9	205.3	131.6	122.7	137.8	
1963	145.6	136.3	123.3	144.0	164.3	230.6	139.5	181.5	157.1	

NOTES AND SOURCES: See p. 320.

TABLE III–A–3

INDEX OF AGRICULTURAL OUTPUT, 1913–55

(1953 = 100)

Year	Output	Year	Output
1913	89.3	1935	103.4
1914	78.2	1936	106.7
1915	76.9	1937	113.5
1916	71.7	1938	102.3
1917	84.8	1939	108.5
1918	74.9	1940	107.8
1919	73.4	1941	97.1
1920	77.8	1942	86.5
1921	68.9	1943	76.4
1922	81.0	1944	80.9
1923	83.9	1945	89.4
1924	87.7	1946	88.2
1925	93.0	1947	90.7
1926	92.3	1948	108.2
1927	88.2	1949	106.0
1928	96.8	1950	101.1
1929	104.4	1951	97.5
1930	96.2	1952	108.5
1931	86.3	1953	100.0
1932	87.2	1954	110.4
1933	98.0	1955	106.7
1934	91.9		

NOTES AND SOURCES FOR TABLES III–A–1, III–A–2, AND III–A–3:   National Bank of Egypt: This is a weighted geometric mean of the quantity of production of 10 major field crops, including clover; weights are average values of each crop over the period 1946–50. See National Bank of Egypt, *Economic Bulletin*, Vol. VII, No. 4 (1954), pp. 252–55. The index has not been published since 1959.

The Department of Statistics and Census indices (col. 2 of Table III–A–1 and cols. 1–9 of Table III–A–2) are Laspeyres indices using as weights prices in the period 1935–39; figures are from *Annuaire Statistique*, various issues. Figures for 1963 for total output, animal products, and food production are all preliminary. The index includes animals as well as field crops and fruits.

The FAO data refer to agricultural years rather than calendar years; 1948 refers to 1948–49, etc. The older FAO index was "constructed by applying uniform world weights based on prewar 1934–38 price relationships to the production figures" (United Nations Food and Agriculture Organization, *Yearbook of Food and Agricultural Statistics*, Vol. X, Part 1: *Production* [Rome, 1956], p. 332). Clover is excluded. The later series uses as weights average prices in the Middle East during 1952–56.

The National Planning Committee memo series underlies the constant-price national income estimates discussed in Appendix I; the estimates are based on output figures from the Ministry of Agriculture, using as weights value added in the different crops in 1954.

The series entitled "Income from Agriculture" is an estimate of the value of output of the whole agricultural sector at 1954 prices; it is taken from United Arab Republic, Department of Statistics and Census, *National Income from the Agricultural Sector for the Years 1958–1960* (Cairo, n.d.), p. 24.

The estimates in Table III–A–3 are a Fisher ideal index covering the period 1913–57, from M. M. el Imam, *A Production Function for Egyptian Agriculture, 1913–1955*, Memo No. 259 (Cairo: Institute of National Planning, December, 1962), p. 43. M. A. Anis has also computed a quantity index covering the period 1914–45, but the weighting he uses makes very little sense ("A Study of the National Income of Egypt," *L'Egypte Contemporaine*, Nos. 261–62 [November-December-1950], p. 920). In view of the diversity of approaches and coverages in these different indices, perhaps the main characteristic which emerges is their overall similarity; divergencies between them are relatively minor, particularly for the postwar period.

TABLE III–A–4

AREA, PRODUCTION, AND YIELD OF MAJOR CROPS

(Area in Thousands of Feddan, Production in Thousands of Metric Tons, Yield in Tons/Feddan)

	Wheat			Maize			Millet			Barley			Rice		
	Area	Production	Yield	Area	Production	Yield	Area	Production	Yield	Area	Production	Yield	Area	Production	Yield
Average, 1915–19	1,304	913	0.70	1,709	1,678	0.98	268	313	1.16	403	271	0.67	249	332	1.33
Average, 1920–24	1,372	981	0.72	1,888	1,722	0.91	240	274	1.14	363	246	0.68	189	228	1.21
Average, 1925–29	1,497	1,090	0.73	2,073	2,026	0.98	246	301	1.22	355	247	0.70	271	355	1.31
Average, 1930–34	1,503	1,173	0.78	1,812	1,748	0.96	299	368	1.23	307	220	0.72	339	428	1.26
Average, 1935–39	1,410	1,248	0.89	1,540	1,606	1.04	358	456	1.27	266	233	0.88	446	684	1.53
Average, 1940–44	1,631	1,197	0.73	1,778	1,440	0.81	617	685	1.11	319	254	0.80	578	736	1.27
Average, 1945–49	1,559	1,127	0.72	1,637	1,436	0.88	560	592	1.06	246	183	0.74	705	1,111	1.58
1950	1,372	1,018	0.74	1,451	1,306	0.90	393	426	1.08	117	91	0.78	700	1,242	1.77
1951	1,497	1,209	0.81	1,655	1,421	0.86	423	517	1.22	118	100	0.85	488	620	1.27
1952	1,402	1,089	0.78	1,704	1,506	0.88	433	522	1.21	137	118	0.86	374	517	1.38
1953	1,790	1,547	0.86	2,015	1,853	0.92	486	582	1.20	116	103	0.89	423	652	1.54
1954	1,795	1,729	0.96	1,904	1,753	0.92	457	549	1.20	122	116	0.95	610	1,118	1.83
Average, 1950–54	1,571	1,318	0.84	1,746	1,568	0.90	438	519	1.18	122	105	0.86	519	830	1.60
1955	1,523	1,451	0.95	1,834	1,714	0.93	437	537	1.23	136	127	0.93	600	1,244	2.07
1956	1,570	1,547	0.99	1,836	1,652	0.90	479	595	1.24	132	129	0.98	690	1,495	2.17
1957	1,514	1,467	0.97	1,769	1,495	0.85	449	566	1.26	133	131	0.98	731	1,624	2.22
1958	1,425	1,412	0.99	1,955	1,758	0.90	423	543	1.28	136	135	0.99	518	1,027	1.98
1959	1,475	1,443	0.98	1,859	1,500	0.81	467	630	1.35	141	141	1.00	729	1,536	2.11
Average, 1955–59	1,501	1,464	0.98	1,851	1,624	0.88	451	574	1.27	136	132	0.97	654	1,385	2.12
1960	1,456	1,499	1.03	1,821	1,691	0.93	453	603	1.33	148	156	1.05	706	1,486	2.10
1961	1,384	1,436	1.04	1,603	1,617	1.01	457	631	1.38	121	133	1.10	537	1,142	2.13
1962	1,455	1,593	1.09	1,832	2,004	1.09	455	659	1.45	131	146	1.12	830	2,029	2.44
1963	1,345	1,493	1.11	1,721	1,867	1.08	484	729	1.51	121	134	1.11	959	2,219	2.31
1964	1,295	1,499	1.16	1,660	1,934	1.17	494	740	1.50	121	141	1.17	962	2,036	2.12
Average, 1960–64	1,387	1,504	1.09	1,727	1,823	1.09	469	672	1.43	128	142	1.11	799	1,782	2.22

(Continued on next page)

TABLE III-A-4—Continued

	Cotton			Beans			Lentils			Onions*			Sugar Cane		
	Area	Produc-tion	Yield	Area	Produc-tion	Yield	Area	Produc-tion	Yield	Area	Produc-tion	Yield	Area	Produc-tion	Yield
Average, 1915–19	1,482	238	0.16	516	417	0.81	69	42	0.61	31	215	6.94	59	1,748	29.60
Average, 1920–24	1,684	278	0.17	459	310	0.68	77	46	0.60	35	232	6.63	57	1,749	30.70
Average, 1925–29	1,761	344	0.20	464	307	0.66	72	42	0.58	45	312	6.93	52	1,646	31.70
Average, 1930–34	1,679	321	0.19	486	320	0.66	84	50	0.60	47	315	6.70	64	2,073	32.40
Average, 1935–39	1,754	411	0.23	393	296	0.75	79	55	0.70	35	243	7.03	67	2,273	33.93
Average, 1940–44	1,120	270	0.24	386	296	0.77	76	55	0.72	25	168	6.87	85	2,432	28.61
Average, 1945–49	1,316	317	0.24	395	295	0.75	74	49	0.66	31	233	6.89	92	2,528	27.48
1950	1,975	383	0.19	356	198	0.56	81	51	0.63	36	255	6.26	81	2,529	31.22
1951	1,979	364	0.18	320	232	0.73	75	47	0.63	37	308	7.61	86	2,810	32.67
1952	1,967	446	0.23	355	250	0.70	58	32	0.55	32	267	7.38	92	3,260	35.43
1953	1,324	319	0.24	299	209	0.70	69	47	0.68	35	304	7.25	104	3,690	35.48
1954	1,579	349	0.22	310	235	0.76	87	60	0.69	45	380	7.29	115	4,215	36.65
Average, 1950–54	1,765	372	0.21	328	225	0.69	74	48	0.65	37	303	7.16	96	3,301	34.39
1955	1,816	335	0.18	358	262	0.73	81	49	0.60	50	415	6.71	111	4,145	37.34
1956	1,653	325	0.20	337	206	0.61	82	48	0.59	46	403	6.75	110	4,091	37.19
1957	1,819	406	0.22	355	254	0.72	83	53	0.64	50	482	6.80	109	4,137	37.95
1958	1,905	446	0.23	360	260	0.72	73	42	0.58	49	463	6.48	113	4,230	37.43
1959	1,760	458	0.26	354	208	0.59	79	48	0.61	56	558	6.57	112	4,329	38.65
Average, 1955–59	1,791	394	0.22	353	238	0.67	80	48	0.60	50	464	6.66	111	4,186	37.71
1960	1,873	479	0.26	362	290	0.80	85	50	0.59	56	545	6.66	111	4,555	41.04
1961	1,986	336	0.17	328	161	0.49	63	34	0.54	64	545	5.99	112	4,188	37.39
1962	1,657	457	0.28	369	328	0.89	79	56	0.71	60	602	6.48	121	4,811	39.76
1963	1,627	442	0.27	360	245	0.68	78	47	0.60	52	659	n.a.	133	5,153	38.74
1964	1,611	504	0.31	408	340	0.83	79	52	0.66	48	647	n.a.	134	5,150	38.43
Average, 1960–64	1,751	444	0.26	365	273	0.74	77	48	0.62	56	600	n.a.	122	4,771	39.07

*Area excludes interplanted crop and is confined to winter crop as of 1963; production excludes green consumption as of 1963; average yield figures refer to winter crop only (fully ripe winter crop as of 1950).

SOURCES: *Annuaire Statistique*, various issues; and Central Bank of Egypt, *Economic Review*, Vol. IV, Nos. 3–4 (1964), pp. 368–69; Vol. V, No. 2 (1965), pp. 212–13.

TABLE III–B–1

Prices of Major Crops

	Cotton (Cantar)	Cotton-seed (Ardeb)	Rice (Dariba)	Wheat (Ardeb)	Maize (Ardeb)	Millet (Ardeb)	Barley (Ardeb)	Sugar Cane (Cantar)	Beans (Ardeb)	Onions (Cantar)	Lentils (Ardeb)
Average, 1920–24	715.1	123.5	1,407.2	207.6	130.0	131.3	126.4	7.0	245.3	28.0	210.9
Average, 1925–29	511.2	95.6	1,079.2	165.7	110.0	108.2	94.6	3.9	198.3	19.4	206.8
Average, 1930–34	236.2	56.6	754.3	126.0	88.4	80.5	70.1	3.6	134.0	16.4	136.5
Average, 1935–39	255.6	61.1	713.1	132.8	92.8	79.6	69.5	3.4	137.9	16.1	153.4
Average, 1940–44	430.6	86.5	1,410.9	258.5	195.1	185.9	175.3	6.8	299.2	29.9	318.6
1945	652.6	101.0	1,908.5	398.0	263.0	263.0	249.0	9.1	402.0	38.0	445.0
1946	747.0	100.7	1,929.5	359.4	235.0	235.0	185.0	9.5	405.0	69.0	445.0
1947	1,205.2	100.7	2,006.5	328.7	235.0	205.0	160.0	9.5	438.0	38.0	445.0
1948	1,117.4	101.6	2,006.5	330.0	235.0	205.0	160.0	9.5	445.0	55.0	445.0
1949	1,500.0	101.6	2,006.5	330.0	235.0	210.0	122.0	11.5	351.0	96.0	460.0
1950	2,511.0	101.6	1,848.5	330.0	245.0	245.0	262.0	11.5	584.0	103.0	611.0
1951	1,865.0	80.0	1,848.5	330.0	245.0	220.0	307.0	11.5	623.0	75.5	624.0
1952	1,242.0	80.0	1,450.0	330.0	270.0	236.0	206.0	11.5	576.0	75.4	908.0
1953	1,209.7	80.0	1,525.0	490.0	270.0	243.0	275.0	11.0	537.0	76.6	915.0
1954	1,253.8	80.0	1,575.0	440.0	264.1	264.8	194.9	11.0	484.7	32.4	915.0
1955	1,421.4	80.0	1,650.0	390.0	377.6	354.7	286.8	10.5	565.8	35.5	629.0
1956	1,702.0	80.0	1,650.0	390.0	419.0	362.0	249.2	10.0	661.3	54.8	915.0
1957	1,479.0	80.0	1,650.0	407.0	350.0	351.0	228.0	11.5	652.0	41.9	912.0
1958	1,363.0	80.0	1,650.0	370.0	330.0	355.4	332.0	10.5	567.0	68.2	921.0
1959	1,497.0	80.0	1,650.0	370.0	330.0	321.0	293.0	10.5	653.0	36.1	915.0
1960	1,424.6	80.0	1,740.0	370.0	330.0	339.9	222.3	10.5	670.6	74.1	943.4
1961	1,264.6	80.0	1,740.0	370.0	330.0	324.8	250.0	10.5	891.2	67.8	1,004.7

NOTES AND SOURCES: *Annuaire Statistique*, various issues, through 1959; 1960 and 1961 are derived by taking the ratio of value to volume of each crop for 1959, 1960, and 1961, as shown in United Arab Republic, Central Statistical Committee, *Basic Statistics*, October, 1963 (in English), p. 81, and using the change in this ratio to indicate change in price on a comparable basis. These are presumably wholesale prices; all are in piasters per unit indicated. (One ardeb = 198 liters; one cantar = 44.928 kilograms; one dariba of rice = approximately 935 kilograms.)

TABLE III-C-1

Total Cropped and Cultivated Areas

(000 Feddan)

	1906-7	1916-17	1926-27	1936-37	1942-43	1946-47	1950-51	1952-53	1956-57	1961-62	1963-64
Summer:											
Cotton	1,603	1,677	1,516	1,978	713	1,254	1,979	1,324	1,819	1,657	1,611
Rice	156	232	358	243	631	758	478	409	717	823	952
Sorghum	n.a.	180	180	223	650	480	379	426	390	398	443
Others	301	163	158	146	289	302	276	360	446	825	868
Total	2,060	2,252	2,212	2,590	2,283	2,794	3,112	2,519	3,372	3,703	3,874
Winter:											
Wheat	1,218	1,076	1,594	1,369	1,917	1,630	1,497	1,790	1,514	1,455	1,295
Clover	n.a.	1,372	1,490	1,742	1,652	1,990	2,122	2,142	2,567	2,442	2,480
Beans	596	472	447	386	381	382	320	299	355	383	408
Barley	458	429	362	261	419	237	118	116	133	131	121
Others	1,591	268	256	262	292	299	265	255	343	411	424
Total	3,863	3,617	4,149	4,020	4,661	4,538	4,322	4,602	4,912	4,822	4,728
Autumn:											
Maize	1,624	1,656	2,115	1,554	1,915	1,578	1,623	1,985	1,721	1,484	1,340
Others	89	125	151	128	214	181	122	164	170	211	237
Total	1,713	1,781	2,266	1,682	2,129	1,759	1,745	2,149	1,891	1,695	1,577
Orchards	27	28	34	66	71	81	91	98	137	145	167
Total cropped area	7,662	7,677	8,661	8,358	9,144	9,167	9,270	9,368	10,312	10,365	10,346
Cultivated area	5,403	5,269	5,544	5,281	5,331	5,761	5,613	5,642	5,756	5,977	n.a.

NOTES AND SOURCES: *Annuaire Statistique,* various issues; and United Arab Republic, Central Agency for Public Mobilization and Statistics, *Statistical Handbook: United Arab Republic, 1952-1964* (Cairo, April, 1965), pp. 20-24.

TABLE III-C-2

LAND OWNERSHIP

Size of Area Owned (Feddan)	Area (Feddan)			Number of Owners		
	1939	1950	1962	1939	1950	1962
Less than 1	153,180	653,016	912,638	373,692	1,901,518	2,164,520
1 to less than 2	275,847	509,866	540,798	204,132	374,595	408,066
2 to less than 3	265,289	347,171	409,498	112,691	145,130	173,225
3 to less than 4	234,628	255,559	339,365	69,824	74,867	101,165
4 to less than 5	199,622	201,948	321,209	45,781	45,641	78,957
5 to less than 10	684,853	615,280	559,604	100,142	89,631	82,457
10 to less than 20	689,081	565,310	610,556	50,543	41,468	45,816
20 to less than 50	833,947	660,184	687,982	27,683	21,694	23,301
50 to less than 100	604,914	488,939	484,630	8,778	7,055	6,946
100 to less than 200	556,113	440,614 }	827,708	4,053 }	3,195 }	2,746
200 to less than 500	598,174	471,467		2,011	1,596	
500 and over	941,231	764,833		733	603	
Total	6,036,879	5,974,187	5,693,988	1,000,063	2,706,993	3,081,249

NOTES AND SOURCES: Years 1939 and 1950 from agricultural censuses. Year 1962 from United Arab Republic, Department of Statistics and Census, *Statistical Yearbook, 1964* (Cairo, 1965) (in Arabic), pp. 58–61. The detailed figures on number of owners in this source, and as given above, add to 3,087,247, rather than the totals shown.

For a thorough and competent discussion of the history of land ownership, see G. Baer, *A History of Landownership in Modern Egypt, 1800–1950* (New York: Oxford University Press, 1962). Baer points out that there is substantial exaggeration in the number of owners shown in these figures, since a land owner with land in two different villages is generally counted twice. In his Appendix 1 (pp. 224–25), he presents annual figures on the distribution of landed property by size, 1896–1950.

TABLE III–C–3

LAND HOLDINGS, BY SIZE

Size of Holding (Feddan)	Area (Feddan)				Number of Holdings			
	1929	1939	1950	1956	1929	1939	1950	1956
Less than 1	206,990	153,180	111,774	142,000	436,873	373,692	214,334	405,300
1 to less than 2	372,042	275,847	335,697	} 1,427,000	} 283,052	204,132	248,336	} 619,800
2 to less than 3	334,328	265,289	373,951		145,837	112,691	161,658	
3 to less than 4	285,398	234,628	328,708		86,843	69,824	99,132	
4 to less than 5	232,445	199,622	272,687		54,189	45,781	63,330	
5 to less than 10	737,315	684,853	818,382	} 1,681,000	} 110,980	100,142	122,356	} 187,700
10 to less than 20	706,761	689,081	705,331		53,154	50,543	52,517	
20 to less than 50	811,427	833,947	792,082	797,000	27,545	27,683	26,468	28,700
50 to less than 100	569,298	604,914	579,053	} 1,040,000	} 8,377	8,778	8,372	} 11,000
100 to less than 200	527,864	556,113	562,943		3,888	4,053	4,075	
200 to less than 500	679,776	598,174	556,218	} 1,125,000	} 2,272	2,011	1,883	} 1,900
500 to less than 1,000	384,934				574	733	562	
1,000 and over	} 1,592,118	941,231	707,098		331			
Total	7,440,696	6,036,879	6,143,924	6,212,000	1,213,915	1,000,063	1,003,023	1,254,400

SOURCE: Agricultural censuses; and National Bank of Egypt, *Economic Bulletin*, Vol. X, No. 1 (1957), p. 46. The figures for 1929 show a suspiciously large total; the whole cultivated area in that year was only 5.5 million feddan.

TABLE III-C-4

Distribution of Holdings by Type of Tenure

Size of Holding (Feddan)	Area (Feddan)				Number of Holdings
	Owned	Leased	Mixed	Total	
1929:					
Total	5,805,395	1,635,301	*	7,440,696	1,213,915
1939:					
1 or less	147,084	5,229	867	153,180	373,692
Above 1 to 2	254,005	14,758	7,084	275,847	204,132
Above 2 to 3	232,332	20,199	12,758	265,289	112,691
Above 3 to 4	197,510	20,748	16,370	234,628	69,824
Above 4 to 5	163,169	19,218	17,235	199,622	45,781
Above 5 to 10	527,339	71,048	86,469	684,853	100,142
Above 10 to 20	501,303	70,854	116,924	689,081	50,543
Above 20 to 50	588,069	82,301	163,577	833,947	27,683
Above 50 to 100	423,095	62,720	119,099	604,914	8,778
Above 100 to 200	402,237	55,399	98,477	556,113	4,053
Above 200 to 500	454,674	59,307	84,193	598,174	2,011
Above 500	859,651	31,573	50,007	941,231	733
Total	4,750,468	513,355	773,056	6,036,879	1,000,063

(Continued on next page)

TABLE III-C-4-Continued

Size of Holding (Feddan)	Area (Feddan)				Number of Holdings
	Owned	Leased	Mixed	Total	
1950:					
Less than 1	91,969	16,911	2,894	111,774	214,334
1 to less than 2	229,904	71,030	34,763	335,697	248,336
2 to less than 3	229,572	84,762	59,617	373,951	161,658
3 to less than 4	190,375	73,456	64,877	328,708	99,132
4 to less than 5	153,935	61,886	56,866	272,687	63,330
5 to less than 10	446,359	182,583	189,440	818,382	122,356
10 to less than 20	377,981	143,958	183,392	705,331	52,517
20 to less than 50	424,427	158,574	209,081	792,082	26,468
50 to less than 100	307,984	134,739	136,330	579,053	8,372
100 to less than 200	318,509	128,422	116,012	562,943	4,075
200 to less than 500	349,871	108,415	97,932	556,218	1,883
500 and more	599,250	57,972	49,876	707,098	562
Total	3,720,136	1,222,708	1,201,080	6,143,924	1,003,023

*Mixed holdings are distributed among the other two categories.

Source: Agricultural censuses. Note that the precise dividing line was changed between 1939 and 1950; a holding of exactly one feddan would be counted in the first bracket in 1939, in the second in 1950.

TABLE III–C–5

RENTED LAND, BY TYPE OF LEASE

	1939		1950	
	Area (Feddan)	Number of Holdings	Area (Feddan)	Number of Holdings
Cash rent....................	635,233	80,543	1,626,167	304,578
Lease in participation..........	50,907	8,545	103,330	15,409
Standing rent in kind..........	n.s.	n.s.	125,682	18,674
Other kinds of leases..........	179,584	18,234	74,106	11,869
Not stated..................	101,618	8,982	0	0
Total...................	967,342	116,304	1,929,285	350,530

NOTES AND SOURCES: Agricultural censuses. The totals correspond to total leased plus the rented portion of mixed holdings shown in Table III–C–4. Leases in participation mean that the landlord gets a fixed percentage of the crop, while standing rent in kind gives the landlord a fixed amount of the crop.

TABLE III–C–6

FRAGMENTATION OF LAND HOLDINGS, 1950

(In Feddan)

Area of Total Holding, in Feddan	In One Piece	In Two Pieces	In Three Pieces	In Four or More Pieces	Total
Less than 1	82,641	22,403	4,739	1,709	111,774
1 to less than 2	134,496	130,676	50,559	19,111	335,697
2 to less than 3	101,145	128,139	96,285	47,296	373,951
3 to less than 4	65,206	114,142	74,402	73,847	328,708
4 to less than 5	45,658	81,496	78,248	66,345	272,687
5 to less than 10	118,404	186,160	218,337	292,685	818,382
10 to less than 20	82,887	109,332	152,425	357,790	705,331
20 to less than 50	103,462	92,789	122,881	469,041	792,082
50 to less than 100	86,601	69,395	74,713	344,204	579,053
100 to less than 200	98,491	60,391	61,547	335,287	562,943
200 to less than 500	99,119	54,132	56,249	338,108	556,218
500 and more	144,703	68,942	46,728	429,169	707,098
Total	1,162,813	1,117,997	1,037,113	2,774,592	6,143,924

SOURCE: Republic of Egypt, Ministry of Agriculture and Department of Statistics and Census, *Agricultural Census, 1950* (Cairo, 1958), p. 25.

TABLE III–C–7

LENGTH OF CANALS AND DRAINS

(Kilometers)

	Canals	Drains	Total
1913.............	24,496	5,926	30,422
1917.............	18,634	6,290	24,924
1927.............	18,711	7,088	25,799
1937.............	20,170	9,168	29,338
1947.............	22,073	12,064	34,137
1954.............	23,471	12,316	35,787
1960.............	24,804	13,330	38,134

NOTES AND SOURCE: From *Annuaire Statistique*, various issues. The drop from 1913 to 1917 results from the exclusion in 1915 and thereafter of the Delta Barrage Directorate, listed earlier as having canals of 8,590 kilometers. This is difficult to understand, unless during this period they counted as canals the branches of the Nile itself; even this, though, can hardly have added eight thousand kilometers.

TABLE III–D–1

LIVESTOCK

(In Thousands)

	Buffaloes	Other Bovines	Horses	Mules	Donkeys	Camels	Pigs	Sheep	Goats
1904	646	605	n.a.	n.a.	n.a.	n.a.	n.a.	n.a.	n.a.
1912	652	620	47	21	691	n.a.	n.a.	n.a.	n.a.
1917	515	566	31	17	586	99	n.a.	808	308
1927	758	740	38	21	751	179	21	1,232	622
1937	956	983	31	23	1,142	155	37	1,919	1,311
1943	1,001	1,202	31	12	827	174	31	1,424	760
1945	1,064	1,265	34	15	851	162	40	1,385	732
1947	1,240	1,321	28	12	1,126	197	50	1,875	1,476
1952	1,212	1,356	39	10	816	165	27	1,254	703
1955	1,323	1,362	42	10	927	162	19	1,237	744
1958	1,395	1,390	45	11	950	157	17	1,259	723
1960	1,524	1,588	48	10	1,011	189	17	1,578	833

SOURCE: *Annuaire Statistique*, various issues; data are based on livestock censuses, undertaken by the Ministry of Agriculture for all years except 1947, which was done by Department of Statistics and Census. We suspect that in all population census years—1917, 1927, 1937, 1947, and 1960—the livestock census was done in conjunction with the population censuses, and that in other years there might be a substantial understatement of the number of donkeys, camels, sheep, and goats.

TABLE III–D–2

SUPPLY OF CHEMICAL FERTILIZERS

(Thousands of Metric Tons)

	Imports	Domestic Production	Total
1902	2.2	0.0	2.2
1907	23.1	0.0	23.1
1912	70.1	0.0	70.1
1917	36.9	0.0	36.9
1922	118.2	0.0	118.2
1927	225.4	0.0	225.4
1932	234.6	0.0	234.6
1937	641.8	n.a.	n.a.
1943	158.6	n.a.	n.a.
1947	459.4	15.0*	474.4
1952	629.0	206.1	835.1
1957	620.1	385.5	1,005.6
1958	715.3	399.9	1,115.2
1959	355.3†	412.3	767.6
1960	625.8	443.2	1,069.0

*Production of superphosphates, in 1946; this was listed as 20,000 tons in 1938. United Nations, Department of Economic and Social Affairs, *The Development of Manufacturing Industry in Egypt, Israel, and Turkey* (New York, 1958), p. 95.

†Excludes imports from Syria, but these are negligible.

SOURCE: *Annuaire Statistique*, various issues. Source also gives (since 1917) breakdown by types of fertilizer.

TABLE III–D–3

LICENSED MOTORS IN AGRICULTURAL WORK

	Irrigation		Drainage		Agricultural Works	
	Number	IHP* (000)	Number	IHP (000)	Number	IHP (000)
1927	13,087	n.a.	335	n.a.	734	n.a.
1937	10,892	299	93	5	1,077	30
1947	12,340	334	107	5	4,895	139
1954	15,326	401	119	6	8,124	247
1960	16,666	455	116	5	10,348	328

*Installed horsepower.

SOURCES: *Annuaire Statistique*, various issues. These figures exclude electrical machinery, but include all other motors, which require a permit from the Department of Mechanical Power and Electricity of the Minisry of Public Works.

TABLE III–D–4

AGRICULTURAL MACHINERY

	1929	1939	1950
Irrigation machinery:			
Irrigation engines and machines.....	n.a.	15,846	15,170
Irrigation pumps..................	n.a.	11,469	5,841
Tambousha:			
Motor-driven..................	n.a.	n.a.	3,500
Cattle-driven..................	n.a.	n.a.	83,436
Tabouts.........................	n.a.	83,673	37,765
Waterwheels:			
European.....................	n.a.	20,869	12,093
Native........................	n.a.	136,669	128,069
Tambours.......................	n.a.	235,027	237,620
Waterlifts (shadoufs).............	n.a.	53,362	44,679
Agricultural instruments:			
Steam ploughs..................	1,008	1,795	648
Tractors:			
Above 35 HP..................	n.a.	n.a.	4,044
Below 35 HP..................	n.a.	n.a.	5,928
Ploughs by tractors..............	2,741	n.a.	7,968
Ploughs by cattle................	n.a.	n.a.	4,475
European ploughs................	n.a.	5,440	n.a.
Native ploughs..................	564,144	603,903	661,919
Leveling scoops.................	n.a.	115,037	97,949
Threshing machines..............	569	2,123	2,951
Winnowing machines.............	2,373*	2,494	2,467
European threshers..............	n.a.	19,082	18,655
Native threshers.................	302,023	301,705	341,499
Segregating machines.............	746	2,083	n.a.

*Excluding 5,303 wooden winnowing fans.
SOURCES: Republic of Egypt, Ministry of Agriculture and Department of Statistics and Census, *Agricultural Census*, various issues. Tambousha and tabouts are different types of waterwheels, while the tambour is an Archimedes screw. On the whole, we have little confidence in the comparability of these figures.

Appendix IV

Industry

TABLE IV–A–1

OFFICIAL INDICES OF MANUFACTURING OUTPUT

(1953 = 100)

| | National Planning Committee | | | | National Bank of Egypt | |
	Basic Industry	Other Industry	Spinning and Weaving	Total	Spinning and Weaving	Total
1945..........	72.2	68.6	54.7	69.8		
1946..........	76.3	68.5	56.8	71.1		
1947..........	82.1	75.6	61.7	77.8		
1948..........	90.0	84.7	71.6	86.5		
1949..........	100.1	93.7	83.2	95.8		
1950..........	105.5	96.7	83.2	99.6		
1951..........	102.3	97.7	88.4	99.2	91.0	95.1
1952..........	101.3	97.1	90.5	98.5	97.4	98.1
1953..........	100.0	100.0	100.0	100.0	100.0	100.0
1954..........	111.7	110.9	105.3	111.2	109.4	106.8
1955.........					116.0	116.9
1956.........					126.1	125.2
1957.........					134.3	131.8
1958.........					147.0	143.3
1959.........					152.0	147.2

NOTES AND SOURCES: National Planning Committee estimates are in Memo No. 1 for the plan; they are based, where possible, on the volume of output and, failing that, on the value of inputs used, or of employment. These estimates are discussed in greater detail in the notes to Appendix Table I–A–5 (pp. 281-85). Weighting is by value added in 1954. "Spinning and weaving" is a component of "other industry."

The National Bank's index is basically similar, using the same weighting and a similar but not identical mixture of output, input, and employment figures; it is described in National Bank of Egypt, *Economic Bulletin*, Vol. X, No. 1 (1957), pp. 6–14.

The United Nations also published an index for the period 1951–59, but this is virtually identical with the National Bank index.

APPENDIX IV–A–2

PRIVATE ESTIMATES OF MANUFACTURING OUTPUT

While the figures in Table IV–A–1 help us to get an overall view of changing aggregate output in manufacturing from 1945 to 1959, we should like to have some idea of developments in this area both before and after these series. We have attempted to compute a rough index of the increase in output during World War II, looking at changes in the volume of output of the main components in each two-digit ISIC category, weighting these by value added in each in 1947. Needless to say, this involves a great deal of guesswork, as output figures are often very crude or not available, but the results imply that if prewar output in manufacturing equals 100, the figure for 1945 is 195. This is higher than other estimates we have seen; Hansen and Marzouk put this figure at 150 (B. Hansen and G. Marzouk, *Development and Economic Policy in the U.A.R.* [*Egypt*] [Amsterdam: North-Holland Publishing Co., 1965], Table V. 2); Anis at 138 (M. A. Anis, "A Study of the National Income of Egypt," *L'Egypte Contemporaine*, Nos. 261–62 [November-December, 1950], p. 685), although according to his estimate it had risen to 154 in 1944. All the estimates are clearly very rough. With regard to the period since 1959, we must rely on current estimates of the value of output from the censuses of industrial production, making allowance for price changes. The figures are as follows:

	1959	1960	1961
Gross output (£E million)............	429	474	549
Index...........................	100	110	128
Net value added (£E million).........	119	127	167
Index...........................	100	107	140
Wholesale price index, industrial products (December figures)....	100	99	95

If we assume that industrial prices were constant, and use the lower growth rate implied by the gross output index, we can extend the National Bank of Egypt total output series in Table IV–A–1 as follows:

$$1960 = 161.9$$
$$1961 = 188.4$$

TABLE IV–A–3

Output Indices of Mining and Quarrying, Construction,
and Electricity

(1953 = 100)

	Mining and Quarrying		Construction	Electricity	
	A	B		A	B
1945	50.0		34.8	59.3	
1946	46.5		58.0	60.9	
1947	50.8		72.5	63.6	
1948	71.0		93.5	66.3	
1949	87.7		118.8	72.2	
1950	102.6		137.7	78.1	
1951	99.9	104.4	129.0	68.7	50.7
1952	100.8	106.1	102.9	89.2	52.4
1953	100.0	100.0	100.0	100.0	100.0
1954	87.7	89.7	110.9	110.8	103.3
1955		92.9			117.6
1956		85.9			128.7
1957		105.5			141.0
1958		137.5			158.7
1959		138.1			177.1

Notes and Sources: Mining and quarrying, series A: S. H. Abdel Rahman, *A Survey of the Foreign Trade of Egypt in the Post-War Period, with Special Reference to its Impact on the National Economy* (Ph.D. dissertation, Faculty of Commerce, Cairo University, 1959). Series is based mainly on quantities produced; where these are not available, volume of materials purchased or employment are taken as substitutes. This index underlies the real income estimate for this sector in National Planning Committee Memo No. 1 (see Table I–A–5 [p. 281]). Series B: National Bank of Egypt, using 1954 weights; series includes only salt, petroleum, and phosphates. See National Bank of Egypt, *Economic Bulletin*, Vol. X, No. 1 (1957), pp. 6–14. Construction: Abdel Rahman, *op. cit.* Based on materials consumed, local and imported. Electricity, series A: From NPC Memo No. 1; series B: National Bank of Egypt. Both are based on electricity production in major companies.

TABLE IV–C–1

EMPLOYMENT AND VALUE ADDED IN MANUFACTURING,
BY SIZE OF ESTABLISHMENT, 1960

Establishments Employing:	Persons Employed (000)	Gross Value Added (£E Million)	Gross Value Added per Person (£E)
Under 10, and outside establishments....	366	100	274
10–49................	55	12	224
50–499...............	97	53	545
500 and over...........	173	82	472
Government establishments.........	21	8	380
Total.............	713	255	358

NOTES AND SOURCES: This table is modeled on Table V. 9 in B. Hansen and G. Marzouk, *Development and Economic Policy in the U.A.R. (Egypt)* (Amsterdam: North-Holland Publishing Co., 1965); these figures differ from those given there in several respects. We refer only to manufacturing (ISIC 2 and 3). All figures for firms of size 10–500 and over are from the 1960 census of industrial production; for the government sector, we have included value added in industry by the government business sector, exclusive of municipal lighting and water, with employment derived by assuming that wage rates there are as in large private firms, as suggested by Hansen and Marzouk. See United Arab Republic, Presidency of the Republic, National Planning Committee, *General Frame of the Five-Year Plan for Economic and Social Development, July 1960–June 1965* (Cairo, 1960), p. 167. Total employment is from United Arab Republic, Department of Statistics and Census, *Population Census, 1960* (Cairo, 1963), Vol. II, p. xiv; total value added from Table 5–3 (p. 104). The first line is derived residually in all cases.

Appendix V

International Transactions

TABLE V–A–1

IMPORTS, BY CATEGORIES, 1885–1929 (Annual Averages, £E Thousand)

	1885–89	1890–94	1895–99	1900–1904	1905–9	1910–14	1915–19	1920–24	1925–29
A. Food, drink, and tobacco:									
1 Animal and food products	342	347	366	795	1,128	1,034	1,796	1,332	1,628
4 Cereals, flour, and agricultural produce	770	737	1,112	1,672	3,261	3,256	1,190	7,557	5,248
5 Colonial products and drugs	420	411	354	476	1,001	1,049	1,638	2,445	3,013
6 Beverages and oils	639	594	609	848	1,133	1,251	3,328	3,753	3,784
15 Tobacco	273	442	524	611	760	1,112	2,176	2,001	1,549
Total	2,444	2,531	2,965	4,402	7,283	7,702	10,129	17,088	15,222
Percent of total imports	30.8	28.5	28.9	27.0	30.6	30.5	28.2	27.5	27.1
B. Other consumer goods:									
2 Hides, skins, and leather	173	169	164	245	378	389	413	3,900	3,423
7 Paper and printed matter	112	121	142	240	363	406	924	1,164	1,054
12 Textiles	2,586	2,981	3,161	4,898	6,296	6,838	13,618	19,526	15,417
14 Miscellaneous	339	380	516	1,036	1,699	1,864	1,569	1,662	1,956
Total	3,210	3,651	3,983	6,419	8,736	9,497	16,524	26,253	21,849
Percent of total imports	40.4	41.0	38.8	39.4	36.7	37.6	46.6	42.3	38.9
C. Producer goods:									
3 Other animal products	76	70	66	84	85	68	89	59	51
8 Wood and coal	911	1,140	1,310	2,215	3,032	3,109	4,245	6,030	4,305
9 Stone, glass, and pottery	180	181	235	411	617	593	468	1,401	1,586
10 Dyes and colors	253	260	244	293	270	255	479	537	387
11 Chemicals, medicines, and perfume	201	208	229	381	662	1,223	1,875	3,363	3,969
13 Metal and metalware	670	829	1,228	2,094	3,118	2,806	2,124	7,336	8,857
Total	2,291	2,688	3,312	5,478	7,784	8,054	9,279	18,727	19,155
Percent of total imports	28.8	30.3	32.3	33.6	32.7	31.9	25.8	30.2	34.1
Total merchandise imports	7,946	8,870	10,260	16,299	23,803	25,253	35,932	62,067	56,227
Specie	2,552	2,913	3,641	5,204	6,569	8,680	826	1,074	1,040
Total imports	10,498	11,783	13,901	21,503	30,372	33,933	36,758	63,141	57,267

NOTES AND SOURCES: See p. 343.

TABLE V–A–2

EXPORTS, BY CATEGORIES, 1885–1929

(Annual Averages, £E Thousand)

Category	1885–89	1890–94	1895–99	1900–1904	1905–9	1910–14	1915–19	1920–24	1925–29
1 Animal and food products	19	25	49	124	136	216	490	479	392
2 Hides, skins, and leather	100	90	87	92	165	221	683	398	347
3 Other animal products	25	29	33	69	86	55	45	68	69
4 Cereals, flour, and agricultural produce	2,316	3,153	2,368	2,560	3,031	4,044	4,174	5,262	5,396
4a (cottonseed)	(1,352)	(1,629)	(1,421)	(1,766)	(2,271)	(2,299)	(2,348)	(3,210)	(2,610)
5 Colonial products and drugs	569	624	635	621	233	212	906	688	92
6 Beverages and oils	4	4	12	33	18	67	234	438	747
7 Paper and printed matter	40	34	15	15	20	23	94	105	83
8 Wood and coal	17	21	19	16	17	18	37	42	22
9 Stone, glass, and pottery	2	1	1	4	3	3	5	7	105
10 Dyes and colors	17	15	16	25	26	28	32	47	21
11 Chemicals, medicines, and perfumes	7	9	12	16	25	90	264	302	220
12 Textiles	7,660	8,645	9,756	14,305	19,828	23,953	37,518	50,158	42,601
12a (Cotton, raw)	(7,548)	(8,561)	(9,683)	(14,228)	(19,700)	(23,788)	(37,186)	(49,851)	(42,306)
13 Metals and metalware	153	76	38	5	28	158	264	268	94
14 Miscellaneous	33	29	26	26	86	108	83	74	46
15 Tobacco	82	157	240	426	429	380	536	597	365
Reexports	275	168	204	258	399	461	1,461	2,855	1,402
Total merchandise exports	11,319	13,080	13,511	18,595	24,530	30,037	46,826	61,787	52,002
Specie	2,154	2,198	1,982	2,277	4,361	7,960	257	115	727
Total exports	13,473	15,278	15,493	20,872	28,891	37,997	47,083	61,902	52,729

NOTES AND SOURCES FOR TABLES V–A–1 AND V–A–2: *Annuaire Statistique*, various issues. Imports are CIF, exports FOB. Before August 3, 1911, all exports are officially stated to show only 90 percent of the market value in each category. The origin of this procedure is uncertain, but it may have been a means for reducing effective tariff rates. This and other weaknesses of these data are discussed in detail in A. E. Crouchley, "The Visible Balance of Trade since 1884," *L'Egypte Contemporaine*, Nos. 155–56 (March–April, 1935), pp. 491–512. Percentages in Table V–A–1 refer to share in total merchandise imports (excluding specie).

TABLE V–A–3

Imports, by Categories, 1931–55

(£E Thousand)

	1931	1932	1933	1934	1935	1936	1937	1938	1939	1940	1941	1942	1943
CONSUMERS													
Food, nonprocessed:													
A. Live animals, chiefly for food	138	74	133	152	124	282	221	279	157	52	138	142	83
B. Fruits and vegetables	764	527	470	555	534	571	542	567	496	324	213	247	390
C. Spices	59	65	52	41	65	39	45	44	45	62	60	173	150
D. Others (including meat, eggs, and honey)	28	21	22	19	40	41	40	40	46	21	20	19	11
Total	989	687	677	767	763	933	848	930	744	459	431	581	634
Food, processed:													
A. Meat and fish preparations	245	229	212	242	276	252	265	282	202	127	90	401	176
B. Dairy products	450	284	254	254	262	275	285	325	250	186	218	183	124
C. Oils and fats	190	212	253	169	192	187	195	166	114	116	62	56	36
D. Vegetables and fruits	199	167	145	177	221	219	268	240	203	200	201	631	510
E. Sugar and sugar preparations	111	63	72	69	74	85	91	90	74	96	174	362	242
F. Others	290	176	142	140	151	153	148	143	136	174	164	247	185
Total	1,485	1,131	1,078	1,051	1,176	1,171	1,252	1,246	979	899	909	1,880	1,273
Beverages and manufactured tobacco:													
A. Coffee	400	404	414	303	313	272	339	287	222	325	418	603	1,147
B. Tea	519	409	367	614	525	645	792	831	758	909	1,242	1,980	959
C. Soft drinks	28	28	28	26	28	25	24	23	23	15	10	17	14
D. Alcoholic drinks	509	452	377	367	417	432	440	395	390	547	1,057	2,233	1,178
E. Tobacco and manufactured tobacco	75	83	81	83	103	150	108	149	165	355	103	1,475	1,129
F. Others	7	3	4	3	2	4	4	2	1	31	2	1	28
Total	1,538	1,379	1,271	1,396	1,388	1,528	1,707	1,687	1,559	2,182	2,832	6,309	4,455
Textiles, ready-made fabrics, footwear, and miscellaneous wearing apparel:													
A. Textiles:													
1. Natural silk textiles	852	715	377	320	272	229	271	222	194	173	122	85	14
2. Artificial silk textiles	......	187	437	554	596	369	415	222	172	146	99	394	26
3. Wool and hair textiles	570	594	804	889	846	993	1,153	867	838	691	1,004	1,836	566
4. Cotton textiles	3,947	3,785	3,965	3,788	3,771	3,486	4,058	3,048	1,985	2,062	2,692	5,548	1,511
5. Others	186	187	216	235	232	243	243	212	253	415	212	702	654
Total textiles	5,555	5,468	5,799	5,786	5,717	5,320	6,140	4,571	3,442	3,487	4,129	8,565	2,771

	1931	1932	1933	1934	1935	1936	1937	1938	1939	1940	1941	1942	1943
B. Ready-made fabrics:													
1. Natural silk	87	54	44	44	53	52	58	61	58	41	98	95	7
2. Artificial silk	151	117	101	113	112	101	83	83	79	81	129	370	33
3. Wool and hair	290	288	299	308	255	269	307	281	210	132	159	281	151
4. Cotton	473	424	429	388	359	299	343	258	195	133	144	344	59
5. Others	61	36	37	37	35	37	39	40	31	23	23	48	16
Total, ready-made fabrics	1,062	919	910	890	814	758	830	723	573	410	553	1,138	266
C. Footwear	130	74	49	48	59	59	63	40	44	14	13	16	4
Total, footwear	130	74	49	48	59	59	63	40	44	14	13	16	4
D. Umbrellas, sticks, and miscellaneous wearing apparel	178	167	211	191	150	147	161	148	82	38	30	55	16
Total, umbrellas, sticks, and miscellaneous wearing apparel	178	167	211	191	150	147	161	148	82	38	30	55	16
Total	6,925	6,628	6,969	6,915	6,740	6,284	7,194	5,482	4,141	3,949	4,725	9,774	3,057
Motion-picture films	55	60	98	107	92	79	93	93	85	89	404	562	585
Total	55	60	98	107	92	79	93	93	85	89	404	562	585
Medicine	274	273	297	328	381	412	423	538	371	357	104	162	122
Total	274	273	297	328	381	412	423	538	371	357	104	162	122
Private means of transportation:													
A. Small cars	406	248	263	443	513	549	731	673	478	307	113	151	92
B. All others	21	14	14	16	28	21	26	34	24	16	6	5	6
Total	427	262	277	459	541	570	757	707	502	323	119	156	98
Kerosene	564	719	763	716	714	725	1,176	1,136	1,144	1,266	1,201	1,438	1,635
Total	564	719	763	716	714	725	1,176	1,136	1,144	1,266	1,201	1,438	1,635

(Continued on next page)

TABLE V-A-3—Continued

	1931	1932	1933	1934	1935	1936	1937	1938	1939	1940	1941	1942	1943
Miscellaneous:													
A. Thread, cotton	157	177	155	164	219	107	168	108	91	100	182	268	253
B. Thread, natural and artificial silk	10	10	13	10	11	13	12	9	7	5	6	5	0
C. Sewing machines	85	25	36	27	46	28	45	38	68	29	59	19	15
D. Household appliances	7	5	6	9	16	16	21	29	20	14	27	14	7
E. Glass and glasswares	66	66	70	80	80	90	108	67	55	37	21	90	19
F. Cutlery and miscellaneous wares, common metals	50	48	55	67	69	87	80	71	59	53	100	215	134
G. Radio receiving sets				156	176	107	125	108	95	41	83	67	33
H. Watches	53	37	54	61	56	72	93	92	69	52	120	445	310
I. Spectacles	8	9	8	10	13	16	16	20	15	11	35	44	6
J. Photography cameras (portable)								52	26	10	21	18	
K. Musical instruments	34	23	18	17	16	17	15	13	12	7	3	2	5
L. Toys, articles for Christmas trees, goods and apparatus	77	78	82	81	85	103	87	86	60	50	59	73	42
M. Others (including wares of stone, works of art, articles for collection, and postal packages)	1,352	1,241	1,227	1,239	1,258	1,304	1,315	1,273	1,103	805	1,035	1,448	754
Total	1,899	1,719	1,724	1,921	2,025	1,960	2,085	1,966	1,680	1,214	1,751	2,708	1,571
Total, consumers	14,156	12,858	13,154	13,660	13,820	13,662	15,535	13,785	11,205	10,758	12,476	23,570	13,430
PRODUCERS													
A. Raw materials:													
1. Cereals	545	515	5	123	281	5	0	103	22	4	147	1,096	53
2. Tobacco	840	740	575	573	628	616	592	605	602	603	863	1,549	3,487
3. Gravel, stones, etc., for building	6	5	8	14	10	8	9	8	5	2	7	7	10
4. Coal	1,399	1,164	1,193	1,379	1,837	1,276	2,120	2,007	2,282	1,273	2,070	2,892	1,438
5. Petroleum		342	227	323	274	258	207	207	19		79		
6. Other mineral and quarrying materials	19	20	19	23	24	21	37	39	49	40	38	42	108
7. Hides and skins	6	6	6	6	16	35	35	56	25	40	27	63	38
8. Crude rubber	1	1	1	2	2	3	5	8	12	20	29	40	53
9. Wool and hair	1	1	2	2	10	10	7	13	10	48	65	77	52
10. Jute				1								9	65
11. Other (including chemicals and fertilizers)	281	246	247	211	242	228	279	217	195	232	333	441	524
Total	3,098	3,040	2,283	2,655	3,324	2,460	3,291	3,263	3,221	2,262	3,653	6,216	5,778

	1931	1932	1933	1934	1935	1936	1937	1938	1939	1940	1941	1942	1943
B. Semifinished products:													
1. Flour	1,167	516	57	40	33	34	34	46	23	24	48	155	39
2. Sugar	11	6	15	16	46	220	197	687	765	817	253	100	4
3. Oils and fats for industry	210	196	273	347	381	402	512	409	286	338	340	318	50
4. Asbestos	1	1	1	1	1	1		1	1	2	2	2	3
5. Chemicals	356	395	440	476	525	495	562	574	634	848	1,259	1,209	860
6. Hides and skins, tanned	105	102	101	99	114	134	141	130	103	91	81	114	14
7. Motion-picture films and other films	19	24	23	28	36	39	39	39	43	16	84	64	45
8. Rubber and rubber products	12	15	13	14	15	17	21	23	19	14	50	19	4
9. Paper and material for paper manufacture	356	345	344	355	453	392	730	526	481	626	1,016	1,165	597
10. Yarn, natural silk	97	130	147	190	194	216	265	229	187	121	126	34	14
11. Yarn, artificial silk	64	83	87	135	107	119	262	226	262	503	1,162	502	169
12. Wool and hair, bleached, dyed, combed, or scoured	3	2	4	9	3	3	1	15	24	65	100	151	120
13. Yarn, wool and hair	19	22	39	44	57	64	74	77	91	53	107	149	101
14. Yarn, cotton	144	89	74	69	97	103	94	112	121	124	263	210	76
15. Yarn, others	26	31	27	24	20	19	20	17	16	13	18	54	16
16. Glass		2	2	3	2	2	4	2	3	3	6	1	2
17. Precious metals	242	70	99	100	123	255	319	234	258	80	166	959	724
18. Marble, stone, and like buildings materials	75	78	74	61	76	27	45	35	31	20	1		1
19. Wood and wooden products	873	842	927	1,240	1,182	1,181	1,339	1,375	1,053	810	325	550	223
20. Iron, cast iron, and steel	305	285	310	441	578	588	748	769	941	915	2,115	3,053	442
21. Copper, cast	154	123	187	243	262	321	335	288	167	87	97	151	63
22. Aluminum, cast	6	8	11	14	19	17	24	21	21	15	8	2	
23. Tin, cast	57	50	79	97	122	96	104	90	77	159	167	236	40
24. Tin, zinc, lead, crude bars, wire, and mercury	79	85	31	43	39	57	65	57	54	62	62	208	47
25. Others	293	261	257	307	336	355	365	335	304	403	451	468	208
Total	4,673	3,759	3,622	4,396	4,821	5,157	6,301	6,317	5,965	6,209	8,307	9,874	3,862
C. Finished products:													
1. Fertilizers	1,800	1,652	1,847	2,171	2,557	2,656	3,390	2,955	2,865	3,267	102	2,737	3,374
2. Oils and lubricants	702	642	588	517	821	700	983	1,053	1,200	1,391	2,864	8,192	8,303
3. Photographic material	34	32	28	29	31	37	29	27	25	32	48	98	26
4. Leather products (belting for machines)	40	27	28	44	41	33	27	36	26	29	19	51	27
5. Rubber products	194	182	176	135	180	177	192	261	251	168	463	283	114
6. Paper and paper articles	199	174	223	203	227	221	349	281	252	254	436	550	97
7. Asbestos products	17	15	14	16	22	17	22	18	16	21	23	39	16
8. Sacks	294	313	425	517	465	504	499	547	489	914	991	1,161	539
9. Cement and products	178	215	147	135	110	62	89	99	86	22	12	1	1
10. Miscellaneous construction material	359	250	259	297	326	406	351	401	430	306	72	55	50
11. Wooden articles	123	66	65	62	74	81	76	86	77	51	33	103	36

(Continued on next page)

TABLE V–A–3—Continued

	1943	1942	1941	1940	1939	1938	1937	1936	1935	1934	1933	1932	1931
12. Iron products	662	930	969	1,420	2,281	2,300	2,243	1,553	1,586	1,493	1,270	1,212	1,698
13. Copper products	10	28	33	25	50	73	81	80	77	85	78	73	159
14. Ropes, wires, cables of aluminum, and manufactures of zinc and lead	1	16	12	6	6	6	9	6	4	4	5	4	5
15. Wires, electric material	82	86	87	98	131	180	129	106	114	82	133	129	133
16. Machinery and equipment (excluding electric machinery)													
17. Parts for machinery and equipment (excluding electric machinery)	176	213	354	382	806	893	1,034	759	658	571	508	665	774
18. Textile machines and looms	283	224	200	297	417	466	356	282	317	241	184	225	251
19. Parts for textile machines and looms	53	175	84	89	375	206	264	111	199	241	66	132	17
20. Electric machines and apparatus	47	63	55	55	66	17	24	18	22	12	18	18	29
21. Articles and detached parts for electric machinery and apparatus	321	226	173	319	421	441	318	331	408	334	422	420	638
22. Railway and tramway equipment	49	166	70	51	56	42	64	56	61	51	43	38	42
23. Parts for railway and tramway equipment	45	4	14	163	191	437	364	336	271	13	18	9	188
24. Aviation and navigation	22	24	15	37	47	44	40	48	30	23	15	65	82
25. Parts for aviation and navigation	145	116	2	6	48	76	20	12	12	3	44	40	164
26. Motor lorries and motor buses	37	4	113	326	122	362	105	36	66	79	88	86	86
27. Parts for motor lorries and motor buses	214	232	55	77	59	228	82		1	2			
28. Other vehicles	2	805	478	396	428	319	290	394	424	167	138	139	222
29. Parts for vehicles, bicycles, and motorcycles	7	3	1	1	9	4	1	49	45	40	1	1	2
30. Precision and other equipment	59	11	14	21	45	47	52	203	171	140	113	111	159
31. Parts for precision and other equipment	10	124	119	151	260	249	203	28	20	18	17	15	17
32. Parts, others	11	24	19	35	17	27	24	19	17	20	14	15	20
33. Cinematographic and nonportable photographic cameras	9	5	6	7	6		57	60	58	30	22	14	15
34. Others	278	732	579	467	518	621	668	571	566	530	482	478	557
Total	15,126	15,498	8,522	10,892	12,227	12,819	12,459	9,953	9,981	8,305	7,512	7,457	9,198
Total, producers	24,766	31,588	20,482	19,363	21,413	22,399	22,051	17,570	18,126	15,356	13,417	14,256	16,969
MISCELLANEOUS													
1. Gold and silver ingots and coins	125	232	27	40	333	250	67	29	26	55	3	160	194
2. Arms and ammunition	789	56	91	1,121	931	300	158	88	73	74	74	70	93
3. Others	84	65	43	108	204	204	222	162	187	149	118	80	115
Total, miscellaneous	998	353	161	1,269	1,468	754	447	279	286	278	195	310	402
Errors, omissions, and rounding	2	1	8	8	5	-4	5	5	7	10	1	1	1
Grand total	39,196	55,512	33,127	31,378	34,091	36,934	38,038	31,516	32,239	29,304	26,767	27,425	31,528

CONSUMERS	1944	1945	1946	1947	1948	1949	1950	1951	1952	1953	1954	1955
Food, nonprocessed:												
A. Live animals, chiefly for food	135	178	419	560	564	579	713	636	332	335	361	495
B. Fruits and vegetables	826	917	1,127	953	1,276	1,343	2,144	3,695	2,804	2,799	2,359	2,558
C. Spices	179	166	327	291	262	313	344	352	299	370	342	274
D. Others (including meat, eggs, and honey)	305	15	447	20	29	24	72	38	15	19	11	309
Total	1,445	1,276	2,320	1,824	2,131	2,259	3,273	4,721	3,450	3,523	3,073	3,636
Food, processed:												
A. Meat and fish preparations	432	372	600	698	843	1,279	1,841	2,054	1,826	1,500	1,440	1,725
B. Dairy products	115	140	182	476	630	865	1,262	1,731	1,699	1,599	1,133	1,122
C. Oils and fats	90	158	142	174	264	258	304	1,110	1,579	1,689	820	743
D. Vegetables and fruits	735	841	662	759	1,017	974	1,386	1,635	1,664	1,104	987	1,177
E. Sugar and sugar preparations	244	485	281	267	395	495	6,499	565	6,769	2,420	855	100
F. Others	360	297	404	318	494	433	523	695	553	596	443	441
Total	1,976	2,293	2,271	2,692	3,643	4,304	11,815	7,790	14,090	8,908	5,678	5,308
Beverages and manufactured tobacco:												
A. Coffee	1,509	1,838	1,615	1,077	1,189	1,601	1,801	1,865	1,770	1,924	1,922	1,245
B. Tea	1,686	1,098	1,158	4,300	4,873	6,237	6,803	7,070	6,481	7,724	8,126	9,801
C. Soft drinks	11	17	64	208	279	361	616	676	538	303	266	319
D. Alcoholic drinks	1,805	1,691	1,338	951	770	668	661	653	443	389	328	334
E. Tobacco and manufactured tobacco	1,333	1,300	1,363	698	956	704	747	691	320	260	327	200
F. Others	9	18	27	14	14	9	21	24	35	29	25	28
Total	6,353	5,962	5,565	7,248	8,081	9,580	10,649	10,979	9,587	10,629	10,994	11,927
Textiles, ready-made fabrics, footwear, and miscellaneous wearing apparel:												
A. Textiles:												
1. Natural silk textiles	13	73	807	272	459	569	409	523	199	162	92	63
2. Artificial silk textiles	13	114	3,033	1,964	2,209	1,666	2,459	2,542	1,387	902	546	374
3. Wool and hair textiles	295	417	1,815	3,392	5,881	5,092	5,324	5,618	3,661	2,101	1,806	1,905
4. Cotton textiles	365	563	3,030	4,600	4,825	4,317	5,278	4,374	2,614	2,765	1,443	1,010
5. Others	543	416	457	860	1,551	590	696	1,142	927	442	478	839
Total textiles	1,229	1,583	9,142	11,088	14,925	12,234	14,166	14,199	8,788	6,372	4,365	4,191

(Continued on next page)

TABLE V–A–3–Continued

	1944	1945	1946	1947	1948	1949	1950	1951	1952	1953	1954	1955
B. Ready-made fabrics:												
1. Natural silk	3	22	165	104	75	57	58	45	41	35	14	13
2. Artificial silk	56	83	437	574	466	489	672	690	506	438	283	239
3. Wool and hair	263	294	504	483	893	1,107	1,312	1,221	622	805	443	461
4. Cotton	101	130	437	538	620	554	794	853	566	533	274	294
5. Others	22	16	88	110	115	131	135	176	104	81	77	152
Total, ready-made fabrics	445	545	1,691	1,809	2,169	2,338	2,971	2,985	1,839	1,892	1,091	1,159
C. Footwear	12	46	53	45	61	75	129	182	78	40	38	45
Total, footwear	12	46	53	45	61	75	129	182	78	40	38	45
D. Umbrellas, sticks, and miscellaneous wearing apparel	24	35	167	255	230	198	264	270	187	157	130	139
Total umbrellas, sticks, and miscellaneous wearing apparel	24	35	167	255	230	198	264	270	187	157	130	139
Total	1,710	2,209	11,053	13,197	17,385	14,845	17,530	17,636	10,892	8,461	5,624	5,534
Motion-picture films	129	113	177	203	221	228	147	340	264	261	312	327
Total	129	113	177	203	221	228	147	340	264	261	312	327
Medicine	735	1,484	1,508	1,739	2,397	2,878	3,978	4,849	4,457	5,091	5,360	6,002
Total	735	1,484	1,508	1,739	2,397	2,878	3,978	4,849	4,457	5,091	5,360	6,002
Private means of transportation:												
A. Small cars	174	128	1,226	2,264	3,085	4,402	3,692	4,771	2,491	1,009	1,577	3,270
B. All others	26	16	209	187	303	232	277	291	277	171	310	395
Total	200	144	1,435	2,451	3,388	4,634	3,969	5,062	2,768	1,180	1,887	3,665
Kerosene	3,201	3,205	2,867	2,392	2,363	4,036	3,788	4,531	6,726	7,000	7,676	4,416
Total	3,201	3,205	2,867	2,392	2,363	4,036	3,788	4,531	6,726	7,000	7,676	4,416

	1944	1945	1946	1947	1948	1949	1950	1951	1952	1953	1954	1955
Miscellaneous:												
A. Thread, cotton	260	600	387	363	947	380	389	525	451	420	371	373
B. Thread, natural and artificial silk	1	1	23	16	21	11	17	22	9	13	8	13
C. Sewing machines	14	21	62	48	176	114	178	259	309	378	423	403
D. Household appliances	1	4	89	186	377	325	440	734	563	362	245	504
E. Glass and glasswares	4	20	158	235	249	240	224	307	247	238	125	87
F. Cutlery and miscellaneous wares, common metals	228	169	234	245	241	272	338	365	235	222	246	286
G. Radio receiving sets	8	6	339	426	516	616	783	1,172	1,120	733	783	848
H. Watches	126	118	155	458	513	714	929	756	994	831	878	927
I. Spectacles	18	58	66	68	87	71	107	123	82	99	105	121
J. Photography cameras (portable)	2	9	25	58	57	57	86	94	93	31	73	75
K. Musical instruments	9	11	17	25	43	36	49	58	73	50	57	57
L. Toys, articles for Christmas trees, goods and apparatus	300	380	226	267	342	301	353	382	245	241	208	258
M. Others (including wares of stone, works of art, articles for collection, and postal packages)	1,729	1,873	3,687	3,694	4,480	4,231	4,971	6,552	4,531	3,941	3,847	4,215
Total	2,700	3,270	5,468	6,089	8,049	7,368	8,864	11,349	8,952	7,559	7,369	8,167
Total, consumers	18,458	19,956	32,664	37,835	47,658	50,132	64,013	67,257	61,186	52,612	47,973	48,982
PRODUCERS												
A. Raw materials:												
1. Cereals	13	2,920	2,196	94	21,443	17,912	18,262	35,432	34,467	22,146	285	2
2. Tobacco	4,916	6,271	5,101	4,328	4,030	4,529	4,873	4,639	4,856	4,709	4,668	4,822
3. Gravel, stones, etc., for building	30	18	9	16	18	25	27	35	50	42	57	60
4. Coal	1,862	1,448	1,180	1,856	1,868	1,804	997	1,921	1,464	485	893	731
5. Petroleum								275	496	249	2,876	5,624
6. Other mineral and quarrying materials	231	56	96	93	206	260	263	372	409	278	251	430
7. Hides and skins	92	43	66	41	38	19	27	14	9	17	47	110
8. Crude rubber	21	4	14	38	18	26	74	109	58	90	105	219
9. Wool and hair	87	60	19	65	96	117	152	71	104	68	179	189
10. Jute	23	24	43	92	178	182	259	187	125	105	203	105
11. Other (including chemicals and fertilizers)	773	711	746	706	976	746	1,004	1,651	1,026	840	755	864
Total	8,048	11,555	9,470	7,329	28,871	25,620	25,938	44,706	43,064	29,029	10,319	13,156

(Continued on next page)

TABLE V-A-3—Continued

	1944	1945	1946	1947	1948	1949	1950	1951	1952	1953	1954	1955
B. Semifinished products:												
1. Flour	21	428	237	760	4,007	213	3,498	3,837	7,151	4,162	2,164	3
2. Sugar	8	3	29	46	652	1,425	817	54	21	15	29	19
3. Oils and fats for industry	60	114	119	344	1,416	994	1,051	2,935	3,265	2,113	2,429	2,796
4. Asbestos	2	9	4	5	24	23	56	76	163	94	134	185
5. Chemicals	1,466	1,627	2,161	1,733	4,039	2,980	3,760	5,808	4,820	3,133	3,685	4,418
6. Hides and skins, tanned	17	60	163	203	206	204	184	196	97	88	98	80
7. Motion-picture films and other films	62	51	193	112	167	157	199	245	226	302	344	252
8. Rubber and rubber products	3	12	36	201	172	110	211	80	106	120	149	90
9. Paper and material for paper manufacture	746	606	2,256	1,770	3,176	1,735	2,807	5,627	4,723	3,617	4,293	4,467
10. Yarn, natural silk	32	230	398	319	410	470	396	243	231	284	187	219
11. Yarn, artificial silk	118	151	853	2,127	2,959	2,520	2,701	2,625	1,454	1,338	1,263	1,190
12. Wool and hair, bleached, dyed, combed, or scoured	321	294	286	480	1,206	1,198	1,560	938	1,577	2,449	2,047	1,804
13. Yarn, wool and hair	139	152	311	264	373	438	445	310	502	553	543	321
14. Yarn, cotton	177	142	145	207	234	130	134	157	144	110	143	230
15. Yarn, others	3	10	12	9	12	7	8	19	31	14	28	34
16. Glass	5	10	15	17	22	27	20	35	31	34	26	76
17. Precious metals	717	1,636	1,841	3,072	1,873	1,772	6,660	4,547	2,263	76	51	63
18. Marble, stone, and like building materials	1	2	22	115	200	197	282	461	328	305	271	364
19. Wood and wooden products	360	890	2,297	6,279	4,374	8,364	8,739	11,228	5,970	7,384	8,145	9,426
20. Iron, cast iron, and steel	346	490	946	1,478	1,755	2,851	2,983	2,636	3,458	2,119	2,891	3,398
21. Copper, cast	86	131	386	212	544	707	993	706	515	766	698	618
22. Aluminum, cast	3	8	92	75	186	168	183	404	328	366	366	474
23. Tin, cast	147	123	274	118	320	341	314	566	566	318	360	427
24. Tin, zinc, lead, crude bars, wire, and mercury	39	105	112	184	168	392	215	330	275	199	256	274
25. Others	328	419	355	526	671	553	646	978	645	653	597	796
Total	5,207	7,703	13,543	20,656	29,166	27,976	38,862	45,041	38,890	30,612	31,197	32,024
C. Finished products:												
1. Fertilizers	5,280	4,169	2,848	5,731	7,936	11,385	12,436	12,238	13,734	11,451	11,237	9,483
2. Oils and lubricants	7,974	7,668	4,964	4,569	5,752	6,036	5,266	8,499	8,726	6,845	7,508	7,118
3. Photographic material	63	137	77	57	72	107	61	91	83	103	101	139
4. Leather products (belting for machines)	34	63	138	117	170	135	92	138	117	65	77	78
5. Rubber products	297	472	567	701	1,046	862	1,725	2,143	2,047	1,551	1,739	2,214
6. Paper and paper articles	70	75	672	592	1,324	815	1,506	2,038	1,555	1,245	1,626	1,682
7. Asbestos products	27	58	72	45	72	85	97	111	120	58	102	132
8. Sacks	1,373	1,261	518	2,340	3,959	3,385	2,910	2,259	2,101	680	1,820	3,434
9. Cement and products	3	4	32	98	117	148	243	252	307	217	129	259
10. Miscellaneous construction material	81	231	868	933	1,536	1,116	1,501	1,591	2,236	1,110	1,230	1,383
11. Wooden articles	60	120	144	206	391	412	600	665	465	326	292	293

	1944	1945	1946	1947	1948	1949	1950	1951	1952	1953	1954	1955
12. Iron products	968	1,716	4,336	4,951	7,959	9,048	10,816	10,479	9,061	8,793	8,884	13,326
13. Copper products	16	34	97	132	296	298	292	412	518	538	397	454
14. Ropes, wires, cables of aluminum, and manufactures of zinc and lead	4	11	16	21	45	15	66	55	67	28	46	35
15. Wires, electric material	127	210	482	609	1,281	1,691	1,390	1,143	2,026	1,904	1,848	1,716
16. Machinery and equipment (excluding electric machinery)	533	860	1,811	2,915	4,476	6,174	6,793	8,169	8,618	5,925	6,911	11,285
17. Parts for machinery and equipment (excluding electric machinery)	424	606	1,085	1,316	2,293	4,083	3,639	3,197	3,926	2,548	3,817	4,105
18. Textile machines and looms	24	48	1,139	2,359	3,016	2,423	1,483	1,573	1,420	845	1,756	4,854
19. Parts for textile machines and looms	79	99	323	619	1,331	756	615	991	1,820	948	867	1,003
20. Electric machines and apparatus	147	378	1,101	1,451	2,374	2,656	3,340	3,659	3,872	3,647	3,406	5,888
21. Articles and detached parts for electric machinery and apparatus	60	54	131	109	441	474	650	1,061	1,115	868	900	1,000
22. Railway and tramway equipment	19	124	81	179	2,294	2,034	1,277	1,103	1,363	2,191	3,007	1,143
23. Parts for railway and tramway equipment	43	92	79	105	319	290	156	174	226	269	227	197
24. Aviation and navigation		34	41	35	45	319	4,813	900	807	2,232	1,832	1,192
25. Parts for aviation and navigation	20	294	115	177	350	492	634	1,246	541	662	757	1,307
26. Motor lorries and motor buses	67	137	375	804	1,440	1,133	973	1,407	2,131	350	901	1,731
27. Parts for motor lorries and motor buses	229	256	544	562	869	1,217	1,319	3,583	3,137	2,503	2,294	3,786
28. Other vehicles	2	1	23	29	25	43	35	21	139	51	63	115
29. Parts for vehicles, bicycles, and motorcycles	6	19	51	72	78	90	132	141	142	116	127	164
30. Precision and other equipment	76	137	384	537	861	1,126	1,156	1,239	1,227	955	1,023	1,541
31. Parts for precision and other equipment	13	25	81	107	113	102	150	165	151	145	144	176
32. Parts, others	9	20	43	36	60	67	78	84	61	59	93	135
33. Cinematographic and nonportable photographic cameras	7	13	42	91	50	18	64	51	32	66	68	85
34. Others	436	734	1,334	1,356	2,431	2,364	2,846	3,342	2,845	2,652	2,941	3,308
Total	18,570	20,160	24,614	33,961	54,822	61,399	69,154	74,220	75,736	61,946	68,170	84,761
Total, producers	31,825	39,418	47,627	61,946	112,859	114,995	133,954	163,967	157,690	121,587	109,686	129,941
MISCELLANEOUS												
1. Gold and silver ingots and coins	525	796	2,154	2,217	11,666	10,710	11,016	44,103	5,110	213	103	11
2. Arms and ammunition	48	121	438	196	191	1,790	3,211	2,894	582	1,118	996	1,056
3. Others	153	185	364	269	497	601	1,105	1,571	1,246	1,485	2,661	2,925
Total, miscellaneous	726	1,102	2,956	2,682	12,354	13,101	15,332	48,568	6,938	2,816	3,760	3,992
Errors, omissions, and rounding	−2	0	1	1	5	2	9	−1	−1	−2	−2	9
Grand total	51,007	60,476	83,248	102,464	172,876	178,230	213,308	279,791	225,813	177,013	161,417	182,924

NOTES AND SOURCES: See p. 357.

TABLE V–A–4

Exports, by Categories, 1931–55
(£E Thousand)

	1931	1932	1933	1934	1935	1936	1937	1938	1939	1940	1941	1942	1943
Raw materials:													
Cotton, cotton waste, burned cotton..	19,690	17,871	21,382	24,792	26,505	25,062	29,102	21,250	24,386	18,905	15,940	14,157	18,430
Rice...................................	351	469	867	590	702	1,180	1,345	685	1,123	1,828	779	39	2,314
Vegetables, fresh:													
1. Onions..........................	717	1,261	772	605	701	590	645	929	916	493	66	46	...
2. Potatoes........................	40	21	5	9	12	9	14	17	29	31	...	...	...
3. Other vegetables...............	96	288	507	58	79	71	67	56	60	185	90	51	2
Subtotal........................	853	1,570	1,284	672	792	670	726	1,002	1,005	709	156	97	2
Phosphate of lime, natural...........	217	368	417	404	438	442	355	307	364	120	199	343	288
Groundnuts...........................	8	7	6	3	8	3	18	5	4	38	27	1	...
Manganese............................	...	...	...	...	...	...	...	...	...	...	7	...	15
Flax and hemp, raw...................	14	9	10	9	81	25	60	80	103	269	655	1,072	1,408
Hides and skins, raw.................	157	167	150	114	140	165	233	140	139	106	114	32	76
Guts, bladders, and stomachs.........	15	14	14	17	16	15	36	39	29	20	10	12	15
Wool, hair, raw......................	125	71	112	77	134	148	178	95	157	73	99	6	4
Fruits, fresh........................	4	6	11	39	61	48	42	67	77	10	1	...	...
Cereals (excluding rice).............	2	31	127	7	28	70	441	112	8	492	300	63	427
Others...............................	1,885	2,082	1,605	1,876	2,359	2,402	2,247	1,824	1,680	1,268	703	389	45
Total, raw materials.............	23,321	22,665	25,985	28,600	31,264	32,030	34,783	25,606	29,075	23,838	18,990	16,211	23,024
Semifinished products:													
Cotton yarn..........................	1	...	40	52	58	51	232	48	6	34	17	...	...
Rags and scraps of textile material..	9	8	16	22	32	58	113	53	68	48	9	50	25
Flour of wheat, spelt, meslin........	...	...	1	...	...	1	28	2	...	12	19	39	2
Molasses, not edible.................	52	98	39	68	69	33	...	52	47	16	...	8	39
Hides and skins, tanned..............	129	115	118	112	103	115	109	61	87	128	60	69	67
Articles exported for completion.....	...	...	9	13	15	8	46	60	45	12	...	...	...
Others (including henna waste scraps and fragments, and iron and steel suitable only for recasting)......	1,682	1,856	903	168	268	220	348	253	201	139	120	87	241
Total, semifinished products....	1,873	2,077	1,126	435	545	486	876	529	454	389	225	253	374

Finished products

	1931	1932	1933	1934	1935	1936	1937	1938	1939	1940	1941	1942	1943
Finished products:													
Onions, dehydrated, powdered, or sliced										9	33	49	44
Oil, cottonseed	288	315	70	109	367	315	300	203	355	277	217	158	1
Cake, cottonseed	790	799	498	743	754	775	889	914	704	504	58	2	
Cake of oleaginons and fruits, n.s.					2	10	5	4	4	2	25	17	1
Cigarettes and manufactured tobacco	248	225	243	208	235	193	212	184	191	95	46	159	203
Cement	1			1	10	5	4	6	10	1	31	9	
Alcohol, ethyl (common), refined	128	124	103	100	103	77	127	135	343	389	157	2	2
Oil, mazout, diesel and solar	80	78	71	100	197	143	191	262	232	254	1,059	1,030	766
Coke, pitch, asphalt	2	2	3	4	5	6	8	7	3	1	8	85	53
Glycerine			1	2								41	
Salt, common (sodium chloride)	15	17	19	62	59	98	107	103	176	84	66	47	48
Piece goods, pure cotton	3	2	1	2	3	4	4	4	3	15	15		3
Cotton fabrics and clothing	4	4	4	5	8	4	4	4	6	38	16	2	25
Wool fabrics and clothing	7	5	6	8	7	3	3	2	1	5	11	10	30
Doors, windows, and furniture		3	3	2	3	4	7	4	9	8	1	2	13
Printed matter	44	54	69	77	93	73	90	83	73	45	29	17	37
Leather and leather products	27	24	32	27	15	14	16	13	15	127	145	105	53
Footwear	3	3	2	2	5	3	2	2	3	8	12	10	4
Films, cinema, positive, talking	1		1				7	10	11		8	10	12
Animal substances, prepared as fertilizers													
Other	422	558	539	519	704	501	754	497	768	1,556	854	408	189
Total, finished products	2,063	2,213	1,664	1,969	2,570	2,229	2,735	2,440	2,907	3,503	2,791	2,161	1,487
Miscellaneous:													
Articles exported for repair	800	14	42	6	1,270	8	1,334	755	1,630				
Gold, accepted by banks													
Others	17	22	33	43	44	23	20	11	13	79	114	121	144
Total, miscellaneous	817	36	75	49	1,314	31	1,354	766	1,643	79	114	121	144
Errors, omissions, and rounding	0	4	−2	3	0	3	5	1	2	1	2	1	1
Total, local products	28,074	26,995	28,848	31,056	35,693	32,979	39,753	29,342	34,081	27,811	22,122	18,748	25,030
Reexports	718	713	671	568	987	896	864	776	741	508	489	537	1,549
Total exports	28,792	27,708	29,519	31,624	36,680	33,875	40,617	30,118	34,822	28,319	22,611	19,285	26,579

(Continued on next page)

TABLE V–A–4—Continued

	1944	1945	1946	1947	1948	1949	1950	1951	1952	1953	1954	1955
Raw materials:												
Cotton, cotton waste, burned cotton	19,498	32,210	46,311	68,494	113,372	106,231	150,002	164,522	126,640	116,666	113,318	107,693
Rice	1,611	4,056	5,933	6,116	16,064	14,442	7,646	14,539	776	20	2,626	7,304
Vegetables, fresh:												
1. Onions	186	440	610	1,400	1,615	1,173	1,997	1,270	2,304	3,647	2,040	2,306
2. Potatoes	98	103	224	325	758	125	98	131	206	116	553	546
3. Other vegetables	90	114	385	102	97	136	115	83	96	122	350	265
Subtotal	374	657	1,219	1,827	2,470	1,434	2,210	1,484	2,606	3,885	2,943	3,117
Phosphate of lime, natural	641	541	684	787	752	325	1,035	899	1,139	1,057	1,118	1,182
Groundnuts	1	....	1	41	71	123	64	10	10	23	510	996
Manganese	2	17	45	96	280	360	313	760	746	872	808	843
Flax and hemp, raw	653	298	339	288	398	286	444	739	377	392	641	437
Hides and skins, raw	2	....	3	2	24	54	72	60	36	64	104	128
Guts, bladders, and stomachs	8	13	14	14	24	51	107	171	129	82	97	122
Wool, hair, raw	7	9	100	74	128	58	188	209	213	162	158	200
Fruits, fresh	32	45	62	46	62	52	55	31	30	21	95	130
Cereals (excluding rice)	691	7	1,821	388	43	172	151	124	53	46	42	38
Others	265	282	508	315	393	355	525	627	394	429	445	548
Total, raw materials	23,785	38,135	57,040	78,488	134,071	123,943	162,812	184,175	133,151	123,719	122,905	122,738
Semifinished products:												
Cotton yarn	....	89	....	6	17	1,852	2,342	6,948	3,453	1,971	4,396	4,383
Rags and scraps of textile material	13	3	180	270	312	203	290	776	282	278	336	418
Flour of wheat, spelt, meslin	24	45	5	9	89	827	321	1,233	331	217	289	175
Molasses, not edible	21	89	63	168	230	89	58	427	320	328	485	511
Hides and skins, tanned	59	....	74	146	104	59	77	78	49	53	53	70
Articles exported for completion	....	....	10	9	....	31	344	132	259	326	552	342
Others (including henna waste scraps and fragments, and iron and steel suitable only for recasting)	269	368	1,015	2,143	524	524	502	741	280	311	574	570
Total, semifinished products	386	594	1,347	2,751	1,276	3,585	5,934	10,325	4,974	3,484	6,685	6,469

Finished products:	1944	1945	1946	1947	1948	1949	1950	1951	1952	1953	1954	1955
Onions, dehydrated, powdered, or sliced	75	64	146	70	311	86	95	252	287	464	296	320
Oil, cottonseed	1	2	78	411	404	94	566	91	4	1,983	497	459
Cake, cottonseed	4	67	1,118	104	327	89	435	230	161	1,334	33	434
Cake of oleaginons and fruits, n.s.	20	109	68	...	11	184	110	86	77	108	105	157
Cigarettes and manufactured tobacco	399	441	351	130	126	50	84	99	102	121	109	70
Cement	6	...	27	16	20	22	23	14	60	615	836	209
Alcohol, ethyl (common), refined	1	6	5	2	1	1	45	154	75	123	95	33
Oil, mazout, diesel and solar	1,128	858	1,078	396	1,228	2,321	1,583	1,867	1,448	812	770	876
Coke, pitch, asphalt	182	66	454	222	210	250	369	384	166	139	98	136
Glycerine	33	16	26	52	2	...	...	...	38	84	62	123
Salt, common (sodium chloride)	96	111	131	575	313	459	316	423	96	259	260	201
Piece goods, pure cotton	...	...	8	270	250	317	262	617	410	497	998	962
Cotton fabrics and clothing	24	8	22	25	35	97	114	118	178	231	228	363
Wool fabrics and clothing	44	9	37	25	16	49	25	27	19	126	157	66
Doors, windows, and furniture	3	8	10	16	19	62	89	62	140	183	212	360
Printed matter	53	60	123	126	136	186	210	344	391	435	550	658
Leather and leather products	127	112	126	123	138	94	97	85	101	155	189	198
Footwear	4	...	269	238	80	96	84	99	183	179	189	141
Films, cinema, positive, talking	23	26	67	109	83	104	120	145	136	157	176	154
Animal substances, prepared as fertilizers	...	...	...	...	2	10	37	65	39	58	64	69
Other	438	930	1,091	1,535	1,627	3,490	1,529	969	555	574	1,142	1,784
Total, finished products	2,661	2,893	5,235	4,445	5,339	8,061	6,195	6,129	4,666	8,637	7,066	7,774
Miscellaneous:												
Articles exported for repair	23	...	...	...	...	1	1	...	...	8	16	1
Gold, accepted by banks	...	...	...	262	...	204	...	...	...	...	...	...
Others	89	7	76	34	50	82	15	9	57	18	34	30
Total, miscellaneous	112	7	76	296	50	287	16	9	57	26	50	31
Errors, omissions, and rounding	1	...	3	-2	5	-1	4	-1	3	-3	3	3
Total, local products	26,945	41,630	63,701	85,978	140,741	135,875	172,959	200,639	142,851	135,863	136,709	137,015
Reexports	3,056	3,529	5,312	3,858	2,361	2,127	2,469	2,438	2,265	1,482	1,566	1,374
Total exports	30,001	45,159	69,013	89,836	143,102	138,002	175,428	203,077	145,116	137,345	138,275	138,389

NOTES AND SOURCES FOR TABLES V–A–3 AND V–A–4: These data are taken from a detailed and careful reclassification of Egypt's trade statistics undertaken at the Social Research Center of the American University at Cairo. The original source of data is United Arab Republic, Department of Statistics and Census, *Annual Statement of Foreign Trade* (Cairo, Annual). The underlying data are discussed at some length in the AUC study; the major weaknesses which emerge are the following:

1. *Timing:* A transaction gets counted in these figures when the forms are forwarded to the Department of Statistics and Census. Sometimes, there is a delay between the presentation of the form and its forwarding to the department, particularly when they are incomplete.

2. *Coverage:* All transit trade with the Sudan is excluded.

3. *Valuation:* This is declared value, not that assessed by the Customs Administration.

In Tables 7–1, 7–7, and 7–8 (pp. 159, 171, and 172, respectively), we have adjusted these figures to be comparable with later data, as follows: cereals, flour, and sugar are included as consumer goods, while small cars are treated as capital goods, which includes, besides these, categories 15–32 of finished producer goods.

TABLE V–A–5

IMPORTS AND EXPORTS BY CATEGORIES, 1953–61

(£E Million)

	1953	1954	1955	1956	1957	1958	1959	1960	1961
Imports:									
0 Food	48.29	21.11	20.17	27.70	43.54	44.27	47.20	42.60	47.25
1 Beverages and tobacco	5.40	5.35	5.39	5.64	5.61	5.63	5.37	5.40	5.23
2 Crude materials, inedible, except fuels	15.39	14.60	14.41	15.32	18.39	19.47	16.28	19.37	22.82
3 Mineral fuels, lubricants, related materials	14.71	19.10	18.06	19.04	21.04	26.37	22.20	24.40	25.51
4 Animal and vegetable oils and fats	3.02	2.96	3.52	4.75	7.94	6.28	3.72	3.65	5.81
5 Chemicals	18.22	20.97	22.39	18.80	27.05	33.06	25.78	25.83	19.64
6 Manufactured goods	35.81	35.40	43.63	43.57	33.72	37.38	33.63	41.97	42.23
7 Machinery and transport equipment	28.21	31.79	45.74	44.47	28.91	52.13	54.00	56.04	64.52
8 Miscellaneous manufactured articles	6.72	6.23	7.12	5.31	3.13	4.54	4.91	3.80	4.66
9 Miscellaneous transactions and commodities	0.86	1.27	1.04	1.11	1.06	1.23	1.32	1.98	0.78
Total*	176.77†	160.15†	182.89	186.11	190.40	230.37	214.40	225.05	238.46
Exports:									
0 Food	6.63	7.36	13.21	17.92	18.92	23.81	11.57	20.66	17.96
1 Beverages and tobacco	0.13	0.12	0.108	0.09	0.11	0.26	0.27	0.25	0.28
2 Crude materials, inedible, except fuels	120.36	117.87	112.89	104.04	129.53	114.91	116.88	140.67	111.31
3 Mineral fuels, lubricants, related materials	0.99	0.91	1.09	1.50	1.24	4.56	4.23	4.56	7.38
4 Animal and vegetable fats and oils	2.05	0.64	0.55	0.59	0.86	0.26	0.20	0.24	0.08
5 Chemicals	0.36	0.38	0.38	0.64	0.78	0.61	0.71	0.62	0.59
6 Manufactured goods	3.80	7.32	6.92	13.29	15.41	15.57	16.03	21.49	20.11
7 Machinery and transport equipment	0.02	0.06	0.03	0.08				0.13	0.14
8 Miscellaneous manufactured articles	1.16	1.46	1.50	2.41	2.83	2.20	2.83	1.92	2.29
9 Miscellaneous transactions and commodities	0.35	0.59	0.36	0.29	0.49	0.31	0.19	0.06	0.10
Total	135.86	136.70	137.01	140.94	170.26	162.58	153.03	190.60	160.26

SOURCE: United Nations, *Yearbook of International Trade Statistics* (New York, annual), various issues.
*Includes British Army stores sold locally (value in millions of Egyptian pounds: 1953, 0.14; 1954, 1.38; 1955, 1.41; 1956, 0.42), not distributed by commodities.
†Revised totals in millions of Egyptian pounds: 1953, 177.54; 1954, 161.29.

TABLE V–A–6

COTTON PRODUCTION AND EXPORTS

	Area (Feddan 000)	Average Yield (Cantar/Feddan)	Production (Cantar 000)	Average Price (£E/Cantar)	Value of Crop (£E 000)	Quantity of Exports (Cantar 000)	Value of Exports (£E 000)
1885	n.a.	n.a.	2,792	n.a.	n.a.	3,189	7,706
1886	n.a.	n.a.	2,872	n.a.	n.a.	3,041	7,121
1887	n.a.	n.a.	2,996	n.a.	n.a.	3,067	7,543
1888	n.a.	n.a.	2,723	n.a.	n.a.	2,692	6,823
1889	n.a.	n.a.	3,238	n.a.	n.a.	3,206	8,548
Five-year average	n.a.	n.a.	2,925	n.a.	n.a.	3,039	7,548
1890	n.a.	n.a.	4,159	n.a.	n.a.	3,328	8,272
1891	n.a.	n.a.	4,765	n.a.	n.a.	4,263	8,989
1892	n.a.	n.a.	5,221	n.a.	n.a.	5,085	8,838
1893	n.a.	n.a.	5,033	n.a.	n.a.	4,480	8,526
1894	n.a.	n.a.	4,619	n.a.	n.a.	5,403	8,181
Five-year average	n.a.	n.a.	4,760	n.a.	n.a.	4,510	8,561
1895	998	5.29	5,276	2.240	11,818	5,264	9,463
1896	1,051	5.60	5,879	2.020	11,876	5,173	9,987
1897	1,128	5.80	6,544	1.576	10,313	5,720	8,916
1898	1,121	4.98	5,588	1.782	9,959	5,990	8,449
1899	1,153	5.64	6,510	2.455	15,981	6,679	11,598
Five-year average	1,090	5.47	5,960	2.010	11,979	5,765	9,683
1900	1,230	4.42	5,435	2.759	14,997	5,427	13,039
1901	1,250	5.10	6,370	2.084	13,275	6,123	11,833
1902	1,276	4.58	5,839	2.729	15,934	6,652	13,886
1903	1,333	4.88	6,509	3.330	21,675	5,589	15,677
1904	1,437	4.39	6,313	2.793	17,633	5,913	16,703
Five-year average	1,305	4.67	6,093	2.738	16,683	5,941	14,288

(Continued on next page)

TABLE V–A–6—Continued

	Area (Feddan 000)	Average Yield (Cantar/Feddan)	Production (Cantar 000)	Average Price (£E/Cantar)	Value of Crop (£E 000)	Quantity of Exports (Cantar 000)	Value of Exports (£E 000)
1905	1,567	3.80	5,960	3.197	19,054	6,627	15,806
1906	1,506	4.61	6,949	3.831	26,623	6,697	20,528
1907	1,603	4.51	7,235	3.641	26,342	6,859	23,598
1908	1,640	4.12	6,751	3.091	20,868	6,348	17,092
1909	1,597	3.13	5,001	4.660	23,303	6,952	21,478
Five-year average	1,583	4.03	6,379	3.642	23,233	6,677	19,700
1910	1,643	4.57	7,505	4.132	31,011	6,009	24,242
1911	1,711	4.32	7,386	3.450	25,483	6,638	22,988
1912	1,722	4.35	7,499	3.655	27,409	8,307	27,529
1913	1,723	4.44	7,664	3.803	29,145	6,973	25,513
1914	1,755	3.67	6,451	2.402	15,494	5,910	18,670
Five-year average	1,711	4.27	7,301	3.521	25,707	6,767	23,788
1915	1,186	4.02	4,775	3.857	18,416	6,899	19,146
1916	1,656	3.06	5,060	7.562	38,267	5,417	29,814
1917	1,677	3.75	6,293	7.703	48,478	4,074	33,495
1918	1,316	3.66	4,821	7.440	35,866	5,020	38,034
1919	1,574	3.54	5,572	17.562	97,849	6,709	65,442
Five-year average	1,482	3.58	5,304	9.007	47,775	5,624	37,186
1920	1,828	3.30	6,036	6.900	41,645	4,001	75,097
1921	1,290	3.37	4,353	6.858	29,853	4,792	28,375
1922	1,801	3.73	6,713	6.142	41,233	6,479	39,715
1923	1,715	3.81	6,531	7.959	51,984	7,473	49,516
1924	1,788	4.07	7,274	7.897	57,443	7,254	56,554
Five-year average	1,684	3.67	6,181	7.188	44,432	6,000	49,851

Year						
1925	1,924	4.14	7,965	6.093	48,529	6,424	51,660
1926	1,786	4.29	7,652	4.306	32,950	6,835	34,371
1927	1,516	4.01	6,087	5.936	36,134	7,383	38,999
1928	1,738	4.64	8,068	5.176	41,760	7,433	45,138
1929	1,841	4.63	8,531	4.072	34,739	7,625	41,361
Five-year average	1,761	4.34	7,661	5.117	38,822	7,140	42,306
1930	2,082	3.97	8,276	2.685	22,216	5,928	23,789
1931	1,683	3.78	6,357	2.337	14,857	7,397	19,688
1932	1,094	4.53	4,956	2.701	13,384	6,699	17,867
1933	1,804	4.75	8,575	2.552	21,886	7,854	21,380
1934	1,732	4.36	7,555	2.900	21,911	8,564	24,788
Five-year average	1,679	4.28	7,144	2.635	18,851	7,288	21,502
1935	1,669	5.11	8,535	2.870	24,492	8,577	26,502
1936	1,716	5.31	9,107	3.243	29,533	7,798	25,020
1937	1,978	5.57	11,009	2.345	25,821	8,900	29,002
1938	1,784	4.67	8,340	2.308	19,244	7,937	21,190
1939	1,625	5.35	8,692	3.192	27,746	9,103	24,330
Five-year average	1,754	5.20	9,137	2.792	25,367	8,463	25,209
1940	1,684	5.44	9,170	3.085	28,290	5,236	18,859
1941	1,644	5.09	8,374	3.550	29,726	4,615	15,924
1942	706	6.00	4,233	5.435	23,003	3,555	14,125
1943	713	5.01	3,569	6.935	24,753	3,241	18,380
1944	853	5.44	4,640	7.935	36,820	2,821	19,461
Five-year average	1,120	5.39	5,997	5.388	28,519	3,894	17,350
1945	982	5.31	5,221	7.487	39,191	4,123	32,162
1946	1,212	5.01	6,066	8.434	51,158	5,711	46,218
1947	1,254	5.08	6,370	12.320	78,480	7,469	68,335
1948	1,441	6.17	8,900	11.046	98,306	7,669	113,327
1949	1,692	5.14	8,704	14.930	129,961	7,979	106,089
Five-year average	1,316	5.34	7,052	10.843	79,399	6,590	73,226

(Continued on next page)

TABLE V-A-6—Continued

	Area (Feddan 000)	Average Yield (Cantar/Feddan)	Production (Cantar 000)	Average Price (£E/Cantar)	Value of Crop (£E 000)	Quantity of Exports (Cantar 000)	Value of Exports (£E 000)
1950	1,975	4.30	8,500	25.144	213,724	8,602	149,756
1951	1,979	4.08	8,076	18.243	147,327	5,674	164,101
1952	1,967	5.04	9,922	12.282	121,868	6,018	126,414
1953	1,324	5.35	7,082	11.990	84,914	7,711	116,348
1954	1,579	4.90	7,746	12.472	96,609	6,406	113,102
Five-year average	1,765	4.73	8,265	16.026	132,888	6,882	133,944
1955	1,816	4.10	7,437	14.214	105,709	6,174	107,438
1956	1,653	4.38	7,230	17.020	123,065	5,227	98,901
1957	1,819	4.96	9,021	14.792	133,441	5,879	124,156
1958	1,905	5.21	9,925	13.633	135,299	6,264	109,860
1959	1,760	5.78	10,175	14.971	152,332	7,074	110,154
Five-year average	1,791	4.89	8,758	14.926	129,969	6,124	110,102
1960	1,873	5.69	10,643	n.a.	n.a.	8,328	134,715
1961	1,986	3.76	7,470	n.a.	n.a.	6,566	104,600
1962	1,657	6.14	10,179	n.a.	n.a.	5,587	83,900
1963	1,627	6.04	9,829	n.a.	n.a.	7,189	121,000

NOTES AND SOURCES: All figures are from *Annuaire Statistique*, various issues. Price and crop value figures refer to cotton-years; e.g., 1900 refers to the period September 1, 1900, to August 31, 1901. All other columns, including export quantities and values, refer to calendar years. Price data show average prices of each type, weighted by area sown in that type of cotton in that year. There have been several changes in the techniques of estimation, explained in detail in the *Annuaire Statistique*. In general, the series gives a comparable measure of average price, weighted by current distribution among staple lengths and qualities. Value figures are simply the product of quantity of production and average price. The *Annuaire Statistique, 1910*, p. 262, also gives annual estimates of the size of the cotton crop from 1821 to 1908–9. (One cantar = 44.928 kilograms.)

TABLE V–A–7

EXPORT AND IMPORT PRICE INDICES AND TERMS OF TRADE, 1910–59

(1953 = 100)

	P_x	P_m	Terms of Trade		P_x	P_m	Terms of Trade
1910	34.2	14.6	235.9	1936	26.5	20.5	129.4
1911	30.1	14.9	202.6	1937	26.1	25.3	103.3
1912	29.3	14.6	201.2	1938	22.4	24.9	90.3
1913	32.2	15.3	212.0	1939	22.4	27.2	82.3
1914	25.8	15.0	172.6	1940	29.6	40.3	73.2
1915	23.5	19.2	123.2	1941	29.6	54.6	54.3
1916	41.9	28.7	146.5	1942	33.4	65.7	50.9
1917	60.5	41.7	145.6	1943	45.4	77.6	58.5
1918	57.1	57.4	99.9	1944	54.2	75.0	72.3
1919	74.4	54.4	137.3	1945	55.8	77.2	72.4
1920	137.9	56.9	243.4	1946	57.5	65.9	87.3
1921	47.6	41.0	116.4	1947	64.1	72.2	88.8
1922	48.8	29.4	166.6	1948	98.5	75.4	130.7
1923	51.7	28.4	182.5	1949	87.9	75.1	117.0
1924	60.3	29.1	207.7	1950	113.5	76.2	149.1
1925	61.6	24.1	256.2	1951	179.1	86.8	206.9
1926	39.6	23.9	166.0	1952	136.5	103.4	132.1
1927	41.3	22.0	188.4	1953	100.0	100.0	100.0
1928	47.1	25.2	187.3	1954	113.3	96.4	117.5
1929	42.3	23.8	178.1	1955	111.1	98.6	112.7
1930	32.1	23.8	135.5	1956	120.9	100.5	120.4
1931	22.8	20.7	111.0	1957	134.3	105.6	127.2
1932	23.2	20.5	113.6	1958	115.7	99.1	116.5
1933	22.8	20.7	110.7	1959	104.6	87.9	119.1
1934	23.8	19.9	119.7				
1935	25.5	19.9	129.0				

NOTES AND SOURCES: See p. 364.

TABLE V–A–8

ALTERNATIVE EARLY IMPORT PRICE INDICES

(Linked with Table V–A–7 at 1938 = 24.9,
(so that 1953 = 100)

Issawi's Estimate	Our Estimate
1848–52 = 14.6	
1853–57 = 16.6	
1858–62 = 16.6	
1863–67 = 21.1	
1868–72 = 18.8	
1873–77 = 18.5	1913 = 22.2
1878–82 = 15.0	
1883–87 = 13.6	1927 = 32.9
1888–92 = 13.9	1928 = 31.8
1893–97 = 12.9	1929 = 29.2
1898–1902 = 14.1	1930 = 20.8
1903–7 = 15.0	1931 = 19.8
1908–12 = 16.0	1932 = 18.6
1913–17 = 21.1	1933 = 18.3
1918–22 = 49.4	1934 = 18.3
1923–27 = 32.4	1935 = 18.1
1928–32 = 26.2	1936 = 18.5
1933–37 = 22.6	1937 = 24.8
1938 = 24.9	1938 = 24.9

NOTES AND SOURCES: See p. 364.

TABLE V–A–9

EXPORT AND IMPORT QUANTUM INDICES, 1910–59

(1953 = 100)

	Q_x	Q_m		Q_x	Q_m
1910	62.3	90.8	1935	99.4	91.2
1911	69.9	102.9	1936	91.6	86.5
1912	86.9	99.9	1937	108.3	84.5
1913	72.4	102.6	1938	93.9	83.0
1914	68.7	81.6	1939	106.6	69.9
1915	84.7	56.8	1940	69.2	43.8
1916	65.8	61.1	1941	55.0	34.1
1917	50.0	44.8	1942	41.3	47.4
1918	58.5	50.2	1943	40.6	28.4
1919	75.1	49.1	1944	36.6	37.9
1920	45.6	100.1	1945	54.9	43.5
1921	56.2	76.2	1946	81.5	69.3
1922	73.5	82.9	1947	98.4	78.2
1923	83.1	89.7	1948	105.2	120.5
1924	80.2	98.0	1949	113.6	125.7
1925	70.7	134.6	1950	112.2	152.1
1926	76.8	122.3	1951	82.5	153.7
1927	85.2	123.6	1952	77.0	120.6
1928	86.1	114.2	1953	100.0	100.0
1929	88.5	130.8	1954	88.8	94.2
1930	71.4	111.2	1955	90.8	104.5
1931	82.8	85.1	1956	85.8	104.3
1932	80.2	74.9	1957	93.3	97.4
1933	90.7	72.8	1958	103.5	135.4
1934	96.0	82.8	1959	107.7	137.4

NOTES AND SOURCES FOR TABLES V–A–7, V–A–8, AND V–A–9: From 1938, this is an official index, computed by the National Bank of Egypt; the index is described in *Economic Bulletin*, Vol. IV, No. 1 (1951), pp. 17–23. The index is a linked-chain index, with changing commodities included in the index each year to reflect changing importance of different categories; each of these chain indices is a Fisher ideal index. Both indices cover only a portion of traded goods; this is a serious problem for imports, where virtually all capital goods imports are excluded, since price changes are too difficult to measure here.

Before 1938, the indices in Table V–A–7 are from A. M. el Tanamli, "Evolution de l'Economie Rurale Egyptienne dans les Cinquante Dernières Années," *L'Egypte Contemporaine*, No. 302 (October, 1960), pp. 78–79. He has followed the same approach as the National Bank, indicating that he includes about 50 percent of all imports in the index. For this earlier period, there are also available two other import price indices. The first was computed by C. Issawi, *Egypt in Revolution: An Economic Analysis* (New York: Oxford University Press, 1963), p. 28; this uses a price index of all manufactured goods exports from the United Kingdom. The second, which we have computed, uses the wholesale prices of Egypt's major imports within the major supplier country. From 1913 to 1930, the commodities included were cereals, iron and steel, minerals, and textiles; after 1930, they were food, manufactures, and raw materials, which include the earlier components. These indices are shown in Table V–A–8, linked together with the official NBE index at 1938. Once again, it is satisfying to find that all these indices show very similar patterns; divergencies appear only during the period 1925–29, and even these are relatively minor.

Finally, taking advantage of one of the characteristics of the Fisher ideal index, we can divide the value of traded goods by the price indices to get a quantity index of imports and exports; this is shown in Table V–A–9.

TABLE V–A–10

Egypt's Regional Balance of Payments, Current Account*

(£E Million)

	American Monetary Area	Sterling Area, Total	United Kingdom	Europe		Middle East	Others	Total
				Western	Eastern			
1927:								
Receipts..........	6.8	20.0	19.1	14.4	1.6	5.5		48.3
Payments..........	2.3	17.3	12.8	16.5	5.9	6.7		48.7
1937:								
Receipts..........	2.6	14.7	12.4	13.6	4.3	4.6		39.8
Payments..........	2.1	10.1	8.3	14.7	5.0	6.1		38.0
1948:								
Receipts..........	4.5	71.6	41.8	29.7	16.5	20.8		143.1
Payments..........	12.4	60.0	36.6	45.1	13.8	41.6		172.9
1954:								
Receipts..........	16.6	71.7	47.5	81.0	21.6	16.3	15.0	222.2
Payments..........	19.6	54.5	38.8	100.3	18.3	17.7	8.2	218.6
1957:								
Receipts..........	11.7	26.1	15.6	57.9	85.2	33.4	22.9	237.2
Payments..........	12.6	20.4	6.9	86.2	84.4	38.0	26.8	268.4
1963:								
Receipts..........	33.2	65.0	46.0	86.6	110.6	34.9	33.5	363.8
Payments..........	124.5	72.9	51.5	115.9	120.8	26.6	26.0	486.7

*The first three years in this table refer to the balance of merchandise trade, since regional balance-of-payments estimates are not available. For these three years, "American monetary area" refers to the United States only.

Sources: *Annuaire Statistique*, various issues; National Bank of Egypt, *Economic Bulletin*, Vol. III, No. 1 (1950), pp. 29–30; Vol. VIII, No. 2 (1955), pp. 98–99; Vol. XI, No. 2 (1958), pp. 146–47; Central Bank of Egypt, *Economic Review*, Vol. IV, No. 2 (1964), pp. 144–45. Eastern Europe includes Austria, Bulgaria, Czechoslovakia, East Germany, Greece, Hungary, Poland, Rumania, Turkey, the USSR, and Yugoslavia.

TABLE V–C–1

BALANCE OF PAYMENTS

(£E Million)

CURRENT	1945	1946	1947	1948	1949	1950	1951	1952	1953	1954
Receipts:										
Proceeds of exports	32.9	52.8	68.5	132.6	140.3	188.5	201.9	145.6	135.3	139.8
Transit trade	1.2	2.0	2.6	1.4	1.9	1.7	2.6	3.2	2.5	4.4
Army expenditure	62.2	20.7	11.5	23.1—	11.5	13.0	14.7	5.8—	9.0	5.6
Insurance	....	....	....	....	0.4	0.2	0.4	1.0	0.7	0.5
Shipping	....	....	....	....	7.9	7.5	7.5	6.8	7.1	7.1
Suez Canal dues	....	....	....	18.4	23.0	26.2	26.4	26.6	29.1	30.6
Interest, dividends, and other	2.9	2.9	3.8	3.7	4.8	4.6	4.9	4.8	6.3	5.0
Travel and maintenance	....	....	....	....	0.1	0.5	....	....	0.6	1.7
Other	26.9	24.6	24.8	15.5	25.5	24.3	33.8	24.9	24.5	27.5
Total	125.9	103.0	111.2	194.7	215.4	266.5	292.2	218.7	215.1	222.2
Disbursements:										
Payments for imports	52.5	88.6	106.1	162.5	158.3	221.7	241.9	210.5	165.2	150.7
Transit trade	1.1	3.3	4.3	4.8*	1.1	0.9	1.5	2.4	1.5	5.2
Films	0.5	0.5	0.2	0.3	0.2	0.3	....	....	0.3	0.3
Other commercial payments	....	....	....	....	1.5	2.0	2.5	2.2	2.2	2.4
Insurance	....	....	....	....	1.3	1.3	1.5	0.9	1.1	1.0
Shipping	....	....	....	....	8.8	7.0	6.1	6.9	6.3	6.8
Interest, dividends, and other	11.3	12.1	8.7	6.8	13.7	15.8	17.4	16.9	17.4	18.1
Travel	3.5	4.7	2.8	7.3	10.4	8.9	15.3	11.6	8.0	11.2
Maintenance	....	....	....	....	....	....	....	....	1.6	1.8
Government expenditures	4.9	6.2	2.3	6.5	6.4	5.1	6.3	5.7	6.6	9.4
Other disbursements	7.2	6.2	6.3	10.3	5.0	14.5	14.9	15.0	12.8	11.7
Total	81.0	121.6	130.7	198.5	206.7	277.5	307.4	272.1	223.0	218.6
Current balance	44.9	−18.6	−19.5	−3.8	8.7	−11.0	−15.2	−53.4	−7.9	3.6

(Continued on next page)

Capital:										
Inflow†	−0.4	....	....	0.8	1.2	....	....	1.9	2.6	....
Outflow†	− 0.8	−12.2	− 8.4	− 5.3	− 4.8	− 4.6	− 2.0	− 2.3	− 2.9	....
Donations	....	....	....	....	....	....	....	....	....	....
Compensations	....	....	....	....	....	....	....	....	....	....
OVERALL, DEFICIT OR SURPLUS	44.5	−19.4	−31.7	−12.2	4.2	−14.6	−19.8	−55.4	−8.3	3.3
Changes in sterling balances	45.3	−11.8	−35.1	− 7.7	−21.7	−29.0	−54.4	−40.1	3.7	2.2
Changes in foreign exchange holdings	....	....	3.9	3.6	19.4	23.0	9.9	−17.7	−7.8	9.1
Changes in N/R bankers' accounts	....	....	....	−10.5	9.5	8.0	− 1.1	− 0.1	−3.9	−2.6
Changes in other N/R accounts	....	....	....	....	....	....	− 0.8	1.9	−0.6	−1.2
Use of IMF resources	....	....	....	....	− 0.7	3.0	....	....	....	....
Monetary gold	....	....	....	....	....	....	26.6	....	....	....
Claims with respect to Suez Canal dues	....	....	....	....	....	....	....	....	....	....
Errors and ommissions, and unrecorded	− 0.8	− 7.6	− 0.5	2.4	− 2.3	− 3.6	....	0.6	0.3	0.2
Total	44.5	−19.4	−31.7	−12.2	4.2	−14.6	−19.8	−55.4	−8.3	3.3

TABLE V–C–1—Continued

CURRENT	1955	1956	1957	1958	1959	1960	1961	1962	1963‡	1964‡
Receipts:										
Proceeds of exports	133.1	129.9	166.0	161.0	164.3	200.2	161.3	142.8 }	228.8	227.6
Transit trade	6.0	2.6	1.0	2.1	3.0	3.5	3.6	2.4 }		0.7
Army expenditure	4.8									
Insurance	0.4	0.4	0.1	0.2	0.6	0.5	0.8	0.5	1.4	8.8
Shipping	9.1	8.7	7.4	8.7	12.5	15.2	8.2	12.3	9.8	8.8
Suez Canal dues	31.8	29.3	24.3	43.0	44.4	50.1	51.2	53.7	71.1	78.4
Interest, dividends, and other	7.3	5.6	4.8	5.0	6.3	5.3	5.8	5.2	6.9	7.2
Travel and maintenance	1.5	1.9	1.4	0.7	1.8	3.8	3.3	6.1	9.3 }	51.0
Other	33.3	40.4	32.2	29.5	32.0	23.1	21.9	23.9	36.5 }	51.0
Total	227.3	218.8	237.2	250.2	264.9	301.7	256.1	246.9	363.8	373.7
Disbursements:										
Payments for imports	190.3	192.3	217.5	214.0	235.3	255.2	237.8	290.0	402.6	399.4
Transit trade	3.6	3.7	1.1	1.5	2.3	2.9	3.6	4.2 }	0.7	0.8
Films	0.3	0.3	0.2	0.5	0.4	0.1	0.1	0.6	5.8	5.2
Other commercial payments	2.5	2.9	2.7	2.9	3.8	3.8	4.5	5.6	0.9	0.6
Insurance	1.0	0.6	0.3	0.3	0.6	0.5	1.0	0.7	9.6	8.9
Shipping	9.3	8.8	9.1	10.7	11.5	14.8	7.8	8.5	9.6	8.9
Interest, dividends, and other	17.1	10.7	2.9	2.2	2.2	3.2	4.5	7.4	11.7	15.0
Travel	8.3	6.1	7.7	3.9	5.8	8.9	6.7	4.8 }	11.5	12.3
Maintenance	1.9	1.9	1.2	1.1	3.1	3.3	3.0	3.6 }		
Government expenditures	11.0	12.9	16.9	21.7	27.9	25.3	30.9	28.4	28.3	36.8
Other disbursements	16.0	11.6	8.8	11.5	8.0	7.3	9.5	10.7	15.6	17.8
Total	261.3	251.8	268.4	270.3	300.9	325.3	309.4	364.5	486.7	496.8
Current balance	−34.0	−33.0	−31.2	−20.1	−36.0	−23.6	−53.3	−117.6	−122.9	−123.1
Capital:										
Inflow†	4.8	3.5	1.3	3.4	19.3§	46.4§	45.2§	92.1§	187.1§‖	188.2‖
Outflow†	− 2.6	− 3.2	− 2.5	− 1.9	− 1.4	− 1.9	− 3.3	− 3.3	−82.1#	−77.1‖
Donations		1.7	1.1						11.3	
Compensations				− 5.3	− 6.5	−33.4	− 8.0	− 8.1	−11.3	

OVERALL DEFICIT OR SURPLUS	−31.8	−31.0	−23.9	−24.6	−12.5	−19.4	−36.9	−29.2	−12.0
Changes in sterling balances	−34.9	−37.7	2.3	−18.9	−27.4	−23.4	−16.8	−1.9	−9.1
Changes in foreign exchange holdings	2.6	−0.6	−12.9	2.1	12.2	0.9	−6.3	−2.0	5.6
Changes in N/R bankers' accounts	0.7	2.1	−7.2	8.3	2.0	3.7	2.2	−18.0	−3.3
Changes in other N/R accounts	0.2	−0.5	0.6	1.4	−6.2	0.9	−20.0	−6.4	−1.9
Use of IMF resources	……	−5.2	−5.1	0.9	……	……	……	……	……
Monetary gold	……	5.0	……	……	……	……	……	……	……
Claims with respect to Suez Canal dues	……	5.4	5.3	……	……	……	……	……	……
Errors and ommissions, and unrecorded	− 0.4	0.5	3.7	− 1.8	6.9	5.9	4.0	− 0.9	− 3.3
Total	−31.8	−31.0	−23.9	−24.6	−12.5	−19.4	−36.9	−29.2	−12.0

*Includes other commercial payments.

†In some years, inflows and outflows are partially offset, and only the net figure is shown.

‡Entries shown at new effective rate of exchange.

§Includes (£E million):

	1959	1960	1961	1962	1963
Capital remittances	17.1				
U.S. counterpart funds and £E loans		2.0	0.8	0.7	0.5
IBRD loan to Suez Canal Authority		33.8	27.7	59.6	57.5
Other inflow		10.6	3.2	5.6	
Foreign loans			13.5	26.2	63.0
Credit facilities					66.1

‖In 1964 the format of the capital account was changed as follows (with 1963 figures given for comparative purposes) (£E million):

	1963	1964
Inflow:		
U.S. counterpart funds and £E loans	57.5	69.1
Foreign loans and credit facilities	90.1	114.8
Other inflow	0.5	4.3
Total	148.1	188.2
Outflow:		
Repayment of foreign liabilities	35.0	50.9
Compensation payments and other outflow	19.4	26.2
Total	54.4	71.1
Net capital transactions	+93.7	+111.1

#Includes (£E million):

Repayment of credit facilities	39.0
Repayment of other liabilities	35.0
Other outflow	8.1

SOURCES: All figures are taken directly from the National Bank of Egypt, *Economic Bulletin*, and Central Bank of Egypt, *Economic Review*, various issues. The inclusiveness of these figures is extensively discussed in the text (pp. 180–90).

Appendix VI

Money and Finance

TABLE VI–A–1

Money Supply and Its Determinants

(£E Million; Year-End Figures)

	1947	1948	1949	1950	1951	1952	1953	1954	1955
Money supply:									
A. Net currency circulation outside banks	141.1	154.8	170.3	188.7	204.1	205.7	189.0	187.0	185.3
1. Net note circulation	132.1	145.7	160.7	178.4	193.8	193.7	178.5	176.7	174.2
2. Subsidiary notes and coins	9.0	9.1	9.6	10.3	10.3	12.0	10.5	10.3	11.1
B. Private demand deposits	176.8	195.2	177.4	171.8	178.8	156.4	157.6	152.9	154.7
C. Time and savings deposits	19.1	23.5	25.0	28.7	35.0	39.2	47.7	59.0	66.0
Total	337.0	373.5	372.7	389.2	417.9	401.3	393.3	398.9	406.0
Factors affecting money supply:									
A. Liabilities:									
1. Post Office Savings Bank deposits	32.2	29.8	30.0	29.7	28.4	27.5	26.8	26.4	27.2
2. Government deposits	94.8	53.2	78.6	67.5	42.8	24.6	26.5	28.9	35.3
a) Government	n.a.	n.a.	n.a.	n.a.	n.a.	16.6	18.1	16.5	11.7
b) Semigovernment	n.a.	n.a.	n.a.	n.a.	n.a.	8.0	8.5	12.4	23.6
3. Other deposits	0.0	0.0	0.0	0.0	0.0	0.2	0.2	16.3	19.2
a) Clearing and other accounts in £E	0.0	0.0	0.0	0.0	0.0	0.0	0.0	16.1	19.0
b) U.S. counterpart funds deposits	0.0	0.0	0.0	0.0	0.0	0.0	0.0	0.0	0.0
c) IMF accounts	0.0	0.0	0.0	0.0	0.0	0.2	0.2	0.2	0.2
Total	127.0	83.0	108.6	97.2	71.2	52.3	53.6	71.6	81.7

B. Assets:

1. Net foreign assets	357.3	346.2	336.5	339.1	331.7	259.4	250.0	252.8	221.9
2. Claims on private sector	72.9	85.4	109.3	121.4	124.3	112.4	119.6	154.7	160.2
a) Loans and advances	62.7	77.2	99.4	110.9	114.4	102.4	109.6	143.5	148.7
b) Securities	9.2	8.2	9.9	9.5	9.9	10.0	10.0	11.2	11.5
3. Claims on specialized banks and other entities	5.7	6.0	9.6	18.0	12.4	18.0	13.0	7.9	11.1
a) Government-guaranteed bonds	n.a.	n.a.	n.a.	n.a.	n.a.	n.a.	n.a.	n.a.	0.0
b) Other claims	n.a.	n.a.	n.a.	n.a.	n.a.	18.0	13.0	7.9	11.1
4. Claims on government	63.4	58.2	60.3	57.8	66.1	100.5	101.0	92.9	136.2
a) Securities	9.4	6.3	9.0	10.5	10.8	26.0	26.1	28.8	26.6
b) Treasury bills	12.5	12.7	11.5	7.0	16.3	34.5	37.3	27.2	71.0
c) Counterpart of subsidiary notes and coins	9.3	9.4	9.8	10.6	10.6	12.5	10.8	10.5	11.4
d) Post Office Savings Bank deposits	32.2	29.8	30.0	29.7	28.4	27.5	26.8	26.4	27.2
Total	499.3	495.8	515.7	536.3	534.5	490.3	483.6	508.3	529.4

C. Balancing items:

1. Capital, reserves, and profits	n.a.	n.a.	n.a.	n.a.	n.a.	−24.7	−24.4	−26.1	−27.5
2. Other items, net	n.a.	n.a.	n.a.	n.a.	n.a.	−12.0	−11.3	−11.7	−14.2
Total	−35.4	−39.3	−34.4	−49.9	−45.4	−36.7	−35.7	−37.8	−41.7

(Continued on next page)

TABLE VI–A–1—Continued

	1956	1957	1958	1959	1960	1961	1962	1963	1964
Money Supply:									
A. Net currency circulation outside banks	226.6	213.0	206.9	200.0	219.8	256.4	276.0	345.0	417.2
1. Net note circulation	214.9	200.3	194.3	186.4	206.8	243.1	262.0	320.6	402.3
2. Subsidiary notes and coins	11.7	12.7	12.6	13.6	13.0	13.3	14.0	14.4	14.9
B. Private demand deposits	170.5	185.4	177.9	189.7	185.0	199.0	166.8	170.7	199.2
C. Time and savings deposits	59.2	55.1	70.1	85.1	80.1	86.1	134.8	173.2	179.3
Total	456.3	453.5	454.9	474.8	484.9	541.3	577.6	688.9	759.7
Factors affecting money supply:									
A. Liabilities:									
1. Post Office Savings Bank deposits	26.6	31.5	34.8	38.6	40.6	43.4	51.6	59.2	68.3
2. Government deposits	36.2	38.5	61.2	65.8	77.4	76.3	60.0	81.1	128.9
a) Government	20.2	11.3	32.1	23.2	28.8	21.8	n.a.	n.a.	n.a.
b) Semigovernment	16.0	27.2	29.1	42.6	48.6	54.5	n.a.	n.a.	n.a.
3. Other deposits	19.7	39.4	52.8	90.1	121.4	129.1	161.9	192.8	210.3
a) Clearing and other accounts in £E	14.3	22.2	36.3	54.1	49.1	62.6	56.6	47.3	53.0
b) U.S. counterpart funds deposits	0.0	6.5	5.8	26.3	53.8	48.9	67.8	101.5	108.8
c) IMF accounts	5.4	10.7	10.7	9.7	18.5	17.6	37.5	44.0	48.5
Total	82.5	109.4	148.8	194.5	239.4	248.8	273.5	333.1	407.5

B. Assets:

	1956	1957	1958	1959	1960	1961	1962	1963	1964
1. Net foreign assets	180.2	142.6	137.6	126.0	112.4	99.3	56.5	54.9	46.7
2. Claims on private sector	175.3	189.8	217.4	251.4	255.8	262.3	291.1	317.1	329.1
a) Loans and advances	161.3	177.4	204.7	239.7	241.3	249.4	270.9	293.6	305.0
b) Securities	14.0	12.4	12.7	11.7	14.5	12.9	20.2	23.5	24.1
3. Claims on specialized banks and other entities	17.9	46.3	54.7	83.5	89.3	96.1	105.1*	109.8*	124.7*
a) Government-guaranteed bonds	0.0	20.0	20.0	20.0	23.0	28.0	n.a.	n.a.	n.a.
b) Other claims	17.9	26.3	34.7	63.5	66.3	68.1	n.a.	n.a.	n.a.
4. Claims on government	217.8	236.3	251.8	269.1	350.6	403.0	463.8	613.4	751.0
a) Securities	33.1	41.4	43.7	41.1	111.6	147.9 }	397.8	539.3	667.2
b) Treasury bills	146.0	150.0	160.0	175.0	185.0	198.0 }			
c) Counterpart of subsidiary notes and coins	12.1	13.4	13.3	14.4	13.4	13.7	14.4	14.9	15.5
d) Post Office Savings Bank deposits	26.6	31.5	34.8	38.6	40.6	43.4	51.6	59.2	68.3
Total	591.2	615.0	661.5	730.0	808.1	860.7	916.5	1,095.2	1,251.5

C. Balancing items::

	1956	1957	1958	1959	1960	1961	1962	1963	1964
1. Capital, reserves, and profits	−29.3	−33.9	−37.8	−43.7	−48.7	−52.0	−66.7	−74.5	−61.8
2. Other items, net	−23.1	−18.2	−20.0	−17.0	−35.1	−18.4	+ 1.3	+ 1.3	+13.5
Total	−52.4	−52.1	−57.8	−60.7	−83.8	−70.4	−65.4	−73.2	−48.3

*These were broken down as follows:

	1962	1963	1964
Investment institutions	44.4	40.9	37.9
Credit institutions	60.7	68.9	86.8

NOTES AND SOURCES: From 1952, these are revised data compiled by the Central Bank of Egypt; they are explained in some detail in *Economic Review*, Vol. III, No. 4 (1963), pp. 371–93. We have shifted time and savings deposits to include them in the money supply rather than as an offsetting liability.

Before 1952, we have made our own estimates, relying on figures for the clearing banks alone; in 1952 the nonclearing banks were estimated to have about 7 percent of total bank deposits in the country. The estimate in Table 8–2 (p. 197) of total bank deposits in 1939 was made by A.A.I. el Gritly, on the basis of special information taken from the commercial banks, in addition to their published balance sheets; see his "Development of Bank Deposits in Egypt," in Egyptian Society of Political Economy, Statistics and Legislation, *Research on the Egyptian Economy during the Past 50 Years* (in Arabic), p. 25

TABLE VI–B–1

INTEREST RATES

End of:	"Long-Term Government Bond Yield"	3½ Percent of 1971–73	Treasury Bill Rate
1937............	3.71		
1938............	3.89		
1939............	5.53		
1948............	2.80		
1949............	3.09		
1950............	3.10		
1951............	3.50		
1952............	3.98		
1953............	3.42	3.14	0.77
1954............	3.11	3.31	0.75
1955............	3.03	2.83	0.75
1956............	3.38	3.66	1.00
1957............	3.81	3.64	1.01
1958............	3.52	3.45	1.03
1959............	3.61	3.61	1.02
1960............	3.39	3.28	1.05
1961............	3.73	4.12	1.01
1962............	4.05	4.02	1.00
1963............	4.89	5.96	1.27
1964............		6.39	1.02

NOTES AND SOURCES: Long-term government bond yield is from International Monetary Fund, *International Financial Statistics*, various issues; and U Tun Wai, "Interest Rates in Underdeveloped Countries," *IMF Staff Papers*, Vol. V (1956–57), p. 255. Earlier figures refer to "annual averages, long-term bonds in most cases." The heading "3½ percent of 1971–73" was "National Loan 3¼ percent (1963–73)" up to August, 1961, when it was converted to the indicated title; this is the redemption yield. "Treasury bill rate" is monthly average of tenders. Both are from Central Bank of Egypt, *Economic Review*, Vol. IV, No. 2 (1964), p. 227, and Vol. V, No. 2 (1965), p. 217.

TABLE VI–C–1

DISTRIBUTION OF OUTSTANDING CREDIT FACILITIES, BY TYPE OF BANK

(£E Million)

	1960		1961		1962
	June	December	June	December	June
Central Bank..............	19.9	33.1	13.4	17.4	15.1
Commercial banks..........	209.7	244.1	224.3	258.4	207.4
Agricultural and Cooperative Credit Bank.........	30.5	19.1	36.3	41.4	60.6
Industrial Bank............	7.3	8.5	8.8	9.2	9.3
Real estate banks.........	21.4	22.6	22.9	23.4	23.6
Total.................	288.8	327.4	305.7	349.8	316.0

NOTES AND SOURCES: All figures from Central Bank of Egypt, Control of Banks Department, *Credit and Banking Developments, January 1961–June 1962,* p. 22. This useful publication also presents complete balance sheets of each of the above groups of financial institutions.

TABLE VI–C–2

DISTRIBUTION OF OUTSTANDING CREDIT FACILITIES, BY SECTORS

(£E Million)

	1960		1961		1962
	June	December	June	December	June
Government business sector..	2.5	3.6	0.9	8.3	1.9
Organized business sector....	124.2	146.2	127.9	160.2	124.2
Corporations of public organizations......	(85.6)	(99.6)	(92.5)	(112.2)	(99.2)
Other corporations.......	(38.6)	(46.6)	(35.4)	(48.0)	(25.0)
Nonorganized business sector..............	37.9	50.1	40.5	35.5	30.2
Public administration sector...............	1.3	1.3	1.0	5.3	6.0
Cooperative societies sector..	26.3	18.3	34.0	42.3	62.2
Individuals sector.........	89.4	100.8	87.3	88.8	71.1
Public organizations sector...	7.2	7.1	14.1	9.4	20.4
Total..............	288.8	327.4	305.7	349.8	316.0

NOTES AND SOURCES: See Table VI–C–1. It is not clear why a small amount of lending to public administration is included in this table, while the great bulk of loans to the government are excluded; Appendix Table VI–A–1 indicates that at the end of 1961, claims of the Central and commercial banks on the government sector amounted to £E403 million.

TABLE VI–C–3

Investments of Insurance Companies

(£E Thousand)

Nationality of Insurance Company	State Bonds and Guaranteed Securities	Foreign Bonds and Guaranteed Securities	Other Securities	Real Estate	Mortgages	Loans on Policies	Other Loans	Fixed Deposits and Current Accounts at Banks	Total
1952....Total.......	8,978	.....	3,331	5,709	2,494	2,446	9	2,874	25,841
1953....Egyptian.....	2,852	424	3,305	3,565	1,313	1,348	18	1,305	14,131
Foreign......	5,579	1,111	1,133	2,615	1,127	1,447	...	2,374	15,385
Total......	8,431	1,535	4,438	6,180	2,439	2,795	18	3,679	29,516
1954....Egyptian.....	3,308	406	3,663	3,596	1,299	1,574	61	1,619	15,525
Foreign......	6,132	1,121	1,126	2,620	1,399	1,693	...	2,689	16,780
Total......	9,440	1,527	4,788	6,216	2,698	3,266	61	4,308	32,305
1955....Egyptian.....	4,663	420	4,069	4,927	1,588	2,119	3	1,798	19,586
Foreign......	6,371	781	1,126	2,245	1,283	1,515	...	2,414	15,734
Total......	11,034	1,201	5,195	7,172	2,871	3,635	3	4,211	35,321
1956*....Egyptian.....	5,954	428	5,027	5,344	1,676	2,262	2	2,037	22,730
Foreign......	5,535	342	1,067	2,640	1,270	1,671	...	1,715	14,240
Total......	11,490	770	6,094	7,984	2,945	3,933	2	3,752	36,970

1957 Egyptian	9,570	525	8,045	7,795	2,337	2,954	…	2,038	33,263
Foreign	2,890	189	157	883	755	911	…	1,065	6,849
Total	12,549	714	8,201	8,678	3,092	3,865	…	3,102	40,112
1958 Egyptian	11,036	655	9,886	9,553	2,891	3,225	…	4,343	41,589
Foreign	2,140	208	122	610	156	761	…	1,587	5,584
Total	13,176	863	10,008	10,163	3,048	3,987	…	5,929	47,174
1959 Egyptian	12,548	463	11,595	10,166	2,642	3,330	605	5,928	47,277
Foreign	2,334	214	124	626	118	733	…	1,360	5,580
Total	14,884	677	11,719	10,791	2,760	4,063	605	7,288	52,785
1960 Egyptian	16,592	462	12,425	11,196	2,603	3,521	620	6,125	53,545
Foreign	2,458	198	77	626	104	707	…	1,301	5,470
Total	19,051	660	12,502	11,822	2,707	4,228	620	7,426	59,015
1961† Egyptian	26,364	419	4,611	12,196	2,504	3,676	613	7,994	58,377
Foreign	2,069	80	95	614	93	676	…	1,413	5,040
Total	28,433	499	4,706	12,810	2,597	4,352	613	9,407	63,417

*The figures for 1956 do not include the investments of English, French, and Australian companies.

†This includes the estimated figures of four non-Egyptian companies.

Source: United Arab Republic, Ministry of Economy, Insurance Department, *Egyptian Insurance Yearbook, 1961* (Cairo, 1963), pp. 44–45.

TABLE VI–E–1

CENTRAL GOVERNMENT RECEIPTS

(£E Thousand)

	1900	1913	1928–29	1933–34	1938–39	1946–47
Land tax..............	4,379	5,041	5,214	5,603	5,200	4,301
Other property taxes.....	242	477	678	2,898	1,795	1,541
Corporate profits and excess profits tax..	0	0	0	0	0	8,867
Customs duties:						
1. Tobacco...........	1,160	1,720	6,219	n.a.	n.a.	21,902
2. Others............	1,258	2,134	6,149	n.a.	n.a.	19,952
Total.............	2,418	3,854	12,368	11,995	15,837	41,854
Government property income:						
1. Interest...........	56	148	2,628	2,551	2,829	1,252
2. Rental of government property....	87	431	906	640	689	1,782
3. Surplus of government enterprises..	1,231	1,687	3,537	1,757	2,803	5,633
Total..........	1,374	2,266	7,071	4,948	6,321	8,667
Individual pension fund contributions......	65	139	323	652	596	813
Other taxes, fees, and miscellaneous receipts..........	1,948	3,245	10,126	8,291	4,224	37,359
Total budgetary receipts..	10,426	15,022	35,780	34,387	33,973	103,402
Exhibit: Extraordinary receipts..........	420	337	3	0	0	0

NOTES AND SOURCES: See p. 381.

TABLE VI–E–2

CENTRAL GOVERNMENT EXPENDITURES

(£E Thousand)

	1900	1913	1928–29	1933–34	1938–39	1946–47
Government current expenditures on goods and services..........	4,101	7,386	20,524	19,993	25,949	64,886
1. General expenditures:						
a) Defense.........	807	1,126	1,187	1,715	2,196	7,276
b) Justice and police.........	687	1,474	5,057	4,571	4,957	6,808
c) All others........	2,249	3,108	7,013	6,084	7,376	27,218
Total.......	3,743	5,708	13,257	12,370	14,529	41,302
2. Developmental expenditures:						
a) Education.......	107	515	2,417	3,057	4,333	10,426
b) Health..........	104	345	989	1,309	2,507	5,113
c) Commerce and industry.......	n.a.	n.a.	42	165	200	794
d) Agriculture and irrigation......	147	818	2,841	1,889	2,221	4,727
e) Communication..	n.a.	n.a.	978	1,203	2,159	2,524
Total.......	358	1,678	7,267	7,623	11,420	23,584
Interest on public debt...	3,675	3,925	4,971	4,195	3,261	5,112
Transfer payments:						
Pensions............	433	561	2,182	1,894	1,960	3,521
Food subsidies........	0	0	0	0	0	5,602
Transfer payments abroad (tribute)...	665	665	0	0	0	0
Total expenditures......	8,874	12,537	27,677	26,082	31,170	79,121
Surplus on current account., ...	1,552	2,485	8,103	8,305	2,803	24,281
Total current expenditures and surplus..	10,426	15,022	35,780	34,387	33,973	103,402
Exhibit: Extraordinary expenditures:						
Irrigation and drainage............	443	722	1,877	3,159	3,633	4,577
Public buildings.......	173	60	453	299	631	696
Railroads and telegraph..........	253	580	849	0	0	856
Army...............	0	0	0	0	2,785	636
Others..............	75	1,414	1,787	1,008	2,174	7,216
Total............	944	2,776	4,965	4,466	9,223	13,981

NOTES AND SOURCES: All figures are from the final accounts of the government budget and from the *Annuaire Statistique*, various issues. We have removed the railroads, telephone, and telegraph from the accounts throughout, entering the current surplus of these organizations under surplus of government enterprises. These entities were originally included in the budget in all the years shown except 1933–34 and 1938–39, when they had separate, annexed budgets. Extraordinary receipts were generally of a capital nature: drawing on funds, or even new borrowing. What we have entitled "extraordinary expenditures" has changed in specific title through time. They were first called extraordinary expenditures; from 1905 to 1914, besides this category there was another entitled "special budgetary expenditures"; from 1914–15, these two were consolidated under the heading "new works." These are supposed to be expenditures of a capital nature; and although this gives only a rough measure of the current capital breakdown of government spending, we have felt it best to follow this breakdown in the table rather than simply adding the components together.

TABLE VI–E–3

CENTRAL GOVERNMENT REVENUE, 1947–48 TO 1956–57

(£E Thousand)

	1947–48	1948–49	1949–50	1950–51	1951–52	1952–53	1953–54	1954–55	1955–56	1956–57
Taxes on production and expenditure:										
Import duties	35,843	45,509	50,227	79,581	60,336	56,746	60,207	62,888	73,402	66,226
Export duties	182	9,611	10,906	23,635	14,145	14,451	17,355	11,955	9,832	5,993
Other customs duties	1,962	2,349	2,961	6,084	5,044	4,756	5,448	5,271	5,383	4,214
Excise and consumption taxes	9,454	12,379	14,296	21,335	14,737	11,886	18,020	18,725	22,834	21,017
Selective commodity taxes	1,200	1,541	1,945	1,837	1,300	1,281	1,263	1,154	1,369	2,125
Monopoly surplus	2,846	1,841	2,277	4,249	4,405	7,120	8,872	9,793	7,368	6,765
Royalties	1,357	1,767	2,643	5,794	3,753	3,490	1,853	7,663	3,783	1,571
Stamp duties	1,614	2,297	2,435	3,243	3,713	5,057	4,809	5,880	6,269	6,328
Licenses	1,366	1,984	2,103	2,785	1,220	1,322	1,498	1,459	1,626	1,694
Property transfer taxes	1,234	1,805	1,851	3,159	2,987	3,075	3,449	3,108	4,114	2,948
Tax on foreign exchange	......	......	......	......	......	200	356	432	447	1,153
Total	57,058	81,083	91,644	151,702	111,640	109,384	123,130	128,328	136,427	120,034
Taxes on income and wealth:										
Personal income taxes	1,746	2,773	2,769	7,758	8,755	9,034	6,783	6,926	7,462	11,190
Business income taxes	9,362	13,953	12,864	16,629	14,211	14,217	13,349	13,098	16,271	16,375
Property tax	5,380	5,586	7,904	9,998	16,013	15,004	16,021	12,931	15,819	12,295
Death duties	342	887	670	923	750	3,253	1,106	1,575	1,626	2,027
Total	16,830	23,199	24,207	35,308	39,729	41,508	37,259	34,530	41,178	41,887

Employee's pension contribution	729	876	885	1,262	974	954	991	962	1,017	1,032
Total	729	876	885	1,252	974	954	991	962	1,017	1,032
Penalties, fines, and forfeitures:										
Court fines	376	599	581	961	798	872	954	992	946	939
Miscellaneous fines, penalties, and forfeitures	124	170	163	287	184	196	175	266	184	244
Total	500	769	744	1,248	982	1,068	1,129	1,258	1,130	1,183
Sales and charges:										
Agriculture	824	1,045	540	791	971	700	540	522	875	2,225
Communication, transportation, and storage	456	671	700	1,032	832	1,008	883	1,341	2,071	1,403
Education	384	705	557	273	261	264	279	498	791	1,088
Health	303	425	440	553	387	357	335	404	525	421
Culture and recreation	196	280	320	489	385	470	92	140	78	1,194
Police and justice	1,421	1,941	2,040	3,022	2,267	2,776	2,795	2,786	2,893	2,583
Miscellaneous	2,546	2,213	2,776	3,587	5,050	5,087	4,075	6,118	11,425	6,666
Total	6,130	7,280	7,373	9,747	10,153	10,662	8,999	11,809	18,658	15,580
Sales of existing capital goods:										
Sales of land	439	1,162	679	1,204	777	861	751	603	612	711
Total	439	1,162	679	1,204	777	861	751	603	612	711
Income from property and enterprise:										
Interest and dividends	1,757	1,903	1,643	3,084	1,334	1,623	2,952	3,759	2,316	1,594
Rent of government buildings and lands	879	986	921	1,353	1,099	1,211	1,124	1,302	1,024	1,017
Receipts of government enterprises	12,933	18,512	21,588	28,850	23,368	24,258	26,816	34,893	42,449	55,504
Receipts from other government property	1,007	1,076	1,003	1,352	1,200	891	1,313	1,177	1,440	768
Total	16,576	22,477	25,155	34,639	27,001	27,983	32,205	41,131	47,229	58,883

(Continued on next page)

TABLE VI–E–3—Continued

	1947–48	1948–49	1949–50	1950–51	1951–52	1952–53	1953–54	1954–55	1955–56	1956–57
Repayment of loans and advances	54	69	68	64	83	82	41	58	56	52
Total	54	69	68	64	83	82	41	58	56	52
Intergovernmental transfers:										
Contribution, appropriation from other accounts and funds	317	5,465	7,490	14,318	2,115	5,030	384	49	7,075	23,934
Reimbursements	27	120	108	242	1,007	975	1,067	943	454	682
Total	344	5,585	7,598	14,560	3,122	6,005	1,451	992	7,529	24,616
Miscellaneous:										
Unspecified receipts	301	5	4	5	3	....	....	....	....	....
Confiscation	....	....	....	....	....	....	....	3	9,043	1,707
Total	301	5	4	5	3	....	....	3	9,043	1,707
Grants:										
Internal	83	24	262	9	20	30	15	16	4,626	63
Total	83	24	262	9	20	30	15	16	4,626	63
Grand total	99,044	142,529	158,619	249,738	194,484	198,537	205,971	219,690	267,505	265,748

NOTES AND SOURCES: See p. 395.

TABLE VI-E-4

CENTRAL GOVERNMENT EXPENDITURES, ORDINARY BUDGET, 1947–48 TO 1956–57

(£E Thousand)

	(1) Wages and Salaries	(2) Rental of Fixed Assets	(3) Other Goods and Services	(4) Military Construction and Equipment	(5) Subsidies	(6) Transfer Payments	(7) New Capital Goods	(8) Existing Capital Goods	(9) Transfers to Capital Account, Domestic Sector	(10) Transfers Abroad	(11) Total Expenditures
For Year 1947–48											
Organ of state	909	1	196				88	3			1,197
Fiscal administration	1,398	13	929			37	15	3			2,395
General economic regulation	492	12	162			1	58				725
Conduct of foreign affairs	243	27	772			517	45				1,604
Other											
Justice and police	5,622	67	1,856			42	72				7,659
General research and scientific services	523	7	94			3	25				652
Defense	2,646	63	4,942	452		6					8,109
Total, general services	11,833	190	8,951	452		606	303	6			22,341
Education	3,938	200	1,664			5,997	434				12,233
Health	1,558	72	2,469			145	375	21	2		4,642
Social security, special welfare services	3,227	38	240		3,988	3,772	244				11,509
Community services	714	3	666			1,236	240		358		3,217
Tourist and cultural services	61	1	110				10	6			188
Total, community and social services	9,498	314	5,149		3,988	11,150	1,303	27	360		31,789
Agriculture and irrigation	2,751	21	3,841			20	1,752	1,208	126		9,719
Mineral resources, manufacturing construction	409	14	780				882	10	23		2,118
Fuel and power	439	14	636				193		2		1,284
Transport, storage, and communications	5,165	48	6,313			54	2,793	3	69		14,445
Other economic services	22		17			26					65
Multipurpose projects											
Total, economic services	8,786	97	11,587			100	5,620	1,221	220		27,631
Interest on public debt						2,208					2,208
Cost-of-living allowances	9,702										9,702
Other unallocable expenses			65								65
Total, unallocable expenditures	9,702		65			2,208					11,975
Grand total	39,819	601	25,752	452	3,988	14,064	7,226	1,254	580		93,736

(Continued on next page)

TABLE VI-E-4, 1948/50—Continued

	(1) Wages and Salaries	(2) Rental of Fixed Assets	(3) Other Goods and Services	(4) Military Construction and Equipment	(5) Subsidies	(6) Transfer Payments	(7) New Capital Goods	(8) Existing Capital Goods	(9) Transfers to Capital Account, Domestic Sector	(10) Transfers Abroad	(11) Total Expenditures
For Year 1948–49											
Organ of state	1,132	1	164				190		3	28	1,518
Fiscal administration	1,868	31	370			18	30		6		2,323
General economic regulation	708	31	1,003			1	41				1,784
Conduct of foreign affairs	379	6	125			155	47			39	751
Other											
Justice and police	8,432	99	1,248			18	275				10,072
General research and scientific services	632	4	228			1	3				868
Defense	4,893	57	24,587	2,367							31,904
Total, general services	18,044	229	27,725	2,367		193	586	9		67	49,220
Education	5,346	202	3,139			5,370	639	33			14,696
Health	2,285	80	2,610			198	434	2			5,640
Social security, special welfare services	3,313		1,015		5,123	7,745	1,556				18,754
Community services	385	3	1,033			7	1,079				2,507
Tourist and cultural services	133	5	277				123				538
Total, community and social services	11,462	290	8,074		5,123	13,320	3,831	35			42,135
Agriculture and irrigation	3,125	30	6,074			20	2,123	463			11,835
Mineral resources, manufacturing construction	605	2	1,177				206				1,990
Fuel and power	595	12	1,255				410	710			2,982
Transport, storage, and communications	6,591	32	6,699			31	2,946	7		501	16,807
Other economic services	29		3			769					801
Multipurpose projects											
Total, economic services	10,945	76	15,208			820	5,685	1,180		501	34,415
Interest on public debt						3,309					3,309
Cost-of-living allowances	13,026										13,026
Other unallocable expenses	2	245	346		1,840		3				2,436
Total, unallocable expenditures	13,028	245	346		1,840	3,309	3				20,611
Grand total	53,479	840	51,353	2,367	6,963	17,642	10,105	1,224		568	144,541

FOR YEAR 1949–50

	(1)	(2)	(3)	(4)	(5)	(6)	(7)	(8)	(9)	Total
Organ of state	1,291	1	208			15	165	33	86	1,799
Fiscal administration	1,987	32	938			42	10	1		3,010
General economic regulation	787	22	170			1	136			1,116
Conduct of foreign affairs	460	82	156			143	50			891
Other										
Justice and police	8,856	117	1,802			44	164			10,983
General research and scientific services	68	1	29							98
Defense	7,918	113	16,589	9,032						33,652
Total, general services	21,367	368	19,892	9,032		245	525	34	86	51,549
Education	6,417	356	4,625			7,358	464			19,220
Health	2,600	105	2,807			258	1,850	10		7,630
Social security, special welfare services	356	5	1,302		3,937	5,345	276			11,221
Community services	1,399	7	1,001			1,455	286	9		4,157
Tourist and cultural services	152	6	185				221			564
Total, community and social services	10,924	479	9,920		3,937	14,416	3,097	19		42,792
Agriculture and irrigation	3,928	29	4,508			940	28,585	474		38,464
Mineral resources, manufacturing construction	1,274	11	1,770			500	1,884			5,439
Fuel and power	394	10	624				2,157			3,185
Transport, storage, and communications	8,015	81	8,203		41	75	11,139	13		27,567
Other economic services	29	1	3			31				64
Multipurpose projects										
Total, economic services	13,640	132	15,108		41	1,546	43,765	487		74,719
Interest on public debt						3,738				3,738
Cost-of-living allowances	13,420									13,420
Other unallocable expenses	3		1,103				6			1,112
Total, unallocable expenditures	13,423		1,103			3,738	6			18,270
Grand total	59,354	979	46,023	9,032	3,978	19,945	47,393	540	86	187,330

(Continued on next page)

TABLE VI-E-4, 1950/52—Continued

	(1) Wages and Salaries	(2) Rental of Fixed Assets	(3) Other Goods and Services	(4) Military Construction and Equipment	(5) Subsidies	(6) Transfer Payments	(7) New Capital Goods	(8) Existing Capital Goods	(9) Transfers to Capital Account, Domestic Sector	(10) Transfers Abroad	(11) Total Expenditures
For Year 1950–51											
Organ of state	1,336		235			194	262		109		2,136
Fiscal administration	2,257	34	288			33	13				2,625
General economic regulation	296	9	104			1	103				513
Conduct of foreign affairs	654	10	481			122	40				1,307
Other:											
Justice and police	10,048	110	1,631			75	275	5			12,144
General research and scientific services	24	2	12				21				59
Defense	9,510	19	10,646	8,761		1					28,937
Total, general services	24,125	184	13,397	8,761		426	714	5	109		47,721
Education	7,014	274	3,512			7,940	1,231	125			20,096
Health	2,941	50	3,370			532	299	49			7,241
Social security, special welfare services	729		1,331		6,348	5,187	286	20			13,901
Community services	2,065	23	2,550			2,480	1,215				8,333
Tourist and cultural services											
Total, community and social services	12,749	347	10,763		6,348	16,139	3,031	194			49,571
Agriculture and irrigation	4,037	11	6,340			80	1,948	911		46	13,373
Mineral resources, manufacturing construction	966	6	1,282			54	7,010	8			9,326
Fuel and power	1,941	5	2,381				2,307	7,216			13,850
Transport, storage, and communications	8,309	66	9,036			214	11,994	61			29,680
Other economic services	176	6	5,863				1				6046
Multipurpose projects											
Total, economic services	15,429	94	24,902			348	23,260	8,196		46	72,275
Interest on public debt						3,606					3,606
Cost-of-living allowances	30,504										30,504
Other unallocable expenses	3		523								526
Total, unallocable expenditures	30,507		523			3,606					34,636
Grand total	82,810	625	49,585	8,761	6,348	20,519	27,005	8,395	109	46	204,203

For Year 1951-52

Organ of state	1,489	1	314		344		293		225	2,666
Fiscal administration	2,415	28	206		37		2			2,688
General economic regulation	654	24	60		45		8			791
Conduct of foreign affairs	657	60	371		217		218			1,523
Other										
Justice and police	10,301	94	6,739		133		462	7		17,736
General research and scientific services	647	6	177		1		79	3		913
Defense	12,934	13	8,549	19,923	242					41,661
Total, general services	29,097	226	16,416	19,923	1,019		1,062	10	225	67,978
Education	13,106	607	4,645		5,176		1,837			25,371
Health	3,032	61	3,335		360		618			7,406
Social security, special welfare services	1,115	23	647		10,473	9,153	261			21,672
Community services	445	4	171		1,741		2,463			4,824
Tourist and cultural services	86	2	51				85			224
Total, community and social services	17,784	697	8,849		17,750	9,153	5,264			59,497
Agriculture and irrigation	3,785	17	5,455		45		1,093			12,459
Mineral resources, manufacturing construction	1,522	5	1,301		2		2,711	2,064		5,541
Fuel and power	1,590	5	1,343				5,068			8,006
Transport, storage, and communications	9,506	135	8,968		95		9,320	522		28,636
Other economic services	43		228		12					283
Multipurpose projects										
Total, economic services	16,536	162	17,295		154		18,192	2,586		54,925
Interest on public debt					3,898					3,898
Cost-of-living allowances	32,742									32,742
Other unallocable expenses			825							825
Total, unallocable expenditures	32,742		825		3,898					37,465
Grand total	96,159	1,085	43,385	19,923	22,821	9,153	24,518	2,596	225	219,865

(Continued on next page)

TABLE VI-E-4, 1952/54—Continued

	(1) Wages and Salaries	(2) Rental of Fixed Assets	(3) Other Goods and Services	(4) Military Construction and Equipment	(5) Subsidies	(6) Transfer Payments	(7) New Capital Goods	(8) Existing Capital Goods	(9) Transfers to Capital Account, Domestic Sector	(10) Transfers Abroad	(11) Total Expenditures
For Year 1952–53											
Organ of state	870	1	296				9				1,563
Fiscal administration	2,514	20	786		30	72	4				3,426
General economic regulation	818	61	123		4	1	29				1,036
Conduct of foreign affairs	550	9	471			224	89			105	1,448
Other											
Justice and police	10,064	102	2,695			48	42				12,951
General research and scientific services	694	10	150			2					856
Defense	9,932		15,679	9,661							35,272
Total, general services	25,442	203	20,200	9,661	34	734	173		105		56,552
Education	9,000	577	7,790			4,394	1,326				23,087
Health	2,972	95	3,044			236	399	4	4		6,750
Social security, special welfare services	494	21	1,721		20,221	6,813	7		3,135		29,281
Community services	337	3	91			1,003	5		3,135		4,574
Tourist and cultural services	109	3	287				35		5		439
Total, community and social services	12,912	699	12,933		20,221	12,446	1,772	4	3,144		64,131
Agriculture and irrigation	3,460	18	2,734			26	1,323	425	80		8,066
Mineral resources, manufacturing construction	850	15	1,078			2	466				2,411
Fuel and power	1,483	12	2,467			178	3,514				7,654
Transport, storage, and communications	9,765	42	8,268			14	6,665	63	377		25,194
Other economic services	71		39			6					116
Multipurpose projects											
Total, economic services	15,629	87	14,586			226	11,968	488	457		43,441
Interest on public debt						1,756					1,756
Cost-of-living allowances	33,525										33,525
Other unallocable expenses			2,760								2,760
Total, unallocable expenditures	33,525		2,760			1,756					38,041
Grand total	87,508	989	50,479	9,661	20,255	15,162	13,913	492	3,706		202,165

Organ of state	538	2	164			433	9			253	1,399
Fiscal administration	2,417	22	775			37	43				3,294
General economic regulation	850	30	133		11	16	8				1,048
Conduct of foreign affairs	555	16	398			454	67				1,490
Other	136	5	2			1	1				144
Justice and police	11,515	106	2,152			98	29				13,900
General research and scientific services	823	10	145			1	1				980
Defense	10,514		15,256	12,008							37,778
Total, general services	27,348	191	19,025	12,008	11	1,039	158			253	60,033
Education	15,458	695	2,838			3,675	879				23,545
Health	3,195	105	2,952			255	390				6,897
Social security, special welfare services	8,169	4	793		7,851	7,842	9		145		24,813
Community services	479	2	126			2,645	2,204				5,458
Tourist and cultural services	90		82				2				176
Total, community and social services	27,391	810	6,791		7,851	14,417	3,484		145		60,889
Agriculture and irrigation	3,153	16	3,091			29	1,244	259	462		8,254
Mineral resources, manufacturing construction	1,062	8	2,886			1	154				4,111
Fuel and power	1,734	13	4,673				842				7,262
Transport, storage, and communications	9,898	61	12,876			15	2,679	47	1		25,577
Other economic services	28		3			5					36
Multipurpose projects											
Total, economic services	15,875	98	23,529			50	4,919	306	463		45,240
Interest on public debt	28,762										28,762
Cost-of-living allowances						4,313					4,313
Other unallocable expenses			55								55
Total, unallocable expenditures	28,762		55			4,313					33,130
Grand total	99,376	1,099	49,400	12,008	7,862	19,819	8,561	306	608	253	199,292

(Continued on next page)

TABLE VI-E-4, 1954/56—Continued

	(1) Wages and Salaries	(2) Rental of Fixed Assets	(3) Other Goods and Services	(4) Military Construction and Equipment	(5) Subsidies	(6) Transfer Payments	(7) New Capital Goods	(8) Existing Capital Goods	(9) Transfers to Capital Account, Domestic Sector	(10) Transfers Abroad	(11) Total Expenditures
For Year 1954–55											
Organ of state	450	1	151		7	1,089	5			59	1,762
Fiscal administration	2,953	28	712			48	23				3,764
General economic regulation	886	55	113			26	9				1,089
Conduct of foreign affairs	601	59	323			304	47			4	1,338
Other											
Justice and police	10,587	57	3,276			164	265				14,349
General research and scientific services	778	6	266			1	1				1,052
Defense	12,583		21,307	19,114							53,004
Total, general services	28,838	206	26,148	19,114	7	1,632	350			63	76,358
Education	17,363	823	3,426			4,032	1,398				27,042
Health	2,954	74	3,829			1,322	255				8,434
Social security, special welfare services	7,794	25	594		4,938	11,095	361				24,807
Community services	885	173	1,187			2,857	1,100				6,202
Tourist and cultural services	202	21	517			138	58				936
Total, community and social services	29,198	1,116	9,553		4,938	19,444	3,172				67,421
Agriculture and irrigation	3,771	21	2,609			34	1,449	254	219		8,357
Mineral resources, manufacturing construction	967	10	6,905			2	14				7,898
Fuel and power	2,671	18	2,423				779				5,891
Transport, storage, and communications	10,983	115	13,063			26	4,029				28,216
Other economic services	32		2			5					39
Multipurpose projects											
Total, economic services	18,424	164	25,002			67	6,271	254	219		50,401
Interest on public debt						4,148					4,148
Cost-of-living allowances	29,176										29,176
Other unallocable expenses			78								78
Total, unallocable expenditures	29,176		78			4,148					33,402
Grand total	105,636	1,486	60,781	19,114	4,945	25,291	9,793	254	219	63	227,582

FOR YEAR 1955–56

									Total
Organ of state	484	2	327			777	22		1,612
Fiscal administration	3,189	23	736			69	5,066	2	9,085
General economic regulation	1,114	63	998			3	67		2,245
Conduct of foreign affairs	692	101	440			254	80		1,567
Other:									
Justice and police	12,367	100	3,301			170	554		16,492
General research and scientific services	861	12	91				253		1,217
Defense	21,337		57,326	3,294					81,957
Total, general services	40,044	301	63,219	3,294		1,273	6,042	2	114,175
Education	20,173	701	3,683			4,964	1,577		31,098
Health	3,527	91	2,749			1,347	580		8,294
Social security, special welfare services	9,634	27	536		6,300	11,957	270		28,724
Community services	701	7	238			3,571	3,413		7,932
Tourist and cultural services	378	41	787			192	50		1,448
Total, community and social services	34,413	867	7,993		6,300	22,031	5,890	2	77,496
Agriculture and irrigation	3,731	18	3,544			39	2,554		9,886
Mineral resources, manufacturing construction	1,499	16	6,698			15	1,008		9,236
Fuel and power	1,894	16	3,607				965		6,482
Transport, storage, and communications	10,661	88	12,316			3	2,754		25,822
Other economic services	35		7			6			48
Multipurpose projects	318						133		451
Total, economic services	18,138	138	26,172			63	7,414		51,925
Interest on public debt						4,242			4,242
Cost-of-living allowances	29,224								29,224
Other unallocable expenses			79						79
Total, unallocable expenditures	29,224		79			4,242			33,545
Grand total	121,819	1,306	97,463	3,294	6,300	27,609	19,346	4	277,141

(Continued on next page)

TABLE VI-E-4, 1956/57—Continued

	(1) Wages and Salaries	(2) Rental of Fixed Assets	(3) Other Goods and Services	(4) Military Construction and Equipment	(5) Subsidies	(6) Transfer Payments	(7) New Capital Goods	(8) Existing Capital Goods	(9) Transfers to Capital Account, Domestic Sector	(10) Transfers Abroad	(11) Total Expenditures
For Year 1956–57											
Organ of state	486	2	343			61	70				962
Fiscal administration	4,533	34	995			181	24				5,767
General economic regulation	1,282	24	328			173	15		7		1,829
Conduct of foreign affairs	868	144	593			666	230				2,501
Other											
Justice and police	11,835	113	5,075			205	125	9	2		17,364
General research and scientific services	1,010	11	159				259				1,439
Defense	22,416		55,593	3,445							81,454
Total, general services	42,430	328	63,086	3,445		1,286	723	9	9		111,316
Education	21,534	700	3,238			4,910	1,747		1		32,130
Health	3,374	77	3,251			1,570	109		498		8,879
Social security, special welfare services	7,536	3	138		7,755	13,994	5				29,431
Community services	1,063	14	1,421		229	3,195	4,021		6,057		16,000
Tourist and cultural services	419	34	683		64	236	31		2		1,469
Total, community and social services	33,926	828	8,731		8,048	23,905	5,913		6,558		87,909
Agriculture and irrigation	5,353	16	2,821			26	143	18	3,454	33	11,864
Mineral resources, manufacturing construction	755	12	1,005				110				1,882
Fuel and power	2,511	22	28,432			26	1,077		118		32,186
Transport, storage, and communications	11,658	66	11,074			163	2,433	8	609		26,011
Other economic services	39		35			6					80
Multipurpose projects			170				273				443
Total, economic services	20,316	116	43,537			221	4,036	26	4,181	33	72,466
Interest on public debt						6,944					6,944
Cost-of-living allowances	30,762										30,762
Other unallocable expenses			67								67
Total, unallocable expenditures	30,762		67			6,944					37,773
Grand total	127,434	1,272	115,421	3,445	8,048	32,356	10,672	35	10,748	33	309,464

NOTES AND SOURCES FOR TABLES VI-E-3 AND VI-E-4: The figures in Tables VI-E-3 and VI-E-4 are taken from an unpublished study by Rasheed Khalid, and we thank him for his kind permission to use them. Khalid is from the Fiscal Division of the United Nations, and spent three years at the Institute of National Planning in Cairo, teaching and doing research on government budgeting procedures. One of his major activities was to supervise the work of reclassifying the closed accounts of the Egyptian ordinary budget for the years 1947–48 to 1956–57, according to an economic and functional cross-classification. The summary tables of this reclassification are reproduced here. We have changed the original figures only by including interest on the public debt with transfer payments, and by shifting high-cost-of-living allowances from the category of transfer payments to wages and salaries. These are wage supplements which we feel should best be included here. The period 1947–48 covers only ten calendar months: May 1, 1947, to February 28, 1948. From 1948–49 to 1950–51 the fiscal year was March 1 to February 28; thereafter, it was changed to run from July 1 to June 30. The three-month period March 1–June 30, 1951, had an interim budget, not included in the expenditure figures, although it was included in the receipts with 1950–51. The classification scheme follows that set out in United Nations, Department of Economic and Social Affairs, *A Manual for the Economic and Functional Classification of Government Transactions* (New York, 1958), although it is far less detailed than the fine breakdown presented in the *Manual*.

TABLE VI–E–5

GOVERNMENT EXPENDITURES IN ANNEXED BUDGETS

(£E Thousand)

	Barlow's Expenditure Number	1948–49	1949–50	1950–51	1951–52	1952–53	1953–54	1954–55	1955–56	1956–57
Expenditures primarily of a current nature:										
Universities	67, 73, and 78	2,524	3,067	3,876	4,349	4,022	3,899	3,989	4,325	4,600
National Research Center	18	.....	15	38	147	301	278	316	323	205
Egyptian Broadcasting	15	205	410	156	196	151	151	77	.....	83
Permanent Council for the Development of National Production	17	.....	.....	.....	.....	4	25	41	81	80
Qalyub Organization and Training Center	16	.....	.....	.....	.....	.....	358	743	334	.....
Mohamed Ali Charitable Society*	180	.....	.....	.....	.....	.....	.....	30	.....	.....
Antituberculosis campaign*	181	.....	.....	.....	.....	.....	.....	277	515	.....
Treatment of diseases*	182	.....	.....	.....	.....	.....	.....	168	112	.....
Combined units*	150	.....	.....	.....	.....	.....	.....	894	6,251	1,790
Rural development*	185	.....	.....	.....	.....	.....	.....	.....	63	.....
Educational services*	186	.....	.....	.....	.....	.....	.....	.....	701	.....
Student aid*	187	.....	.....	.....	.....	.....	.....	.....	156	.....
Public service Projects:										
Administration*	189	.....	.....	.....	.....	.....	.....	93	309	.....
Montaza Palace*	190	.....	.....	.....	.....	.....	.....	1	2	.....
Sudanese health and education*	193	.....	.....	.....	.....	.....	.....	.....	97	.....
Grants to social organizations*	194	.....	.....	.....	.....	.....	.....	.....	136	.....
Prison improvement*	195	.....	.....	.....	.....	.....	.....	.....	14	.....

No.	Item									
196	Civil defense*									500
197	Contribution to Army*									1,000
10	Institute of Public Administration							10	20	20
59	Higher Council for Industrial Training and Efficiency								20	57
128	National Criminological Institute									18
70	Egyptian Library									77
71	Arabic Language Academy									21
23	Higher Council for Youth Welfare									840
85	Higher Council for Public Health									1,556
	Total, current expenditures	2,729	3,492	4,070	4,692	4,478	4,711	6,639	14,959	9,347
	Expenditures primarily of a capital nature:									
159	Granaries†							4,311	5,455	251
160	Irrigation, dams, etc.†							1,521	1,804	3,096
161	Agricultural expansion†					79		108	132	628
162	Wadi el Natroun†					36			1,197	139
163	Behera and Fayum†					7		1,826	3,058	310
164	Liberation Province†					23		1,495	3,711	5,362
165	Agriculture and livestock†							3,506	34	460
166	Pasture improvement†							25	850	28
167	Land Reclamation Authority†								451	1,345
168	Aswan High Dam project†						14,577		7,858	443
169	Electrification projects†						4,577	6,587	10,066	7,432
170	Communications projects†					52		7,127	3,530	11,610
171	Oil refinery, etc.†							1,242	717	1,663
172	Fertilizer factory†							10		1,000
174	Economic Organization†						417		116	4,110
175	Other independent projects†							1,212	400	50
176	General research†						611	24	779	212
69	Public Buildings Foundation							500		988

(Continued on next page)

TABLE VI-E-5—Continued

	Barlow's Expenditure Number	1948-49	1949-50	1950-51	1951-52	1952-53	1953-54	1954-55	1955-56	1956-57
Hospitals†	177	.....	.....	.....	.....	.....	.....	47	671	.....
Public health laboratories†	178	.....	.....	.....	.....	.....	.....	.....	16	.....
College of Dentistry†	179	.....	.....	.....	.....	.....	.....	.....	28	.....
Public Health Institute†	85	.....	.....	.....	.....	.....	.....	30	.....	.....
Drinking water projects†	183	.....	.....	.....	.....	.....	.....	1,303	4,077	.....
Rural police stations†	184	.....	.....	.....	.....	.....	.....	.....	.....	.....
Student housing†	188	.....	.....	.....	.....	.....	.....	7	75	.....
Workers' housing†	191	.....	.....	.....	.....	.....	.....	.....	441	.....
Civil servants' housing†	192	.....	.....	.....	.....	.....	.....	550	420	.....
Total, capital		0	0	0	0	197	20,182	31,431	46,179	39,127
Grand total		2,729	3,492	4,070	4,692	4,675	24,893	38,079	61,138	48,474

*Projects of the Permanent Council for Public Services.
†Projects for the Development of National Production.
SOURCES: One of the weaknesses of the data in Tables VI–E–3 and VI–E–4 is that they include only expenditures in the ordinary budget. In order to make a more complete estimate of government expenditures, we have used estimates in the doctoral dissertation of Robin Barlow. Barlow has presented a completely consolidated set of government revenue and expenditure accounts; fortunately for us, he has also provided detailed figures which permit us to compute total expenditures of entities with annexed budgets. Unfortunately, this yields only total expenditures, whether for current, capital, or transfer purposes. We have assumed that none of these expenditures are for transfers. As between current and capital expenditures, we have looked at the heading of the expenditure category and attempted to make a rough breakdown; thus, for example, expenditures of the Arabic Language Academy were assumed to be current, while expenditures in electrification and communications projects were treated as wholly capital. Of course, this is rough, but it is probably the best that can be done at present. The figures are from Robin Barlow, *Intersectoral Income Redistribution in Egypt* (unpublished Ph.D. dissertation, University of Michigan, 1961). Appendices A and E. Barlow also presents figures for a number of other agencies with annexed budgets, but these did not start spending money until after the period shown in this table.

TABLE VI–E–6

TOTAL CENTRAL GOVERNMENT CURRENT EXPENDITURES, 1947–48 TO 1956–57

(£E Thousand)

	1947–48	1948–49	1949–50	1950–51	1951–52	1952–53	1953–54	1954–55	1955–56	1956–57
1. Wages and salaries..........	39,819	53,479	59,354	82,810	96,159	87,508	99,376	105,636	121,819	127,434
2. Rent.......................	601	840	979	625	1,085	989	1,099	1,486	1,306	1,272
3. Current purchases..........	25,752	51,353	46,023	49,585	43,385	50,479	49,400	60,781	97,463	115,421
4. Military expenditures........	452	2,367	9,032	8,761	19,923	9,661	12,008	19,114	3,294	3,445
5. Minus current expenditures of enterprises in budget....	9,927	11,238	13,612	13,918	15,822	14,632	18,921	20,020	19,112	18,890
6. Total current expenditures in budget..............	56,697	96,801	101,776	127,863	144,730	134,005	142,962	166,997	204,770	228,682
7. Plus current expenditures, annexed budgets..........	2,000	2,729	3,492	4,070	4,692	4,478	4,711	6,639	14,959	9,347
8. Total current expenditures...	58,697	99,530	105,268	131,933	149,422	138,483	147,673	173,636	219,729	238,029
9. Exhibit: Cost-of-living allowances............	9,702	13,026	13,420	30,504	32,742	33,525	28,762	29,176	29,224	30,762

NOTES AND SOURCES: Rows 1–4 are from Table VI–E–4. Row 1 includes cost-of-living allowances, also shown separately in row 9. Row 5 includes railroads, telephone and telegraph, and the post office; the figures are taken from the detailed work sheets underlying Table VI–E–4, except for the years 1954–55 to 1956–57, when they are estimated using share of current in total expenditures in these organizations in 1953–54, and estimates of their total spending in these years from the budgets. Row 7 is from Table VI–E–5, except for 1947–48, which is very roughly estimated by extrapolation.

TABLE VI–F–1

Price Indices

(1953 = 100)

	1939	1940	1941	1942	1943	1944	1945	1946	1947	1948	1949	1950	1951
Cost-of-living index	34	38	47	62	82	94	99	97	94	95	94	99	108
Retail price index	31	35	44	60	81	96	100	96	92	92	93	101	110
Wholesale price index	28	37	46	51	77	88	93	90	86	93	88	97	108
A. Foodstuffs:													
1. Cereals	35	34	51	68	80	91	100	99	87	86	84	89	94
2. Dairy products	27	32	41	56	83	102	114	108	100	96	102	113	120
3. Oils	27	39	47	61	80	102	95	95	111	106	97	95	115
4. Meat and fish	34	37	44	63	92	100	99	105	103	106	110	114	123
5. Sugar, tea, and coffee	29	37	43	48	59	69	67	69	69	69	70	80	83
6. Others*	27	34	43	72	96	101	101	106	97	98	91	102	105
Total	30	…	…	…	…	…	…	…	89	89	86	95	101
B. Industrial products:													
1. Fuels	32	41	69	72	77	82	82	80	79	83	84	87	87
2. Soap and chemicals†	27	41	49	67	82	95	102	101	100	106	101	99	106
3. Paper	19	43	63	81	177	355	301	138	83	81	74	72	138
4. Building materials	22	41	54	62	69	79	121	94	90	92	83	77	89
5. Fertilizer	27	43	57	69	89	99	96	81	72	96	99	100	100
6. Metals	23	44	62	86	105	113	109	82	82	87	86	90	105
7. Textiles	22	32	34	42	54	63	67	63	65	77	71	83	100
8. Hides and skins	29	39	50	70	83	117	120	110	96	98	95	100	109
9. Pharmaceuticals	32	39	42	45	48	85	97	97	97	96	91	98	100
Total	26	…	…	…	…	…	…	…	81	96	89	99	116

	1952	1953	1954	1955	1956	1957	1958	1959	1960	1961	1962	1963	1964
Cost-of-living index	107	100	96	96	98	102	102	102	103	103	100	101	105
Retail price index	107	100	101	102	104	110	110	111	112	113	113	115	122
Wholesale price index	105	100	97	99	110	119	117	117	118	120	119	118	123
A. Foodstuffs:													
1. Cereals	91	100	105	111	121	119	113	114	114	119	118	117	122
2. Dairy products	112	100	104	108	109	121	120	115	117	123	128	136	150
3. Oils	107	100	91	91	100	103	107	107	107	107	104	107	105
4. Meat and fish	117	100	102	105	108	113	108	107	108	110	114	117	124
5. Sugar, tea, and coffee	95	100	112	117	116	124	126	124	122	122	129	137	136
6. Others*	104	100	83	80	97	106	112	106	108	122	121	112	123
Total	98	100	98	101	110	116	118	117	115	122	122	120	127
B. Industrial products:													
1. Fuels	97	100	103	105	111	140	135	128	121	121	123	119	117
2. Soap and chemicals†	108	100	88	86	89	105	103	102	104	105	107	109	112
3. Paper	120	100	94	91	92	98	108	110	105	100	99	103	104
4. Building materials	108	100	94	97	111	115	112	109	113	115	117	116	118
5. Fertilizer	100	100	101	100	101	118	119	119	107	101	101	95	95
6. Metals	114	100	89	96	108	123	130	138	141	146	153	158	165
7. Textiles	115	100	99	102	105	112	109	106	107	105	105	113	115
8. Hides and skins	105	100	102	104	105	123	153	159	157	154	155	170	181
9. Pharmaceuticals	100	100	100	100	100	100	100	100	100	n.a.	n.a.	n.a.	n.a.
Total	113	100	97	97	109	121	116	117	120	116	114	115	118

*Includes rice, potatoes, beans, peas, starches, chick-peas, molasses, salt, onions, dried dates, olives, pepper, and garlic.

†Includes soap, matches, jute, sulfuric acid, caustic soda, and alcohol.

NOTES AND SOURCES: As we indicate in the text, price data in Egypt are all suspect due to the existence of price controls and the use of official prices for index purposes, which may diverge from actual prices. We have found no evidence of any conscious attempt to present a misleading picture either by choosing the index items with price controls or by putting controls on items already in the index. Some divergence between actual developments and the official index surely does exist; as we indicate in the text, however, we have found no reason to question the overall price picture presented in these indices, at least up through 1960; thereafter, we are inclined to believe that the gap may be widening—that prices have risen fairly sharply since then, rather than staying roughly constant, as the figures imply.

The wholesale price index is an unweighted geometric average of a large number of price relatives computed monthly and chained together with June-August, 1939 = 100. Perhaps the word "unweighted" is too strong; if a commodity is felt to be of some importance, several different grades or varieties are chosen; thus, 29 different price series for raw cotton enter the index, 15 for wheat, five for sugar, etc., making a total of 192 different series, each of which enters with equal weight. The decision as to which series to include in the index, and how many series for a given commodity, was made within the Department of Statistics and Census on the basis of its evaluation of the "relative importance" of the different commodities. The department reserves the right to change the inclusions as different commodities gain or lose in relative importance, although there is no indication that it has done so. The index is explained in *Annuaire Statistique, 1946–47*, pp. 659–63.

With regard to the cost-of-living or consumer price index, the weighting for this as well seems to have been based on armchair guesses within the Department of Statistics and Census as to the normal expenditure patterns of a lower middle-class urban worker. More precisely, these were armchair readjustments, done in 1939, of a 1920 survey of expenditure patterns of this group, the adjustments being to take account of the "probable" changes in expenditure patterns which had taken place in the interim. It was hoped that the 1958–59 household budget survey would yield figures which could be used as a basis for a new and better index, but it seems that this has not been the case; if we make a rough comparison of weighting in the cost-of-living index and in these expenditure surveys, the divergencies are fairly substantial.

The retail price index is simply the food, fuel, and soap component of the cost-of-living index.

The figures are annual averages of the monthly figures.

Bibliography

BOOKS

ABDEL RAHMAN, S. H. *A Survey of the Foreign Trade of Egypt in the Post-War Period, with Special Reference to Its Impact on the National Economy.* Ph.D. dissertation, Faculty of Commerce, Cairo University, 1959.

ALLEN, R. L. *Middle Eastern Economic Relations with the Soviet Union, Eastern Europe and Mainland China.* Charlottesville: University of Virginia Press, 1958.

AMIN, G. A. *Food Supply and Economic Development with Special Reference to Egypt.* London: Frank Cass & Co. Ltd., 1966.

AMMAR, A. M. *A Demographic Study of an Egyptian Province (Sharqiya).* Monographs on Social Anthropology, No. 8. London: Percy Lund, Humphries & Co., Ltd., 1942.

AYROUT, H. *The Felaheen.* Cairo: R. Schendler, 1945.

BAER, G. *A History of Landownership in Modern Egypt, 1800–1950.* New York: Oxford University Press, 1962.

BARLOW, ROBIN. *Intersectoral Income Redistribution in Egypt.* Ph.D. dissertation, University of Michigan, 1961.

BROWN, C. H. *Egyptian Cotton.* London: Leonard Hill, Ltd., 1953.

CLELAND, W. *The Population Problem in Egypt.* Lancaster, Pa.: Science Press Printing Co., 1936.

CRAIG, J. I., and ABDEL KARIM, M. *Cereals Consumption in Egypt.* Cairo, 1947.

CROMER, EARL OF. *Modern Egypt.* London: Macmillan & Co., Ltd., 1908. 2 vols.

CROUCHLEY, A. E. *The Economic Development of Modern Egypt.* New York: Longmans, Green & Co., Inc., 1938.

FARRAG, ABDELMEGID MOUSTAFA. *Demographic Developments in Egypt during the Present Century.* Ph.D. dissertation, London School of Economics and Political Science, 1957.

GADALLA, S. M. *Land Reform in Relation to Social Development: Egypt.* Columbia: University of Missouri Press, 1962.

GARZOUZI, E. *Old Ills and New Remedies in Egypt.* Cairo: Dar el Maaref, 1958.

403

HANSEN, B., and MARZOUK, G. *Development and Economic Policy in the U.A.R. (Egypt).* Amsterdam: North-Holland Publishing Co., 1965.

HARBISON, F., and IBRAHIM, I. A. *Human Resources for Egyptian Enterprises.* New York: McGraw-Hill Book Co., Inc., 1958.

HURST, H. E. *The Nile.* London: Constable & Co., 1952.

HURST, H. E.; BLACK, R. P.; and SIMAIKA, Y. M. *The Future Conservation of the Nile.* Cairo: Société Orientale de Publicité Press, 1946.

INTERNATIONAL COTTON ADVISORY COMMITTEE. *Cotton—World Statistics,* Special Base Book Issue, Vol. XVI, Nos. 9–10, Part II (April, 1963.)

ISSAWI, C. *Egypt in Revolution: An Economic Analysis.* New York: Oxford University Press, 1963.

KARDOUCHE, G. K. *Monetary Developments and Policy in the U.A.R. (Egypt), 1952 to 1962.* Ph.D. dissertation, Brown University, June, 1965.

KIRK, G. E. *A Short History of the Middle East.* London: Methuen & Co., 1955.

LACOUTURE, J., and LACOUTURE, S. *Egypt in Transition.* London: Methuen & Co., 1958.

MAREI, S. *Agrarian Reform in Egypt.* Cairo: S.O.P. Press, 1957.

MEYER, A. J. *Middle East Capitalism.* Cambridge: Harvard University Press, 1959.

MIKESELL, R. F., and BEHRMAN, J. N. *Financing Free World Trade with the Sino-Soviet Bloc.* Princeton Studies in International Finance, No. 8. Princeton: Princeton University Press, 1958.

O'BRIEN, P. K. *The Revolution in Egypt's Economic System, 1952–1965.* London: Oxford University Press, 1966.

SABRI, A. *The Years of Socialist Transformation: An Evaluation of the First Five-Year Plan.* Cairo: Dar el Maaref, 1966, in Arabic.

RIZK, H. *Fertility Patterns in Selected Areas in Egypt.* Ph.D. dissertation, Princeton University, 1959.

WARRINER, D. *Land and Poverty in the Middle East.* New York: Royal Institute of International Affairs, 1948.

————. *Land Reform and Development in the Middle East.* New York: Oxford University Press, 1962.

WHEELOCK, K. *Nasser's New Egypt.* New York: Frederick A. Praeger, Inc., 1960.

YOUNG, G. *Egypt.* London: Ernest Benn, Ltd., 1927.

ARTICLES

ABDEL MALEK, A. "La Question Agraire en Egypte et la Réforme de 1952," *Tiers-Monde,* Vol. III, Nos. 9–10, January-June, 1962.

ABU-LUGHOD, J. L. "Urbanization in Egypt: Present State and Future Prospects," *Economic Development and Cultural Change,* Vol. XIII, No. 3 (April, 1965).

AMIN, S. "Financing Investment in the Egyptian Region of the UAR," *L'Egypte Contemporaine,* No. 297 (July, 1959).

ANIS, M. A. "A Study of the National Income of Egypt," *L'Egypte Contemporaine,* Nos. 261–62 (November-December, 1950).

EL BADRY, M. A. "Some Demographic Measurements for Egypt Based on the Stability of Census Age Distributions," *Milbank Memorial Fund Quarterly,* Vol. XXXIII, No. 3 (July, 1955).

_____. "Trends in the Components of Population Growth in the Arab Countries of the Middle East: A Survey of Present Information," *Demography,* Vol. II (1965).

BLANCHARD, G. "Du Redressement de la Balance Commerciale de l'Egypte en Temps de Crise," *L'Egypte Contemporaine,* No. 157 (May, 1935).

CRAIG, J. I. "Statistics of the Yield of Cotton," *L'Egypte Contemporaine,* No. 8 (November, 1911).

CRAWFORD, J. M. *National Income Statistics.* Mimeographed report to United Nations Technical Assistance Board, File No. TAA/173/20/-06, 1955.

CROUCHLEY, A. E. "The Visible Balance of Trade since 1884," *L'Egypte Contemporaine,* Nos. 155–56 (March-April, 1935).

DARLING, SIR MALCOLM. "Land Reform in Italy and Egypt," *Yearbook of Agricultural Cooperation,* Oxford: Basil Blackwell, 1956.

"Egypt's Rural Welfare Centers," *International Labor Review,* Vol. LXI, No. 1 (January, 1950).

EZZAT, M. A. W. "The Land Tenure System in Egypt," In PARSONS, K. H., *et al.* (eds.). *Land Tenure.* Madison: University of Wisconsin Press, 1956.

EL GHONEMY, M. R. "The Investment Effects of the Land Reform in Egypt," *L'Egypte Contemporaine,* No. 278 (October, 1954).

EL GRITLY, A. A. I. "The Structure of Modern Industry in Egypt," *L'Egypte Contemporaine,* Nos. 241–42 (November-December, 1947).

HANSEN, B. *Planning and Economic Growth in the U.A.R. (Egypt).* Mimeographed paper presented to Conference on Egypt since the Revolution, School of Oriental and African Studies, University of London, September, 1966.

HUSEIN, HASAN H. *Manpower Sample Survey in the U.A.R.: A Descriptive and Critical Review.* Mimeographed paper presented to the Regional Seminar on Problems of Planning the Labor Force and Its Employment, Cairo, 1963.

I.E.D.E.S., UN GROUPE D'ETUDE. "La Société Urbaine Egyptienne," *Tiers-Monde,* Vol. II, No. 6 (April-June, 1961).

Issawi, C. "Egypt since 1800: A study in Lopsided Development," *Journal of Economic History*, Vol. XXI, No. 1 (March, 1961).

————. "The Entrepreneur Class," in Fisher, S. N. (ed.), *Social Forces in the Middle East*. Ithaca: Cornell University Press, 1955.

Khallaf, H. "Financing Economic Development in Egypt," *Middle East Economic Papers*, 1955.

Kiser, C. V. "The Demographic Position of Egypt," in Milbank Memorial Fund. *Demographic Studies of Selected Areas of Rapid Growth*. Proceedings of the Round Table on Population Problems. New York, 1944.

Lévi, M. I. G. "Le Commerce Extérieur de l'Egypte: Mouvement de l'Année 1913," *L'Egypte Contemporaine*, No. 19 (May, 1914).

Lotz, J. R. "Taxation in the United Arab Republic (Egypt); International Monetary Fund *Staff Papers*, Vol. XIII, No. 1 (March, 1966).

Mahhouk, A. "Trends in Egypt's National Income, 1913–1956," *Middle East Economic Papers*, (Periodical) 1962.

Marei, S. "The Agrarian Reform in Egypt," *International Labor Review*, Vol. LXIX, No. 2 (February, 1954).

Marzouk, G. "Monetary and Financial Analysis in the Egyptian Region," *L'Egypte Contemporaine*, No. 300 (April, 1960).

McDiarmid, O. J. "Capital Inflow in Economic Development," in *Arab Development in the Emerging International Economy*. Fifteenth Annual Near East Conference, Princeton University. Princeton: Princeton University Press, 1963.

el Naggar, S. *Foreign Aid and the Economic Development of the U.A.R.* Preliminary Research Paper No. 1964(8). Princeton Program in Near Eastern Studies, Princeton: Princeton University Press, 1964.

Nakaoka, S. "A Note on the Evaluation Work of the Agrarian Reform in the U.A.R. (Egypt)," *The Developing Economics*, Vol. I, No. 1 (January-June, 1963).

O'Brien, P. K. "Industrial Development and the Employment Problem in Egypt, 1945–1965," *Middle East Economic Papers*, 1962.

Oweis, J. S. *Agricultural Development in the United Arab Republic (Egypt)*. Working paper prepared for U.S. Department of Agriculture, Economic Research Service, Development and Trade Analysis Division. Washington, D.C.: U.S. Government Printing Office, n.d. Mimeographed.

Owen, W. F. "Land and Water Use in the Egyptian High Dam Era," *Land Economics*, Vol. XL, No. 3 (August, 1964).

Parsons, K. H. "Land Reform in the United Arab Republic," *Land Economics*, Vol. XXV, No. 4 (November, 1959).

Porter, R. S. "Comment," *Kyklos*, Vol. XI, Fasc. 2 (1958).

"Recent Developments in Social Insurance in the United Arab Republic," *International Labor Review,* Vol. LXXXV, No. 5 (May, 1962).

SAAB, G. "Rationalization of Agriculture and Land Tenure Problems in Egypt," *Middle East Economic Papers,* 1960.

EL SAATY, HASSAN. "Changes in the Industrial Organization of Egypt," in INTERNATIONAL SOCIOLOGICAL ASSOCIATION. *Transactions of the Third World Congress,* Vol. II. London, 1956.

SAID, GAMAL EL DIN. "Productivity of Labor in Egyptian Industry," *L'Egypte Contemporaine,* Nos. 259–60 (May-June, 1950).

EL SHAFEI, A. M. N. "The Current Labor Force Sample Survey in Egypt (U.A.R.)," *International Labor Review,* Vol. LXXXII, No. 5 (November, 1960).

STERN, R. M. "The Price Responsiveness of Egyptian Cotton Producers," *Kyklos,* Vol. XII, Fasc. 3 (1959).

TADROS, H. "The Balance of Payments," in INSTITUT DES ETUDES BANCAIRES. *Série de Conférences Donnés durant la Deuxième Année.* Cairo: Imprimerie Mondiale, 1956.

————. "Recent Developments in Egypt's Balance of Payments," *Middle East Economic Papers,* 1957.

EL TANAMLI, A. M. "Agricultural Credit and Cooperative Organization," *L'Egypte Contemporaine,* No. 310 (October, 1962).

THWEATT, W. "The Egyptian Agrarian Reform," *Middle East Economic Papers,* 1956.

EL TONBARY, A. A., and EL EZZ, M. S. A. "Economics of Water Supply and Control in the Southern Region of the United Arab Republic: An Outline," *International Journal of Agrarian Affairs,* Vol. III, No. 1 (1961).

WEIR, J. M., and ASSOCIATES. "An Evaluation of Health and Sanitation in Egyptian Villages," *Journal of the Egyptian Public Health Association,* Vol. XXVII, No. 3 (1952).

EGYPTIAN PUBLICATIONS, OFFICIAL AND SERIAL

NOTE: Official government publications are generally printed either by the Government Printing Office (more recently, General Organization for Government Printing Offices), by the Société Orientale de Publicité (S.O.P.) Press, or by Dar Memphis Press. Almost invariably, however, they are not available from the publisher, but may be procured either from the Central Documents Office (Opera Square, Cairo) or from the ministry or office responsible for producing them.

BANK MISR. *Economic Review.* Quarterly.

BANK OF ALEXANDRIA. *Bulletin.* Quarterly.

BANQUE BELGE ET INTERNATIONALE EN EGYPTE. *25 Ans au Service de l'Economie Egyptienne, 1929–1954.* Cairo, 1954.

Banque de Port Said. *Revue Economique Trimestrielle.*

Central Bank of Egypt. *Credit and Banking Developments.* Annual.

————. *Economic Review.* Quarterly.

Chambre de Commerce Suisse en Egypte. *Bulletin.* Quarterly.

Federation of Industries in the United Arab Republic (earlier: Federation of Egyptian Industries). *Industrial Egypt.* Quarterly.

————. *Yearbook.* Annual.

National Bank of Egypt. *Economic Bulletin.* Quarterly.

————. *The Economy of the U.A.R. during the 1950's.* Cairo, 1963.

Republic of Egypt, Department of Statistics and Census. *National Income of Egypt for 1953: "Official Estimate."* Cairo, 1955.

Republic of Egypt, Ministry of Agriculture. *Agricultural Census of Egypt, 1929, 1939, and 1950.*

Republic of Egypt, Ministry of Commerce and Industry. *Opportunities for Industrial Development in Egypt.* Report of survey by Arthur D. Little, Inc. Cairo, 1955.

Republic of Egypt, Permanent Council of Public Services. *The Population Problem of Egypt.* Cairo, 1955.

Sherif, A. F. *General Tendencies in the Development of the National Economy in the Last Quarter Century.* Memo No. 121. Cairo: National Planning Committee, January, 1959.

United Arab Republic. *Central Statistical Committee.* Cairo, September, 1961.

United Arab Republic, Administration of Public Mobilization. *Statistical Pocket-Book of the U.A.R. 1952–1961,* Cairo, 1962.

United Arab Republic, Central Agency for Public Mobilization and Statistics. *Statistical Handbook: United Arab Republic, 1952–64.* Cairo, April, 1965.

United Arab Republic, Central Statistical Committee. *Basic Statistics.* Twice yearly in Arabic; was published in English in June, 1962, and October, 1963.

————. *Household Budget Survey in the Egyptian Region, 1958–59.* Cairo, April, 1961.

————. *The Labor Force Sample Survey in the Egyptian Region of the U.A.R.* Cairo, 1959.

————. *Population Trends in the U.A.R.* Cairo, 1962.

United Arab Republic, Department of Statistics and Census. *Annuaire Statistique.*

————. *Annual Return of Shipping, Cargo and Passenger Traffic.*

————. *Annual Statement of Foreign Trade.*

————. *Census of Industrial Production,* 1944, 1947, 1950, 1952, 1954; yearly since 1956. (Since 1962, there is also a quarterly mimeographed survey of all firms employing five hundred or more workers.)

_____. *Monthly Bulletin of Agricultural and Economic Statistics.*

_____. *Monthly Summary of Foreign Trade.*

_____. *National Income from the Agricultural Sector for the Years 1958–1960.* In Arabic. Cairo, n.d.

_____. *Population Census,* 1882, 1897, 1907, 1917, 1927, 1937, 1947, 1960.

_____. *Statistical Pocket Year-Book.* Annual.

_____. *Statistique Scolaire.* Triennial.

_____. *Statistics of Employment, Wages, and Working Hours.* Twice yearly.

_____. *Statistics of Officials and Employees in the Government and Public Enterprises.* Annual through 1956; irregular since then.

_____. *Ten Years of Revolution: Statistical Atlas,* Cairo, July, 1962.

_____. *Vital Statistics.* Annual.

UNITED ARAB REPUBLIC, GENERAL CONGRESS OF THE NATIONAL UNION. *Address by Mr. Abdel Latif el Boghdadi on the Five-Year-Plan.* Cairo, 1960.

UNITED ARAB REPUBLIC, INSTITUTE OF NATIONAL PLANNING. *Research Project on Employment and Unemployment among the Educated.* 8 vols., Cairo, 1963.

UNITED ARAB REPUBLIC, MINISTRY OF AGRICULTURE. *Monthly Bulletin of Agricultural Economics and Statistics.* In Arabic.

UNITED ARAB REPUBLIC, MINISTRY OF AGRICULTURE, DEPARTMENT OF AGRICULTURAL ECONOMICS AND STATISTICS. *Agricultural National Income.* Annual.

UNITED ARAB REPUBLIC, MINISTRY OF ECONOMY, INSURANCE DEPARTMENT. *Egyptian Insurance Yearbook.* Annual.

UNITED ARAB REPUBLIC, MINISTRY OF EDUCATION, DEPARTMENT OF STATISTICS. *Comparative Statistics of Education.* Cairo, 1961.

UNITED ARAB REPUBLIC, MINISTRY OF PUBLIC WORKS, ELECTRICITY COMMISSION. *Electrical Power Projects in the U.A.R.* Cairo, November, 1962. Mimeographed.

UNITED ARAB REPUBLIC, MINISTRY OF THE TREASURY. *The Budget Report.* Annual.

UNITED ARAB REPUBLIC, PRESIDENCY OF THE REPUBLIC, NATIONAL PLANNING COMMITTEE. *General Frame of the Five-Year Plan for Economic and Social Development, July 1960–June 1965.* Cairo, 1960.

UNITED ARAB REPUBLIC, SUEZ CANAL AUTHORITY. *Monthy Report.*

_____. *Suez Canal Report.* Annual.

MEMOS OF THE INSTITUTE OF NATIONAL PLANNING

DEIF, N. A. *Some Uses of Economic Accounting in Planning Economic Development of the U.A.R.* Memo No. 210. Cairo, September, 1962.

————. *The System of Follow-Up of the First Five-Year Economic and Social Plan.* Memo No. 141. Cairo, February, 1962.

EL DINE, H. KHEIR. *The Cotton Production Function in the U.A.R. and Its Relation to Technical Progress and to Disguised Unemployment.* Memo No. 370. Cairo, September, 1963.

ELIESH. G. E. *The Applicability and Utilization of the Input-Output Model in a Developing Economy: The Case of Egypt Examined.* Memo No. 168, Cairo, March, 1962.

————. *An Introduction to the Input-Output Model.* Memo No. 176. Cairo, April, 1962.

EL-ISAWY, I. H. *The Development of the U.A.R.'s Foreign Exchange Policy.* Memo No. 452. Cairo, June, 1964.

HANSEN, B. *The Distributive Shares in Egyptian Agriculture, 1897–1961.* Memo No. 583. Cairo, June, 1965.

————. *Marginal Productivity Wage Theory and Subsistence Wage Theory in Egyptian Agriculture.* Memo No. 547. Cairo, March, 1965.

————. *The National Outlay of the U.A.R. (Egypt), 1937–39 and 1945–1962–63.* Memo No. 377. Cairo, December, 1963.

————. *Savings in the U.A.R. (Egypt), 1938–39 and 1945–46–1962–63.* Memo No. 551. Cairo, March, 1965.

HANSEN, B., and MEAD, D. *The National Income of the U.A.R. (Egypt), 1939–1962.* Memo No. 355. Cairo, July, 1963.

HOSNI, A. *Financing Capital Formation in the U.A.R.* Memo No. 211. Cairo, 1962.

EL IMAM. M. M. *Models Used in Drafting the 20-Year Plan (1959–1978).* Memo No. 255. Cairo, December, 1962.

————. *A Production Function for Egyptian Agriculture, 1913–1955.* Memo No. 259. Cairo, December, 1962.

EL-NAGGAN, S. *Foreign Aid to the United Arab Republic.* Memo No. 382. Cairo, December, 1963.

TECHNICAL OFFICE. *List of Memoranda Issued by the I.N.P.C.* Memo No. 500. Cairo, March, 1965.

EL TOMY, M., and HANSEN, B. *The Seasonal Employment Profile in Egyptian Agriculture.* Memo No. 501. Cairo, October, 1964.

OTHER OFFICIAL PUBLICATIONS

UNITED KINGDOM, DEPARTMENT OF OVERSEAS TRADE. *Report on the Economic and Financial Situation of Egypt.* London: H.M.S.O., April, 1924.

UNITED KINGDOM, FOREIGN OFFICE. *Reports on the Finances, Administration and Condition of Egypt, and the Progress of Reforms.* London: H.M.S.O., May, 1898.

UNITED NATIONS. *The Development of Manufacturing Industry in Egypt, Israel, and Turkey.* New York, 1958.

UNITED NATIONS, DEPARTMENT OF ECONOMIC AND SOCIAL AFFAIRS. *Economic Developments in the Middle East* (annual).

UNITED NATIONS, ECONOMIC COMMISSION FOR AFRICA. *Industrial Growth in Africa: A Survey and Outlook.* U.N. Document E/CN.14/-INR/1. New York, October 15, 1962.

INDEX

This book has been set in 10 and 9 point Caledonia, leaded 2 points. Chapter titles are in 18 point Bradley. The size of the type page is 25 by 43½ picas.